Modern Investment Management
and the Prudent Man Rule

Modern Investment Management and the Prudent Man Rule

BEVIS LONGSTRETH

New York   Oxford
OXFORD UNIVERSITY PRESS
1986

Oxford University Press

Oxford New York Toronto
Delhi Bombay Calcutta Madras Karachi
Petaling Jaya Singapore Hong Kong Tokyo
Nairobi Dar es Salaam Cape Town
Melbourne Auckland
and associated companies in
Beirut Berlin Ibadan Nicosia

Published by Oxford University Press, Inc.,
200 Madison Avenue, New York, New York 10016

Oxford is a registered trademark of Oxford University Press

Library of Congress Cataloging-in-Publication Data
Longstreth, Bevis.
Modern investment management
and the prudent man rule.
Includes index.
1. Legal investments—United States.
2. Portfolio management—United States. I. Title.
KF1083.L66 1986   346.73′07   86-16294
ISBN 0-19-504196-8   347.3067

2 4 6 8 10 9 7 5 3 1
Printed in the United States of America
on acid-free paper

Statement of Advisers

We have examined the study entitled *Modern Investment Management and the Prudent Man Rule* directed by Bevis Longstreth in collaboration with the Salomon Brothers Center for the Study of Financial Institutions at New York University's Graduate School of Business Administration. In our opinion this study identifies and thoroughly explores the gap that exists between legal notions of prudence in investment management by fiduciaries, on one hand, and the teachings of financial economics and sound practices of investment professionals, on the other. The development of a modern legal standard of prudence contained in Chapter 4 is generally sound. It deserves serious consideration by fiduciaries subject to some form of prudent man rule and by others, including judges, lawyers, and investment managers, who are called upon to interpret and apply that legal standard.

Foreword

It is axiomatic that fiduciaries must be prudent in the investment of funds for which they are responsible. Defining prudence may always have been a challenging matter, but in a time of rapidly changing investment markets, with new investment opportunities, new financial products, and proliferating investment methods and strategies, the task is even more difficult.

Finding an appropriate legal framework in which to manage funds has become particularly important to today's manager of endowment funds, especially those devoted to charitable, educational, and other eleemosynary purposes. Faced by increasing financial pressures, institutions have looked to their endowment managers to use energy and imagination to increase total return. Excessive caution and failure to take advantage of new financial products and new investment opportunities, methods, and strategies can adversely affect the charitable or educational enterprise's ability to accomplish its purposes as surely as can excessive risk taking. Responsive legal guidance that permits active management and timely decision-making is a necessity for many institutions.

However, legal counsel for many charitable institutions have too often found themselves unable to respond adequately to questions posed by their officers and trustees in this new and evolving investment environment. The innovative approaches to endowment management are sophisticated and complex, and existing statutes and case law do not provide clear guidance.

In the course of discussing this matter, the four of us, in our capacities as legal counsel respectively for Columbia, Harvard, Princeton, and Stanford Universities, with encouragement from colleagues at other institutions, came to the view that a study of this subject had the possibility of providing clarification and better understanding of the issues. We believed that a thorough legal analysis of the law of prudence and a review of current economic theory on the subject of risk management, supplemented by a "real world" survey of investment activities by institutional investors, could point the way to more solid ground. Bevis Longstreth's familiarity with the relevant legal principles and his experience as a legal adviser to several kinds of charitable institutions, together with his recent service as a Commissioner of the Securities and Exchange Commission, fitted him well for the role of directing such a study. We were pleased to find that the foundations to which we took our proposal agreed about the importance and promise of such a study.

We have been influenced from the beginning, in our vision of this study, by the contribution of William Cary and Craig Bright in their creative work, *The Law and Lore of Endowment Funds* (and *The Law and Lore Revisited*). These studies changed in important ways the manner in which certain legal principles applicable to the management of institutional endowments are viewed. Those changes have, of course, now been largely codified and adopted in many states, in the Uniform Management of Institutional Funds Act. But it was changes in perceptions of lawyers, judges, legislators, and fiduciaries that made possible the recodifications that occurred.

We do not, of course, know exactly what effects this study will have. We believe that the study squarely addresses the central issues and consequently considerably advances the reader's understanding of the law of prudence and provides a useful analytic framework for considering and answering the legal questions posed by the fiduciary in today's world. We are optimistic that this thoughtful work will lead to a substantial clarification in what seems to us now to be an unnecessarily vague and outdated understanding of the meaning of "prudence" with regard to the responsibilities of fiduciaries and in particular their management of educational and charitable endowments.

May 1986

John Mason Harding
Columbia University

Daniel Steiner
Harvard University

Thomas H. Wright
Princeton University

John J. Schwartz
Stanford University

Acknowledgments

There are many deserving of thanks for helping to bring this book into being. Thomas H. Wright, General Counsel of Princeton University, and Daniel Steiner, General Counsel of Harvard University, share parentage of the idea that the prudence standard be addressed. They, together with their counterparts at Columbia and Stanford Universities, John Mason Harding and John J. Schwartz, initiated early planning for the study, selected the author as study director, and advanced funds to support the preparation of a "prospectus" to test the idea's utility against the opinions of possible users and funding sources.

The five foundations supporting the study, and those at the foundations whose special interest led to support, include the Alfred P. Sloan Foundation and its President, Albert Rees, the Carnegie Corporation of New York and its Vice President, David Z. Robinson, The Ford Foundation and its Vice President, Louis Winnick, The William and Flora Hewlett Foundation and its President, Roger W. Heyns, and The Rockefeller Foundation and its Treasurer and Chief Investment Officer, Jack R. Meyer, and its Vice President, Alberta B. Arthurs. Sloan provided 50 percent of the budget and the others 12½ percent each.

While acknowledging the generous support of these universities and foundations, I should emphasize that they bear no responsibility for the book's analysis and conclusions.

New York University's Graduate School of Business Administration and, in particular, its Salomon Brothers Center for the Study of Financial Institutions, administered the study. The Center's Director, Dr. Arnold W. Sametz, became the study's associate director, lending his important support and that of the Center to the effort. In addition to assuring the interest in the project of several economists at the Center, including Professors Edwin J. Elton and Martin J. Gruber, the authors of Appendix A, and Professor Kose John, who wrote a research paper, Dr. Sametz provided able advice and reassuring support throughout the study.

In Professor Jeffrey N. Gordon, I enjoyed not only a contributor, whose essay appears in Appendix B, but an adviser as well, who interested himself in all aspects of the study and provided important guidance along the way.

Over the course of writing this book, I was fortunate to have the advice of a number of experienced professionals. They included Jonathan R. Bell, Carolyn K. Brancato, Craig B. Bright, Robert L. Bunnen, Richard T. Chase, Andrea Corcoran, Charles Ellis, Mark D. Fitterman, Beverly Gordon, Jon L. Hagler, Albert G. Hart, Scott Irwin, Richard G. Ketchum, Robert Kopprasch, Theodore A. Kurz, Dwight Lee, Paul Lowenstein, Burton G. Malkiel, Robert A. G. Monks, Roger Murray, Frank Peabody, Joel Seligman, Jack Treynor, Kimberly Walton, James B. Welles, Malcolm Wiener, and Kevin Winch.

Research assistance was ably provided by a number of people, including Peter Eisenstadt, an historian with the New York Stock Exchange's archives department, and several lawyers and (then) law students at Debevoise & Plimpton, including Nancy Heller, Eugenia McGill, Jane W. Meisel, Alan Michaels, Richard Painter, Eric Sippel, and Marshall Sonnenshine. Many of the staff of the firm, and particularly Lester Stroh, also deserve thanks for their assistance.

Debevoise & Plimpton, however, warrants further mention. The intellectual elbowroom and more tangible support accorded to me in pursuing this study was extraordinary in every sense except that, for those who know the ethos of the place, it would not be terribly surprising. The time commitment required was considerable, far more than anticipated at the outset. Yet, the firm remained quietly supportive and encouraging throughout the undertaking, both with respect to my time and the time of Thomas M. Kelly, a colleague in the firm whose time commitment to this project was roughly equal to mine. Beyond that, one of my partners, Richard D. Kahn, was present at the first meeting with university counsel, assisted in developing the idea, and labored through the first draft of the manuscript to spot weaknesses and generally provide well-aimed comment.

To Francis H. Burr, Esq., Professor Robert Charles Clark, Judge Frank H. Easterbrook, Nicholas de B. Katzenbach, Esq., Dean LeBaron, Hilda Ochoa-Brillembourg, Professor Myron S. Scholes, Dean Richard R. West, and James D. Wolfensohn, the Advisers whose names appear below their statement of support at this book's beginning, I acknowledge a profound appreciation for their willingness to contribute freely their time and important counsel. They made this book better than it otherwise would have been, and by their support, importantly strengthened the authority with which it speaks.

I return to Messrs. Wright and Steiner to acknowledge to them my sense of great good fortune in having their continuous focused interest during the study. The care with which they approached my questions and their close reading of the manuscript were valuable resources along the way.

In hindsight, the single most important, and rewarding, decision made was to ask Tom Kelly to work with me on this study when he commenced practice at Debevoise & Plimpton in the fall of 1984. Although his major effort was directed to the legal review of the prudent man rule contained in Chapter 1, his contributions to the study permeate the book. He was a constant source of intelligence and sound judgment, but that's not all. He seemed always ready at the right moment with encouragement, wit, and boundless good humor.

My secretary, Mary Ann Canuso, had the creative task of divining the meaning of an often obscure hand that carried the drafting work forward without aid from a word processor. To suggest that, without both the alert intelligence and technical skills that she brought to this task and many others involved with the project, the study would never have been completed, is not to exaggerate one bit.

Finally, I should like to thank my wife, Clara, and children, Katie, Tom, and

Ben, for their abiding indulgence and support. Their patience with my long and distracting affair with the prudent man rule competed, often and unduly, with their reasonable demands on the time of a husband and father.

April 1986 Bevis Longstreth

Contents

APPENDICES

Modern Investment Management
and the Prudent Man Rule

Introduction

In recent years the field of finance has exploded with innovation. New investment products and services abound. New investment techniques are constantly being tested and applied. The risks of inflation, the volatility of interest rates, the deregulation of financial intermediaries, and the unbundling of financial services have combined to present investment managers with challenges and opportunities far greater than have existed in the past. Recent experience shows how difficult it is to beat the averages.[1] For managers subject to the prudent man rule[2] in one form or another—fiduciaries we will call them—the task of meeting the challenges and exploiting the opportunities is much more difficult. They must measure their investment decisions against constrained interpretations of a legal standard that have lagged far behind changes in investment theory and in the marketplace.

Nothing in the origins of the prudent man rule would have predicted its present condition. While its ancestry lies in the ancient principle of trust law that a trustee must exercise, on pain of personal liability, a fiduciary duty of care with respect to the funds entrusted to him, the prudent man rule is a creation of American law issuing from the 1830 Massachusetts case of *Harvard College v. Amory*.[3] The *Harvard College* decision framed the trustee's duty as one of "conduct[ing] himself faithfully and exercis[ing] a sound discretion[,] observ[ing] how men of prudence, discretion and intelligence manage their own affairs, not in regard to speculation, but in regard to the permanent disposition of their funds, considering the probable income, as well as the probable safety of the capital to be invested."[4]

This timeless and adaptable formula serves as the basis for the legal standards that now govern most trustees of personal trusts, educational and foundation endowments, and pension funds—consituting more than $1,384 billion in assets.[5] Some sense of the magnitude of this figure is conveyed by comparing it to the total market value of all stocks listed on the New York Stock Exchange—$1,586.1 billion at the end of 1984[6]—or to the value of gross personal assets held by all people in the United States—$5,644 billion as of 1976 (the most recent year for which such data is available).[7]

3

Much of the flexibility of the original *Harvard College* standard was diminished by later cases and commentary, and those encrustations have been slow to change. As interpreted by courts, the rule has looked to established practices to determine prudence. Innovators are suspect precisely because they are ahead of the crowd. As the rate of change in portfolio management increases, so too must the rate at which the prudence standard adjusts to these new realities. Yet this process of adjustment lags. In part this is true simply because court decisions typically appear years after the events in question. The problem is more difficult, however, than this explanation alone suggests.

A review of the literature addressing the investment process leads one to conclude that, despite a broad array of writings in the field, little attention has been paid to the legal constraints of the prudence standard. This subject is addressed by few of the important books on investment management written over the past ten years.[8] Yet the principles of modern investment theory would seem to collide with those of the classic prudent man rule on many fronts.

Options and futures, short-selling, repurchase agreements, securities lending, currency hedging, venture capital, use of nonproductive assets such as precious metals, leverage through margin accounts or second mortgages (in contrast to the often greater leverage acquired through ownership of common stock) are suspect to varying degrees under such traditional statements of prudence as can be found in the late Professor Austin Wakeman Scott's time-honored treatise on trusts[9] and the American Law Institute's venerable Restatement of Trusts, for which the same pre-eminent scholar served as the Reporter.[10] These works are referred to throughout this book as the Treatise and the Restatement, respectively.

The first edition of the Treatise was published in 1939; it has gone through two editions since then, the last in 1967. The first Restatement was completed in 1935 and the second in 1959. It is significant that the rules developed by Scott for investment management by trustees have remained virtually unchanged since the Restatement appeared over fifty years ago and continue to command widespread support.

The prudent man rule of the Treatise and the Restatement only applies directly to trustees for private trusts, and then only in the absence of directions to vary from this standard, which may be included in the trust instrument. Moreover, recently various legislative and regulatory efforts have been made explicitly to depart from the traditional prudence standard in defining the duties of fiduciaries outside the province of private trusteeship. Examples include the Uniform Management of Institutional Funds Act of 1972 (UMIFA), applicable to charitable organizations, the regulations under Section 4944 of the Internal Revenue Code, applicable to private foundations, and the Employee Retirement Income Security Act of 1974 (ERISA) and its regulations, applicable to pension funds. In 1985, the law changed for California trustees of private trusts when that state enacted a new and substantially more flexible version of the prudent man rule.

These developments are important and useful, as are the leading personal trust cases in New York, which emphasize the importance of a sound process for investment decision-making, treating it as the chief determinant of prudence. These advances are insufficient, however, to erode the constraining influence of the Treatise and the Restatement, even in areas outside the law of personal trusts. These works are supported by, and in turn support, a large body of doctrine and case law. In contrast, there are virtually no important cases construing the recent attempts to modernize the law of prudence. Fiduciaries are understandably concerned that a court, reaching for precedent, will apply anachronistic rules drawn from trust law. Counsel to fiduciaries are similarly fettered. The absence of forward-looking, authoritative judicial statements requires counsel to strain over opinions intended to give comfort to fiduciaries and scope to their ingenuity and resourcefulness. These efforts are costly, duplicative, and seldom sufficiently reassuring.

Traditional interpretations of the prudent man rule define "prudence" negatively as the absence of "speculation" and then label particular products and techniques as speculative for all time and purposes. These interpretations suggest that the prudence of each investment should be judged in isolation, without particular reference to its intended function in the overall design of the portfolio. They also suggest that, while fiduciaries should preserve the nominal value of their funds, they need not seek to increase that value, even when inflation makes the steady erosion of purchasing power a near certainty.

There have been some isolated efforts to bring the use of new products and techniques within the ring of prudence. Unfortunately, with the important exception of the Labor Department's flexible interpretation of the ERISA standard, these efforts have tended to focus on specific techniques, such as the writing of calls against long stock positions, without recognizing that equivalent techniques (for example, the writing of puts against cash or cash equivalent positions) may be equally appropriate. Recent actions of both the New York State Department of Insurance[11] and the Board of Governors of the Federal Reserve System[12] illustrate the point. The negative implications of this piecemeal approach have been unfortunate.

Another problem arises out of the special vocabulary associated with some of the new products. On the futures markets, one is either a "hedger" or a "speculator," but never an investor. For those reared with the traditional notion that prudent money managers must not speculate, this terminology may give pause. So too may the use of the term "margin" to describe the initial good faith deposit made on acquiring a futures position. And it is the customary use of "naked" to describe the writer of puts (even when written against cash) that worries fiduciaries who have only recently grown accustomed to "covered" call writing.

Widely accepted lessons of modern economics push hard against these constraining notions of prudence. Indeed, it would not be an exaggeration to observe that today the prudent man rule as elaborated in the Treatise, the Restatement, and much of the case law would virtually compel a fiduciary to act imprudently in terms of economic reality.

Survey Results

It is widely believed that a serious gap exists between what is permitted under traditional legal notions of prudence and what fiduciaries would like to do in the exercise of their best judgment. To test this proposition, a survey was conducted by the author of 200 fiduciaries subject to one or more versions of the prudent man rule. The fifty largest bank trust departments, corporate pension funds, foundations, and private universities were mailed the questionnaire included in Appendix C, which also reports the specific results of the survey. The principal findings, based on a response rate of 45 percent (54 percent for the bank trust departments, 54 percent for the corporate pension funds, 34 percent for the foundations, and 49 percent for the universities), follow.

1. A significant number of fiduciaries believe that the law precludes certain investment opportunities that they would otherwise seek to pursue in what they believe to be the proper discharge of their duties.

2. Many new or unconventional investment products and techniques are considered either legally precluded or questionable by a significant number of fiduciaries.

3. Although some less conventional investments (such as venture capital, real estate, and foreign equities) have gained acceptance in the portfolios of most respondents, others (such as options, futures, and index funds) are not used by most of the respondents.

4. Significant differences exist among groups of fiduciaries regarding the extent of perceived constraint. The spectrum of opinion corresponds to what would be predicted by the relevant legal standards: Bank trust departments, subject in their management of personal trust assets to the most rigid version of the prudent man rule, report the most constraint; at the opposite extreme, corporate pension fund sponsors, subject to ERISA, the most liberal version of the prudence standard, report the least; educational and philanthropic endowments, subject to standards of intermediate liberality, fall roughly in the middle.

5. Delegation of investment authority, a major legal stumbling block before statutory and regulatory reforms over the last fifteen years, is both widespread and apparently unproblematic for the great majority of fiduciaries other than bank trust departments. A significant proportion of these nonbank fiduciaries has retained consultants to assist in selecting investment managers.

6. Developments in financial theory over the last two-and-one-half decades have made a distinct but not overwhelming impression on the attitudes of fiduciaries. For example, while fiduciaries appear to concur with most financial economists that markets are so efficient that it is extremely difficult to achieve consistent superior performance, most fiduciaries still believe it possible to beat the market and worthwhile to try. Further, although modern portfolio theory has significantly influenced the measurement of portfolio risk by fiduciaries, the most popular investment strategy remains that theory's precursor, value-oriented fundamental analysis.

Study Thesis and Goal

The empirical data developed by the survey support the intuition that a gap exists between legal and marketplace notions of prudence, that the law has been left far behind by economic advances in understanding how markets behave and by the dramatic changes in those markets and in the intermediaries who serve the needs of suppliers and users of capital. This is the thesis of the study. Real tensions can and do arise from the possibility that the legal view of prudence sometimes fails to accommodate the sound investment judgments of fiduciaries. The result is that fiduciaries are either exposed to liability for pursuing their best judgment or constrained against the exercise of that judgment to avoid liability. The absence of strong authority to offset the traditional view of prudence constrains counsel to fiduciaries as well, making it hard to bless new investment products and techniques with more than a "pale green" opinion formulated on the basis of what the law should be rather than what judicial and other legal authorities tell counsel it is.

The goal of this study is to bridge the gap by offering a modern paradigm of prudence. The key to this approach is process. Prudence is to be found principally in the process by which investment strategies are developed, adopted, implemented, and monitored in light of the purposes for which funds are held, invested, and deployed. Prudence is demonstrated by the process through which risk is managed, rather than by the definition of specific risks that are imprudent. Under a modern paradigm, no investment is imprudent per se. The products and techniques of investment are essentially neutral. It is the way in which they are used, and how decisions as to their use are made, that should be examined to determine whether the prudence standard has been met. Even the most aggressive and unconventional investment should meet that standard if arrived at through a sound process, while the most conservative and traditional one may not measure up if a sound process is lacking.

The process-based paradigm developed in this study requires more than just procedures and a paper trail to show that they were followed. By emphasizing the importance of process, we do not mean to empty the reviewing function of all substantive content. Process should not be allowed to paper over incompetence or irrationality. The prudence standard has long embraced a duty of caution, which the modern paradigm advanced in this study does nothing to disturb. In examining the prudence of a fiduciary's investment record, a court may be expected to scrutinize the substantive elements of the decision-making process, not to substitute its judgments for those of the fiduciary, but to assure that some rational basis for the fiduciary's judgments existed.

The modern paradigm of prudence applies to all fiduciaries who are subject to some version of the prudent man rule, whether under ERISA, the private foundation provisions of the Code, UMIFA, other state statutes, or the common law. It seeks a synthesis, by emphasizing and developing the dominant themes linking these variations, without dwelling significantly on the differences in language. The purposes for which funds subject to the prudent man rule are held vary infinitely in terms of income needs, time horizons, and capacity to withstand volatility. Accordingly, the portfolio decisions resulting from application of the prudence standard differ from case to case. However, the broad outlines of a fiduciary's duty of prudent investing should be the same regardless of whether he is a director of a foundation, a college or pension fund trustee, or the trustee of a private trust.

Organization

Chapter 1 addresses prudence as defined by the law. After a brief review of its origins, the scope and meaning of the rule are illuminated by a survey of the different forms of the rule in effect today and their elaboration by case law, commentary, and administrative interpretation. It concludes with a summary of the major aspects of the rule that stand in contrast to the lessons of economics and the marketplace.

Chapter 2 briefly sketches the development of financial markets, products, and intermediaries from the sparse investment landscape at the time of the *Harvard College* decision to the richly diverse and crowded marketplace of today. It does not purport to account for the vast changes that occurred, as an economic history devoted to the subject would. Instead, drawing on the available scholarship and data, it attempts to uncover some insights as to why those glosses on the rule that trouble us now made more sense in earlier times and why they should no longer apply. Snapshots of two institutional portfolios at various points over more than 150 years add texture to this account.

Chapter 3 develops through examples the main points of restraint and conflict between legal doctrine, on one hand, and financial theory and marketplace realities, on the other. It begins with the principal conclusions that can be drawn from the economics essay included as Appendix A. That essay, written for this study by Professors of Finance Edward J. Elton[13] and Martin J. Gruber,[14] explores the lessons of modern portfolio theory for prudence. Although intended for noneconomists, the essay is written in some detail. It develops the various alternative asset pricing models and other elements of portfolio theory at a sufficiently technical level to permit the reader to understand the assumptions on which the more prominent pricing models rest and to appreciate not only the complexity of the subject but the underlying reasons for that complexity.

The placement of this essay in an appendix does not imply that it is any less important than the main chapters of this study. Because the goal is law reform, with economics playing a contributing role, it seemed sufficient to draw upon the economic lessons in summary form as needed throughout the main legal argument, while setting forth their full explication in Appendix A. Reading Appendix A, a rewarding exercise in its own right, contributes to the thesis of this study as well. As the economic theories examined by Professors Elton and Gruber become more accessible, readers will recognize the difficulty for the well-informed fiduciary of arriving at a single compellingly correct formula for the exercise of prudence.

Chapter 4 contains the study's principal effort at law reform. Drawing upon the main lessons of earlier chapters, it advances a modern paradigm of prudence and illustrates its application by reference to various investment products and techniques (including securities lending, real estate, venture capital, options and futures, and repurchase agreements) and to two recent cases that applied the constrained version of the prudent man rule.

Chapter 5 is a summary of the study's main conclusions, followed by a recommendation that the American Law Institute undertake a new Restatement of the law of fund management by fiduciaries, which would elaborate and refine the principles of prudence advanced in this study and supersede the corresponding portions of the present Restatement of Trusts. This recommendation draws strength from an essay written for this study by Professor of Law Jeffrey N. Gordon,[15] included as Appendix B. In this essay, which also lends support to other parts of the study's main legal argument, Professor Gordon searches for an explanation of why the prudent man rule has failed to keep pace with the advances in economic learning and the dramatic changes occurring in the marketplace. He finds the answer chiefly in the constrained but authoritative notion of prudence adopted by the Treatise and the Restatement and the complexity of the economic models on which a modern paradigm of prudence could be based.

The study does not address the important issue of whether and to what extent a fiduciary can sacrifice expected monetary return on fund investments in order to achieve other purposes, for example, divestment and avoidance as expressions of protest against corporations doing business in South Africa or investment as an expression of approval regarding a corporation's hiring or environmental policies. Analysis of this issue begins with the purpose for which a fund is held and invested, but a full exegesis of the subject is beyond the scope of this study.[16]

NOTES

[1]SEI Funds Evaluation Services, a pension fund consultant, says that the S&P 500 index outperformed 87 percent of all managers in the decade ending in 1979 and 66 ⅔ percent for the decade ending in 1982. *See* "S&P 500 Index Bests Money Managers in '83, Sharpening Debate on Investment Tactics," Wall St. J., 20 Jan. 1984. Indata, a Southport, Connecticut investment analysis firm, reports that in 1983 the S&P 500 index rose 22.4 percent, outperforming 73 percent of the 622 stock portfolios run by some 200 money managers it monitors. *Id.* More recent data from the same firm indicates that 1985 was the first year since 1982 when the average investment adviser's equity portfolio outperformed the S&P. *See* "Professional Stock Pickers Are Beating S&P 500 for First Time in Three Years," Wall St. J., 19 Dec. 1985; "Investment Advisers Beat S&P 500 Index in Magic Year," Wall St. J., 2 Jan. 1986. However, SEI Funds Evaluation Services reports that the S&P 500 index outperformed 64 percent of all pension accounts in 1983, 75 percent of such accounts in 1984, and 66 percent of such accounts in 1985. *See* "Fund Tracks S&P 500 Index," N.Y. Times, 12 March 1986.

[2]This book uses the term "prudent man rule," rather than the gender-neutral "prudent person rule." Because "prudent man" has been used over the years and this book examines the history of that use, there is some logic to retaining it.

[3]26 Mass. (9 Pick.) 446 (1830) [hereinafter cited as Harvard College].

[4]*Id.* at 461.

[5]The sum of the estimated value of assets held by (i) pension funds subject to ERISA; (ii) personal trust funds managed by banks and trust companies; (iii) endowment funds of all universities, colleges, and other educational institutions, and (iv) endowment funds of all private foundations, derived from the sources indicated:

	Billions
i. pension funds subject to ERISA	$1,000
Source: R. A. Ippolito, *Pensions, Economics, and Public Policy* (1986) Table 1–1, at 5.	
ii. personal trust funds managed by FDIC-insured banks with trust powers and non-federally insured trust companies affiliated with bank holding companies	295.6
Source: Federal Financial Institutions Examination Council, *Trust Assets of Banks and Trust Companies* (1984) (Tentative)	
iii. endowment funds of universities, colleges, and other educational institutions	25.5
Source: *NACUBO 1984 Comparative Performance Study,* Business Officer (April 1985) at 23	
iv. endowment funds of private foundations	63.1
Source: *The Foundation Directory* (10th ed. 1985) at xv	
	$1,384.2

This sum is somewhat understated because it proved impossible to obtain a good estimate of the size of funds held by individually managed personal trusts, religious organizations, and charitable or other nonprofit institutions not specifically covered above.

[6]New York Stock Exchange, *1985 Fact Book* at 79.

[7]U.S. Department of Commerce, Bureau of the Census, *Statistical Abstract of the United States* (105th ed. 1985) Table No. 775, at 463.

[8]*See, e.g.*, R. Brealey & S. Myers, *Principles of Corporate Finance* (2d ed. 1984) (no treatment of prudent man rule); T. E. Copeland & J. F. Weston, *Financial Theory and Corporate Policy* (2d ed. 1983) (same); A. Rudd & K. K. Clasing, Jr., *Modern Portfolio Theory: The Principles of Investment Management* (1982) (same); F. Sharpe, *Investments* (2d ed. 1981) (same). Some explanation of prudent man standards appears in F. J. Fabozzi & F. G. Zarb, eds., *Handbook of Financial Markets* (1981) at 527–44 and 593–607 and S. N. Levine, ed., *Investment Manager's Handbook* (1980) at 567–602, 650–86, 794–96.

[9]A. W. Scott, *Law of Trusts* (3d ed. 1967).

[10]Restatement (Second) of Trusts (1959).

[11]N.Y. Dep't of Insurance Regulations No. 72, § 174.3, and No. 111, § 175.6.

[12]Fed. Banking L. Rep. (CCH) ¶ 35,318. *See* discussion in Chapter 3, *infra* commencing at 89.

[13]Professor of Finance, Graduate School of Business Administration, New York University.

[14]Professor of Finance, Graduate School of Business Administration, New York University.

[15]Associate Professor of Law, New York University School of Law.

[16]*See* Troyer, Slocombe, & Boisture, "Divestment of South Africa Investments: The Legal Implications for Foundations, Other Charitable Institutions and Pension Funds," 74 Geo. L. J. 127 (1985).

CHAPTER 1

The Prudent Man Rule Today—
Variations on a Single Theme

The prudent man of trust law, like his sibling the reasonable man of tort law,[1] is a relatively recent figure in Anglo-American jurisprudence. The roots of the fiduciary relation toward a fund of money known as trusteeship extend back over several centuries of English common law,[2] but the legal fiction of the "prudent man" did not appear until 1830, when the Massachusetts Supreme Judicial Court decided the case of *Harvard College v. Amory.*[3]

The question before the court in the *Harvard College* case, the duty of a trustee in regard to the investment of trust funds, had a relatively straightforward answer in English law at the time. The English Court of Chancery had developed a "court list" of presumptively proper investments that principally directed trustees to invest in government securities.[4] The trustees in the *Harvard College* case were directed by the terms of the $50,000 testamentary trust to "loan the same upon ample and sufficient security, or to invest the same in safe and productive stock, either in the public funds, bank shares of other stock, according to their best judgment and discretion . . [,]"[5] paying the income to the testator's wife for her lifetime and thereafter to deliver the principal to Harvard College and Massachusetts General Hospital in equal shares.[6] The trustees invested in several bank and insurance stocks as well as those of two manufacturing companies. Pointing to the English rule, the two charitable remaindermen sought to surcharge the trustees for declines in value of the insurance and manufacturing stocks (roughly, from $41,000 in total to $29,000) on the ground that they were not proper trust investments. Justice Putnam, who delivered the opinion of the court, rejected the English rule as having "very little or no application"[7] to American trust law for the reason that American government securities were both "exceedingly limited in amount, compared with the amount of trust funds to be invested"[8] and in any event not necessarily a safe investment.[9] Noting that other supposedly "safe" investments such as mortgage lending and real estate ownership were also subject to fluctuation, he concluded: "Do what you will, the capital is at hazard."[10] He then announced what has come to be known as the prudent man rule:

All that can be required of a trustee to invest, is, that he shall conduct himself faithfully and exercise a sound discretion. He is to observe how men of prudence, discretion and intelligence manage their own affairs, not in regard to speculation, but in regard to the permanent disposition of their funds, considering the probable income, as well as the probable safety of the capital to be invested.[11]

The court found that the trustees had satisfied this standard and accordingly refused to hold them liable for the investment losses. In reaching this conclusion the court sounded a related theme that recurs up to the present in any discussion of when a trustee should be liable despite having acted in good faith:

Trustees are justly and uniformly considered favourably, and it is of great importance to bereaved families and orphans, that they should not be held to make good, losses in the depreciation of stocks or the failure of the capital itself, which they held in trust, provided they conduct themselves honestly and discreetly and carefully, according to the existing circumstances, in the discharge of their trusts. If this were held otherwise, no prudent man would run the hazard of losses which might happen without any neglect or breach of good faith.[12]

Despite its appealing flexibility and open-textured capacity to adjust to changing circumstances, the prudent man standard failed to attain wide acceptance outside Massachusetts until the 1940s.[13] The competing desire for certainty about which investments were absolutely safe and prudent and which were not resurfaced in such cases as *King v. Talbot,*[14] decided by the New York Court of Appeals in 1869. In this case, the court declared that common stock investments were essentially per se imprudent.[15] State legislatures began to adopt "legal list" statutes, specifying permissible investments, in the second half of the nineteenth century.[16] By 1900 both the majority of states and the great majority of trust funds were subject to such statutes.[17] The legal lists, like the analogous English statutes, were primarily composed of fixed income securities. One historian of these developments remarks: "Equity participations were almost universally excluded. Common stocks were emphatically 'taboo.' The trustee who purchased or retained unauthorized securities became in substance a guarantor against depreciation."[18]

The collapse of bond values in the depression, among other things, led to disaffection with the legal lists and a trend toward replacement of these statutes with some form of the prudent man standard beginning around 1940.[19] Today, the prudent man rule is overwhelmingly the standard for investment of private trust funds. With different modifications, it has also come to govern the investment of most educational, philanthropic, and other endowment funds (through the Uniform Management of Institutional Funds Act of 1972 (UMIFA) and the regulations pursuant to Section 4944 of the Internal Revenue Code) and private pension funds (through the Employee Retirement Income Security Act of 1974 (ERISA)). The current state of the law of prudence is revealed through an examination of each of these standards.

State Law of Personal Trusts

The Shift from Legal Lists to the Prudent Man Rule

The triumph of the prudent man standard over the legal list approach in state law governing the management of personal trust funds is nearly complete. By judicial decision or, more commonly, by legislative action, forty states have adopted the prudent man rule as the standard governing the investment decisions of these fiduciaries in the absence of language to the contrary in the trust instrument.[20] Almost all of the statutory standards are variations of the Model Investment Statute developed by the Trust Division of the American Bankers Association in the 1940s.[21] The model statute was intended to enact the rule of the *Harvard College* case and adopts that case's language almost verbatim:

> In acquiring, investing, reinvesting, exchanging, retaining, selling and managing property for the benefit of another, a fiduciary shall exercise the judgment and care, under the circumstances then prevailing, which men of prudence, discretion and intelligence exercise in the management of their own affairs, not in regard to speculation but in regard to the permanent disposition of their funds, considering the probable income as well as the probable safety of their capital.[22]

The statute, known as the Model Prudent Man Investment Act, authorizes specifically certain kinds of investments subject to the general prudence standard. The list includes real estate, bonds, common and preferred stock, and mutual funds, "which men of prudence, discretion and intelligence acquire or retain for their own account."[23]

The model statute was meant to emancipate. Its principal draftsman described the prudent man rule that the statute enacted as "a bright star in a newly discovered galaxy."[24] However, interpretations of the rule have made a black hole the more likely metaphor. A growing body of commentary argues that the rule has become rigid and anachronistic in application, particularly in light of modern portfolio theory and investment techniques.[25] One writer suggests that "in some respects, the rule has become nearly as inflexible as the legal lists it replaced."[26]

The Influence of the Treatise and the Restatement

The source of this rigidity is to be found not in the open-textured language of the rule itself, but in the glosses upon it by courts and commentators. In this respect it would be almost impossible to underestimate the influence of the Treatise and the Restatement. They have both achieved canonical standing in the law of private trusts.[27]

The Treatise[28] and the Restatement[29] charge the trustee with a duty to administer the trust with such care and skill as a man of ordinary prudence would exercise in dealing with his own property. The standard governing investment decisions, however, adds a further requirement of caution to the general duties of care and skill.[30] It is no longer sufficient simply to ask how a prudent man would deal with his own property, "since men of prudence may well take risks in making investments which trustees are not justified in taking."[31] Rather, a "trustee must use the caution in making investments which is used by prudent men who have primarily in view the preservation of their property, of men who are safeguarding property for others."[32] Thus, instead of the "prudent man," the test becomes one of the "prudent trustee." In the Treatise, Scott concedes the circularity of exhorting the trustee to act as a prudent trustee and suggests the objective standard of a "prudent family man."[33]

The Treatise and the Restatement also articulate the distinction between prudent and imprudent investments in terms of the prohibition against "speculation." The Treatise states that the following are almost universally permitted: bonds of the United States or of the state or of municipalities in the state, first mortgages on land within the state, and corporate bonds "of certain classes which are supposed to be especially free from risk."[34] Generally impermissible investments, on the other hand, include margin trading, "speculative shares of stock," bonds selling at a large discount because of uncertainty as to whether they will be paid at maturity, securities in "new and untried enterprises," or "land or other things [purchased] for the purpose of resale."[35]

The Comment to the Restatement offers little guidance on the question of what is a "speculative" stock beyond the statement that "the purchase of shares of preferred or common stock of a company with regular earnings and paying regular dividends which may reasonably be expected to continue is a proper trust investment if prudent men in the community are accustomed to invest in such shares when making an investment of their savings with a view to their safety."[36] The Comment goes on to list a number of factors for the trustee to consider in selecting an investment in addition to the factors of safety of principal and amount and regularity of income.[37] In effect these factors seek to reconcile the often conflicting interests of income beneficiaries and remaindermen by balancing maximization of income against preservation of principal, thus assuring contending beneficiaries of the trustee's impartiality.

Pervasive changes in the financial marketplace (as sketched in Chapter 2) and advances in financial theory and practice (as developed in Appendix A) have rendered the Restatement's quarter-century-old prescriptions for prudent conduct self-contradictory and sometimes self-defeating. Persistent inflation and volatile interest rates have expanded and reordered the universe of "prudent" investments, while modern portfolio theory and its refinements have redefined the first principles of investment management. As a result, a trustee wishing to carry out certain of the Restatement's directions, such as those to consider the likelihood of inflation or to exercise skill greater than that of a man of ordinary prudence if he has or claims to have such special skills, would find that other, antiquated sections of the Restatement stand in his way.

The "likelihood of inflation" is listed in the Comment to Section 227 of the Restatement as the last of the ten factors a trustee should consider in selecting an investment.[38] The experience of the last fifty years certainly justifies giving that concern a more prominent place in the investment calculus.[39] However, the Restatement, written in a period when one court could categorize an assumption of future inflation as "speculation,"[40] does not recognize a duty to preserve the purchasing power of a trust's assets. Indeed, in the Comment to Section 227 every illustration of the duty to preserve principal is stated in terms of preventing nominal, rather than purchasing power, loss. Conversely, investment strategies intended to increase the dollar value of principal are discussed primarily in connection with the prohibition against speculation.[41].

Some courts have responded positively to inflation-conscious investment strategies, but none has imposed a duty to guard against depreciation in purchasing power.[42] Indeed, it has been suggested that the common law of trusts either forbids or seriously constrains the practice of every important traditional hedge against inflation.[43] Investments in rental real estate may be construed as the conduct of a trade or business and therefore are forbidden; precious metals and collectibles are suspect as unproductive assets; even a portfolio of common stocks, while clearly not prohibited per se, is more problematic than investments less likely to withstand the ravages of inflation (such as traditional debt investments).[44]

Some decisions have recognized inflation as a "changed circumstance" of sufficient magnitude to justify departing from directions in trust instruments to invest only in debt securities. In the leading case of *In re Mayo,*[45] the Supreme Court of Minnesota granted the petition of a beneficiary of two personal trusts, created in 1917 and 1919, to allow the trustees to deviate from a provision restricting investments to "real estate mortgages, municipal bonds or any other form of income bearing property (but not real estate nor corporate stock)."[46] The trust assets were invested primarily in municipal bonds and between 1939 (the year of the donor's death) and 1958 lost half of their value in inflation-adjusted dollars. During the same period, the market value of common stocks almost doubled. In reaching its holding that "unless deviation is ordered the dominant intention of the donor to prevent a loss of the principal of the two trusts will be frustrated[,]"[47] the court relied upon the unforeseeability of significant inflation at the time of the donor's death, the high likelihood of future inflation, and the evolution of common stocks as a suitable and widely held trust investment.[48]

The express holding of the *Mayo* decision stopped far short of imposing a duty to preserve real as well as nominal values. The court simply granted the trustees permission, in their discretion, "to invest a reasonable amount of the trust assets in corporate stocks of good, sound investment issues."[49] However, the *Mayo* trustees, including one bank that commonly invested the assets of its trusts in corporate stocks, had opposed the trust beneficiary's petition, arguing, among other things, that the donor was well aware of the possibility of inflation. The court rejected the trustees' arguments in dicta, suggesting that a complete refusal to consider inflation in investment decisions disserves trust beneficiaries:

> Through an investment in bonds and mortgages of the type designated by the donor, plus corporate stocks of good, sound investment issues, in our opinion, the trusts will, so far as possible, be fortified against inflation, recession, depression, or decline in prices. Corporate trustees of the kind here are regularly managing trusts consisting of corporate stocks, bonds, and mortgages, on a successful basis. There appears to be no sound reason why they cannot do the same thing here.[50]

The highest court of Kentucky followed the reasoning of the *Mayo* decision in *Carlick v. Keiler.*[51] The testator in the *Carlick* case died in 1913 leaving a will that called for investments in "good, interest-bearing securities."[52] The trustees had invested in preferred and common stock as well as bonds and debentures, and the estate's value increased fourfold. Nonetheless, various guardians ad litem challenged an accounting, seeking to restrict investments to debt securities as provided in the will.

The court found that the settlor's overriding intention of providing adequately for the income beneficiaries of the trust would be frustrated by adherence to the investment restrictions found in the will:

> To assure a comparative income as well as to preserve the comparative value of a capital fund, the contemporary prudent investor, as were the trustees of this fund, seeks recognized stocks paying dividends from the corporate profits whose values will float with the inflationary tide rather than bonds of a value and interest rate forever pegged as of the time of their issue.[53]

A similar case in the charitable trust area is *Davison v. Duke University,*[54] in which the Supreme Court of North Carolina construed the governing instruments of the Duke Endowment. The endowment's trustees sought a broadening of investment powers beyond the categories of Duke Power Company securities, U.S. government bonds, and certain state and municipal bonds. The North Carolina Attorney General and certain beneficiaries opposed the petition. Reasoning that "the ravages of inflation and other economic pressures threaten[ed] to destroy the dominant purposes"[55] of the endowment, the court affirmed the trial court's modification of the investment restrictions.

While these cases would provide some comfort to a trustee seeking to make inflation hedging an important factor in portfolio decisions, they bless only the most timid inflation hedge: highly conservative common stocks. Further, none of them tests the robustness of inflation hedging as a defense to a surcharge action brought to recover investment losses. Finally, there is case law contrary to the *Mayo* rationale.[56]

The Restatement undercuts itself in another way when it directs that "if the trustee has or procures his appointment as trustee by representing that he has greater skill than that of a man of ordinary prudence, he is under a duty to exercise such skill."[57] Corporate or "professional" trustees such as bank trust departments may safely be assumed to profess special skills and, accordingly, to be subject to this more stringent standard.[58] While just how substantial a degree of additional skill must be exercised is an open question, the intensity of the interest shown by professional trustees in New York's recent adoption of a special skills standard[59] suggests that the distinction has meaning.

Assuming that "skill" denotes acquaintance with the more sophisticated methods of investment management and the prudent adaptation of those methods to the needs of the trust beneficiaries, the problem for a trustee held to possess this skill is that the general framework of the Restatement codifies premises of investment management that today would find few adherents among skilled investment managers. As has already been discussed, the exercise of skill in investment management has for some time entailed understanding risk as containing both systematic and unsystematic components and accordingly judging any particular investment in terms of its place in the overall portfolio.

The notion of a tradeoff between risk and return is neither revolutionary nor foreign to the Restatement.[60] Diversification is mandated as a general practice by Section 228: "Except as otherwise provided by the terms of the trust, the trustee is under a duty to the beneficiary to distribute the risk of loss by a reasonable diversification of investments, unless under the circumstances it is prudent not to do so."[61] However, the analytical method of the Comment to Section 227, concerning proper trust investments, is to classify types of investments as either more or less imprudent in themselves, without regard for the possibility that the same investment might be an imprudent addition to one portfolio and a prudent selection for another depending on the other assets in the portfolio.[62] Consequently, the Restatement discourages investments that appear "imprudent" in isolation, but which would reduce the riskiness of the overall portfolio.

Review of Case Law

A review of recent case law reveals that reported decisions testing the prudence of novel investment strategies or even discussing the basic precepts of modern portfolio theory that give rise to those strategies are virtually nonexistent. Although the body of legal scholarship urging the acceptance of modern portfolio theory by the courts and legislatures has grown since the early 1970s to include three student notes and two major articles and a book by leading legal academics, the cry for reform appears to have fallen upon deaf ears. Based upon a Lexis search of state court decisions, it appears that no court has ever considered any of these arguments in any detail. Indeed, this scholarship is almost never cited at all.[63] Perhaps counsel for trustees in surcharge actions have decided against advancing novel economic arguments for a change in the law in order to avoid the implication that the trustee's conduct is insupportable under existing law. In any event, the depth of judicial indifference to new learning in trust investment law stands in stark contrast to an embrace of the efficient market theory in the field of securities law by some federal courts and the Securities and Exchange Commission.[64]

Further, the relatively small number of reported decisions on the prudence of investments of any kind suggests that litigation challenging trustees' investment decisions is rare. It has been suggested that, at least in cases involving institutional trustees, the courts are so lenient toward trustees that beneficiaries are simply discouraged from suing to recover for investment losses.[65]

Even if that were true for widely accepted categories of permissible investments, a more likely explanation for the absence of cases testing the prudence of innovative strategies is the reluctance of trustees to engage in such strategies in light of the conservative interpretations of the prudent man rule by the Treatise and the Restatement and the absence of judicial precedent. A 1978 report by the Committee on Investment by Fiduciaries of the Trust Section of the American Bar Association, for example, in its discussion of the prudence of option trading, notes that while many investment advisers and professional money managers practice option trading, no court had yet sanctioned the practice. The report asked "who wants to be the fiduciary to provide litigation and decision?"[66]

The same report predicts in its conclusion that some trust investments of the future would have surprised the fiduciaries of the era of the *Harvard College* case, but concludes "fiduciaries will do well not to be 'the first by whom the new are tried, nor yet the last to cast the old aside.'"[67]

Many of the cases on prudent investment standards are actually decided according to some more lenient standard posited by the trust instrument involved and therefore superseding the prudent man rule.[68] The frequency with which the drafters of trust instruments attempt to displace the prudence standard may indicate a perception that the standard as currently interpreted is an obstacle to effective investment strategies. It may also explain the general scarcity of case law concerning investments by trustees,[69] which may in turn suggest that the prudent man rule is easily circumvented. On the other hand, specific authorizations in the trust instrument to invest in certain innovative or novel forms of investment are apparently frequently ignored by trustees unless the investment category is otherwise generally accepted.[70]

Decisions actually surcharging trustees are indeed rare. Some in fact seem to turn on bad faith or gross negligence bordering on bad faith, rather than imprudence alone. For example, in *In re Estate of Collins*,[71] the California Court of Appeal reversed the trial court's finding that the trustees of a personal trust had not acted imprudently in investing two-thirds of the trust principal in a loan to a builder secured by a second trust deed. The entire investment of $50,000 was lost when the builder declared bankruptcy and the holder of the first trust deed foreclosed. Applying California's statutory prudent man rule, the appellate court concluded that the trustees failed to follow that standard, "first, by investing two-thirds of the trust principal in a single investment, second, by investing in real property secured only by a second deed of trust, and third, by making that investment without adequate investigation of either the borrowers or the collateral."[72] The builder who received the loan was a client of one of the trustees, the settlor's lawyer. While this fact surely influenced the court's decision, no discussion of it or of the duty of loyalty problems it raises appears in the court's statement of its reasoning and legal conclusions.

A surcharge case involving conduct that would offend even a much more permissive standard than the prudent man rule is *In re Estate of Dwight*.[73] In that case the Supreme Court of Hawaii affirmed the surcharge of a bank trustee of a personal trust on facts that probably would have supported a finding of gross negligence. The trustee had purchased a decrepit fifty-year-old building with numerous serious physical defects and safety code violations, yet had failed to secure any structural or termite inspections or even to inquire about conformity with building, health, safety, and fire code requirements. Following the refusal of a new tenant to pay further rent due to the building's substandard condition, the building lay idle and yielded no income for a thirty-nine-month period, after which it was finally sold at public auction. Applying Hawaii's statutory prudent man standard, the court concluded that the trustee had acted imprudently in purchasing the property and had breached its duty to preserve the property and make it profitable.

The other recent surcharge cases, because they involve more sophisticated trustees and less clearly imprudent conduct, supply a more appropriate body of evidence against which to measure the soundness of the differing perceptions of the prudent man rule. Considered against this evidence, neither of the two most stringent characterizations of the rule, discussed below, appears to be well-founded. On the whole, the recent reported decisions fail to support the view that trustees are never surcharged except for dishonesty or outrageous neglect. Neither do they justify the opposite notion: That courts, gifted with twenty-twenty hindsight, are deeply suspicious of any investment more "speculative" than the safest fixed-income securities and frequently impose liability for honest mistakes of judgment. Not surprisingly, a more accurate account of these cases falls somewhere between these two polar views.

Only one recent decision applies the rule so harshly as to justify its reputation for backwardness and irrationality. In *First Alabama Bank of Montgomery, N.A. v. Martin*,[74] the Supreme Court of Alabama affirmed the trial court's surcharge of a bank trustee for losses incurred by two large common trust funds due to investments in common stock and real estate investment trust (REIT) debentures. The plantiffs' expert, citing a treatise by Benjamin Graham that is not named in the decision, testified that a trustee should not purchase stocks of companies that failed to meet any one of eight criteria for testing the safety of investments. Those criteria were:

(1) A minimum of $100 million in annual sales; (2) a current ratio of at least two to one (current assets should be twice current liabilities); (3) a net working capital to long-term debt ratio of at least one to one (net working capital being current assets less current liabilities and long-term debt meaning obligations that mature in more than one year); (4) earnings stability (positive earnings for the last ten years); (5) a good dividend record; (6) an earnings growth measure of at least one-third per share over a ten-year period, averaging the first three years and the last three years to remove extremes; (7) a moderate price earnings ratio of no more than fifteen to one; and (8) a moderate ratio of price to assets of no more than one and one half to one.[75]

On cross-examination, the same expert conceded that only five of the thirty stocks in the Dow Jones industrial average would meet all eight criteria. The bank then called an expert witness who testified to the soundness of investing in growth companies as an inflation hedge. The same expert testified that Standard and Poor's ratings were not intended to be used as investment recommendations and were not used as a guide to sound investments by experienced analysts. The trust investment officer who made the investments in question testified as to his investment policy. He said that because in 1971 and 1972, the time of the purchases, the "favorite fifty stocks" were selling at very high prices, he sought securities that were relatively undervalued. He testified further that he did not rely on prospectuses, saw little difference in stocks rated B (speculative) and B+ (medium), believed that the rating services did not understand their business, and attempted to buy securities of companies in their growth cycles rather than after they had matured.

The evidence considered sufficient by the court to support a finding of imprudence consisted of: (1) the plaintiffs' expert witness's testimony that most of the common stock investments failed to meet all eight of his criteria; (2) the fact that the defendant's expert witness, although he testified that he believed the stock purchases were prudent, could not say that he, as an investment adviser for a number of trust companies, had ever recommended the purchase of any of those stocks; and (3) the testimony of the trust investment officer. The court considered the investment officer's testimony that he "tried to buy undervalued stocks instead of the higher priced, more established ones"[76] evidence of imprudence. The collapse of the higher priced, more established stocks—the "favorite fifty"— in the bear market of 1973 to 1974 goes undiscussed in the court's opinion.[77]

The remaining surcharge cases employ an approach that, compared to the Alabama court's, is less doctrinaire, more reluctant to second-guess a trustee's investment judgments, and consequently more permissive. In *Chase v. Pevear*,[78] the highest court of Massachusetts reduced the surcharge amount imposed by a lower court on a trustee, who was a professional investment adviser, for losses on investments in common stocks and debt securities, including debentures of a REIT. In an opinion by Justice Braucher, the court agreed that no investment should automatically be held improper because of "lack of 'seasoning' for some minimum period, because of the line of business, such as Real Estate Investment Trusts (REITS) or 'conglomerates,' because of ratings by services such as Moody's or Standard & Poor's, because of the recommendations of the investment adviser, or because of price history."[79] However, the court said, those elements might properly be taken into account as factors in determining the prudence of an investment.

The court's analysis of each of the particular investments in question suggests that the chief test of prudence is whether a particular investment is commonly held by other trustees. In almost every instance, the primary reason cited by the court to support the prudence of an investment was the fact that it was widely held by other common trust funds and by institutional investors.[80] For example, the court stated its reasoning for rejecting the probate judge's findings as to the prudence of investment in Penn Central common stock in favor of the master's findings as follows:

> The judge characterized the Penn Central investment as a "speculation" primarily because the trustee relied on real estate and other non-rail values and earnings. But the

master found that others did the same, and that the stock was widely held, in 1968, by financial institutions and common trust funds. We accept those findings, and the conclusion follows that the investment was properly made.[81]

The court concluded that none of the investments in question were imprudent from the outset, but that the trustee had held some of them for too long after they had become imprudent. As a result, the total surcharge for failure to make timely sales was less than $12,000, although the total losses on the investments in question appear to have been much larger.

The notion that prudence is determined chiefly by whether an investment is one commonly held by trustees entails greater judicial deference to trustees' expertise than is found in the *Martin* decision and similar cases. Although the rationale of the *Chase* decision implies that innovative or unconventional investments are inherently suspect, it has the virtue of preventing a court from imposing notions of prudence that are drastically out of step with those in practice among trustees. Recent decisions in New York suggest a similar reluctance by courts to judge the substantive or inherent wisdom of trustees' investment decisions. These cases reflect a tendency to uphold the prudence of investment decisions as long as the trustee can provide a record of diligence and informed deliberation in reaching them.

The most frequently cited of these decisions is *In re Bank of New York (Spitzer)*,[82] a New York Court of Appeals case that upheld the prudence of four common stock investments made by a bank trust department on behalf of its common trust fund during the 1960s. The case is most frequently cited for its ambiguous dictum concerning the extent to which individual investments should be judged in relation to their place in the overall portfolio:

> The fact that this portfolio showed substantial overall increase in total value during the accounting period does not insulate the trustee from responsibility for imprudence with respect to individual investments for which it would otherwise be surcharged.... To hold to the contrary would in effect be to assure fiduciary immunity in an advancing market such as marked the history of the accounting period here involved. The record of any individual investment is not to be viewed exclusively, of course, as though it were in its own water-tight compartment, since to some extent individual investment decisions may properly be affected by considerations of the performance of the fund as an entity, as in the instance, for example, of individual security decisions based in part on considerations of diversification of the fund or of capital transactions to achieve sound tax planning for the fund as a whole. The focus of inquiry, however, is nonetheless on the individual security as such and factors relating to the entire portfolio are to be weighed only along with others in reviewing the prudence of the particular investment decisions.[83]

In rejecting the guardian ad litem's challenge to the trustee's investment decisions, the court did not elaborate its reasoning in detail, remarking that "procedures we now find acceptable with respect to these investments at the time of this accounting may not be satisfactory at another time in other circumstances."[84] The opinion suggests, however, that a record of diligence and good faith by the trustee heavily influenced the court's holding:

> It was not shown in any instance that the losses to the trust fund resulted from imprudence or negligence. There was evidence of attention and consideration with reference to each decision made. Obviously, it is not sufficient that hindsight might suggest that

another course would have been more beneficial; nor does a mere error of investment judgment mandate a surcharge. Our courts do not demand investment infallibility, nor hold a trustee to prescience in investment decisions.[85]

Similarly, in *In re Morgan Guaranty Trust Co. of New York,*[86] the Surrogate's Court analyzed the prudence of transactions involving three common stocks and one convertible preferred stock solely in terms of the process by which the investment decisions were made. After describing in great detail the bank trust department's elaborate system of investment committees, stock research, daily meetings, and so forth, the court concluded:

> The elaborate description of the formal proceedings disclosed in the record before the court as well as the extensive investigations and considerations of the aforementioned securities by the appropriate committees, as revealed on this record, support no other conclusion than that the investment transactions were not imprudent.[87]

Similar analysis and a similar result appear in *Stark v. United States Trust Company of New York,*[88] a federal court diversity case applying New York law. The plaintiffs in *Stark* were trust beneficiaries who sought to surcharge the trustee for its failure to sell shares in three common stocks that were present in the trust at the time of the settlor's death in 1972 and that fell in value from approximately $940,000 to $93,000 within three years.[89] Judge Weinfeld's opinion devotes several pages to describing the trustee's internal decision-making processes, which included an investment policy committee that made general portfolio strategy recommendations and a portfolio manager responsible for the day-to-day handling of accounts, and the application of those processes to the investment decisions in question. Stressing the dangers of hindsight judgments of trustees, the court concluded: "The trustee's retention decisions were results of careful and informed deliberations; the fact that in retrospect they may have been wrong or unwise is no ground for surcharge."[90]

With regard to the erroneous recommendations of the investment policy committee, the court said:

> Indeed, daily we witness instances of public officials and financial experts, specialists in the field of economics, fiscal and monetary affairs, whose forecasts of events are far wide of eventualities. Given the breadth of information and analyses the [committee] reports contain, their predictions were certainly not without a reasonable basis—which is all that is required.[91]

These cases suggest that a trustee is most likely to avoid surcharge if he invests trusts' funds exactly as other trustees do and takes care to build a record of his decision-making process. Thus, the law encourages trustees to pursue safety in numbers regardless of how misguided the prevailing wisdom of the moment might be (as illustrated by the Nifty Fifty craze) or how substantively sound and prudent an innovative or unorthodox strategy might be. Given the general reluctance among trustees to offer themselves as test cases, development of legal standards in ways that would give comfort to trustees wishing to adapt imaginatively to development in investment theory and financial markets appears unlikely. It should not occasion surprise, then, that the most dramatic initiative toward revision of the prudent man rule, like the adoption of the rule in the 1930s and 1940s, has been legislative rather than judicial. Effective January 1, 1985, California replaced its statutory prudent man standard (drawn, like most states', from the *Harvard College* case) with language drawn from the ERISA standard:

> (a) *Degree of care, skill, prudence and diligence.* (1) Subject to paragraph (2), when investing, reinvesting, purchasing, acquiring, exchanging, selling and managing property for the benefit of another, a trustee shall act with the care, skill, prudence, and diligence under the circumstances then prevailing, specifically including, but not by way of limitation, the general economic conditions and the anticipated needs of the trust and its beneficiaries, that a prudent person acting in a like capacity and familiar with such matters would use in the conduct of an enterprise of a like character and with like aims, to attain the goals of the trustor as determined from the trust instrument. Within the limitations of the foregoing and considering individual investments as part of an overall investment strategy, a trustee is authorized to acquire every kind of property, real, personal or mixed, and every kind of investment.
>
> (2) The trustor may expand or restrict the standards set forth in paragraph (1) by express provisions in a trust instrument. Any trustee acting for the benefit of another under that instrument shall not be liable to anyone whose interests arise from that trust for the trustee's good faith reliance on those express provisions.[92]

The most striking features of the new statute are the elimination of the classic language prohibiting "speculation," the specific directions to take into account general economic conditions (presumably including inflation) and the particular needs of the trust, and, most strikingly, the instruction to consider individual investments as part of an overall investment strategy. It is impossible to discover with any certainty the intentions of the new statute's drafters because of what one commentator has described as the "virtually complete absence of official legislative history."[93] There are as yet no cases interpreting the new statute. At a minimum, however, California's legislative initiative appears to signal a desire to encourage adaptability to changing circumstances and a perception that, in the hands of the courts, the broad, flexible, and apparently timeless language of *Harvard College* has become a less suitable vehicle for promoting that adaptability than a standard containing more specific directions for investment management.

State Law Governing Trustees of Endowments and Other Charitable Corporations: The Uniform Management of Institutional Funds Act

As discussed previously, liability for imprudent investments is relatively rare in the personal trust area. In the law governing fiduciaries of educational and foundation endowments and other similar charitable corporations, it is practically nonexistent. New York's Assistant Attorney General responsible for the supervision of charities, citing Professor Joseph Bishop's assertion that "a search for cases in which the directors [of business corporations] have been held liable. . . .for negligence uncomplicated by self-dealing is a search for a very small number of needles in a very large haystack[,]"[94] remarked recently that "Professor Bishop's observation remains substantially accurate. In the nonprofit area, to extend his metaphor, there would be *no* needles in the haystack (although it is a considerably smaller haystack)."[95]

The absence of needles can most plausibly be explained first, by the scarcity of plaintiffs possessing both standing and incentive to sue, and second, by judicial reluctance to surcharge a trustee who acted in good faith and who received little or no compensation for his service to the nonprofit institution. The author of a leading article in this field once observed that the law of charitable institutions stands as an exception to the law's usual "reliance on those who are most immediately interested in the property or enterprise administered by a fiduciary to call [its] enforcement machinery into action."[96] Beneficiaries occupy this place in the sphere of private trusts, as shareholders do in that of business corporations. But, the author noted, "there is no beneficiary in a comparable position who is sufficiently interested as an individual to call the charitable fiduciary to account."[97]

In most states, only the attorney general, co-trustees, and successor trustees possess standing to challenge the decisions of the trustees of a charitable corporation.[98] In addition, as New York's Attorney General observed in the course of arguing for a higher standard of care for directors of nonprofit corporations than for those of business corporations, nonprofit institutions enjoy insulation from marketplace discipline for mismanagement: "The stock will not plummet; the organization will not report a decline in earnings or sales—there is no easy way to measure or control the quality of performance."[99]

The apparent infrequency of litigation against trustees of charitable corporations, comforting as it might be expected to be for those fiduciaries, has in one sense worked the opposite effect. In contrast to the law of trusts, on the one hand, and the law of business corporations on the other, the law governing the duties of trustees of charitable corporations is comparatively recent and undeveloped. From the perspective of fiduciaries of large nonprofit institutions that resemble business corporations in their need for flexible and sophisticated management, the primary danger in this is that courts might mechanically and inappropriately apply trust law doctrine to the management of endowments that differ radically from private trusts.

Private colleges and universities typically operate as nonprofit corporations.[100] Other charitable endowments such as foundations may be organized either as charitable trusts or nonprofit corporations, but the latter form is decidedly more common.[101] Charitable trust doctrine, however, is more elaborated by case law; one author has remarked that "[w]hile both charitable trusts and charitable corporations have been used for centuries, only the former has involved many litigated disputes."[102] The principal point of tension for large charitable trusts has been the courts' tendency to apply trust law principles to charitable trusts and corporate law principles to charitable corporations. Kenneth Karst attacked this formalistic distinction in a 1960 article entitled "The Efficiency of the Charitable Dollar: An Unfulfilled State Responsibility":[103]

> [T]here is no good reason for making different rules for the managers of two large foundations simply becuase one is a corporation and the other a trust. The law should recognize that the charitable trust and the charitable corporation have more in common with each other than each has with its private counterpart. The important differences among charities relate not to their form but to their function. In the area of fiduciary duties, a law of charities is needed.[104]

In ensuing years, a number of other commentators have repeated the call for a unitary standard.[105]

At the same time, the tendency to apply corporate principles to charitable corporations has been less than reliable. One commentator states:

> Some courts apply trust standards of loyalty and care to charitable trusts and corporations while others apply corporate principles to both. Courts have applied different standards to the same organization, or have applied the stricter trust standards while reject-

ing some of the specific requirements accompanying this standard as being too onerous or unrealistic. Courts sometimes complicate the situation by concluding that a corporation is holding property in trust.[106]

The Restatement offers a similarly murky picture of the status of charitable corporations. Section 379 states: "The duties of the trustee of a charitable trust are similar to the duties of the trustee of a private trust"; the Comment to Section 379 adds: "In the case of a charitable corporation duties of a somewhat similar character rest upon the members of the controlling board, whether they are called directors or trustees."[107]

The narrower question of what rules govern the investment decisions of fiduciaries for educational endowments and other charitable corporations has enjoyed no exemption from the general confusion so characteristic of the law of charitable corporations. The portfolio constraints affecting these institutions differ so dramatically from those governing the typical private trust that one would expect appropriately different rules to apply. The trustee of a private trust must be impartial as between successive beneficiaries: he must produce a reasonable income for the life beneficiary, but must also preserve the capital for ultimate delivery, at an uncertain date, to the remainderman. Thus, it is said, he must avoid investments that are non-income producing, wasting, or highly volatile. The antagonistic interests of the income beneficiary and the remainderman imbue the characterization of investment returns as income or principal with a flesh-and-blood immediacy.

A foundation or university endowment also faces regular income needs and should also, it is generally agreed, be held to some requirement of caution in its investments. However, the need for impartiality as between successive beneficiaries has no application in the endowment context; the principal-income distinction, lacking economic significance, becomes a pallid accountants' quarrel. The portfolio's time horizon is perpetual. It may therefore tolerate fairly high risk levels for the sake of higher long-term return; it must as a practical matter assume a risk level sufficient to avoid eventual extinction through loss of the fund's purchasing power.

Presumably because of at least some of these numerous and fairly obvious differences, the legal lists dictating permissible investments for trustees, in those states possessing such statutory lists, have generally been assumed not to apply to trustees of charitable corporations.[108] The Restatement states:

> Where money is given to a charitable corporation for its general purposes, it may make such investments as a prudent man would make. Even in a State in which trustees are restricted, by statute or otherwise, to certain kinds of investments, the restriction is not applicable.[109]

Thus the law has long acknowledged that, at least to some extent, endowments ought to be treated differently from private trusts under rules governing permissible investments. But the view persisted that the law might apply inappropriate trust doctrines to endowment funds, culminating in the "total return" debate of the late 1960s. By that time inflation had seriously eroded the purchasing power of traditionally fixed-income-laden endowment portfolios. "Growth" stocks were thought to be a good inflation hedge because of their potential for substantial long-term appreciation; however, they typically pay low dividends and yield most of their investment return through capital appreciation. "Endowment" funds are funds the principal of which must be kept intact in perpetuity; only the income may be spent to meet current operating expenses. Trust law treats capital gains as principal rather than income. In the 1960s many endowment fiduciaries assumed or feared that the same rule governed them and therefore considered themselves unable to spend any part of capital appreciation.

The Ford Foundation sponsored a study of the problem by William L. Cary and Craig B. Bright, published in 1969, entitled *The Law and the Lore of Endowment Funds.* Proceeding from the premise that "room exists for great improvement" in the investment of endowment funds, the study set out to "examine the law governing endowment funds in an attempt to determine its bearing on . . . a sound investment policy."[110] Although some leading institutions had adopted a "total return" policy permitting the expenditure of a portion of capital gains, the results of a survey conducted in connection with the study suggested that many, if not most, endowment fiduciaries believed that "as a matter of law the capital gains of endowment funds may not be expended, because the principal of endowment funds must be maintained intact and in perpetuity and capital gains are part of that principal."[111]

In the course of determining the soundness of the notion that the law prohibits endowments from pursuing a total return policy, the authors of *The Law and the Lore* undertook to examine the law of charitable corporations generally and in particular the legal standards governing investments of those institutions' assets. Their conclusions must have surprised many. They determined that "the only body of learning which treats realized gains as anything other than income is the law of trusts, which was developed to accommodate the divergent interests of income beneficiaries and remaindermen;"[112] that while "[n]o jurisdiction treats charitable corporations exactly like business corporations or exactly like trusts for all purposes,"[113] in the area of administration, "particularly financial administration, courts uniformly tend to apply the more flexible principles found in corporate law;"[114] and that "there is no substantial authority under existing law to support the widely held view that the realized gains of endowment funds of educational institutions must be treated as principal."[115] The authors found that the very few reported cases regarding liability for imprudent investment decisions generally apply a test similar to the business judgment rule despite frequent invocations of a more exacting standard:

> In summary, neither directors nor trustees are liable under the law for reasonable mistakes of judgment or for failure to foresee events which are not generally anticipated. A trustee may be liable for actual negligence, but directors have not even been held to that standard. As a practical matter courts require proof of bad faith or gross or wilful neglect before imposing personal liability upon directors of business corporations, and the little authority in point indicates that this is true also in respect of directors of charitable corporations.[116]

On balance, the authors reported, "legal impediments which have been thought to deprive managers [of educational endowment funds] of their freedom of action" were "more legendary than real."[117]

Cary and Bright's confident conclusion that a charitable corporation director's duty with respect to investments is defined by a standard substantially similar to the business judgment rule rested upon the facts and results of the cases analyzed more than upon the standards the courts purported to apply in those cases. In this conclusion Cary and Bright followed the entirely sensible and well-credentialed view of the law as "prophecies of what the courts will do in fact."[118] Still, the number of cases invoking a higher standard was large enough to produce some discomfort among counsel for charitable corporations when called upon to say what the law is.

The case law in California provides an apt illustration. California is the home of the celebrated *Pepperdine*[119] case, which Cary and Bright discuss as a dramatic example of judicial leniency. George Pepperdine, after endowing the Pepperdine Foundation with a gift of about $3 million, served as its president, as a director, and as the controlling force behind investments that resulted eventually in the loss of the $3 million. The decision, which affirmed the dismissal of a suit by successor directors against Pepperdine and his fellow directors, never identifies the specific investments but takes for granted that they were "improvident and ill-conceived."[120] Pepperdine's good faith and the fact that the fund would never have existed but for his benevolence were sufficient:

> Each director sought only the public good. Not a chirp in the voluminous pleading intimates that a corrupt motive marred the character of or inspired the acts of one of them.... Although a director of [a charitable] corporation is held to the highest degree of honor and integrity, he is not personally liable for mistake of judgment.[121]

The opinion goes on in a similarly colorful vein to decry the injustice of Pepperdine and "his patriotic associates [being] plundered of their personal possessions to fill the never-to-be gratified maw of charity"[122] and to hold that plaintiffs even lacked capacity to sue, such capacity residing exclusively in the attorney general.[123]

Later California cases complicate the picture. A 1964 California Supreme Court decision not involving investments declared in an opinion by Justice Traynor that "[r]ules governing charitable trusts ordinarily apply to charitable corporations"[124] and overruled *Pepperdine* concerning the capacity of co-trustees to sue.[125] A 1970 decision in a suit by the California Attorney General against foundation directors whose in-fighting had led to the accumulation for some five years of large amounts of cash in a non-interest-bearing account directly applied trust cases concerning the duty to invest assets in reaching its conclusion that the trustees should be surcharged for the lost interest. In marked contrast to the *Pepperdine* decision, the court declared that "members of the board of directors of [a charitable] corporation are essentially trustees"[126] and that "good faith is no defense in an action against trustees based on negligence."[127] Because failure to invest funds at all would presumably violate even a gross negligence standard, the case failed to provide a test of whether California courts really would treat charitable corporations as strictly as private trusts.

Dissatisfaction with the common law's failure to provide a developed and consistent body of doctrine led to calls for legislative treatment of the problems Cary and Bright had addressed. Their arguments and findings strongly influenced the drafting of the Uniform Management of Institutional Funds Act (UMIFA), which was approved by the National Conference of Commissioners on Uniform State Laws in 1972 and has since been adopted in twenty-eight states. The Commissioners' prefatory note to the statute observes at the outset that "[t]here is substantial concern about the potential liability of the managers of . . . institutional funds even though cases of actual liability are virtually nil."[128]

UMIFA governs any "incorporated or unincorporated organization organized and operated exclusively for educational, religious, charitable, or other eleemosynary purposes, or a governmental organization to the extent that it holds funds exclusively for any of these purposes."[129] The statute provides fairly clear and permissive guidelines for the expenditure of capital appreciation[130] and the delegation of investment authority,[131] sets out a general standard of care[132] and a procedure for the release of obsolete restrictive provisions in gift instruments,[133] establishes the inapplicability of legal lists,[134] and grants specific authority to make certain investments (such as property that does not produce a current return) that are especially suspect under trust law.[135]

UMIFA's standard of care is drawn in part from the Internal Revenue Code's private foundation regulations under Section 4944 and the "ordinary business care and prudence" formula found in those regulations:

> In the administration of the powers to appropriate appreciation, to make and retain investments, and to delegate investment management of institutional funds, members of a governing board shall exercise ordinary business care and prudence under the facts and circumstances prevailing at the time of the action or decision. In so doing they shall consider long and short term needs of the institution in carrying out its educational, religious, charitable, or other eleemosynary purposes, its present and anticipated financial requirements, expected total return on its investments, price level trends, and general economic conditions.[136]

The Commissioners' Comment to this section states in part:

> The section establishes a standard of care and prudence for a member of a governing board. The standard is generally comparable to that of a director of a business corporation rather than that of a private trustee, but it is cast in terms of the duties and responsibilities of a manager of a nonprofit institution.
>
> Officers of a corporation owe a duty of care and loyalty to the corporation, and the more intimate the knowledge of the affairs of the corporation the higher the standard of care. Directors are obligated to act in the utmost good faith and to exercise ordinary business care and prudence in all matters affecting the management of the corporation. This is a proper standard for the managers of a nonprofit institution, whether or not it is incorporated.[137]

Some objected to UMIFA's standard of care language as effecting a significant and unwarranted relaxation of fiduciary duties. A Report of the Committee on Charitable Giving of the American Bar Association's Section of Real Property, Probate and Trust Law indicates that a minority of the committee believed the standard was "too loosely stated."[138] The report asserts: "[T]here appears to be no settled law that the fiduciary duties of directors of a charitable corporation in the investment of funds are or ought to be any different from those of the trustees of a charitable trust."[139] In Michigan, opposition from an assistant attorney general led proponents of UMIFA to stress the similarities between UMIFA's standard of care and Michigan's statutory prudent man rule.[140]

Of course, just how significant a departure UMIFA's prudence standard makes from the classic prudent man rule depends upon its interpretation by the courts, which seem not to have had much opportunity. The last fifteen years have witnessed more aggressive and innovative investment practices by foundations and universities, as well as some large and highly publicized investment losses by some of those institutions.[141] However, the reported cases indicate no accompanying increase in litigation against directors based on investment losses.

Research has uncovered only a handful of decisions interpreting any section of UMIFA. These cases recognize and speak approvingly of UMIFA's central premise that corporate law principles are more suitable than those of trust law.[142] Doubtless they have reinforced the impression, expressed with some frequency in recent years, that the application of corporate principles represents both the "modern trend" and the majority view.[143] None of these cases, however, arose out of an attack on directors' investment decisions. In fact, the only major decision of that kind since the promulgation of UMIFA arose in the District of Columbia in 1974, three years before that jurisdiction adopted UMIFA.

The decision, *Stern v. Lucy Webb Hayes National Training School for Deaconnesses and Missionaries,*[144] has been described as "the first reported case in which a court has made an exhaustive review of [the duties of trustees of charitable institutions] and handed down useful guidelines to be followed."[145] The suit was a class action brought by patients of Sibley Memorial Hospital, a nonprofit charitable corporation, against several of the hospital's trustees and a number of financial institutions with which those trustees were affiliated. The plaintiffs claimed, among other things, that the trustees had violated their duties of loyalty and care by maintaining unnecessarily large amounts of the hospital's funds in savings and checking accounts at banks with which some trustees were affiliated. In one year, for example, more than one-third of the roughly $4 million available for investment was deposited in checking accounts.[146] The plaintiffs claimed not only mismanagement and self-dealing, but also abdication of fiduciary duty. For about fifteen years all aspects of the hospital's affairs were managed by its administrator and treasurer, with perfunctory ratification by the other trustees. During the period of the claimed financial mismanagement, the treasurer exercised "almost exclusive"[147] control over financial matters; for eleven years the board's finance committee, as well as its investment committee, never met at all:

> All of the defendant trustees testified that they approved [the Treasurer's] recommendations as a matter of course, rarely if ever read the relevant details of audits critically, and generally left investment decisions to the presumed expertise of [the Treasurer]. Several also commented that the Treasurer regarded their suggestions as "interference" in these matters and none forced the issue.[148]

Applying the District of Columbia's nonprofit corporation statute, the court aligned itself with "the modern trend [which] is to apply corporate rather than trust principles in determining the liability of the directors of charitable corporations, because their functions are virtually indistinguishable from those of their 'pure' corporate counterparts."[149] The court contrasted the two rules, characterizing them as simple and gross negligence standards:

> Both trustees and corporate directors are liable for losses occasioned by their negligent mismanagement of investments. However, the degree of care required appears to differ in many jurisdictions. A trustee is uniformly held to a high standard of care and will be held liable for simple negligence, while a director must often have committed "gross negligence" or otherwise be guilty of more than mere mistakes of judgment.[150]

Citing Cary and Bright's work, among others, the court stated: "directors of charitable corporations are required to exercise ordinary and reasonable care in the performance of their duties, exhibiting honesty and good faith."[151] In appraising the plaintiffs' claim of failure to supervise investments, the court again chose the corporate standard rather than the strict antidelegation rule of trust law, but noted that "[t]otal abdication of the supervisory role, however, is improper even under traditional corporate principles."[152]

After a bench trial, the court held that each of the defendant trustees had breached his duties of care and loyalty, particularly in supervising the management of the hospital's investments, but chose to order steps to prevent the repetition of past abuses rather than to remove or surcharge any of the trustees. The leniency of the result has led one commentator to suggest that "there is implicit in the decision a belief that a trustee of a charitable institution should not be held to even as strict an accountability as a director of a business corporation."[153]

The developments of the last fifteen years—Cary and Bright's work, the passage of UMIFA in most states, and the *Stern* decision—should significantly lessen the discomfort of a charitable corporation investment manager contemplating investments that would be suspect under the law governing trustees of private trusts.[154] Investment policies that are both widely practiced by other institutional fiduciaries and specifically blessed by UMIFA, such as the adoption of the total return method, are in fact quite uncontroversial even if forbidden under trust law. However, for nonconventional investment products and techniques not specifically permitted by UMIFA, the dearth of case law is likely to discourage their use unless they become widely accepted by similar institutions. For example, one commentator advised educational endowments in an article published in 1980 to avoid dealing in commodities because their speculative aura and their lack of acceptance by educational institutions would make it difficult to justify an unsuccessful investment, "even if the institution showed that it had obtained the advice of the most sophisticated experts who devoted all of their time to managing the institution's commodity investments."[155]

The disturbing implication of the commentator's advice is, of course, that the courts remain significantly likely to attach a near-irrebuttable presumption of imprudence to innovative or traditionally speculative investment products and techniques regardless of the strength of the case for their prudence in the particular institution's portfolio. However, as Chapter 3 argues more fully, a fixation on "seasoning" as the touchstone of prudent investing practically guarantees substandard investment performance. As long as safety in numbers remains a prominent feature of the practical wisdom for the investment of charitable corporation funds, the law will continue to hobble institutional portfolio management.

Federal Law Governing Private Foundations: Section 4944 of the Internal Revenue Code

Another variant of the prudent man standard, and the one which provided the source for the UMIFA standard, is found in the regulations promulated pursuant to Section 4944 of the Internal Revenue Code. Section 4944 is part of a series of sections in the Code governing private foundations.[156] Section 4944 imposes a graduated series of excise taxes on both the private foundation and participating foundation managers if the foundation "invests any amount in such a manner as to jeopardize the carrying out of any of its exempt purposes."[157] The severity of the penalties increases depending upon how long the foundation continues to hold the "jeopardizing" investment after receiving notice of its jeopardizing status from the Internal Revenue Service.[158] In addition, the foundation must include the prohibition against jeopardizing investments in its charter, thus converting any violation of Section 4944 into a charter violation as well.[159]

Section 4944 is only one of a series of fairly harsh provisions governing private foundations enacted in the Tax Reform Act of 1969. These provisions, which include prohibitions against self-dealing, mandatory annual payout requirements, and restrictions on "excess" business holdings, political lobbying, and grants to individuals, were enacted in response to a wide array of perceived abuses by foundations of their tax-exempt status.[160] The investment standards of Section 4944 were intended to overlay whatever state corporate or trust standards applied to the private foundation, establishing a separate and distinct test uninfluenced by state law.

In the case of Section 4944, the legislative history suggests that Congress considered the possibility of "speculation" with foundation assets to pose a serious threat to a foundation's ability to carry out its charitable purposes, as well as a serious distraction of the energy and attention of foundation managers.[161] For example, the Senate Report, in discussing why the Code's preexisting prohibition on jeopardizing investments of accumulated income should be extended to all of the foundation's assets, noted:

> *General reasons for change.*—The grant of current tax benefits to donors and exempt organizations usually is justified on the basis that charity will benefit from the gifts. However, if the organization's assets are used in a way which jeopardizes their use for the organization's exempt purpose this result is not obtained. Present law recognizes this concept in the case of income, but not in the case of an organization's principal.
>
> Under the present law a private foundation manager may invest the assets (other than accumulated income) in warrants, commodity futures, and options, or may purchase on margin or otherwise risk the corpus of the foundation without being subject to sanction. (In one case a court held that the consistent practice of making such investments constituted operation of the foundation for a substantial non-exempt purpose and would result in loss of tax exemption).[162]

Further, the 1965 Treasury Department Report on Private Foundations recommended that the tax legislation include a "specific interdiction of devices ordinarily deemed inherently speculative—as, for example, the purchase of 'puts,' 'calls,' 'straddles,' 'spreads,' 'strips,' 'straps,' and 'special options,' selling short and trading in commodity futures."[163]

The excerpts quoted above, in their emphasis on prohibiting speculation and on categorizing investments as imprudent in the abstract, are reminiscent of the most conservative interpretations of the prudent man rule. For example, the Treasury report's recommendation represents a call for return to a variation on the generally discredited legal list approach to prudence regulation. Even on its own terms it represents an unusually arbitrary legal list, since it forbids, among other things, the purchase of puts and calls, but not seemingly equally risky activities, such as the writing of puts and calls. However, one commentator, writing before the promulgation of regulations in 1972, concluded after a review of the legislative history that Congress intended essentially to provide a federal enforcement mechanism for requiring foundations to adhere to the prudent man rule rather than to "establish any new generally applicable standard of care and skill for foundation managers."[164] The Treasury Department, in promulgating the final regulations under Section 4944, appeared to adopt an even more flexible reading of the legislative history.

The regulations fashion a quasi-corporate standard of care that expressly permits the foundation to consider the need to protect against inflation and to consider each investment's place in the whole portfolio. They provide that an investment jeopardizes the carrying out of the foundation's exempt purposes "if it is determined that the foundation managers, in making such investment, have failed to exercise ordinary business care and prudence, under the facts and circumstances prevailing at the time of making the investment, in providing for the long- and short-term financial needs of the foundation to carry out its exempt purposes."[165] Foundation managers "may take into account the expected return (including both income and appreciation of capital), the risks of rising and falling price levels, and the need for diversification within the investment portfolio (for example with respect to type of security, type of industry, maturity of company, degree of risk and potential for return)."[166] Whether an investment is a jeopardizing one "shall be made on an investment by investment basis, in each case taking into account the foundation's portfolio as a whole."[167]

Rejecting the Treasury Department's earlier recommendation that a "per se speculative" rule be adopted for products and techniques deemed inherently imprudent, the regulations provide that "[no] category of investments shall be treated as a per se violation of Section 4944."[168] The legislative concern for particular types of investments is expressed in the regulations sotto voce, by a call for "special scrutiny":

> However, the following are examples of types or methods of investment which will be closely scrutinized to determine whether the foundation managers have met the requisite standard of care and prudence: Trading in securities on margin, trading in commodity futures, investments in working interests in oil and gas wells, the purchase of "puts," "calls," and "straddles," the purchase of warrants, and selling short.[169]

The regulations also incorporate the familiar principle that a trustee is to be judged not by his performance but by his conduct: "[t]he determination whether the investment of any amount jeopardizes the carrying out of a foundation's exempt purposes is to be made as of the time that the foundation makes the investment and not subsequently on the basis of hindsight."[170]

The three examples provided in the regulations defining jeopardizing investments, by suggesting circumstances in which a foundation's investment in unimproved real estate, a new and untried venture, or a stock with an uneven earnings record would not violate Section 4944,[171] offer further confirmation that the "ordinary business care and prudence" standard effects a significant departure from the traditional prudent man rule as interpreted by the Treatise, the Restatement, and the private trust cases.

Although no formal public record of the Treasury Department's deliberative process exists, it appears that the final regulations reflect the success of the affected constituency in persuading their regulators, first, that Congress' primary goal in Section 4944 was to foster effective portfolio management and, second, that that goal would best be served by a departure from trust law doctrine in favor of modern notions of investment prudence. Even more than the specific references to inflation, diversification, and "portfolio as a whole" concerns, the phrase "ordinary business care and prudence" signals a rejection of what one foundation group's submission to the Treasury Department called the "judicially encrusted prudent man rule."[172] For instance, the same submission cites Cary and Bright's conclusion, discussed previously, that courts tend strongly to apply corporate rather than trust principles to charitable corporations in order to allow these institutions a necessary flexibility of operation.[173]

Nothing in the application of the regulations since their adoption in 1972 suggests that the Service has retreated from their liberalizing tenor. An early revenue ruling to the effect that the Service deemed it impossible to approve investment procedures governing investments to be made in the future[174] accounts for a general paucity of revenue rulings interpreting the regulations. At the same time, however, research has uncovered no reported case holding an investment to be jeopardizing. One commentator has asserted that, as of 1985, the Service had issued only one revenue ruling and three private letter rulings in which it determined that particular investments violated Section 4944. In each of those rulings, the commentator observes, the Service found that the risk of loss from the investment approached a certainty.[175]

Federal Law Governing Pension Funds: Employee Retirement Income Security Act of 1974

The version of the prudent man rule found in the Employee Retirement Income Security Act of 1974 (ERISA), as elaborated by administrative and judicial interpretation, bears the imprint of modern investment theory far more than do the prudence standards of private trust law, UMIFA, or the Section 4944 regulations. Three prominent features of the ERISA standard probably account for its relative sophistication. First, it is the most recent of the four versions studied here: ERISA was enacted in 1974, and regulations interpreting its prudence standard were not issued until 1979. Second, the staggering size of the funds to which it applies, and the sizable public interests in their efficient management, ensures that legal constraints affecting those assets will receive intense scrutiny. The assets of America's private, noninsured pension plans—the plans covered by ERISA—exceeded $130 billion in 1973;[176] the comparable 1984 figure is $1,000 billion[177] (a figure that represents 63 percent of the market value of the stocks listed on the New York Stock Exchange).[178] Third, an administrative apparatus exists that is well-suited to the continual process of adapting the standard in light of changing circumstances: The entire web of ERISA regulations is administered by an office of the Labor Department capable of providing more guidance to fiduciaries, through advisory opinions and otherwise, than could a system that relied entirely on judicial interpretation.

It is generally said that Congress passed ERISA in response to "widespread concern about exploitation of pension funds by employers and unions."[179] Accordingly, ERISA's prudence standard stands as only one facet of a long and complicated statute designed to assure that workers receive the pensions they are promised. It receives much less attention than do concerns over the duty of loyalty, which are principally addressed through a general direction to act "solely in the interest of the participants and beneficiaries"[180] of the plan, and a list of transactions, most of which would involve conflicts of interest, which are specifically prohibited.[181]

The duties of an ERISA fiduciary relating strictly to prudence are twofold. First, he must act in all matters regarding the pension plan (not simply its investments) "with the care, skill, prudence, and diligence under the circumstances then prevailing that a prudent man acting in a like capacity and familiar with such matters would use in the conduct of an enterprise of a like character and with like aims[.]"[182] Diversification, which trust law treats as one facet of the general duty of prudent investment, appears in ERISA as a separate statutory duty. The fiduciary must "diversif[y] the investments of the plan so as to minimize the risk of large losses, unless under the circumstances it is clearly prudent not to do so."[183]

All of these duties belong to a "fiduciary," defined by the statute in a way that embraces a pension fund's investment managers as well as its trustees:

> (21)(A) Except as otherwise provided in subparagraph (B), a person is a fiduciary with respect to a plan to the extent (*i*) he exercises any discretionary authority or discretionary control respecting management of such plan or exercises any authority or control respecting management or disposition of its assets, *(ii)* he renders investment advice for a fee or other compensation, direct or indirect, with respect to any moneys or other property of such plan, or has any authority or responsibility to do so, or *(iii)* he has any discretionary authority or discretionary responsibility in the administration of such plan. Such term includes any person designated under Section 1105(c)(1)(B) of this title.[184]

Although the statute does allow some compartmentalization of fiduciary duties in order to limit one fiduciary's liability for the acts of another,[185] ERISA posits an otherwise formidable scheme of sanctions for breach of fiduciary duty. A fiduciary who makes an imprudent investment or violates the duty to diversify plan assets is personally liable for any losses[186] and is subject to suit in federal court by the Secretary of Labor, a plan participant or beneficiary, or another fiduciary.[187] Unlike the trustee of a private trust, moreover, the ERISA fiduciary cannot contract out of ERISA's prudent man rule; any specific instructions contained in a pension plan are effective only if consistent with the statute,[188] and exculpatory provisions are void.[189] Recovery of attorney's fees is also specifically authorized.[190]

The Labor Department did not adopt regulations to clarify ERISA's prudence standard until 1979. As with Section 4944's "jeopardy investments" standard, a debate ensued over the extent to which Congress intended to embrace and federalize the common law of trusts and in what ways Congress intended to depart from that body of doctrine.[191] A particularly heated debate, instigated by spokesmen for small businesses and venture capital firms, ensued over the permissibility of investments in such new and untried enterprises.[192]

Although the legislative history contains remarks such as that of then Solicitor of Labor (now a Judge of the United States Court of Appeals for the District of Columbia Circuit) Lawrence Silberman that ERISA's "statutory scheme ... is along the lines and direction which the courts have gone in the development of trust law[,]"[193] some departure from trust law was clearly intended. The prudent man appears in the ERISA standard, but the rest of the classic *Harvard College* formula is gone, replaced by a specific instruction to consider "the circumstances then prevailing" and the "character" and "aims" of the "enterprise." Moreover, the conference report says of the ERISA prudence standard that "[t]he conferees expect that the courts will interpret this prudent man rule (and the other fiduciary standards) bearing in mind the special nature and purpose of employee benefit plans."[194] As commentators have observed, pension plans differ from private trusts in three important ways. The pension fund trustee does not have to weigh the competing interests of an income beneficiary and a remainderman; second, he typically receives continual infusions of new funds; and finally, as his fund is tax-exempt, he can invest with limited regard to tax considerations.[195] As a result, he operates without the constraints relating to non-income-producing property, illiquid assets, and tax holding periods that a trustee of a private trust must typically face.

The regulation interpreting ERISA's prudent man standard reflects these differences and on balance represents the most sophisticated expression of prudence to have attained the force of law. Crafted as a "safe harbor," the regulation provides that the statutory duty to act as would a prudent man will be satisfied with respect to a particular investment if the fiduciary has thoroughly considered the investment's place in the whole portfolio, the risk of loss and the opportunity for gain, and the diversification, liquidity, cash flow, and overall return requirements of the pension plan:

> (b) Investment Duties. (1) With regard to an investment or investment course of action taken by a fiduciary of an employee benefit plan pursuant to his investment duties, the requirements of section 404(a)(1)(B) of the Act set forth in subsection (a) of this section are satisfied if the fiduciary:

> (i) Has given appropriate consideration to those facts and circumstances that, given the scope of such fiduciary's investment duties, the fiduciary knows or should know are relevant to the particular investment or investment course of action involved, including the role the investment or investment course of action plays in that portion of the plan's investment portfolio with respect to which the fiduciary has investment duties; and

> (ii) Has acted accordingly.

> (2) For purposes of paragraph (b)(1) of this section, "appropriate consideration" shall include, but is not necessarily limited to,

> (i) A determination by the fiduciary that the particular investment or investment course of action is reasonably designed, as part of the portfolio (or, where applicable, that portion of the plan portfolio with respect to which the fiduciary has investment duties), to further the purposes of the plan, taking into consideration the risk of loss and the opportunity for gain (or other return) associated with the investment or investment course of action, and

> (ii) Consideration of the following factors as they relate to such portion of the portfolio:

> (A) The composition of the portfolio with regard to diversification;

> (B) The liquidity and current return of the portfolio relative to the anticipated cash flow requirements of the plan; and

> (C) The projected return of the portfolio relative to the funding objectives of the plan.[196]

The release that announced the regulation's adoption rejects trust law as the exclusive source of interpretation and suggests a limited embrace of the teachings of modern portfolio theory and the efficient market hypothesis. Observing that the common law of trusts "should not be mechanically applied to employee benefit plan[s],"[197] the Labor Department expressed the opinion that:

> (1) generally, the relative riskiness of a specific investment or investment course of action does not render such investment or investment course of action either *per se* prudent or *per se* imprudent, and (2) the prudence of an investment decision should not be judged without regard to the role that the proposed investment or investment course of action plays within the overall plan portfolio.[198]

The Labor Department specifically adopted the view that an investment is not necessarily imprudent "merely because the investment, standing alone, would have, for example, a relatively high degree of risk."[199] In response to commentators who asked for clarification concerning the prudence of the classes of investments "such as, for example, investments in small or recently formed companies, or non-income producing investments that are not securities (such as, for example, certain precious metals and objects of art) [that] have not been viewed with favor, traditionally, as trust investments,"[200] the Labor Department replied that while it did not intend to suggest a "legal list," it did believe "that the universe of investments permissible under the prudence rule is not necessarily limited to those permitted at common law."[201] The release suggests some retreat from a too explicit endorsement of portfolio theory, however. It refers to a modification of the proposed regulation, changing "diversification of risk" to "diversification" (and adding that the word "is to be given its customary meaning as a mechanism for reducing the risk of large losses")[202] and deleting a reference to "volatility" because it might be read "according to some comments, as suggesting that only certain portfolio management techniques are appropriate."[203] Finally, the release suggests that prudent use of an index fund would require a "screen" or "filter" process to delete companies experiencing "significant, adverse financial developments."[204]

In light of the vastly larger class of potential plaintiffs and sums of money at stake, it might be expected that ERISA's prudence standard would be far better defined by case law than the other forms of the prudent man rule. Judging from the reported cases, however, the first ten years of litigation under ERISA have produced very little judicial elaboration of pure prudence issues (uncomplicated by conflicts of interest, self-dealing, and bad faith) and no testing at all of the prudence of new products or, for that matter, of more typical stock and bond investments. While this may be partly explained by frequent settlement of cases before they result in published decisions, the Labor Department's liberal interpretation of the standard, the absence of any severe stock market collapses since 1975, and the relative newness of techniques such as options and futures strategies probably play a very large part as well.

Pure prudence cases are hard to find. Most interpretations of the prudence standard to date involve some clearly abusive self-dealing, resulting in a "prohibited transaction" and/or gross negligence bordering on bad faith. The conflict of interest may involve use of the pension plan to help fend off a hostile tender offer[205] or some other manipulation of the plan to serve the interests of company management[206] or union trustees.[207] Typical of the gross negligence cases is one in which the court remarked that the challenged investment (a $2 million loan by a $58 million fund to a bank that later failed, leaving $1.625 million principal amount unpaid) was "a loser from its inception"[208] and would have been revealed as such had the trustees undertaken even a minimal independent inquiry into the bank's creditworthiness. In other cases, courts held the prudence and diversification duties violated by the loan of about 25 percent of a plan's assets to the developer of a time-sharing project (characterized by the court as a "single, speculative real estate venture")[209] and by loans of over half of a fund's assets to companies "engaged in high-risk real estate development and sales programs" and "substantially or wholly owned and controlled"[210] by one person.

Some themes relevant to more typical (or typically atypical) investments do emerge from these cases. First, while the cases always acknowledge trust law as a source of interpretation and sometimes apply it directly in the context of issues such as the duty to dispose of improper investments[211] and when a trustee may resign,[212] none of the reported cases exhibit the "labeling" or per se style of analysis characteristic of the Treatise, the Restatement, and most private trust cases. Instead, the courts have rested findings of imprudence less on the type of investment at issue than on the fiduciary's failure to undertake the kind of careful, independent inquiry into the merits of the investment that would have revealed its unsuitability to the particular fund[213] and the existence of alternative investments offering a more favorable risk/return trade-off.[214] These cases demonstrate an emphasis on competence reflected by one court's comment that "[w]hile there is flexibility in the prudence standard, it is not a refuge for fiduciaries who are not equipped to evaluate a complex investment."[215] They tend also to emphasize process in language similar to business judgment rule cases. One example is the district court opinion in the case involving the loan described on appeal as a "loser": "Here, the manner in which the loan ... was proposed and presented was designed to discourage inquiry into the merits. Urgency and speed overrode the need for calm deliberate inquiry and discussion."[216]

The Labor Department's flexible interpretation of the statutory language, coupled with the absence of narrow judicial interpretations, would appear to leave pension funds significantly less constrained than other fiduciaries to use unconventional investment products and techniques. One commentator wrote shortly after the issuance of the prudence regulation that it seemed likely to "precipitate increased use of alternative investments, such as options, real estate, nonincome producing investments, and index funds."[217] Indeed, the results of the questionnaire used in this study indicate that, in general, pension funds consider themselves less inhibited by the law in their choice among investment alternatives than do other groups of fiduciaries.

Nevertheless, even the liberality of ERISA's prudence standard has proved insufficient to overcome the craving for safety in numbers (and the attendant bias against innovation) that characterizes fiduciaries subject to less sophisticated versions of the prudent man rule. One writer remarked as recently as 1983 that "if the objective of the investment fiduciary is to avoid liability, there is some safety in numbers."[218] Another, also writing well after the promulgation of the prudence regulation, said of venture capital investments: "As in the case of other innovative investment techniques, it might also be appropriate to follow the principle of safety in numbers and make such investments only in the company of other comparable institutional investors."[219] The same commentator, the general counsel of a major investment manager, also advised:

> [T]he Department of Labor does not sanction particular investments so an awareness of what other plan fiduciaries are doing with respect to a new investment vehicle or technique is important. A careful study of the new investment vehicle or technique over a period of time and its utilization by other plans should effectively rebut claims of imprudence in the event that the new investment or technique fails.[220]

The Related Doctrine of Delegation

The so-called anti-delegation doctrine of trust law, while not strictly speaking a branch of the prudent man rule, also figures importantly in the fabric of legal constraints on investment management by trustees. As with the prudence standard, conservative interpretations of the anti-delegation doctrine have been widely criticized for inhibiting efficient portfolio management by fiduciaries, especially outside the personal trust area.

According to Section 171 of the Restatement, "the trustee is under a duty to the beneficiary not to delegate to others the doing of acts which the trustee can reasonably be required personally to perform."[221] Like the duty to act as would a prudent man, the duty not to delegate applies to all of the trustee's responsibilities, not solely those involving investment management. The commentary to Section 2 of the Restatement underscores the fundamental character of the duty not to delegate by including it, along with duty of loyalty doctrines, as a basic component of a "fiduciary relation."[222] A trustee who wrongly delegates authority to an agent, or who fails properly to supervise an agent to whom he properly delegated authority, is absolutely liable for any resulting losses.[223] While the Restatement commentary concedes that generally a multi-factor analysis is necessary because no "clear-cut line"[224] distinguishes delegable from nondelegable acts, it states flatly that: "A trustee cannot properly delegate to another power to select investments."[225]

The simple, undeniable logic of the delegation doctrine lies in the observation that if the trustee can escape all liability by delegating his responsibilities to a third party, the entire purpose of the trust is frustrated. In the words of a highly respected commentary on the law of delegation,

> Trustees are typically chosen as such because the settlor of the trust places special confidence in their judgment and ability. If trustees are allowed casually to surrender the administration of the trust to strangers, there seems little point in having designated the trustees to act in the first place; indeed, the reason for establishing the trust itself may have been lost. It has therefore become an established precept of trust law that the trustee must attend personally to the most important aspects of administering the trust.[226]

In view of the pervasiveness of delegation in any complex economy, however, the interpretation of the doctrine to require "the trustee" personally to select each trust investment appears so unrealistic as to render virtually unworkable any fiduciary relationship other than the management of a small trust by an individual trustee such as a friend of the family.

Not surprisingly, then, the anachronistic premises of the delegation doctrine as applied to investment management have clashed repeatedly with the realities of the marketplace. In the nineteenth century, New York courts considered investment in corporate stock an improper delegation to the corporation's directors;[227] much more recently, investments in mutual funds and REITs have been considered legally suspect on similar grounds.[228]

Although the delegation doctrine's shortcomings are most glaring when measured against the organizational requirements of endowed institutions, its central premise of personal judgment as the basis for a trustee's selection appears to have little application even in the private trust area. The typical "trustee" is a bank or trust company, a corporation that can act only through its officers, many of whom typically play some part in the investment research and selection process for any given trust. The Restatement accommodates this pervasive de facto delegation as follows: "Although a corporate trustee cannot properly delegate the administration of the trust, it can properly administer the trust through its proper officers."[229]

What Professor Scott in the Treatise calls "the element of reliance upon personal judgment and discretion,"[230] while of questionable applicability in the case of a corporate trustee, appears even less relevant to the trustees or directors of a charitable corporation. First, an institution such as a university or a foundation is in a sense both trustee and beneficiary of its own endowment. Second, as the authors of *The Law and the Lore of Endowment Funds* noted in a subsequent work that reexamined the delegation doctrine,

> Directors are chosen for a variety of reasons, few of which have anything to do with expertise in portfolio management. Once elected they face a myriad of responsibilities, most of them unrelated to portfolio management. And those responsibilities must be met on a part-time basis by men who are typically fully occupied in other endeavors.[231]

This second work by Cary and Bright, entitled *The Developing Law of Endowment Funds: "The Law and the Lore" Revisited,* systematically addressed the question of whether delegation of investment responsibility by the board of a charitable corporation was legal, particularly in light of trust law's seemingly unambiguous prohibition on delegating the selection of individual investments. By 1974, most nonprofit institutions had apparently determined either that delegation was not legally questionable or that such questions as did hover around its legality were not compelling enough to override the self-evident need to delegate. Cary and Bright reported survey results to the effect that less than 5 percent of the surveyed colleges and universities required buy-sell decisions to be made by the full governing board and cited a Harris Survey finding that only one-third of the colleges and universities polled managed their entire endowments internally.[232]

In states that have adopted UMIFA, such delegation is no longer troublesome. UMIFA specifically authorizes both internal and external delegation of authority to "act in place of the board in investment and reinvestment of institutional funds."[233] In states whose statutes do not specifically address the propriety of delegation, either through UMIFA or some other statute applicable to nonprofit institutions, the answer is less certain. The Restatement indicates in commentary that some more relaxed standard applies to the administration of charitable corporations: "It may be proper, for example, for the board to appoint a committee of its members to deal with the investment of the funds of the corporation, the board merely exercising a general supervision over the actions of the committee."[234] Cary and Bright concluded after a lengthy survey of both corporate and trust law principles that both internal and external delegation were proper, assuming appropriate supervision, regardless of which branch of law was applicable.[235] Their view is cautiously seconded by Professor Fratcher, in a 1983 supplement to the Treatise. Fratcher remarks that internal delegation is both pervasive and proper and that although external delegation is more problematic, "it seems reasonable to permit it"[236] even in the absence of specific statutory permission.

The other legal standards surveyed in this chapter also reflect modern thinking about delegation. As previously discussed, the Section 4944 regulations accord a "foundation manager" (but not the foundation itself) protection from liability if he relies on the advice of "qualified investment counsel."[237] Thus, while the regulations do not explicitly grant permission to delegate, they clearly contemplate that delegation will occur.

In the case of ERISA, an express authority to delegate issues directly from the statute:

> Any employee benefit plan may provide: ... that a person who is a named fiduciary with respect to control or management of the assets of the plan may appoint an investment manager or managers to manage (including the power to acquire and dispose of) any assets of a plan.[238]

The statute requires an "investment manager" to be a registered investment adviser under the Investment Advisers Act of 1940, a "bank" as defined in that Act, or an insurance company qualified as a money manager under the laws of more than one state;[239] further, as discussed previously, an investment manager under ERISA is a "fiduciary" and therefore subject to its scheme of fiduciary duties.

Conclusions

The following conclusions emerge from the foregoing survey of the law of prudence today.

1. Trust investment law has exhibited from the beginning a tension between a desire for flexibility and openness to changing circumstances, on the one hand, and for certainty as to which investments will give rise to liability on the other. *Harvard College* has come to stand for a flexible, adaptable standard, while the traditional English rule, the *King v. Talbot* decision, and the legal lists have come to stand for the opposite.

2. The legal standard known as the prudent man rule, first announced in the 1830 Massachusetts decision in *Harvard College,* in one form or another governs the overwhelming majority of the funds held by trustees of one kind or another in the United States today.

3. Although, like the reasonable man rule of tort law, the prudent man rule looks for its content to prevailing investment practices, courts and commentators have always assumed that a trustee must behave more conservatively than the average investor. The primary qualification thus placed upon the use of the average investor as an objective source of meaning for the rule has focused upon the preservation of the nominal value of the principal and has been expressed in a prohibition against "speculation."

4. In the state law of private trusts, the prudent man rule is the applicable legal standard in the overwhelming majority of states. However, as a result of restricting commentary and case law, this standard has become widely perceived as rigid and anachronistic. Recent commentators have especially criticized private trust law's failure to take sufficient account of the risk of inflation, its tendency to label entire categories of investments (such as junior mortgages or the securities of new and untried enterprises) prudent or imprudent in the abstract, and its insistence upon considering the prudence of investments on an individual basis rather than with regard to the role they were expected to play in the overall portfolio. Although litigation against trustees is rare and findings of liability even rarer, some recent decisions support critics' assertions that the tendency of private trust law doctrine is to impose liability for certain economically prudent conduct and to excuse economically imprudent conduct that is harmful to the interests of the trust beneficiaries.

5. As a result of the reputation for unjustified and counterproductive conservatism attaching to the prudent man rule of private trust law, subsequent legislative and administrative adoptions of prudence standards have departed somewhat from the language of the *Harvard College* decision in order to emphasize the intention to enact a more flexible standard and specifically to signal a concern for inflation risk, a rejection of the tendency to label investments as prudent or not in the abstract, and an acceptance of the "portfolio as a whole" approach. Thus, in different ways, the California prudence statute,

UMIFA, the Section 4944 regulations, and ERISA vary from the *Harvard College* formula, as it has been constrained by the Treatise, the Restatement, and judicial interpretations.

6. In state law governing charitable corporations, where legal standards while somewhat indefinite have always been generally considered to be more liberal than those of trust law, the drafters of UMIFA sought to emphasize their departure from trust law by making reference to the standards governing directors of business corporations and by specifically authorizing use of the total return method.

7. Like UMIFA, the regulations defining jeopardy investments under Section 4944 of the Code indicate a departure from the rigid standards of trust law by invoking the flexibility of the business judgment rule. Thus both UMIFA and the Section 4944 regulations speak in terms of "ordinary business care and prudence."

8. In the case of ERISA, the most recent of the prudence standards and the most economically significant, similar desires to depart from archaic interpretations of the prudent man rule led to a statutory standard framed in terms of "a prudent man acting in a like capacity" and to regulations that represent the most liberal and sophisticated expression of prudence to date.

9. An emerging theme in the law of prudence, most evident in recent New York personal trust cases, the Section 4944 regulations, and in interpretations of the ERISA standard, is an emphasis on a sound process for investment decision-making as the principal determinant of investment prudence.

10. Recent commentary indicates that in all the areas studied here, even those governed by more flexible interpretations of the prudence standard, the paucity of case law in general and in particular the absence of cases rejecting outdated interpretations of prudence or approving more current interpretations have led to a preoccupation among fiduciaries with "safety in numbers" and, accordingly, to a powerful reluctance to innovate.

11. The anti-delegation doctrine of private trust law, as contained in the Restatement, has over the last fifty years stood as a significant obstacle to the practice of modern investment techniques by fiduciaries of various kinds. Today many of these tensions have been relieved somewhat by statute or regulation governing fiduciaries other than the trustees of personal trusts.

12. With the exception of the new California statute governing trustees of personal trusts, efforts at reinterpretation of the prudent man rule have taken place in the context of standards governing other classes of fiduciary funds: educational and philanthropic endowments and pension funds. This has occurred even though most of the arguments for reform, such as the insights of portfolio theory and the emergence of inflation as a more serious threat than in the past, logically apply with equal force to the portfolio needs of trust beneficiaries.

Unable to rework directly the authoritative sources of trust law, the drafters of UMIFA, ERISA, and the Section 4944 regulations concentrated their analytical energies on distinguishing the portfolio needs of the funds subject to those statutes from those of personal trusts. Unfortunately, the law of personal trusts remains by far the more fully developed body of doctrine in comparison to the rarely litigated standards of UMIFA, Section 4944, and to a lesser extent ERISA. As a result, endowment and pension fund fiduciaries continue to operate under uncertainty as to whether a court, searching for precedent, will apply anachronistic prudence rules drawn from trust law. In this way the rigid interpretations of prudence found in the Treatise and the Restatement continue to exert a constraining influence over all fiduciaries, including those not expressly within the scope of those works.

NOTES

[1]Professor Prosser reports that the "reasonable man of ordinary prudence" made his first appearance in the English case of Vaughn v. Menlove, 3 Bing.N.C. 468, 132 Eng. Rep. 490 (1837). *See* W. L. Prosser, *Law of Torts* 150 (4th ed. 1971).

[2]The "use," the predecessor of the modern trust, originated in England in the Middle Ages. *See* G. G. Bogert & G. T. Bogert, *Trusts and Trustees* (2d ed. rev. 1984) § 2, at 13 [hereinafter cited as Bogert].

[3]26 Mass. (9 Pick.) 446 (1830) [hereinafter cited as "Harvard College"]. A search of the archives and other records of Harvard University and the court records of Massachusetts Supreme Judicial Court failed to produce briefs or other documents pertaining to the case.

[4]*See* Langbein & Posner, "Market Funds and Trust Investment Law," 1976 A.B.F. Res. J. 1, 3; Friedman, "The Dynastic Trust," 73 Yale L.J. 547, 553 (1964)[hereinafter cited as Friedman]; Shattuck, "The Development of the Prudent Man Rule for Fiduciary Investment in the United States in the Twentieth Century," 12 Ohio St. L.J. 491, 492 (1951)[hereinafter cited as Shattuck].

[5]*Harvard College, supra* note 3, at 447.

[6]*Id.*

[7]*Id.* at 460.

[8]*Id.*

[9]*Id.*

[10]*Id.* at 461.

[11]*Id.*

[12]*Id.* at 465.

[13]*See* Friedman, *supra* note 4, at 554 for a more detailed discussion.

[14]40 N.Y. 76 (1869).

[15]*Id.* at 88–9.

[16]*See* Bogert, *supra* note 2 (2d ed. rev. 1980) § 613, at 55.

[17]*See* Shattuck, *supra* note 4, at 499.

[18]*Id.*

[19]*Id.* at 501.

[20]Johnston, "Prudence in Trust Investment," 8 Mich. J.L.Ref. 491, 491–2 (1975) [hereinafter cited as Johnston].

[21]Fleming, "Prudent Investments: The Varying Standards of Prudence," 12 Real Prop. Prob. & Tr. J. 243, 245 (1977) [hereinafter cited as Fleming]; Shattuck, *supra* note 4, at 501.

[22]Shattuck, *supra* note 4, at 509–10.

[23]*Id.*

[24]*Id.* at 508.

[25]Johnston, *supra* note 20; H. Bines, *The Law of Investment Management* (1978); Note, "The Regulation of Risky Investments," 83 Harv. L. Rev. 603 (1970) [hereinafter cited as Note, "Risky Investments"]; Hirsch, "Inflation and the Law of Trusts," 18 Real Prop. Prob. & Tr. J. 601 (1983) [hereinafter cited as Hirsch].

[26]Johnston, *supra* note 20, at 508. It has been suggested that the new standard proved frustrating from its inception:

Important though this movement was in unshackling trustees and allowing them to invest funds in accordance with prevailing notions of prudence in the financial community, it immediately began to suffer from that very attribute. As Charles W. Buek of the U.S. Trust Company in New York once observed, it was almost like prisoners who had sawed their way out of their cells only to find themselves still within the prison walls. The certainty of the old "legal list" had been replaced by an amorphous standard which read well on first impression and seemed to sanction flexibility and selection according to concepts current at the time of investment but which, in fact, created problems because the standard was so very general and devoid of specific guidance to the trustee.

Fleming, *supra* note 21, at 245, *citing* Buek, " 'Qualified' Trustee Performance Calls for Full Investment Freedom," 99 Tr. & Est. 194 (1960).

[27] *See, e.g.,* Canfield v. Security-First Nat'l Bank of Los Angeles, 87 P.2d 830, 844–45 (Cal. 1939) ("[I]n the absence of a contrary statute or decision in this state, [the Restatement] is entitled to great consideration as an argumentative authority.").

[28] 2 A.W. Scott, *Law of Trusts* § 174 (3d ed. 1967) [hereinafter cited as Treatise].

[29] Restatement (Second) of Trusts § 174 (1959) [hereinafter cited as Restatement]. The Restatement further requires that "if the trustee has or procures his appointment as trustee by representing that he has greater skill than that of a man of ordinary prudence, he is under a duty to exercise such skill." *Id.*

[30] 3 Treatise, *supra* note 28, § 227. The Restatement incorporates this duty by positing the preservation of the estate as the trustee's primary concern:

In making investments of trust funds the trustee is under a duty to the beneficiary

(a) in the absence of provisions in the terms of the trust or of a statute otherwise providing, to make such investments and only such investments as a prudent man would make of his own property having in view the preservation of the estate and the amount and regularity of the income to be derived;

(b) in the absence of provisions in the terms of the trust, to conform to the statutes, if any, governing investments by trustees;

(c) to conform to the terms of the trust, except as stated in §§ 165–168.

Restatement, *supra* note 29, § 227.

[31] 3 Treatise, *supra* note 28, § 227, p. 1806.

[32] *Id.* It has been argued that this criterion, along with the emphasis in Scott and the Restatement on a hypothetical prudent man rather than the *Harvard College* standard based upon how men of prudence actually manage their own affairs, is to a large degree responsible for narrow interpretations of the prudent man rule and consequent reliance on over-cautious strategies such as overpriced "favorite-fifty" lists. *See* Fleming, *supra* note 21, at 245–47; *but see* Hirsch, *supra* note 25, at 625 ("I have found no case in which the 'permanent disposition' aspect of the *Harvard College* rule led to a different decision than would have been reached under the phrase 'preservation of the estate' in Scott's statement of the rules.").

[33] 3 Treatise, *supra* note 28, § 227.3, p. 1812.

[34] *Id.* at § 227.6.

[35] *Id.* The commentary and illustrations in the Restatement are to substantially the same effect. Restatement, *supra* note 29, § 227, p. 532. Washington State amended its trustee investment statute in 1984 explicitly to permit limited investment in "new, unproven, untried . . . enterprises . . ." Wash. Rev. Code § 11.100.023.

[36] Restatement, *supra* note 29, § 227, p. 534.

[37] (1) the marketability of the particular investment; (2) the length of the term of the investment, for example, the maturity date, if any, the callability or redeemability, if any; (3) the probable duration of the trust; (4) the probable condition of the market with respect to the value of the particular investment at the termination of the trust especially if at the termination of the trust the investment must be converted into money for the purpose of distribution; (5) the probable condition of the market with respect to reinvestment at the time when the particular investment matures; (6) the aggregate value of the trust estate and the nature of the other investments; (7) the requirements of the beneficiary or beneficiaries, particularly with respect to the amount of the income; (8) the other assets of the beneficiary

or beneficiaries including earning capacity; (9) the effect of the investment in increasing or diminishing liability for taxes; (10) the likelihood of inflation.
Id. at p. 535.

[38]*Id.*

[39]*See generally* B. Malkiel, *A Random Walk Down Wall Street* 18–19 (4th ed. 1985); Hirsch, *supra* note 25, at 601 ("Though not a penny of principal was lost [from 1967 to 1983], inflation turned fortunes into livings and modest estates into mementos.").

[40]Toledo Trust Co. v. Toledo Hospital, 187 N.E.2d 36, 39 (Ohio 1962).

[41]*See, e.g.,* Restatement, *supra* note 29, § 227, p. 531:

> In making investments, however, a loss is always possible, since in any investment there is always some risk. The question of the amount of risk, however, is a question of degree. No man of intelligence would make a disposition of property where in view of the price the risk of loss is out of proportion to the opportunity for gain. Where, however, the risk is not out of proportion, a man of intelligence may make a disposition which is *speculative in character with a view to increasing his property instead of merely preserving it.* Such a disposition is not a proper trust investment, because it is not a disposition which makes the preservation of the fund a primary consideration.

(emphasis supplied); *see also* Headley, "Trust Investments," 91 Tr. & Est. 739 (1952):

> The rules of law governing investment have evolved in forms designed to accomplish the basic purpose of family security by the method which experience has devised. The method of the common law trust requires a permanent source of income and a continuous flow. The permanent source is provided by placing a capital fund in the hands of a trustee. *The trustee is charged with a duty to preserve its dollar value.* I know of no case where a trustee has been surcharged for a failure to enlarge the size of the trust. In fact the hazards of attempting it are so great that the usual methods of doing so, through business and speculation, are normally prohibited to a trustee by law.

(emphasis supplied).

[42]Hirsch, *supra* note 25, at 628; Note, "Risky Investments," *supra* note 25, at 623.

[43]*See* Hirsch, *supra* note 25; *see also* Comment, "Investment and Management of Trust Funds in an Inflationary Economy," 126 U. Pa. L. Rev. 1135 (1978).

[44]Hirsch, *supra* note 25, at 625. Hirsch cites trust law's emphasis on preservation of the dollar value of principal, item-by-item consideration of the prudence of investments, and "anti-netting" damages rule as obstacles to investments in common stock.

[45]105 N.W.2d 900 (Minn. 1960).

[46]*Id.* at 902.

[47]*Id.* at 904.

[48]The court attributed much of the increased suitability of common stock as a trust investment to the Securities and Exchange Commission's regulations forbidding practices that were thought to have contributed to the stock market crash of 1929. *Id.* at 905–06.

[49]*Id.* at 906.

[50]*Id.* at 906–07; *accord* Dennis v. R.I. Hosp. Trust Nat'l Bank, 744 F.2d 893, 900 (1st Cir. 1984) (Breyer, J.) ("For one thing, it seems reasonable for the court—in devising a remedy for the trustee's violation of its duty of impartiality—to assume that a fair trustee would have maintained the property's *real* value from 1950 through 1982." (citing *Mayo*)).

[51]375 S.W.2d 397 (Ky. 1964).

[52]*Id.* at 397.

[53]*Id.* at 398.

[54]194 S.E.2d 761 (N.C. 1973).

[55]*Id.* at 776. The Duke Endowment was created in 1924. The court contrasted the spiraling costs faced by the major beneficiaries of the fund (Duke University and two hospitals) with the fund's dismal performance. Of the twenty-six foundations with assets greater than $100 million, the Duke Endowment "had, by far, the worst cumulative investment performance for the years 1967, 1968 and 1969." *Id.* at 773, *citing* W. A. Nielsen, *The Big Foundations* (1972).

[56]*See* Toledo Trust Co. v. Toledo Hospital, 187 N.E.2d 36, 39 (Ohio 1962) (affirming denial

of trustee's petition for permission to deviate from provision limiting investments to federal, state, and municipal bonds and characterizing the *Mayo* decision's assumptions about the likelihood of future inflation as "speculation"); *see also* In re Kilmer's Will, 186 N.Y.S.2d 120 (Surr. Broome Co. 1959) (rejecting claim that trustees' failure to make any investments in common stock as an inflation hedge represented imprudence and stating that "[f]ailure to diversify investments is not improvident per se," *id.* at 129, and that "a conservative investment plan in itself is not a basis for the imposition of liability in a court of law," *id.* at 131); Troost Avenue Cemetery Co. v. First Nat'l Bank, 409 S.W.2d 632, 637 (Mo. 1966) (considering the *Mayo* argument but concluding that "the evidence in this case is not sufficient to show at this time the accomplishment of the purposes of the trust would be defeated or substantially impaired unless deviation from the trust restrictions on investment is authorized.").

[57]Restatement, *supra* note 29, at § 174.

[58]*See* 3 Treatise, *supra* note 28, at § 227.2, p. 1811.

[59]N.Y. E.P.T.L. § 11–2.2(a).

[60]Restatement, *supra* note 29, at § 227, p. 531 ("Where, however, the risk is not out of proportion [to the opportunity for gain], a man of intelligence may make a disposition which is speculative in character with a view to increasing his property instead of merely preserving it.").

[61]Restatement, *supra* note 29, at § 228, p. 541.

[62]The third edition of the Treatise, published in 1967 (when modern portfolio theory was beginning to gain wider acceptance), does evidence some awareness of the growing conflict between legal doctrine and investment practice:

> Undoubtedly in recent years there has been a more scientific study of investments, but the results of this study are not always reflected in the cases. The courts are also likely to treat each individual investment separately, instead of considering it in relation to the whole of the trust estate.

3 Treatise, *supra* note 28, at § 227, p. 1809.

[63]No case citations at all appeared for Bines, "Modern Portfolio Theory and Investment Management Law: Refinement of Legal Doctrine," 76 Colum. L. Rev. 721 (1976); Langbein & Posner, "Market Funds and Trust Investment Law," 1976 A. B. F. Res. J. 1; Note, "The Regulation of Risky Investments," 83 Harv. L. Rev. 603 (1970); or Note, "Trustee Investment Powers: Imprudent Application of the Prudent Man Rule," 50 Notre Dame Law. 519 (1975). Two other works are cited only in passing and only by two cases. *See* In re Newhoff, 435 N.Y.S.2d 632, 637 (Surr. Ct. 1980) (*citing* H. E. Bines, *The Law of Investment Management* (1978) and Johnston, "Prudence in Trust Investment," 8 Mich. J.L. Ref. 491 (1975)), *aff'd,* 486 N.Y.S.2d 956, 959 (App. Div. 2d Dept. 1985) (*citing* Johnston, "Prudence in Trust Investment," 8 Mich. J.L. Ref. 491 (1975)). Hamilton v. Nielsen, 678 F. 2d 709 (7th Cir. 1982), in which Judge Posner suggests in dicta that plaintiffs should have based their surcharge claim in portfolio theory, appears to be the only reported case thus far to reflect the influence of this scholarship.

[64]*See generally* Gordon & Kornhauser, "Efficient Markets, Costly Information, and Securities Research," 60 N.Y.U. L. Rev. 761 (1985).

[65]"Unless the trustee actually has been lining his pockets with their assets, disgruntled beneficiaries . . . can expect little aid from the courts if a trust performs poorly." "The Meaning of Prudence," *Forbes,* 28 January 1985, at 81.

[66]"Current Investment Questions and the Prudent Person Rule," 13 Real Prop. Prob. & Tr. J. 650, 654 (1978). The report's authors predicted judicial hostility to innovative financial products and techniques:

> No reported court cases have been located dealing with options. But the classification of margin and short sell investments by one court as "rank gambles" signals a less than enthusiastic reception for "modern portfolio techniques."

Id. at 653 (*citing* Merrill Lynch, Pierce, Fenner & Smith, Inc. v. Bocock, 247 F. Supp. 373, 379 (S.D. Tex. 1965) (broker negligent in making short sale investments for account of a trust when trust instrument indicated trust funds could not be used for speculative purposes: "A margin account and a short sale are speculative to the extent that they can be termed 'rank gambles.'")).

[67]*Id.* at 671.

[68]*See, e.g.,* Jackson v. Conland, 420 A.2d 898, 900 (Conn. 1979); Hartford Nat'l Bank and Trust Co. v. Donahue, 402 A.2d 1195 (Conn. Super. Ct. 1979); Perling v. Citizens and Southern Nat'l Bank, 300 S.E.2d 649 (Ga. 1983); Estate of McCredy, 470 A.2d 585 (Pa. Super. Ct. 1983); Estate of Niessen, 413 A.2d 1050 (Pa. 1980); Hoffman v. First Virginia Bank of Tidewater, 263 S.E.2d 402 (Va. 1980).

[69]With the law so out of phase with economic reality, we would predict that the draftsmen of trust instruments would commonly include language waiving the limitations that are imposed by trust law in the absence of appropriate language. And indeed most current trust instruments waive the detailed limitations of trust law and vest broad discretion in the trustee—hence the paucity in recent years of reported litigation involving the investment duties of trustees.

R. Posner, *Economic Analysis of Law* at 330 (1973).

[70]*Fleming, supra* note 21, at 251.

[71]139 Cal. Rptr. 644 (Cal. Ct. App. 1977).

[72]*Id.* at 648.

[73]681 P.2d 563 (Hawaii 1984).

[74]425 So. 2d 415 (Ala.), *cert. denied,* 461 U.S. 938 (1983).

[75]*Id.* at 419–20.

[76]*Id.* at 428.

[77]The court also surcharged the bank for its purchase of unsecured debentures of six real estate investment trusts, relying in part on the testimony of the same plaintiff's expert witness, who again based his opinion on the work of Benjamin Graham. The expert testified that the test set out in Graham's *Security Analysis* (4th ed. 1962) required examination of a company's record over a period of seven to ten years, which was impossible because all six of the REITs were too young. The witness "concluded it was a poor decision to purchase REITs because there were other options available that were less risky." *Id.* at 422. No discussion of the trade-off between risk and return follows this statement in the court's opinion.

A New York intermediate appellate court quoted the *Martin* decision's reasoning approvingly in affirming the surcharge of an individual, nonprofessional trustee for investments in real estate investment trusts. *See* In re Newhoff, 486 N.Y.S.2d 956, 963 (App. Div. 2d Dep't 1985).

[78]419 N.E.2d 1358 (Mass. 1981).

[79]*Id.* at 1366.

[80]*Id.* at 1367–69.

[81]*Id.* at 1369.

[82]364 N.Y.S.2d 164 (1974).

[83]*Id.* at 168 (citations omitted). *See also* In re Kemske Trust, 305 N.W.2d 755, 759 (Minn. 1981) ("Evidence from [one] trust would have been relevant on the question of investment objectives, since a short-term income emphasis in [that] trust strengthens the propriety of a long-term growth strategy in the [other] trust.").

[84]*Id.* at 169–70.

[85]*Id.* at 169 (citation omitted).

[86]396 N.Y.S.2d 781 (N.Y. Surr. 1977).

[87]*Id.* at 787.

[88]445 F. Supp. 670 (S.D.N.Y. 1978).

[89]*Id.* at 672.

[90]*Id.* at 680.

[91]*Id.* at 680–81.

[92]Cal. Civ. Code § 2261.

[93]Wade, "The New California Prudent Investor Rule: A Statutory Interpretive Analysis," 20 Real Prop. Prob. & Tr. J. 1, 13 (1985). This article does note, however, that the bill was proposed by the California Bankers Association in cooperation with the Estate Planning, Trust and Probate Law Section of the California Bar Association. *Id.* at 1.

[94]Bishop, "Sitting Ducks and Decoy Ducks: New Trends in the Indemnification of Corporate Directors and Officers," 77 Yale L.J. 1078, 1101 (1968).

[95]*See, e.g.,* D. Kurtz, "Non-Traditional Revenue Ventures of Tax Exempt Organizations: The Role of Trustees," 39 Rec. A.B. City N.Y. 129, 137 (1984) [hereinafter cited as Kurtz].

[96]Karst, "The Efficiency of the Charitable Dollar: An Unfulfilled State Responsibility," 73 Harv. L. Rev. 433, 436 (1960) [hereinafter cited as Karst].

[97]*Id.*

[98]Christie, "Legal Aspects of Changing University Investment Strategies," 58 N.C.L. Rev. 189, 209 (1980) [hereinafter cited as Christie]; *see also* Restatement, *supra* note 29, at § 391 (concerning charitable trusts).

[99]Abrams, "Regulating Charity—The State's Role," 35 Rec. A.B. City N.Y. 481, 486 (1980) [hereinafter cited as Abrams]; *see also* R. Posner, *Economic Analysis of Law* 391–92 (1973) (charitable foundation's lack of stockholders and freedom from need to compete in any product market or the capital markets create need to strengthen incentives to efficient management of foundation assets).

[100]*See* Brown, *The Not-for-Profit Corporation Director: Legal Liabilities and Protection,* F.I.C.Q. 57, 58 (Fall 1977).

[101]*See* Karst, *supra* note 96, at 456 ("We know from prominent authority that approximately three-quarters of all American foundations are organized in corporate form, and that the 'usual framework for foundations in recent years' is the corporation.").

[102]Velde, "Corporate Management of Endowment Funds," 31 Bus. Law. 398, 404 (1975).

[103]Karst, *supra* note 96.

[104]*Id.* at 436.

[105]*See* Fremont-Smith, "Duties and Powers of Charitable Fiduciaries: The Law of Trusts and the Correction of Abuses," 13 U.C.L.A. L. Rev. 1041, 1044 (1966); Committee on Charitable Trusts, "Duties of Charitable Trust Trustees and Charitable Corporation Directors," 2 Real Prop. Prob. & Tr. J. 545, 546 (1967); Note, "The Fiduciary Duties of Loyalty and Care Associated with the Directors and Trustees of Charitable Organizations," 64 U. Va. L. Rev. 449 (1978) [hereinafter cited as Note, "Fiduciary Duties"].

[106]Note, "Fiduciary Duties," *supra* note 105, at 455–56.

[107]Restatement, *supra* note 29, § 379 and comment b; *see also* Treatise, *supra* note 28, § 379.

[108]*See, e.g.,* 1951 Op. Atty. Gen. 159, 161 (N.Y.), *cited in* W. L. Cary & C. B. Bright, *The Law and the Lore of Endowment Funds* (1969) [hereinafter cited as *The Law and the Lore*] at 68 n. 53; Pasley, "Non-Profit Corporations: Accountability of Directors and Officers," 21 Bus. Law. 621, 638 (1966); Christie, *supra* note 98, at 198–201.

[109]Restatement, *supra* note 29, § 389 comment b.

[110]*The Law and the Lore, supra* note 108, at 1.

[111]*Id.* at 6.

[112]*Id.* at 30.

[113]*Id.* at 33.

[114]*Id.*

[115]*Id.*

[116]*Id.* at 61.

[117]*Id.* at 66.

[118]Holmes, "The Path of the Law," 10 Harv. L. Rev. 457, 461 (1897).

[119]Pepperdine Found. v. Pepperdine, 271 P.2d 600 (Cal. Dist. Ct. App. 1954).

[120]*Id.* at 604.

[121]*Id.* at 603–04 (citations omitted).

[122]*Id.* at 604.

[123]*Id.* at 605.

[124]Holt v. College of Osteopathic Physicians & Surgeons, 394 P.2d 932, 937 (Cal. 1964).

[125]*Id.*

[126]Lynch v. John M. Redfield Found., 88 Cal. Rptr. 86, 89 (Cal. Ct. App. 1970).

[127]*Id.* at 91.

[128]Uniform Management of Institutional Funds Act (hereinafter cited as UMIFA), Commissioners' Prefatory Note.

[129]*Id.* at § 1(1).

[130]*Id.* at §§ 2, 3.

[131]*Id.* at § 5.

[132]*Id.* at § 6.

[133]*Id.* at § 7.

[134]*Id.* at § 4.

[135]*Id.*

[136]*Id.* at § 6.

[137]*Id.,* Commissioners' Comment.

[138]Committee on Charitable Giving, "The Uniform Management of Institutional Funds Act—A Commentary," 8 Real Prop. Prob. & Tr. J. 405, 409 (1973).

[139]*Id.*

[140]Letter dated March 26, 1976 from Hill, Lewis, Adams, Goodrich, and Tait to the Honorable Paul A. Rosenbaum, Chairman, House Judiciary Committee, Michigan House of Representatives, at 3.

[141]Christie, *supra* note 98, at 193–194 and 216–21.

[142]*See* Alco Gravure, Inc. v. The Knapp Found., No. 50, slip op. (N.Y. Ct. App. March 28, 1985) (holding that the "quasi-cy-pres" principle governing the release of gift instrument restrictions had not been followed by the lower court but acknowledging the statute's primary intent to establish corporate rather than trust law principles); Midlantic Nat'l Bank v. Frank G. Thompson Found., 405 A.2d 866, 871 (N.J. Sup. Ct. Ch. Div. 1979) (the standard of appropriate compensation for investment management services to a charitable trust should not be applicable to trustees of a charitable corporation because in adopting UMIFA the legislature expressed its intent that "in the area of investment management, the responsibilities of members of governing boards of charitable corporations are to be considered more under the developed law of corporations than of trusts." (citations omitted)); Opinion of the Justices, 306 A.2d 55 (Sup. Ct. N.H. 1973) (holding that the adoption of UMIFA would not violate the state constitution by encroaching on the powers of judiciary, and stating that eleemosynary institutions "are in a situation with regard to their endowment funds similar to that of directors of a business corporation with respect to the administration of its property." (citations omitted)).

[143]*See* Kurtz, *supra* note 95, at 136; Abrams, *supra* note 99, at 485; Ward, "The Charitable Fiduciary Liability Question," 17 Real Prop. Prob. & Tr. J. 700, 700 (1982).

[144]381 F. Supp. 1003 (D.D.C. 1974) (Gesell, J.).

[145]Porth, "Personal Liability of Trustees of Educational Institutions," 2 J. C. & U. L. 143, 143 (1975) [hereinafter cited as Porth].

[146]*Stern,* 381 F. Supp. at 1010.

[147]*Id.* at 1010–11.

[148]*Id.* at 1011.

[149]*Id.* at 1013.

[150]*Id.*

[151]*Id.*

[152]*Id.* at 1014.

[153]Porth, *supra* note 145, at 155.

[154]*See* Cusack, "Managing Institutional Funds: Major Changes," 51 N.Y. St. B. J. 386, 386 (1979) ("Counsel who do the legal worrying for the governing boards of New York's colleges, universities and hospitals and the thousands of other New York not-for-profit organizations have been able to sleep better since [the adoption of UMIFA in New York]."). In an apparent response to liability insurance concerns, in 1986 New York relaxed the standard of care applicable to uncompensated directors of not-for-profit corporations in certain circumstances to a gross negligence standard. N.Y. N.P.C.L. § 720-a.

[155]Christie, *supra* note 98, at 218–219.

[156]*See* I.R.C. § 509 (private foundation defined).

[157]*Id.* § 4944(a)(1).

[158]*Id.* § 4945.

[159]*Id.* § 508(e).

[160]Kahn, "Regulation of Privately Supported Foundations: Some Anomalies," 4 Ind. Legal F. 271, 271–72 (1970) [hereinafter cited as Kahn].

[161]H.R. Rep. No. 91-413, 91st Cong., 1st Sess. 4 (1969); S. Rep. No. 91-552, 91st Cong., 1st Sess. 6 (1969) [hereinafter cited as Senate Report].

[162]Senate Report, *supra* note 161, at 45.

[163]House Comm. on Ways and Means, 89th Cong., 1st Sess., Treasury Dep't Rep. on Private Founds. 76-717 (Comm. Print 1965) at 45–50.

[164]Kahn, *supra* note 160, at 291.

[165]Treas. Regs. § 53.4944-1(a)(2)(i).

[166]*Id.*

[167]*Id.*

[168]*Id.*

[169]*Id.*

[170]*Id.*

[171]*Id.* at § 53.4944-1(c).

[172]"Investments Which Jeopardize Charitable Purpose—A Framework for Regulations" (unpublished memorandum, April 5, 1971) at 13.

[173]*Id.* at 14.

[174]Rev. Rul. 74-316, I.R.B. 1974-26, 17.

[175]Troyer, Slocombe, & Boisture, "Divestment of South Africa Investments: The Legal Implications for Foundations, Other Charitable Institutions and Pension Funds," 74 Geo. L.J. 127, 153 (1985) [hereinafter cited as Troyer].

[176]Note, "Fiduciary Standards and the Prudent Man Rule Under the Employment [sic] Retirement Income Security Act of 1974," 88 Harv. L. Rev. 960, 960 n.1 (1975) [hereinafter cited as Note, "Fiduciary Standards"].

[177]*See* R.A. Ippolito, *Pensions, Economics, and Public Policy* (1986) Table 1-1, at 5.

[178]New York Stock Exchange, 1985 Fact Book, at 79.

[179]Troyer, *supra* note 175, at 154 n. 99.

[180]ERISA § 404(a)(1), 29 U.S.C. § 1104(a)(1) (1985).

[181]ERISA § 406, 29 U.S.C. § 1106 (1985).

[182]ERISA § 404(a)(1)(B), 29 U.S.C. § 1104(a)(1)(B) (1985).

[183]ERISA § 404(a)(1)(C), 29 U.S.C. § 1104 (a)(1)(C) (1985).

[184]29 U.S.C. § 1002 (21)(A)(1985).

[185]*See* ERISA § 405, 29 U.S.C. § 1105 (1985); 29 C.F.R. § 2550.404a-1(b)(3)(1985).

[186]ERISA § 409, 29 U.S.C. § 1109 (1985).

[187]29 U.S.C. § 1132 (a) (2) (1985).

[188]ERISA § 404 (a)(2), 29 U.S.C. § 1104 (a)(2) (1985).

[189]ERISA § 410(a), 29 U.S.C. § 1110 (a)(1985).

[190]29 U.S.C. § 1132(g)(1) (1985).

[191]Crawford, "Prudent Investments for Plan Fiduciaries and Plan Administrators," 40 Inst. on Fed. Tax'n 5-1, 5-13–5-14 (1982) (ERISA Supp.) [hereinafter cited as Crawford].

[192]*Id.* at 5-14.

[193]*Hearings on H.R. 16462 Before the General Subcomm. of the House Comm. on Educ. and Labor,* 91st Cong., 1st & 2d Sess. 521 (1969–1970), *cited in* Hutchinson, "The Federal Prudent Man Rule Under ERISA," 22 Vill. L. Rev. 15, 16 n.9 (1976).

[194]H. Conf. Rep. No. 93-1280, 93d Cong., 2d Sess. (1974), *reprinted in* 1974 U.S. Code Cong. & Ad. News 5038, 5083.

[195]Note, "Fiduciary Standards," *supra* note 176, at 966–68; Crawford, *supra* note 191, at 5-12.

[196]29 C.F.R. § 2550.404a-1(b) (1985).

[197]44 Fed. Reg. 37,221, 37,222 (June 26, 1979).

[198]*Id.*

[199]*Id.* at 37,224.

[200]*Id.*

[201]*Id.* at 37,225.

[202]*Id.* at 37,223.

[203]*Id.*

[204]*Id.* at 37,224.

[205]*See* Donovan v. Bierwirth, 680 F.2d 263 (2d Cir.), *cert. denied,* 459 U.S. 1069 (1982).

[206]*See* Eaves v. Penn, 587 F.2d 453 (10th Cir. 1978) (agreement for sale of company provided for purchaser to use assets of the company's pension plan as part of the purchase price); Freund v. Marshall & Ilsley Bank, 485 F. Supp. 629, 636 (W.D. Wis. 1979) (loan of "virtually all of the Plan's assets . . . back to the sponsoring companies in exchange for unsecured promissory notes"); Marshall v. Kelly, 465 F. Supp. 341 (W.D. Okla. 1978) (Loans to employer).

[207]*See* Donovan v. Mazzola, 716 F.2d 1226 (9th Cir. 1983) , *cert. denied*, 464 U. S. 1040 (1984). (loan to another union fund at below-market interest rates and hiring of consultant at inflated fee).

[208]Katsaros v. Cody, 744 F.2d 270, 280 (2d Cir.), *cert. denied*, 105 S. Ct. 565 (1984).

[209]Marshall v. Glass/Metal Ass'n & Glaziers & Glassworkers Pension Plan, 507 F. Supp. 378, 381 (D. Hawaii 1980).

[210]Donovan v. Schmoutey, 592 F. Supp. 1361, 1395 (D. Nev. 1984); *see also* Marshall v. Teamsters Local 282 Pension Trust Fund, 458 F. Supp. 986, 992 (E.D.N.Y. 1978) (investment of 36 percent of fund's assets in financing of the building of a Las Vegas hotel and gambling casino, while "[g]overnment-guaranteed Ginnie Mae certificates [were] available bearing approximately the same interest rates as provided in the permanent mortgage.").

[211]*See* Morrissey v. Curran, 567 F.2d 546, 548–49 (2d Cir. 1977); *accord* Buccino v. Continental Assurance Co., 578 F. Supp. 1518, 1521 (S.D.N.Y. 1983); Marshall v. Craft, 463 F. Supp. 493, 497 (N.D. Ga. 1978).

[212]Freund v. Marshall & Ilsley Bank, 485 F. Supp. 629, 635 (W.D. Wis. 1979).

[213]*See* Katsaros v. Cody, 744 F.2d 270, 275–76 (2d Cir.), *cert. denied*, 105 S. Ct. 565 (1984). Donovan v. Cunningham, 716 F.2d 1455, 1469 (5th Cir. 1983), *cert. denied*, 467 U. S. 1251 (1984); Donovan v. Schmoutey, 592 F. Supp. 1361, 1397 (D. Nev. 1984); Marshall v. Glass/Metal Ass'n & Glaziers & Glassworkers Pension Plan, 507 F. Supp. 378, 384 (D. Hawaii 1980).

[214]*See* Marshall v. Teamsters Local 282 Pension Trust Fund, 458 F. Supp. 986 (E.D.N.Y. 1978); Marshall v. Glass/Metal Ass'n & Glaziers & Glassworkers Pension Plan, 507 F. Supp. 378, 384–85 (D. Hawaii 1980).

[215]*Marshall v. Glass/Metal, supra* note 214, at 384.

[216]Katsaros v. Cody, 568 F. Supp. 360, 367 (E. D. N. Y. 1983).

[217]Note, "Fiduciary Responsibility: Prudent Investments Under ERISA," 14 Suffolk U.L. Rev. 1066, 1084 (1980).

[218]Kelly, "Fiduciary Duties Related to Pension Fund Investment in Real Estate," 14 Loy. U. Chi. L.J. 253, 277 (1983).

[219]Crawford, *supra* note 191, at 5-46.

[220]*Id.* at 5-55.

[221]Restatement, *supra* note 29, § 171.

[222]*Id.,* § 2.

[223]*Id.,* § 218.

[224]*Id.,* § 171 and comment d.

[225]*Id.,* comment h.

[226]W.L. Cary & C. B. Bright, *The Developing Law of Endowment Funds: "The Law and the Lore" Revisited* (1974) at 36–37 [hereinafter cited as *Law and Lore Revisited*].

[227]*Id.* at 38.

[228]*Id.*

[229]Restatement, *supra* note 29, § 171 and comment e; *see also* 2 Treatise, *supra* note 28, § 171.4.

[230]2 Treatise, *supra* note 28, § 171.4.

[231]*Law & Lore Revisited, supra* note 226, at 21–22.

[232]*Id.* at 24.

[233]UMIFA, *supra* note 128, § 5.

[234]Restatement, *supra* note 29, § 379 and comment b.

[235]*Law & Lore Revisited, supra* note 226, p. 48.

[236]4 Treatise, *supra* note 28, § 379, 1985 Supp. at 101.

[237]Treas. Regs. § 53.4944-1(b)(2)(v).

[238]ERISA § 402(c)(3), 29 U.S.C. § 1102(c)(3)(1985).

[239]29 U.S.C. § 1002(38)(1985).

CHAPTER 2

Historical Sketch of the Investment Landscape from 1830 to Today[1]

This chapter sketches the changing marketplace for investments from the sparse landscape of 1830, when *Harvard College v. Amory* was decided, to the richly diverse and crowded markets of 1984. It does not purport to account for the vast changes that occurred over this period, as an economic history would. Instead, drawing on the available scholarship and data, the effort is to reach some conclusions about why those glosses on the prudent man rule that are now troublesome may have made more sense in earlier times and why they are out of place in today's very different marketplace. The principal conclusions can be summarized as follows:

1. This study reveals a circular journey from Justice Putnam's awareness in 1830 that risk was pervasive (exemplified by his famous dictum in the *Harvard College* case that "Do what you will, the capital is at hazard"), through a long period in which "safe" investments were thought to exist and fiduciaries were expected to find them, often with the help of labels affixed to specific products by commentators, courts, and legislatures, to the present era, in which safety as an investment concept has become an anachronism, emptied of meaning by a growing awareness that uncertainty is the central factor at work in the marketplace and that the management of risk, rather than its avoidance, is the primary task of the fiduciary.

2. Growth in the size and complexity of the marketplace, particularly since World War II, has been accompanied by (a) remarkable improvements in financial reporting and in the fairness of the trading markets, as insider trading increasingly became an unacceptable practice, and (b) the growth in professionalism among fiduciaries and other financial intermediaries, including security analysts, investment managers, broker-dealers, and investment management consultants. In the face of these changes, marketplace prudence often compels a fiduciary to delegate management responsibilities to specialists.

The Changing Landscape Traced Through Statistics

The sweep of change that has occurred at an ever-increasing rate over the period from 1830 to 1984 needs no elaborate proof, for it is intuitively obvious. However, it can be usefully displayed in a number of ways through statistics.

The New York Stock Exchange

Table 2.1 uses a number of different barometers to gauge growth and change in the securities markets, taking snapshots of the scene at the New York Stock Exchange as it existed in 1830 (the year *Harvard College v. Amory* was decided in Massachusetts), 1869 (the year *King v. Talbot* was decided in New York), and then, somewhat arbitrarily, 1884, 1904, 1924, 1940, 1960, 1970, 1975, 1980, and 1984. The enduring dominance of the "Big Board" makes its record over the decades a reasonable surrogate for the country's auction marketplace for securities.

The numbers displayed in Table 2.1 chart a course of consistent growth at the New York Stock Exchange in every category over the entire period. However, the most remarkable developments have occurred since 1970. In the fourteen years between 1970 and 1984, trading in equities, whether measured by share volume or dollar volume, increased by 650 percent, rivaling the 800 percent growth in trading that tracked the industrial revolution as it continued in the post-Civil War period from 1869 to 1884. Listed securities grew by 65 percent from 1970 to 1984, almost doubling the growth of the previous thirty years and exceeding all other periods except for 1830 to 1869, when the rate of increase was approximately the same, and 1869 to 1884, when listed securities grew by 172 percent.[2]

Asset Allocations by Harvard and Princeton

Tables 2.2 and 2.3 and Figure 2.1 show for each of the years used in Table 2.1 the asset allocations of the Harvard and Princeton University endowments, capturing the large shifts that occurred over this long period.

The allocation to equities by Harvard and Princeton over the span of years since 1830 generally tracks the trends displayed by the New York Stock Exchange records. Both universities allocated significant assets to equities in the early period (32.8 percent for Harvard by 1869, 96.6 percent for Princeton in 1830); both thereafter reduced their equity shares until sometime early in the twentieth century; and then, reversing the trend, both increased equities to within a percentage point of each other at just below the 50 percent level in 1940, to over 50 percent by 1960 (56 percent for Harvard, 66.6 percent for Princeton) and to post-World War I highs in 1970 (60.1 percent for Harvard, 79.4 percent for Princeton). In 1975 both universities held lower shares of equities, with Princeton showing continued declines in 1980 and 1984 and Harvard showing increases, as each moved toward a two-thirds equity allocation.

As the ensuing discussion elaborates, in very rough terms the holdings of Harvard and Princeton correspond to the wisdom of the day and trace the evolution of security capitalism in the United States.[3] Until the westward movement began to create a national need for turnpikes, canals, and railroads and the capital to build and sustain them, investments were typically limited to real estate and other local enterprises. In the case of Harvard in 1830, that meant local real estate in the Boston area (98.6 percent of assets); for Princeton it meant equity investments

Table 2.1 NEW YORK STOCK EXCHANGE Selected Statistics 1830–1984

Year	Equity Securities Share volume (millions)[1]	Equity Securities Dollar volume (market value) (millions)[1]	Debt securities dollar volume (par value) (millions)[1]	Number of all securities[2]	Market value of all securities (millions)[3]	Number of equity securities[2]	Market value of equity securities (millions)[3]	Number of equity securities as % of all securities
1830	N/A	N/A	N/A	115	N/A	92	N/A	80
1869	10.5	N/A	N/A	340	N/A	145	N/A	42.6
1884	96.2	5,939.5	517.6	925	N/A	315	N/A	34
1904	186.9	N/A	1,032.6	1,286	N/A	383	N/A	29.8
1924	284.0	N/A	3,801.9	2,151	60,684	889	27,072	41.3
1940	207.6	7,166	1,669.4	2,628	92,723	1,233	41,890	46.9
1960	766.6	37,959	1,346.4	2,719	415,224	1,528	306,967	56.2
1970	3,123.1	102,494	4,494.9	3,669	749,002	1,840	636,380	50.1
1975	4,839.4	131,705	5,178.3	4,733	1,000,515	2,111	685,110	44.6
1980	11,561.5	382,447	5,190.3	5,265	1,750,573	2,228	1,242,803	42.3
1984	23,308.6	773,426	6,982.3	6,070	2,607,946	2,319	1,586,155	38.2

N/A—Not Available.

1. The figures for 1884 are from Francis L. Eames, *The New York Stock Exchange* (New York, 1894), p. 95. The other figures, for debt volume in par value and equity volume in market value, are from the 1940 and 1984 New York Stock Exchange (NYSE) Fact Books.

2. No figures for 1830 are available. Figures shown for 1830 represent the average of figures for 1825 and 1835, respectively. 1825 and 1835 computed from NYSE manuscript call books, in NYSE archives. Figures for 1869, 1884, 1904, 1924, and 1940 (January 1, 1940) from NYSE 1940 Year Book, p. 49. Figures for 1960, 1970, 1975, 1980, and 1984 from NYSE Fact Book 1985, p. 79.

3. Figures from the 1960 and 1948 NYSE Fact Books.

Table 2.2 HARVARD UNIVERSITY PORTFOLIO ASSET ALLOCATIONS 1830–1984[1,2,3]

Year	Mortgages and other interests in real estate	U.S. debt	State and local debt	Corporate Debt					
				Bank and finance	Canal, bridge, and barge	Railroads	Utilities	Industrial and other	Total
1830	98.6	0	0	0	0	0	0	0	0
1869	33.1	15.1	5.3	0	0	13.7	0	0	13.7
1884	34.6	0	1.0	0	0	49.5	0	0.4	50.9
1904	33.1[5]	0	0	0	0	44.7	9.3	4.7	58.7
1924	29.4[6]	1.3	0	0	0	18.6	23.9	13.9	56.4
1940	6.3[7]	0	2.2	1.9	0	6.5	20.0	16.8	45.2
1960	0.5	18.0	0	3.8	0	2.6	10.2	8.9	25.5
1970	1.5	4.6	0	2.9	0	0.3	16.0	14.6	33.8
1975	0.9	17.1	0	7.8	0	1.2	5.8	8.5	23.3
1980	0	6.2	0	7.3[4]	0	0.3	7.6	13.2	28.4
1984	3.5	20.3	0	—	—	—	—	—	9.7

Table 2.2 HARVARD UNIVERSITY PORTFOLIO ASSET ALLOCATIONS 1830–1984[1,2,3]

Year	Bank and finance	Canal, bridge, and barge	Railroads	Utilities	Industrial and other	Total	Preferred	Common
					Corporate Stock			
1830	0	1.4	0	0	0	1.4		100
1869	4.3	0	0.3	0	28.2	32.8		100
1884	3.3	0	7.4	0	3.8	14.5		100
1904	0	0	6.1	1.8	0.3	8.2		100
1924	0.6	0	3.1	3.2	6.0	12.9	48.7	51.3
1940	3.2	0	1.0	9.4	32.7	46.3	22.4	77.6
1960	1.5	0	0.7	10.4	43.4	56.0	2.7	97.3
1970	2.6	0	0.5	11.1	45.9	60.1	4.8	95.2
1975	1.2	0	0	5.1	52.4	58.7	0	100
1980	0[4]	0	0	3.1	62.3	65.4	0	100
1984	—	—	—	—	—	66.5[8]	0.2	99.8

1. *Source:* Archives of Harvard University.

2. Unless otherwise noted, each figure is the percentage of all assets in the general fund of the university allocated to the specified type of investment. Where market value is unavailable, book value is used. Where book value is also unavailable, income from the specified type of investment as a percentage of total income from all assets in the general fund is used.

3. Obligations under security lending and options transactions are excluded.

4. Allocations within corporate debt and stock categories for 1984 could not be made because records were not maintained that way. Mark-to-market futures positions with respect to debt and equities are included.

5. Includes real estate trust stocks equal to 5.3% of total assets.

6. Includes real estate trust stocks equal to 2.2% of total assets.

7. Includes real estate trust stocks equal to 1.1% of total assets.

8. 26% of total corporate stock constituted an index fund.

54

Table 2.3 PRINCETON UNIVERSITY PORTFOLIO ASSET ALLOCATIONS 1830–1984[1,2]

Year	Mortgages and other interests in real estate	U.S. debt	State and local debt	Corporate Debt					Total
				Bank and finance	Canal, bridge, and barge	Railroads	Utilities	Industrial and other	
1830	4000 acres in Pa. 1000 acres in NY House in Pa.[3]	0.6	2.8	0	0	0	0	0	0
1872[4]	30.5	0.4	12.6	0	15.1	25.4	0	12.6	53.1
1884	5.5	0	4.8	0.4	8.1	68.4	0	9.7	86.6
1904	2.2	0	.5	0	0	73.7	7.5	13.2	94.4
1924	4.7	24.7	1.3	0	0	50.5	4.7	11.4	66.6
1940	5.9	1.6	1.0	0	0	5.5	21.8	17	44.3
1960	3.3	3.5	0	3.7	0	0	6.5	16.4	26.6
1970	1.3	6.7	0	3.4	0	0	6.0	3.2	12.6
1975	2.3	3.0	0	2.1	0	0	3.6	10.6	16.3
1980	5.9	5.5	0	6.6	0	0.7	1.7	10.6	19.6
1984[5]	7.5	16.0	0	4.4	0	0.1	0.4	2.3	7.2

Table 2.3 PRINCETON UNIVERSITY PORTFOLIO ASSET ALLOCATIONS 1830–1984[1,2]

Year	Bank and finance	Canal, bridge, and barge	Railroads	Utilities	Industrial and other	Corporate Stock		
						Total	Preferred	Common
1830	77.8	18.8	0	0	0	96.6	0	100
1872[4]	2.7	0	0	0.7	0	3.4	0	100
1884	0.3	0	2.3	.5	0	3.1	0	100
1904	0.1	0	2.7	0.1	0	2.9	3.4	96.6
1924	0.2	0	0.8	0	1.7	2.7	26	74
1940	2.3	0	1.3	11.0	32.6	47.2	42	58
1960	1.2	0	0.1	15.7	49.6	66.6	5.4	94.6
1970	1.2	0	0	9.4	68.8	79.4	0.5	99.5
1975	1.5	0	0	8.5	68.4	78.4	0.6	99.4
1980	1.6	0	1.5	9.5	56.4	69.0	0.5	99.5
1984[5]	3.6	0	0.5	5.0	59.8	68.9	1.7	98.3

1. *Source:* Archives of Princeton University.

2. Unless otherwise noted, each figure is the percentage of all assets in the pooled (or combined) accounts of the university allocated to the specified type of investment. For 1975, 1980, and 1984, the real estate investments in the Princeton Forrestal Center are included. The secondary pool of invested funds, separately invested funds, and student, parent, and faculty loans have been excluded. Where market value is unavailable, book value is used. Where book value is also unavailable, income from the specified type of investment as a percentage of total income from all assets in the general fund is used.

3. For 1830 all assets are used, consisting of "real estate" and "personal estate," divided into a "general fund," a "vice president's fund," and a "charitable fund." No income or value, book or market, is shown for real estate, so it is simply referred to by location and excluded from the computation of percentages.

4. No records exist for 1869 that would permit the asset allocations displayed for other years. The closest year for which numbers are available is 1872, for which the asset allocations are shown above. They apply to what was then called "permanent funds."

5. For 1984, 0.4% of the combined accounts was invested in gold, for which there is no column shown.

56

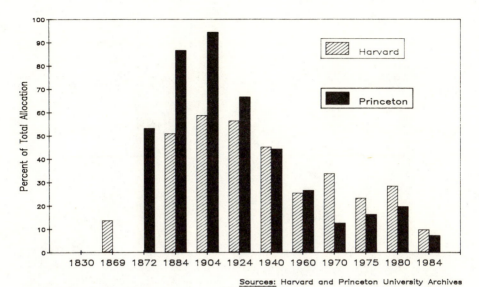

Sources: Harvard and Princeton University Archives

Figure 2.1(a) Comparison of Harvard and Princeton University Portfolio Asset Allocations, Corporate Debt 1830–1984

Figure 2.1(b) Comparison of Harvard and Princeton University Portfolio Asset Allocations, Corporate Stock 1830–1984

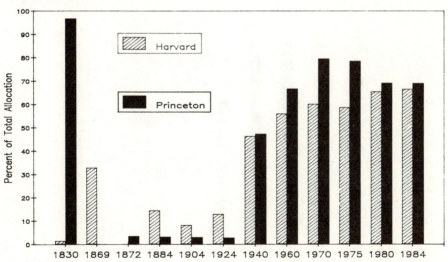

Sources: Harvard and Princeton University Archives

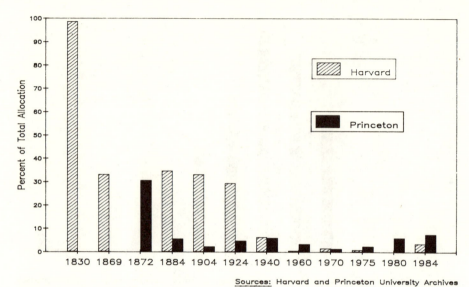

Sources: Harvard and Princeton University Archives

Figure 2.1(c) Comparison of Harvard and Princeton University Portfolio Asset Allocations, Real Estate 1830–1984

Figure 2.1(d) Comparison of Harvard and Princeton University Portfolio Asset Allocations, Railroad Securities (Debt plus Equity)

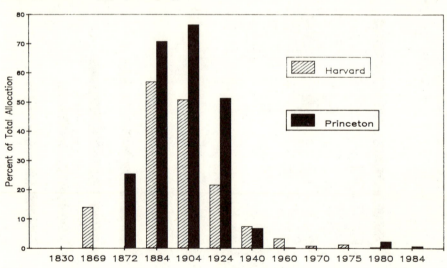

Sources: Harvard and Princeton University Archives

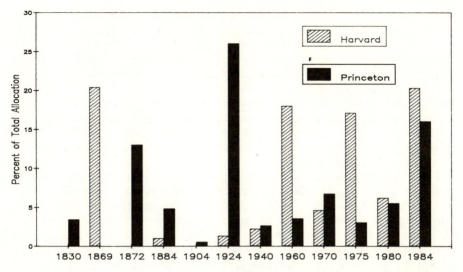

Figure 2.1(e) Comparison of Harvard and Princeton University Portfolio Asset Allocations, United States, State, and Local Debt

in banking enterprises in nearby Trenton and New York City (76 percent of assets).

Before 1820 federal government bonds were about the only form of traded securities available to an investor. The New York Stock Exchange, organized in 1816, began trading principally in federal and state debt securities. Trading expanded gradually to include some bank and insurance company securities and then, with the expansion westward, canal and, most importantly, railroad securities, which came to dominate the market for corporate securities until the twentieth century. This point is well-illustrated by the university profiles. In 1884 Harvard's portfolio was dominated by investments in railroads, with 49.5 percent allocated to railroad bonds and another 7.4 percent to railroad equities—a total of almost 57 percent to this single industry. Princeton was even more severely concentrated in railroading, with 68.4 percent allocated to debt issues and another 2.3 percent to equities for a total commitment to the industry of over 70 percent of its portfolio. If Harvard's significant allocation to real estate in 1884 (34.6 percent) is removed, the share of the remainder represented by railroad securities increases to 87 percent.

It is noteworthy that both universities showed marked preferences for railroad debt securities over equities, despite the substantial use by railroads of equities for external financing. Railroad stock outstanding constituted about 55 percent of that industry's total external financing in 1855, 50 percent in 1880, and 40 percent in 1900.[4]

By 1904 Princeton's commitment to railroads had increased to 76.4 percent, while Harvard's had fallen to just over half of its assets. It was not until 1940 that both universities showed only a small (less than 10 percent) commitment to the railroads. The theoretical value of diversification is to some degree intuitive and, therefore, must have been available to the managers of these university portfolios during the late nineteenth and early twentieth centuries. Because a more diversified portfolio was probably recognized as desirable, the limited number of investment alternatives explains in part these unusual levels of concentration.

Rapid development of a national trading market for securities had to await such technological advances as the Atlantic cable (opened in 1866), the stock ticker (started in 1867), and the installation of telephones on the floor of the New York Stock Exchange (in 1878).

Until the last decade of the nineteenth century, there were less than 300 corporations whose equities traded publicly, and those that did were chiefly engaged in banking and railroading. "Industrials," a term that came to embrace manufacturing, distribution, extraction, and processing, was not used until the late 1880s. With the exception of coal companies and New England textile companies, for which public markets dated from the early years of the industry (accounting for Harvard's having 28.2 percent of its portfolio invested in the common stock of New England industrial companies in 1869 and the Boston Stock Exchange being the country's leading market for industrials in the 1880s), industrial securities were almost unknown. Messrs. Dow and Jones did not start to publish stock averages until the mid-1890s and John Moody did not begin the first manual of industrial securities until 1900.[5] By 1903, however, there were at least 136 industrial common stocks and eighty-three industrial preferreds being traded on the New York Stock Exchange and on the so-called Curb Exchange.[6]

Legal advances, too, were a necessary precondition to growth in security capitalism and, in particular, the use of publicly offered equity securities. Although the concept of the corporation as a flexible means of housing business enterprise and attracting capital without exposing investors to personal liability for its debts was well known in the early nineteenth century, it did not become widely accepted as the preferred structure until the middle of the nineteenth century. Following the panic of 1873, the corporate form came to dominate the shape of business enterprise and, to some observers, the character of the nation as well.[7]

Inflation

Any portrait of change in the financial marketplace would be incomplete without some reference to inflation. The persistence of inflation since World War II and, particularly, the high levels of inflation over the past fifteen years, are well known. Yet statistics add force to the point. The average rates of inflation per year for the ten-year periods ending in 1980, 1981, 1982, 1983, and 1984 were 7.87 percent, 8.44 percent, 8.72 percent, 8.46 percent, and 7.79 percent, respectively.[8] In no other ten-year period since 1800 has the average rate of inflation per year been close to the lowest of these percentages, with the exception of two ten-year periods bracketing World War I, from 1910 to 1919 and 1911 to 1920, when the annual rate averaged 6.93 percent and 8.14 percent, respectively,[9] driven up to these high levels by a four-year spike of double-digit inflation from 1917 to 1920.

It is important to remember that before World War I periods of deflation were as common as those of inflation. During the long deflationary period from 1864 to 1900, when much American corporate and trust law was developed and a public market for industrial securities commenced, the value of the dollar in purchasing power almost doubled. Bonds offered a good return for income beneficiaries and a marked increase in the real value of the principal. It is no surprise that over this period they grew in importance on the New York Stock Exchange and came to be viewed as inherently safe.

The past fifteen years stand in stark contrast to the last half of the nineteenth century. The effects of this period of high inflation on fixed-dollar investments have been brutal. A $1,000 fifteen-year note issued in 1969, upon repayment in 1984, would have an inflation-adjusted principal value of $350, a loss in purchasing power of 65 percent.[10]

Adding to the uncertainties created by the high inflation rates of the past fifteen years has been the failure of the stock averages to act as a good hedge against inflation. Total annual return for common stock, adjusted for inflation, was a negative 1.5 percent for the decade of the 1970s and only 1.6 percent for the period from 1970 through 1983.[11] This result is contrary to the long experience of the earlier part of the twentieth century. For example, looking at the fifty years from 1926 to 1976, with inflation averaging 2.3 percent per year, the total annual return for common stock, adjusted for inflation, was 6.9 percent.[12]

Post-World War II inflation (as discussed in Chapter 1) was accepted by a few courts as a "changed circumstance" of sufficient importance to warrant departing from directions in trust investments to invest only in debt securities. The "inflation" cases hastened the demise of the legal list approach to prudence. The higher levels of inflation over the past fifteen years triggered vastly greater changes, however, including a strong deregulatory bias favoring competition in the financial marketplace, an expanding search by investors for products and services designed to cope with the new inflationary era, and, in response to these changes, a profusion of new financial products and techniques, a number of which are briefly described in the following section.

Derivative Financial Products

The most remarkable developments over the past fifteen years have been in the design and use of financial futures and options. Scholars, noting that the largest increases in the number of futures markets occur amid market turbulence, have suggested that the increased uncertainty associated with high levels of inflation leads to the creation of additional futures markets.[13] If so, perhaps the growth in these derivative products during the recent period of unprecedented inflation is not so remarkable after all. The statistics, in any event, are striking. Until 1972 when currency futures began trading on the International Monetary Market of the Chicago Mercantile Exchange, no financial futures existed. Before 1972, foreign exchange was regulated under the Bretton Woods accord. Rates were fixed from time to time by agreement of the contracting countries; they did not fluctuate in response to market conditions. When the accord was dropped in 1972, exchange rates began to float freely in the marketplace, volatility increased, and the need for a method of hedging this enhanced risk of future exchange rate fluctuation became intense. Growth in the use of currency futures is displayed in Table 2.4 and Figure 2.2.

Following the creation of the Commodity Futures Trading Commission (CFTC) in 1974, the Chicago Board of Trade was designated in 1975 as the contract market for trading futures in Government National Mortgage Association

Table 2.4 Selected Currency Futures Contracts Traded on International Monetary Market 1972–1984

Year	British pound	Deutschemark	Japanese yen	Swiss franc
1972	14,790	19,320	43,989	17,722
1973	31,412	77,272	125,660	22,013
1974	14,033	49,447	7,239	42,505
1975	15,015	54,793	1,790	69,933
1976	33,465	44,887	1,449	37,246
1977	78,701	134,368	82,261	106,968
1978	240,099	400,569	361,731	321,451
1979	513,682	450,856	329,645	493,944
1980	1,263,750	922,608	575,073	827,884
1981	1,491,102	1,654,891	960,598	1,518,767
1982	1,321,701	1,792,901	1,762,246	2,653,332
1983	1,614,993	2,423,508	3,442,262	3,766,130
1984	1,444,492	5,508,308	2,334,764	4,129,881

Figure 2.2 Selected Currency Futures Contracts, Traded on International Monetary Market 1972–1984

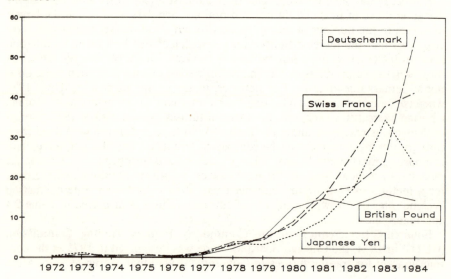

certificates (GNMAs or Ginny Maes). After currency futures, GNMAs were the first financial futures contracts to be traded, and they quickly became a popular mechanism for risk management. Other financial futures followed as the uses of these derivative instruments were discovered by a growing group of investors and financial intermediaries. Table 2.5 and Figure 2.3 capture the stunning growth of the more prominent of these new products.

The surge of volume in GNMA, Treasury bill, and Treasury bond futures that has occurred since 1979 can be attributed primarily to the decision of the Federal Reserve Board in October of that year to alter its anti-inflation strategy from controlling the level of key interest rates to limiting the growth of the nation's money supply. With interest rates free to reach market levels, volatility increased, creating a corresponding increase in the use of futures to hedge the uncertainty of future interest rate movements.

Another measure of activity in derivative financial instruments is found in the sheer number of new products approved for trading by the CFTC since 1975, when the Chicago Board of Trade was designated to trade the GNMA futures contract. Before the end of that year a futures contract on ninety-day Treasury bills had been approved. In succeeding years the CFTC approved two new financial instruments in 1977, four in 1978, six in 1979, three in 1980, ten in 1981,

Table 2.5 Selected Financial Futures Contracts Traded on All Exchanges, 1975–1984

Year	GNMA[1]	Treasury bills[2]	Treasury bonds[1]	Eurodollar[2]
1975	20,125	—	—	—
1976	128,568	110,223	—	—
1977	422,421	321,703	32,101	—
1978	953,161	768,980	555,350	—
1979	1,371,078	1,930,482	2,059,594	—
1980	2,325,892	3,338,773	6,489,555	—
1981	2,292,882	5,631,290	13,907,988	15,171
1982	2,055,648	6,598,848	16,739,695	323,619
1983	1,692,017	3,789,864	19,550,535	891,066
1984	862,450	3,292,817	29,963,280	4,192,952

Year	S&P 500 index[2]	S&P 100 index[2]	Major market index[1]	NYSE composite index
1975	—	—	—	—
1976	—	—	—	—
1977	—	—	—	—
1978	—	—	—	—
1979	—	—	—	—
1980	—	—	—	—
1981	—	—	—	—
1982	2,935,532	—	528,743	1,432,913
1983	8,101,697	—	724,979	3,506,439
1984	12,363,592	1,514,737	910,956	3,456,798

Source: Futures Industry Association Statistics

[1] Volume on Chicago Board of Trade

[2] Volume on Chicago Mercantile Exchange

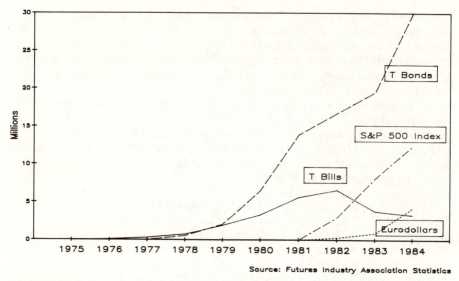

Source: Futures Industry Association Statistics

Figure 2.3(a) Selected Financial Futures Contracts Traded on All Exchanges, 1975–1984

Figure 2.3(b)

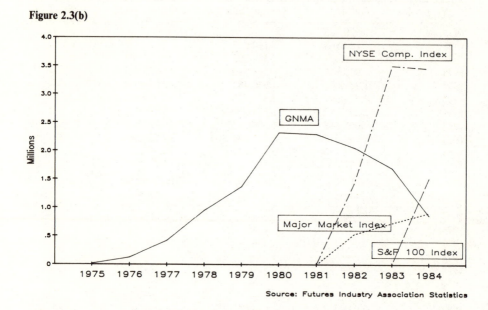

Source: Futures Industry Association Statistics

nine in 1982, five in 1983, and three in 1984, for a total of forty-four. By 1984 these financial futures instruments, none of which existed before 1975, accounted for 40 percent of the total number of contracts traded on all futures exchanges in the United States. If the currency futures that have traded only since 1972 are added, financial futures accounted for 49.3 percent of the total volume of all futures contracts traded in 1984.

Turning to options, the growth in recent years is no less remarkable. Exchange-listed options on individual issues of common stock began trading in 1973. As shown in Table 2.6 and Figure 2.4, growth in this derivative product has been impressive, despite a moratorium on new equity option products imposed by the Securities and Exchange Commission (SEC) from July 1977 until the spring of 1980.

Options on individual securities, while of some use to fiduciaries investing for the long-term, continue to serve primarily the needs of those bent on gain through short-term trades. Of greater significance to this study is the very recent growth in the use of options on stock indices. The first stock index options were approved for trading by the SEC in November 1982. Litigation initiated by the Chicago Board of Trade blocked the commencement of trading until the following year. On March 11, 1983, the Chicago Board Options Exchange (CBOE) opened trading of options on its Standard & Poor's (S&P) 100 index, which is made up of 100 "blue chip" corporations in the S&P 500 with stock options listed on the CBOE. In 1983 contract volume in this option was 10.6 million. Contract volume for 1984 increased dramatically to 64.3 million, representing about 87 percent of trading in broad-based stock index options on all exchanges; further growth in the use of this product has occurred in 1985. For the first three quarters of 1985 contract volume was 71.6 million, compared with 45.3 million for the comparable period of 1984.[14] Although many stock index option products have been approved for trading since 1982 (including, by the SEC, options on various broad-based indices and options on narrow-based indices such as computer technology stocks, oils, airlines, and high technology, and, by the CFTC, options on currency and

Table 2.6 Options Contract Volume on All Exchanges 1973–1984

Year	Options volume	Options volume in shares as % of NYSE volume
1973	1,119,177	2.8
1974	5,682,907	16.2
1975	18,102,569	38.6
1976	32,373,927	60.4
1977	39,637,328	75.2
1978	57,231,018	79.4
1979	64,264,863	78.8
1980	96,728,546	85.2
1981	109,405,782	92.3
1982	137,264,816	83.4
1983	135,658,976	62.8
1984	118,925,239	51.5

Source: Market Statistics 1985 Chicago Board Options Exchange

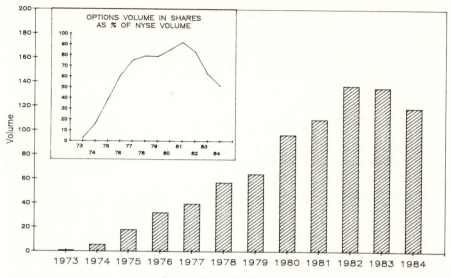

Source: Market Statistics 1985 Chicago Board Options Exchange

Figure 2.4 Options Contract Volume on All Exchanges, 1973–1984

stock index futures), none has even approached the level of trading interest enjoyed by the CBOE's option contract on the S&P 100 index.[15]

These derivative products have been developed and are being used, mainly, as means of managing overall market risk, hedging a diversified portfolio, and participating fully in the market across a broad spectrum of risk from a leveraged long position to a short position, goals founded upon widely accepted notions of modern portfolio theory (as explored by Professors Edwin J. Elton and Martin J. Gruber in Appendix A).[16] Empirical evidence supports the growing use of derivative financial products by fiduciaries. Greenwich Research Associates reports that demand for financial futures has increased from 5 percent of the institutional investors interviewed by that firm in 1981 to 13 percent in 1984. Some 29 percent more indicated in 1984 that they were planning to start using financial futures.[17] The results of the questionnaire used in this study (Questionnaire) confirm this trend: 42 percent of all respondents indicated they were using options; 35 percent said they were using futures.

Mutual Funds

Change in the mutual fund industry illustrates the themes being emphasized in this chapter. In 1940 there were sixty-eight mutual funds with $448 million in assets and 296,000 shareholder accounts.[18] By 1984 there were 1,246 mutual funds with $371 billion in assets and more than 28 million shareholder accounts.[19] In addition to this dramatic growth, there has been vast change in asset allocation within the funds. In 1970 there were only 361 mutual funds; money market funds hadn't been invented. In 1974 money market funds had just entered the market, accounting for only 5 percent of mutual fund assets. By 1984 their share was over 56 percent and their number—426—substantially exceeded the total number of funds in 1970.[20]

The diversity of mutual funds has expanded greatly as the investor's demand for specialized investment products has grown. Commencing with the July 1985 issue, the Investment Company Institute's *Trends in Mutual Fund Activity* was changed to reflect the more diverse range of investment objectives offered. Five new categories were added to the eight classifications of investment objective previously employed (consisting of aggressive growth, growth, growth-and-income, balanced, income, option/income, corporate bond, and long-term municipal bond). The new categories included two equity funds, precious metal and international, and three bond and income funds, government, GNMA, and state municipal bond.

Another measure of change appears in the dramatic increase in the use of mutual funds by institutional investors, whose share of mutual fund assets rose from 7 percent in 1960 to 38 percent in 1984.[21] The lessons of modern portfolio theory are reflected in the success of mutual funds designed to replicate the market by tracking some suitable surrogate efficiently and at low cost to investors choosing to be passive. There has been a growing acceptance of the index fund idea, particularly among the larger institutional pools. Greenwich Research Associates reports that among companies with pension plan assets over $1 billion, 45 percent used index funds in 1983, 53 percent used them in 1984, and another 4 percent are planning to start using them.[22]

Evidence of marketplace change can also be observed in legislation (H.R. 3397) introduced in the House of Representatives on September 20, 1985 to amend subchapter M of the Internal Revenue Code, which governs the taxation of mutual funds, defining the parameters within which a fund must operate to achieve conduit tax treatment. The bill would repeal the requirement that less than 30 percent of a fund's gross income be derived from the sale of securities held for less than three months. As explained by Congressman Flippo in introducing the bill:

> This rule was enacted at a time when products such as index options and futures, financial futures and other new investment products did not exist and, indeed, were not contemplated. However, in today's environment, the rule thwarts a mutual fund's fiduciary responsibility to act in the shareholder's best interest.
>
> First, the rule prohibits a mutual fund from taking advantage of these new investment products, even though they are used extensively by other investors. Second, it imposes an unwarranted restriction on the fund's ability to react and benefit from rapid changes in the market, that is, periods of volatile interest rates or when the value of securities increase abruptly, thereby precipitating an artificial investment decision that may not be in the best interest of the mutual fund shareholder.[23]

Another change in subchapter M would broaden the definition of qualifying income, which must make up at least 90 percent of a fund's gross income for the fund to enjoy conduit tax treatment. The new categories proposed by H.R. 3397 would be gains from options and futures contracts and from foreign currency transactions.

Technology

Computer technology has been an important contributing factor to the accelerating growth in new financial products and services over the past fifteen years. The creation of synthetic securities backed by the collective cash flows of a pool of assets, such as home mortgages, consumer loans, and business equipment loans, has only been made possible with the programming capabilities of the computer. The securitization of mortgage pools and other hitherto illiquid assets has opened up to public investors a range of new products geared precisely to their needs. By avoiding the intermediation of lending institutions, these instruments have achieved loan placement at lower cost to borrowers. The collateralized mortgage obligation (CMO) is perhaps the most prominent example of this development. CMOs consist typically of several classes of securities with varying interest rates and maturities (ranging from "fast pay" to "slow pay" and usually including the popular zero coupon bond), backed by a pool of mortgages, the debt service from which is allocated among the classes, first to meet interest due on all, then to repay the principal of the class with the shortest maturity and severally to each succeeding class in order of maturity until all classes are paid in full.

Computerization has also lowered the transaction costs of fund transfers among accounts. These effects have ushered in discount brokerage and cash management products designed to achieve higher returns on short-term fund deposits through, for example, money market mutual funds and cash management sweep accounts at banks.

Improvements in Financial Reporting

The importance of the securities laws in helping to achieve a "fair game" by requiring issuers to furnish the financial community with a reliable body of reasonably uniform financial data can hardly be overstated. William O. Douglas, a law professor at Yale University and later to become the third chairman of the SEC, wrote (with George Bates) in the year of its passage that the Securities Act of 1933 would, among other things "plac[e] in the market during the early stages of the life of a security a body of facts, which, operating indirectly through investment services and expert investors, will tend to produce more accurate appraisal of the worth of a security if it commands a broad enough market."[24]

The transformation of the marketplace wrought by the securities laws is prosaically demonstrated by a shift in the subject matter covered by Graham and Dodd in the third edition of *Security Analysis,* published in 1951, from that covered in the first and second editions, published in 1934 and 1940, respectively. The preface to the third edition tells the story:

> Another significant modification of our approach lies in the dropping of nearly all the detailed references to the corporate abuses prior to 1940; the space saved has made possible the expansion into a full division of the book of the material on stockholder-management relations. This change reflects a shift in the nature of the investment problems growing out of the purchase and ownership of securities. Prior to the creation of the Securities and Exchange Commission, the more pressing problems grew out of the inadequacy or misleading character of corporate information, and the manipulation of securities both in corporate setups and on the market. The reforms in these areas have been sweeping and efficacious. It is a source of satisfaction to note that the great majority of the abuses to which we called attention in the first (1934) edition of this work have now all but disappeared. In turn, this cleansing of the financial stables, coupled with the

improvement in the financial condition of the typical enterprise, has largely improved the investment status of common stocks, viewed as a whole.

All told, about 200 pages, or 24 percent, of the second edition were dropped for this reason.

Just as those who grew up with hot and cold running water, central heating, and refrigeration find it hard to imagine life without those amenities, so too do today's investors and financial intermediaries have trouble putting themselves in the shoes of their late nineteenth or early twentieth century counterparts. George W. Edwards, in his study of the evolution of finance capitalism,[25] writes of this period:

> Financial statements in this period were unreliable, and the issuing of untrue earning statements was a common practice. When the Atchison, Topeka and Santa Fe went into receivership in 1894, an independent audit revealed that while the statements from 1891 to 1894 showed satisfactory surpluses, actually the books had been falsified to cover an average annual deficit of over $1,250,000 for these years.[26]

Despite the exposure of these practices, the unsettling effects of the financial panics of 1903 and 1907, the reforming efforts of Presidents Theodore Roosevelt and Woodrow Wilson, and the findings of the House Committee on Banking and Currency in the so-called Money Trust Investigation headed by Arsene Pujo of Louisiana,[27] inadequacies remained the dominant characteristic of financial reporting. Indeed, until the securities laws of 1933 and 1934 took hold, less than half of the publicly traded industrial corporations supplied annual income statements displaying such minimum data as sales, net earnings, depreciation (and depletion), interest charges, nonoperating income, income taxes, dividends paid, and surplus adjustments. Railroads and public utilities, however, uniformly did so, but only after they became subject to government regulation.

Issuers with securities traded "over-the-counter," which were not made subject to the reporting requirements of the Securities Exchange Act of 1934 until 1964, continued the understandable tendency to disclose only what they wanted to have the investing public see. Graham and Dodd reported, as of 1940, that although the great majority of over-the-counter issuers supplied both a balance sheet and an income statement, exceptions were fairly numerous. As one amusing example, Dun & Bradstreet Corporation, whose business it was to supply financial information to the public, was one of those who refused to reveal its own earnings to stockholders.

Although the amount of sales or gross revenues is generally regarded as the most important item in the financial statement, after net earnings, in the late 1920s Laurence H. Sloan of Standard Statistics Company found it possible to compare the gross incomes and net profits of only 235 out of the 545 leading industrial corporations studied, some 43 percent. Gross incomes were simply not reported by 57 percent of the companies. In its 1935 study of the securities markets, the special staff of the Twentieth Century Fund found that "despite some improvement during the past few years, a majority even of those companies whose issues are listed on the New York Stock Exchange do not disclose enough information to render their balance sheets and income statements intelligible to the average, well-informed investor."

Evolving Notions about Insider Trading

Another way to examine change in the investment landscape is to look at how attitudes regarding insider trading have shifted and, roughly in parallel, how the profession of security analysis has developed. Opinion about trading in securities on the basis of information not generally available in the marketplace has changed greatly since the early nineteenth century. At the time of *Harvard College* and, indeed, until the early twentieth century, it would have been hard to find anyone who questioned the idea that corporate directors and officers might freely trade in the shares of their corporations while in possession of material, nonpublic information.[28]

It is not surprising that, in the early years of our public securities markets, the owners of business enterprises, in parting with some portion of that ownership (in the case of the early industrials, typically in the form of preferred stock), should continue to view the enterprise essentially as theirs to deal with as they saw fit. Henry Manne notes, for example, that before 1910, no one had ever publicly questioned the morality of "insider trading." In a *New York Times* survey of 1915, 90 percent of the business executives interviewed admitted to trading regularly in stock of their own corporations.[29] To the same effect was a statement by the SEC appearing in its 1944 annual report:

> Prior to the enactment of the Securities Exchange Act, profits from "sure thing" speculation in the stocks of their corporations were more or less generally accepted by the financial community as part of the emolument for serving as a corporate officer or director notwithstanding the flagrantly inequitable character of such trading.[30]

If corporate insiders, who presumably were thought even in those early days to owe some kind of duty to their stockholders, could so trade, then surely those they chose to inform—tippees—could do so too. In the extensive hearings of 1933 and 1934 before the Senate Committee on Banking and Currency that led to adoption of the securities laws, evidence of widespread insider trading was adduced, leading specifically to the sanction against short-swing profits by directors, officers, and substantial stockholders contained in Section 16(b) of the Securities Exchange Act of 1934.[31] Nothing specific, however, was done to address the question of whether those with special access to insiders could freely trade on nonpublic information furnished to them in this way. In fact, the antifraud provisions of the securities laws were not extended to tippees until 1961, when, in *Cady, Roberts & Co.*, a case of first impression, the SEC applied Rule 10b-5 to a selling broker who acted on behalf of clients (including his wife) after receiving nonpublic information about a corporation's dividend action from one of its directors.[32] Before *Cady, Roberts & Co.*, special access to corporate management played a leading role in successful investing. It was commonplace for investors, whether trading for their own account or as fiduciaries, to use inside information in the investment process. Access to nonpublic information was a critically important tool to the investor—more important in fact than skill, industry, and foresight combined. Fiduciaries and other money managers were often chosen precisely because of their multiple positions on the boards of corporations and the ready access to corporate developments that these positions allowed.

Following the *Cady, Roberts & Co.* decision, attitudes among investors, and particularly among the growing cadre of financial intermediaries who served them, began to change.

Evidence of this change abounds. Boards of directors of public companies have adopted and enforced policies against insider trading. The stock exchanges and other self-regulatory organizations are on record with unequivocal rules against the practice. Investment advisers, broker-dealers, and banks have developed policies against insider trading and procedures for policing those policies, including so-called Chinese walls where necessary to permit multi-purpose firms to continue their businesses by sealing off the flow of nonpublic information from one department to another. Investment companies and other institutional investors have likewise adopted formal policies prohibiting insider trading. And law and accounting firms have followed suit. The breadth of these changes is cogent evidence of a basic shift in perception that places insider trading outside the bounds of lawful behavior.[33]

While trading on the basis of material nonpublic information derived from someone having special access to a corporation continues to occur, and probably always will despite the increased sanctions against it provided by Congress in the Insider Trading Sanctions Act of 1984,[34] the practice is no longer acceptable. Financial intermediaries have written policies against it, institutional investors do not expect to profit from it (sometimes expressly prohibiting their managers from resorting to it), and neither fiduciaries nor the investment managers who serve them are marketed or selected because of their access to inside information. Indeed, so complete has been this change that special access is often viewed negatively because of its potential for preventing investments to be made in corporations where access exists or preventing rapid disinvestment when it becomes desirable.

These conclusions hold despite the reoccurrence of claims in the popular press that insider trading cannot be stopped.[35] That insider trading has become an unattractive but inevitable by-product of the takeover phenomenon, which itself is the dominant corporate event of recent years, cannot be gainsaid.[36] Takeovers inevitably involve prices well above market and access to knowledge of those prices well in advance of public disclosure by very large working groups responsible for effecting the takeovers. It is not surprising that some within those groups submit to the temptations of greed. However, no evidence has been found to rebut the accuracy of the broad trends in the fiduciary and investment manager behavior depicted in this study. The extent to which unusual trading in potential takeover targets is based on rumor, attempted manipulation, or inside information is unclear. Regardless of the ultimate findings on this point, the fact remains that the bulk of fiduciaries and professional investment managers are not playing that game.

Professionalizing of Security Analysis

The shrinking use since 1961 of inside information as a feasible tool of the investment trade coincides with the emerging dominance through the decade of the 1960s of the institutional investor,[37] the coming of age of the financial intermediary,[38] and the recognition that our capital markets are in a broad sense efficient.[39] As a profession, security analysis developed slowly following enactment of the securities laws in 1933 and 1934 and the coincidental publication in 1934 of *Security Analysis: Principles and Techniques* by Benjamin Graham and David Dodd.[40] By making mandatory a uniform system of financial disclosure, the securities laws provided the grist for the security analyst's mill. The machinery for that mill came from Graham and Dodd.[41] In the preface to their third edition, published in 1951, Graham and Dodd could say "Security analysis is on the verge of attaining some measure of formal recognition as a professional discipline."[42] Today, the efficiency of our capital markets is much more a product of rapid dissemination of information, its analysis by professionals, and the investment decisions of institutional investors relying on that analysis than of the trading by insiders and those with special access to insiders. Over the years, the security analyst has replaced the inside source as the key to sound investment choice within an actively managed portfolio.

The Rule Against Delegation

Of what significance to the prudent man rule are these shifts? They particularly affect the matter of delegation, which (as discussed in Chapter 1) was sharply proscribed by the Treatise and the Restatement. Before World War II, it made sense for several reasons to restrict the ability of a fiduciary to delegate investment selection to others. It was thought to be relatively simple and even routine to manage a portfolio.[43] Until the post-war period, the idea of selecting and holding "permanent investments" prevailed, particularly for fiduciaries. It was reasonable to expect the fiduciary chosen to do the selecting. Moreover, there were not others who demonstrably knew more about the limited field of available investment products than the typical fiduciary of that era. There did not exist either an accepted body of learning about market behavior and security pricing or a cadre of professionals to hold, enlarge, and apply that learning. There were no easy and reliable performance measures with which to select among fiduciaries. The most obvious reason for selecting one fiduciary over another, beyond friendship and family, was his potential for special access to securities information. In short, there was no need to delegate and, lacking a need, the marketplace had not provided anyone to delegate to. The antidelegation rule was simply an expression of concern over the possibility that the fiduciary would not be sufficiently diligent and attentive to his task; that he might abandon it to others. In the modern context, however, it is precisely a keen sense of diligence that the fiduciary exhibits in searching out the best to whom to delegate the execution of a particular investment strategy.

In this connection, it is worth recalling that the profession of investment adviser (or counsel) did not exist until the post-World War I decade and by 1928 could claim only about twenty firms. Logically enough, following the stock market crash in 1929, the number and types of clients seeking the services of investment advisers increased rapidly, as did the number of advisers available to meet this rising demand. By 1934 there were about 3,000 in the field; today there are over 9,000 registered with the SEC under the Investment Advisers Act of 1940.[44] They offer a wide variety of specialized skills and investment strategies, to which fiduciaries have increasingly turned for help in fund management. Indeed, so complex has the marketplace become that fiduciaries are even using delegees for help in the search for able investment managers.

A revealing creation of the past twenty years has been the "investment management consultant," whose business it is to assist fiduciaries, particularly those responsible for pension funds subject to the Employee Retirement Income Security Act of 1974 (ERISA), in asset allocation, the evaluation and selection of managers, and the measurement of their performance. *Pensions & Investment Age,* which conducts an annual survey of this new profession, profiled sixty-nine firms in its August 6, 1984 issue.[45] Frank Russell Company of Tacoma, Washington was probably the first firm of this kind, starting business in 1969.[46]

As the marketplace has grown more complex, and the skills required to master even small segments of it more demanding, it is not surprising to find fiduciaries seeking help not only to deploy the assets under their charge, but to find those most capable of undertaking the deployments. With many economists arguing that no one should be able consistently to outperform the indices, the burden of trying to accomplish that feat became heavy. For fiduciaries reluctant to yield to economists' logic by shifting to the index fund, it was natural to turn to those who claimed the ability to pick the managers who could produce superior results. The Questionnaire results indicate that 30 percent now employ investment management consultants to aid in selecting investment managers and 37 percent employ them to monitor and evaluate performance. This trend is likely to continue as the demand for specialization in investment management increases and the general level of sophistication among fiduciaries rises. Indeed, the services offered by investment management consultants have been expanding since 1969 to track the increasingly complicated universe of investment products and techniques. Initially, the services offered simply helped in selecting capable managers and measuring their performance. Here is a typical description of the much broader range of services offered in 1984:

> [The firm] offers manager evaluation and selection, asset allocation guidance and assists in setting investment objectives. It also provides performance measurement for domestic stocks and bonds, real estate and venture capital investments, as well as international investments. The firm offers performance analysis and diagnosis.

> [The firm] has expertise in real estate, international investing, venture capital and issues related to public funds. It assists its clients in the evaluation and selection of managers within these asset categories.

> The firm also provides pension asset and liability simulation; manager structure determination; identification of the impact of passive investment strategies; on-line manager monitoring and performance measurement; and endowment and foundation consultations.

In addition to explaining the antidelegation rule, the absence of professionalism and professionals before World War II may help to explain the attractions of a labeling approach to prudence, wherein legislatures, judges, and commentators sought to limit fiduciaries in the discretion they might otherwise have exercised, presumably for the purpose of preventing them from making investment errors and incurring losses. As discussed previously, legislatures adopted legal lists from which the fiduciary was required to choose. Courts, influenced by events of the time, labeled particular securities imprudent per se, as the New York Court of Appeals did in 1869 for *all* common stock in *King v. Talbot* and as the Pennsylvania Supreme Court did in 1852 for stock of the Bank of the United States in *Hemphill's Appeal.*[47] And the Treatise and the Restatement superimposed the labeling approach on Justice Putnam's pristine statement of the prudent man rule. Underlying the tendency to label was a confident belief in the existence of "safe" investments.

The Notion of a Safe Investment

In 1830, as Justice Putnam recognized, all investments, even government bonds,[48] were risky. In this environment, it was not unexpected that investors would be attracted to securities offering a dynamic share of entrepreneurial returns. Thereafter, recurring financial panics and scandals, combined with a long period of deflation and a growth in capital seeking assured safety as the paramount goal, led to an expanding use of the bond, particularly by fiduciaries. Not only was it widely believed through the latter half of the nineteenth and first half of the twentieth centuries that safe investments existed, it was also thought that they could be identified.[49] In *Investment and Speculation,* written in 1931 by Lawrence Chamberlain and William Wren Hay, two acknowledged experts in finance, the view is expressed that "[a] pure investment is always a loan."[50] Elsewhere in this book the nature of equity is addressed: "Common stocks, as such, are not superior to bonds as long-term investments, because primarily they are not investments at all. They are speculations."[51] Given the fiduciary's emphatic duty to conserve principal, it was logical, if safe investments could be described, to limit his discretion to selecting only from among them.

An awakening to the impossibility of listing those investment products or techniques that are safe was a long time in coming and, as noted in Chapter 3 (devoted, in part, to the endurance of that fallacy), in some respects has yet to be fully accepted. (Most remarkably, for example, the constitutions of Alabama and Montana to this day forbid their legislatures from authorizing trust investments in corporate stock.[52]) It is interesting, therefore, to observe the prescience of Graham and Dodd on the subject, as expressed in their first edition of *Security Analysis* published in 1934:

> It is not the wild gyrations of the common-stock averages but the precipitate decline in the bond averages . . . which constitutes the really novel and arresting feature of recent financial history—at least from the standpoint of investment logic and practice. The heavy losses taken by conservative investors since 1928 warrant the serious question, Is there such a thing as a sound and satisfactory investment? . . . [F]or years prior to 1928, there had been developing a realization that bonds did not afford sufficient protection against loss to compensate for the surrender of the profit element. The years 1917–1920 were marked by a tremendous decline in all bond prices as the result of war financing followed by the postwar inflation and collapse. . . .

> It was the natural dissatisfaction with their experiences as bond owners which predisposed investors to embrace the new doctrine of common stocks as the superior form of investment. . . . Today the doctrine of common stocks as long-term investments seems discredited, but this fact does not in itself restore the bond to its old estate as the sound investment *par excellence,* nor does it explain away the unhappy history of the bondholder in recent years.

> If we were to regard the record of the bond list since 1927 as indicative of what the future has in store, the considered conclusion would be warranted that sound investment as formerly conceived—meaning generally the purchase of bonds at prices close to par—no longer exists.[53]

The wisdom of this statement took many years gradually to be reflected in investor choice betweeen equities and debt. SEC statistics on securities registrations for public sale are revealing on the point, at least to the extent that issuers' preferences for the public sale of debt or equity reflect investors' preferences as well (a plausible theory since an issuer's cost of capital is likely to be lower if the securities floated are those preferred by investors). In the prewar years from 1935 to 1940, the dollar value of equity registrations (preferred and common) was only 19 percent of the total dollar value of equity and debt registered during that period.[54] Following World War II the spread began to narrow until (in 1952) equity registrations for the first time exceeded those of debt, with common stock offerings alone falling only $14 million, or .4 percent, shy of equalling the $3.346 billion of debt registered in that year. From that point on equity offerings dominated the marketplace, although there were six years (1954, 1958, 1975, 1979, 1980, 1982) in which the dollar value of debt offerings exceeded that of equities.

The comparative return studies of stocks, government and corporate bonds, Treasury bills, and inflation over the period from 1926 to 1984 are also instructive.[55] If one had invested $1,000 in long-term government bonds in 1926, and reinvested all interest, one would have experienced low risk in the sense of volatility (a standard deviation[56] of 7.5 percent) and a correspondingly low rate of return. The investment would have grown to $8,420 by 1984, but only $1,390 when adjusted for inflation. Selecting corporate bonds would have produced $12,642 by 1984, or a real growth of $2,092 after the inflation adjustment, with only a slight increase in volatility (standard deviation of 7.6 percent). Treasury bills, virtually riskless for the short-term investor in that they never experienced a negative nominal total return over the entire fifty-eight-year period, exhibited a strong tendency to track the rate of inflation, so that the $1,000 investment would have shown near zero real growth, reaching only $1,155 by 1984.

In marked contrast, $1,000 invested in common stocks (based upon the S&P composite index), while exhibiting much greater volatility (standard deviation of 21.2 percent), would have grown to $211,200 by 1984, or $35,436 after adjusting for inflation. Volatility is demonstrated by the fact that the investment would have been worth $35,620 in 1972, its all-time high in real terms, indicating that an investor in common stocks would have realized a slight loss in real terms over the past twelve years.

If the $1,000 was invested only in small stocks (essentially those in the fifth quintile of New York Stock Exchange listings by market capitalization), the volatility would have been even greater over the fifty-eight-year period (standard deviation of 36.3 percent), but so too the growth. By 1984 the investment would have been worth $168,573 adjusted for inflation. The striking superiority of small stock returns is even more remarkable because, as recently as ·1960, one would find that the small stock investment had grown about the same as the investment in the broader index of common stocks. In real terms, a $1,000 investment made in 1926 in either equity group would have been worth about $17,000 in 1960. Since that year small stocks have increased in real terms by a multiple of ten compared to only a twofold increase for the broader index of common stocks.

These long-term market results add empirical support to the conclusion that inherently safe investments do not now exist nor, with the benefit of hindsight, did they exist in the past. (The results also tend to support one of the major lessons drawn from modern portfolio theory in Appendix A—that the only way to increase return in an efficient portfolio is to increase risk.)

The uncertainty signaled by Graham and Dodd in 1934 continues to dominate today's much richer investment landscape. Indeed, the very high rates of inflation through the 1970s followed by lowering inflation and increased real rates of interest,[57] an unprecedented growth in the country's domestic debt (relative to gross national product) and in its international trade deficit, and the remarkable burst in financial innovation over the past fifteen years have conspired to increase the sense of uncertainty,[58] while at the same time (through innovation) increasing the tools available to the investor to bear the greater risk.[59]

In a sense, this sketch of the investment landscape brings us full circle to the timeless and essentially unheeded words of Justice Putnam: "Do what you will, the capital is at hazard."[60]

NOTES

[1]This chapter draws generally on a number of works of economic and financial history and specifically on memoranda prepared for this study by Peter Eisenstadt, an historian employed by the Archives Department of the New York Stock Exchange. Among the principal source books are Carosso, *Investment Banking in America: A History* (1970) (including selected materials from its richly appointed bibliography); Kross & Blyn, *A History of Financial Intermediaries* (1971); U.S. Securities and Exchange Commission, *Annual Reports; U.S Securities and Exchange Commission, Investment Trusts and Investment Companies:* Report (5 pts., Washington, 1939–42); U.S. Securities and Exchange Commission, *Institutional Investor Study Report* (7 pts., Washington, 1971); Goldsmith, *Financial Institutions* (1968); *Financial Intermediaries in the American Economy Since 1900* (1958); B. Graham & D. Dodd, *Security Analysis* (4 eds. 1934, 1940, 1951, 1960); Edwards, *The Evolution of Finance Capitalism* (1967). The discussion of the historical composition of the Harvard and Princeton portfolios is drawn from unpublished data in the archives of those universities.

[2]The growth, maturity and widespread acceptance of NASDAQ as a viable competitor to the Big Board that has occurred since 1971, when trading on NASDAQ began, reinforces the point. NASDAQ's listings (including foreign issuers) grew from 2,969 in 1971 to 4,728 in 1984, its volume grew from 2,221 million shares in 1972 to 15,159 million in 1984, and the market value of its listings grew from $78,190 million in 1976 (the first year for which this information was made available) to $206,955 million in 1984.

[3]Report of the National Bureau of Economic Research on Institutional Investors and Corporate Stock [hereinafter cited as NBER Report] (H.R. Doc. No. 92-94, Part 6, 92d Cong., 1st Sess., 1971) prepared for and as part of the Institutional Investor Study Report of the SEC [hereinafter cited as SEC Institutional Investor Study] (H.R. Doc. No. 92-94, Parts 1–6, 92d Cong., 1st Sess., 1971) contains statistical data supportive of this conclusion. Table 2.4 from the NBER Report, tracing the shifting allocation of corporate stock outstanding among different sectors of the economy from 1835 to 1949, is set forth on the following page.

Meaningful comparisons between the portfolio shifts of Harvard and Princeton, on the one hand, and other institutional investors, on the other, over the period 1830 to 1984 are difficult. Data for such plausibly comparable institutions as personal trust departments of commercial banks and trust companies, and particularly their common trust funds, is scarce and of limited reliability before the late 1950s. NBER Report, *supra* note 3, at 68. Investment companies were of negligible importance until the early 1920s, with earlier data hard to uncover, and in any event, were not subject to a form of prudent man rule. Instead, as vehicles primarily designed for common stock investing on a diversified basis, their portfolios were always dominated by common stock. *Id.* at 61–2. Life insurance companies operating in New York, after legislative reforms brought on by the Armstrong-Hughes investigation of 1905, were sharply restricted in the stockholdings permitted by law. Previously, from 1860 to 1880, approximately 2 percent of their assets were in equities, railroads accounting for 25 percent and banks a significant (but uncertain) portion of the balance. *Id.* at 54. From 1880 to 1906 stockholdings of life insurance companies increased to a peak of 6 percent. Property insurance companies, with liabilities of intermediate length and much less regulatory constraint than life insurance companies, were the only group of financial institutions that held a substantial proportion of their total assets in corporate stock until well into the twentieth century. In 1860 fire and marine insurance companies held nearly one-quarter of their assets in equities, consisting primarily of bank stocks. The commitment to equities dropped to 11.5 percent in 1880, but then rose to 25.7 percent in 1900. *Id.* at 58. Of

Industrial Distribution of Corporate Stock Outstanding 1835–1949 (percent)

	1835	1859[1]	1871	1890	1900	1912	1922	1929	1939	1949
Railroads	2	15	19	20	39	26	10	6	4	3
Other transportation	7	8	5	3						
Gas & electricity	0	5	4	8	7[2]	7[2]	5[2]	11[2]	12[2]	10[2]
Banks & insurance	64	39	26	21	20	15	16	11	9	8
Manufacturing & mining	18	24	38	39	34	52	69	72	75	79
Other	9	9	8	9						
Total	100	100	100	100	100	100	100	100	100	100

1. For 1860 alternate and for some groups substantially different estimates of the value of corporate stock (rather than dividends) may be derived from *Hunt's Merchants Magazine*, 1863, p. 23. According to these estimates railroads accounted for 45 percent of the total, public utilities for 13 percent, and banks and insurance companies for 44 percent, no entries being shown for corporations in manufacturing, mining, trade, and service.

2. All public utilities except railroads.

course, given their different functions, neither life nor property insurance companies provide especially useful comparative data.

[4]NBER Report, *supra* note 3, at 41.

[5]Navin & Sears, "The Rise of a Market for Industrial Securities, 1887–1902," XXXIX Bus. His. Rev. (June 1955) at 105, 106.

[6]*Id.* at 134 n.42.

[7]In 1923, for example, Thorstein Veblen wrote that the corporation had become no less than "the master institution of civilized life." T. Veblen, *Absentee Ownership and Business Enterprise* (1923) at 86, *cited in* Edwards, *The Evolution of Finance Capitalism* (1967) at 162 n.4. Reference to Edwards, particularly Part II at 140–222, is made for a good description of the evolution of American capitalism over the nineteenth century and up to the depression years of the twentieth century.

[8]Hirsch, "Inflation and the Law of Trusts," 18 Real Prop. Prob. & Tr. J. 601 (1983); Ibbotson Associates, *Stocks, Bonds, Bills and Inflation: 1985 Yearbook* (1985).

[9]Hirsch, *supra* note 8, at 605–610.

[10]Table No. 789, "Consumer Price Indexes, by Major Groups: 1950 to 1984," *1985 Statistical Abstract of the United States* at 475.

[11]Ibbotson Associates, *Stocks, Bonds, Bills, and Inflation: 1985 Yearbook* (1985) at 90, 100.

[12]*Id.*

[13]Carlton, *Futures Markets: Their Purpose, Their History, Their Growth, Their Successes and Failures,* Working Papers Series #CSFM-78, Columbia Center for the Study of Futures Markets (April 1984) at 25–6.

[14]Market statistics of the Chicago Board Options Exchange.

[15]Statistics compiled by the SEC's Division of Market Regulation in November 1985 indicate that trading on narrow based indices declined from an aggregate of 511,879 contracts in the first quarter of 1984 to only 89,953 contracts in the first quarter of 1985. Of some seventy-four stock index option products filed with the SEC for approval since 1982, forty have been withdrawn or delisted or are not trading, sixteen are not yet approved, and only eighteen continue to be traded.

[16]*See* Jaffee, *The Impact of Financial Futures and Options on Capital Formation,* Working Paper Series #CSFM-84, Columbia Center for the Study of Futures Markets (April 1984), for insightful discussion of role played by financial futures and conclusion that no substantive basis (theoretical or empirical) exists for believing that financial futures contracts will have a negative impact on capital formation. Jaffee attributes acceptance and pursuit of modern finance and portfolio theory by investors as a primary source of the success of stock index futures. *Id.* at 21–2. *See also A Review and Evaluation of Federal Margin Regulations, A Study by the Staff of the Board of Governors of the Federal Reserve System* (December 1984), in which the argument that exchange-traded futures and options have encouraged a material shift of "risk capital" away from potentially more productive use in business enterprises is rejected. *Id.* at 10–11.

[17]Greenwich Research Associates, *Report to Participants on Institutional Equity Services 1985* at 56. Largely due to the popularity of interest rate futures, trading volume in futures and options on futures rose by more than 28 percent in the first half of 1986. *See* "Trading in Futures Increases by 28%," N.Y. Times, 7 July 1986.

[18]*1985 Mutual Fund Fact Book* at 23–4.

[19]*Id.*

[20]*Id.*

[21]*Id.* at 42.

[22]Greenwich Research Associates, *Report to Participants on Large Corporate Pensions 1985* at 23.

[23]131 Cong. Rec. H7699–700 (daily ed. Sept. 20, 1985) (statement of Rep. Flippo).

[24]Douglas & Bates, "The Federal Securities Act of 1933," 43 Yale L.J. 171, 172 (1933).

[25]Edwards, *The Evolution of Finance Capitalism* (1967).

[26]*Id.* at 187.

[27]This inquiry was authorized by a House resolution "to obtain full and complete information on the banking and currency conditions of the United States for the purpose of determining what regulation is needed." H.R. Res. 429, extended by H.R. Res. 504, February 24, 1912.

[28]Evidence of some early concern over speculation by issuers in their own securities, perhaps more on grounds of market manipulation than misuse of nonpublic information, can be found. In its 1908 listing agreement with the New York Stock Exchange, the National Lead Company agreed that "the company will not speculate in its own securities or those of the constituent companies, nor permit similar speculations by any of its constituent companies." This practice was followed by duPont and American Woolen Company in 1909. *See* unpublished paper entitled "How the New York Stock Exchange Went Public," prepared for this study in November 1985 by Peter Eisenstadt.

[29]H. Manne, *Insider Trading and the Stock Market* (Free Press, New York 1966) at 1, 2. Manne attributes to Professor H. L. Wilgus (at 4) the first public argument against insider trading, advanced in a 1910 article entitled "Purchase of Shares of Corporation by a Director From a Shareholder," in the Michigan Law Review.

[30]10 Securities and Exchange Commission Annotated Report 50 (1944).

[31]*Stock Exchange Practices, Report of Com. on Banking & Currency,* S. Rep. No. 1455, 73d Cong., 2d Sess. (1934).

[32]*In the Matter of Cady, Roberts & Co.,* Sec. Exch. Act Rel. No. 6668 (Nov. 8, 1961).

[33]The SEC is chiefly responsible for these changes. Through a combination of rule-making, monitoring, hectoring, lecturing, and enforcing, the SEC succeeded in bending the norms of business behavior toward the "disclose or refrain from trading" rule. This is not the place to mark all the steps along the path. However, one example may be useful. In 1973, the SEC censured certain broker-dealers and investment advisers for the misuse of inside information relating to a drop in quarterly earnings of Faberge, Inc., the well-known cosmetics firm. In its order the SEC chose to address virtually the entire financial community when it said:

> This case emphasizes the importance and *necessity* of broker-dealers, investment advisers and institutional investors, as well as issuers, instituting and implementing effective procedures calculated to *deter* and *detect* the misuse of inside information [emphasis supplied]. *In re Certain Trading in the Common Stock of Faberge, Inc.,* Sec. Exch. Act Rel. No. 10174 (May 25, 1973).

This statement sensitized both the securities bar and the investment community it serves. In response to the SEC's direction, fiduciaries and other institutional investors did, in fact, adopt procedures against insider trading—procedures which, over time, have had an effect.

[34]Pub. L. No. 98-376, 98 Stat. 1264 (August 10, 1984).

[35]*Barron's* (July 1981) (Editorial headline: "Want a Hot Tip? There's No Way to Prevent Trading on Inside Information."); *Fortune* (July 1981) ("The Unwinnable War on Insider Trading").

[36]As this book goes to press, Michael David, a former associate of a major New York law firm, and four colleagues from the ranks of Wall Street professionals were indicted by a Federal Grand Jury on insider trading charges. This indictment comes on the heels of the widely publicized case brought by the SEC against Dennis B. Levine, a managing director and merger specialist at Drexel Burnham Lambert (and formerly with two other major Wall Street investment banking firms). Mr. Levine is charged by the SEC with having earned $12.6 million in illegal profits through insider trading made possible for the most part out of Mr. Levine's access to nonpublic information involving takeover activity.

[37]*See* Coffee, "Market Failure and the Economic Case for a Mandatory Disclosure System," 70 Va. L. Rev. 717, 732 (1984) [hereinafter cited as Coffee] (noting that "[t]he volume of institutional trading on the New York Stock Exchange rose during the 1960s from a low of 17 percent to a high of 59 percent in 1969).

[38]Clark, "The Four Stages of Capitalism: Reflections on Investment Management Treatises," 94 Harv. L. Rev. 561 (1981).

[39]The seminal work on the Efficient Capital Market Hypothesis appeared in 1970. *See* Fama, "Efficient Capital Markets: A Review of Theory and Empirical Work," 25 J. Fin. 383 (1970). Appendix A takes a current reading on the subject.

[40]B. Graham & D. Dodd, *Security Analysis: Principles and Techniques* (1st ed. 1934).

[41]*See* Coffee, *supra* note 37, at 729 n.35 and accompanying text for an equation between Graham and Dodd's influence on security analysis and Freud's influence on psychoanalysis.

[42]B. Graham & D. Dodd, *Security Analysis: Principles and Techniques* (3d ed. 1951) at viii.

[43]Shattuck, "The Development of the Prudent Man Rule for Fiduciary Investment in the United States in the Twentieth Century," 12 Ohio St. L.J. 491 (1951).

[44]Securities and Exchange Commission 1985 Annual Report.

[45]*Pensions & Investment Age* (August 6, 1984) at 39–48.

[46]*Id.* at 39.

[47]18 Pa. 303 (1852).

[48]Harvard College v. Amory, 26 Mass. (9 Pick.) 446, 460 (1830).

[49]Of course, it was early recognized that market manipulators could do harm to even the safest investment. In March 1792, when the stock market was in its first major decline, Thomas Jefferson wrote to a friend: " . . . the credit and fate of the nation seem to hang on the desperate throws and plunges of gambling scoundrels." As explained by Senator Thomas H. Kuchel in hearings on S.510 (which became the Williams Act) before the Subcommittee on Securities of the Senate Committee on Banking and Currency on March 21, 1967 (at p. 42):

> Jefferson was referring to a small organization of investors of that day—"The Six Per Cent Club"—that had carelessly speculated on debt securities issued by the Federal Government and had operated with great mystery behind the scenes. They had overextended themselves in the expectation of sharply rising prices and were left with obligations that could not be met. Neither the Government nor the market was prepared to deal with the situation. Indeed, were it not for Alexander Hamilton's intervention and encouragement, the panic that resulted could well have brought complete disaster to Wall Street and the Nation.

[50]Chamberlain & Hay, *Investment and Speculation* (Holt 1931) at 8.

[51]*Id.* at 55.

[52]*See* G. G. Bogert & G. T. Bogert, *Trusts and Trustees* (2d ed. rev. 1980) §§ 616, 642.

[53]B. Graham & D. Dodd, *Security Analysis* (1st ed. 1934) at 3–6.

[54]Securities and Exchange Commission 50th Annual Report 1984, Table 24 at 114. The Securities Exchange Commission Institutional Investor Study concluded (at 58): "In the first half of this century the issuance of equity securities was never a major source of financing or even a major source of external financing for U.S. corporations." It further concludes (at 78) that, over the period 1952 to 1969, corporations in the aggregate relied very little on security issues, especially stock issues, to finance capital formation, turning instead to internal funds, including depreciation reserves, and bank loans, trade credit, commercial paper, and other short-term financing.

[55]*See* Ibbotson Associates, *Stocks, Bonds, Bills and Inflation: 1985 Yearbook* (1985). The statistics set forth in the text are drawn from Exhibits 3 and 6 at 23 and 28, respectively.

[56]*See* the Introduction to Appendix A for an explanation of standard deviation.

[57]The real interest rate, measured as the Treasury bill return less the inflation rate for the year, averaged 5.835 percent for the four-year period 1981 to 1984. It would be necessary to go back to 1932 to find the first year before that period in which the real interest rate was higher than any of those four years. Ibbotson Associates, *Stocks, Bonds, Bills and Inflation: 1985 Yearbook* (1985) at 26.

[58]*See generally* Sametz, "The "New" Financial Environment of the U.S.," Introductory Chapter, *Financial Handbook* 1986; Sametz, "The New Financial Environment," Chapter 1; Sametz, ed., *The Emerging Financial Industry: Implications for Insurance Products, Portfolios and Planning* (Lex., Mass. 1984); and Friedman, "The Effect of Large General Deficits on Interest Rates and Equity Returns," 1 Oxford Rev. Econ. Pol. 58 (1985).

[59]*See* Silber, "Recent Structural Change in the Capital Markets—The Process of Financial Innovation," Am. Econ. Rev. 89 (May 1983) (attributing financial innovation from 1970 to 1982 to five primary exogenous causes: (1) inflation, (2) volatility of interest rates, (3) technology, (4) legislative initiative, and (5) internationalization and describing the social utility of such innovation to include improved ability to bear risk (e.g., futures markets), lowered transaction costs (e.g., automatic teller machines), and circumvention of outmoded regulations (e.g., money market funds and Regulation Q)).

[60]Harvard College v. Amory, 26 Mass. (9 Pick.) 446, 459 (1830).

CHAPTER 3

Points of Restraint and Conflict

This chapter gathers together the main points of restraint and conflict between what the constrained prudent man rule tolerates and what prudence as defined by financial economics and the marketplace suggests. The goal is not to resolve the tension created by this gap between law, on the one hand, and financial theory and investment practice, on the other, but simply to illustrate it in preparation for the effort at resolution that follows in Chapter 4.

Previous chapters have demonstrated that the legal authorities, consisting of the Treatise and the Restatement, as well as judicial pronouncements regarding the prudent man rule,[1] have not incorporated the important economic advances in portfolio theory of the past thirty-five years since Harry Markowitz first invented the concept.[2] Nowhere is this legal tendency toward tunnel vision more striking than in the continuing effort to find prudence in the absence of speculation and to find speculation in the apparent riskiness of individual investment products or techniques, viewed in isolation and labeled accordingly.

Hopeful signs of some interdisciplinary peripheral vision on the part of law-makers and some regulators, however, have been noted. The message of the Labor Department in interpreting the version of the rule found in the Employee Retirement Income Security Act of 1974 (ERISA)[3] and of the Treasury Department in interpreting the version applicable to private foundations[4] is that no category of investment should be treated as per se imprudent. In both sets of regulations, and also in the statutory language of the Uniform Management of Institutional Funds Act (UMIFA), support for the idea that the prudence of any investment should be determined by reference to its intended use in the portfolio can be found with varying degrees of conviction. The fact is, however, that the influences of the Treatise and the Restatement remain powerful, creating serious restraints and conflicts that the modern fiduciary is hard put to avoid.

The Lessons of Modern Portfolio Theory

In Appendix A, Professors of Finance Edwin J. Elton and Martin J. Gruber have set forth the principal lessons of modern portfolio theory for fiduciaries subject to some form of the prudent man rule. Although their essay was written for non-economists, it pursues the subject in considerable detail, developing alternative asset pricing models and other elements of portfolio theory at a sufficiently technical level to permit the reader to understand the assumptions on which the more prominent pricing models rest and to appreciate not only the complexity of the subject but the underlying reasons for that complexity.

The principal conclusions to be drawn from Appendix A follow:

1. In publicly traded capital markets, security prices generally are efficient, in the sense that most information material to investment choice is rapidly and cheaply made available to investors and rapidly reflected in security prices. The more a market is scrutinized and used, the higher its level of pricing efficiency. The converse is also true. Opportunities for superior performance through skill, industry, and foresight increase as the pricing efficiency of particular markets decreases. The more conventional the product or the more plausible the strategy, the less likely one can achieve above-average results. Accordingly, since the prudence standard was not intended to be intolerant of those seeking superior performance, it must be defined to accommodate the innovator who proceeds alone but with diligence and informed deliberation.

2. By holding a well-diversified portfolio, one can remove issuer-specific risks, leaving only the systemic risk of the particular market for which the securities in the portfolio are a proxy. The lesson for prudence is that the standard should be applied to the portfolio as a whole, rather than, as suggested in *Spitzer,*[5] to each security in the portfolio. The volatility of each individual security is only important in its impact on the volatility of the whole portfolio and should be so tested in evaluating the prudence of holding it. Therefore, it is meaningless to discuss in the abstract the prudence of a "type" of investment, such as stock in a new and untried enterprise, or of a technique, such as the writing of put options.

3. While risk continues to be viewed as the possibility of capital loss, the symmetry of security return distributions permits risk to be better understood as the variability of expected returns around a mean. All investors are assumed (reasonably enough) to be risk-averse and, accordingly, to pay more for an investment with less variance of possible return around an expected return than for one with more variance. Paying more for an expected return is another way of saying the yield on an investment with less variance is lower than the yield on an investment with more variance. This, in combination with the point made in the previous paragraph, leads to the widely accepted thesis that the higher the systematic or undiversifiable risk the higher the expected returns. For prudence, the implications are that efforts to equate "speculation" with imprudence and to distinguish it from "investment," except perhaps at the marginal extremes, are doomed to failure. Since higher expected returns can only come from exposure to higher risks, the choice of risk depends critically on one's time horizon, one's cash flow needs, and one's tolerance for volatility. There is a broad, indeed nearly infinite, spectrum of possiblities in establishing economically defensible risk levels. Across that spectrum, it is not possible to find some Plimsoll line[6] where speculation commences, nor is it socially useful for courts or other governmental bodies to try to do so.

4. Despite major advances in understanding how financial markets operate and the validity of the important implications for investment behavior summarized in the previous paragraphs, uncertainties remain. Neither the capital asset pricing model (CAPM) nor any of the other asset pricing models commands universal acceptance as an explanation of the expected return of assets.[7] Greater understanding, while creating a widely accepted framework for analysis of market behavior, has produced many models (each having some validity) and more complexity overall. Although the most actively traded markets display a general efficiency, anomalies (e.g., the small firm effect, the low P/E effect, and the January effect, among others) continue to be uncovered, creating uncertainty as to whether they result from an inability to measure risk properly or are true market inefficiencies. Whether, and to what extent, the various equilibrium models for explaining expected return rest on the efficiency of markets is unclear. And, despite the central importance of the "market portfolio" to portfolio theory, its composition remains unclear because of many open questions about what to include in the pool of "all risky assets" for which it is a surrogate. (For example, is the pool limited to assets in the domestic economy or does it include foreign assets, and if so, which ones?) For the fiduciary, the lesson is that there are no entirely satisfactory formulae to guide investment behavior within the accepted framework of portfolio theory. As informed by that theory, prudence tolerates many alternative strategies while dictating none.

5. Although ex post it can be observed that some investment managers have achieved consistently superior performance, economics offers no system for identifying them, ex ante. In particular, despite its broad appeal to those diligently seeking the best managers, past superior performance is not a reliable predictor of future superior performance.

6. In measuring a manager's performance and comparing it with the performance of others, the levels of risk assumed in the manager's portfolio and in those with which it is being compared should be taken into account. Doing so is difficult, however, because of the number of different asset pricing models available to establish a benchmark for measuring risk and comparing performance.

The Individual Investment Approach

As stated by the highest court in New York in the 1974 *Spitzer* decision, "[t]he fact that this portfolio showed substantial overall increase in total value during the accounting period does not insulate the trustee from responsibility for imprudence with respect to individual investments for which it would otherwise be surcharged. . . ."[8] This is an application of the anti-netting rule that bars the balancing of losses arising from one or more breaches of trust against gains from any source. As Professor Gordon reasons in Appendix B, this rule is not inconsistent with modern portfolio theory's insistence that each investment be examined in light of its impact on the portfolio, not in isolation. However, *Spitzer* is believed by some to carry forward the idea that the prudence of a portfolio is judged through an examination of its individual investments, with each being tested on its own merits.[9]

Scrutiny of investments, item by item, poses severe problems for the fiduciary. Consider, for example, the index fund concept, which proceeds on the notion that the market is too efficient for any investor to be likely, ex ante, to outperform it over the long run and that the transaction costs of trying to accomplish this feat will contribute to a performance inferior to what the market fund offers. The key to holding a market portfolio is low transaction costs, derived from an ability to avoid any effort to evaluate individual securities. Thus, a market fund could expect to include at any moment one or more corporations vulnerable to bankruptcy (e.g., Penn Central, W.T. Grant, Chrysler, Continental Illinois, Braniff). The conflict is clear enough. This passive strategy is calculated sooner or later to run afoul of item-by-item scrutiny. Legal advisers have sought to duck the issue by recommending sufficient analytical input to avoid insolvency-prone companies. The Labor Department has reinforced this idea by suggesting that fiduciaries subject to ERISA who wish to use index funds should develop a "screen" to cull out companies experiencing "significant, adverse financial developments."[10] Doing so, of course, involves costs that the market fund theory is designed to avoid.

The idea that no investor can systematically "beat the market" and that, accordingly, marketplace prudence dictates the use of a market fund, absent compelling evidence of market inefficiencies, is not only plausible, but supported by a large body of empirical data.[11] Indeed, it is at least as plausible as the contrary claim that some investment professionals can consistently outperform the market and that, ex ante, they can be identified. And yet, by focusing on individual securities in a portfolio, the prudent man rule tilts powerfully in favor of the security-picking claim. Legal advisers have no difficulty in assuring fiduciaries that they will incur no liability for below-market performance achieved through a careful (and, relatively speaking, expensive) security analysis approach. The law seems to echo the old American adage "it is better to have tried and failed than never to have tried at all." As one of many possible outcomes, mediocrity is accepted by this society, but as an objective, it's hard to square with an American ethos forged on the Darwinian anvil and steeped in legends of rugged individualism.

The rule's preoccupation with individual securities poses problems even for the fiduciary who seeks actively to manage the portfolio. Selecting more volatile securities, each viewed in isolation, may appear imprudent; yet if they have a strong negative correlation (e.g., umbrella manufacturers versus sunscreen makers), collectively they may be less risky than other less volatile securities. Viewed in isolation, raw land or commodity futures are highly suspect as unproductive assets under the constrained rule. Considered as part of a portfolio designed to hedge against inflation, these investments can well be justified by historical data showing their sensitivity to rising price levels.

Another example might be the use of a well-diversified pool of below-investment-grade corporate bonds—junk bonds. Empirical evidence over the period from January 1982 through May 1984 showed lower quality bonds experiencing less volatility than higher grade corporates or equities,[12] suggesting that a pool of them may not represent an especially risky investment, even though each component is highly volatile and, accordingly, suspect under the item-by-item approach of the constrained rule.

Venture capital shows the constrained rule's capacity for mischief in a different way. Consider a large insititution with excellent staff capability to analyze and invest in start-up business enterprises. Suppose the costs of committing, for example, 5 to 10 percent of the portfolio to this kind of venture capital investment, if done through its own staff, would be substantially cheaper than the typical alternative of investing in a venture capital limited partnership managed by outsiders and offered to other investors seeking the same type of exposure. Comparing the talents of the in-house staff with those of the available venture capital pool managers indicates no advantage to going outside, nor does the institution believe any outside management group would be likely to see a better selection of investment opportunities or be able to achieve better diversification. In addition to cost savings, important advantages of using internal staff include the ease of monitoring and the absence of potential for conflicts of interest. In short, all elements of the investment analysis strongly support the use of internal staff to carry out this deployment of assets—only the legal analysis stands in the way.

The constrained rule, with its emphasis on individual selection, is likely to examine each investment made by the staff on its own merits. By definition it will be in a "new and untried enterprise," suspect under traditional notions of prudence. Venture capital investing invariably involves some failures, a result fiduciaries must reasonably anticipate and include in their analysis before embarking on a venture capital program, whether conducted internally or externally. Figure 3.1 illustrates the point with reference to the actual (and not atypical) results over eight years of a venture capital fund that became fully invested in thirty-one issuers. Of these, five, aggregating over $4 million in original cost, were complete losses, while another five, also aggregating over $4 million in original cost, increased in value by more than a factor of ten to an aggregate of over $42 million. Although another seven investments, constituting 21 percent of the original cost of all investments, suffered a greater than 50 percent write-off, the fund overall increased in value more than five times from $32 million to over $177 million.[13]

Legal advisers aware of *Spitzer* must caution against the risk of being held liable for losses due to individual failures, despite the overall success of a venture capital program. However, were the program effected through an investment in a venture capital limited partnership, the alternative shown in the hypothetical case to be inferior in all other respects, the legal adviser could offer comfort instead of caution. His argument would be that the institution has made but a single investment (in a partnerhsip), which has resulted in no loss at all. Just as a fiduciary investing in Warner Communications would not be surcharged for Atari's losses in 1983 (although that subsidiary accounted for most of Warner's net loss for that year), so too should the institution be immune from liability for failures among the enterprises selected for investment by the venture capital pool.

However sound this legal analysis (and it *is* supportable under present rules),[14] the distinctions made are nonsense in the practical world of investment. Taken seriously, they restrain the exercise of sound judgment.

Finally, financial futures and options offer stunning examples of the restraining influence of the rule on a fiduciary's freedom to pursue his best judgment. As "wasting assets," such products are highly suspect when considered in isolation, even though they can be deployed to manage and lower risk[15] or carry out other

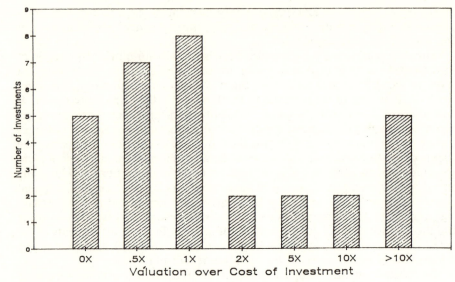

Figure 3.1 Venture Capital Fund, Total Number of Investments: 31

strategies at less cost and greater efficiency than other available alternatives.[16] These matters are touched on in the next section and then developed more extensively in Chapter 4.

The Enduring Fallacy of Labels

Since *Harvard College v. Amory,* prudence has been found principally in the absence of "speculation." From that time, a grasp of the difference between speculation and investment became more than a semantic quibble to fiduciaries, for on that distinction turned their personal liability of trustees for losses. While the cynic's definition—that an investment was a successful speculation and a speculation simply an unsuccessful investment—had much to commend it, fiduciaries were not charmed by its logic, for if an unsuccessful investment were a speculation, the prudent man rule would hold the fiduciary personally liable for losses.

Chapter 1 traced the modern triumph of the prudent man rule over the legal list approach, begun by the New York legislature in the mid-nineteenth century.[17] Unfortunately, the promised flexibility of the judicial standard has been seriously undermined, first by the Restatement's penchant for labeling investment products and techniques as speculative or not based on their inherent riskiness when viewed in isolation, and second by the willingness of even modern judges to accept those labels as immutable,[18] almost as if they constituted a kind of legal list enshrined not by statute but in the Treatise and Restatement, and equally enduring.

This section traces the labeling phenomenon through its early development in the Restatement and then notes its current hold (to varying degrees) on the thinking of regulators at the Board of Governors of the Federal Reserve System (FRB), the Securities and Exchange Commission (SEC), and the Commodity Futures Trading Commission (CFTC).

The Treatise's Legacy

The Oxford English Dictionary[19] defines "speculation" as "the action or practice of buying and selling goods, land, stocks and shares, etc., in order to profit by the rise or fall in the market value, as distinct from regular trading or investment; engagement in any business enterprise or transaction of a venturesome or risky nature, but offering the chance of great or unusual gain."

This definition would appear to cover the widespread practice among active money managers of identifying undervalued stocks, holding them for a market rise as the mispricing becomes more widely recognized and is corrected, and then selling them for a gain when their true value is reflected in market price. The dictionary definition is picked up in a 1952 article by Louis S. Headley, appearing in *Trusts and Estates*[20] and cited with approval in *First Alabama Bank of Montgomery, N.A. v. Martin* in 1983. Mr. Headley, however, turns it inward as a matter of subjective intent:

> What constitutes speculation is one of the most difficult questions in trusteeship. Any attempted definition must be based chiefly on the attitude of the person making the investment. If he buys for the purpose of selling at a later day at an expected profit he is speculating.

As the Treatise puts it,

> [C]ertain kinds of investments are universally condemned. It is improper for a trustee to purchase securities for the purpose of speculation, although the line between what constitutes speculation and what constitutes a businessman's risk and what constitutes a prudent investment is drawn in different places by different courts. It is clear of course that a trustee cannot properly purchase securities on margin; nor can he properly purchase speculative shares of stock, or bonds selling at a large discount because of uncertainty as to whether they will be paid at maturity.
>
> A trustee cannot properly purchase securities in new and untried enterprises.[21]

Here one can observe the tendency to label investment products and techniques as speculative per se, without regard to the reasoning behind their use or their role in the portfolio.

In 1934, one year before the Restatement first appeared, two professors of finance at Columbia University, Benjamin Graham and David L. Dodd, published *Security Analysis,*[22] a treatise that, in its own sphere of investment management, was fully as influential and enduring as the Treatise and the Restatement were in the sphere of law. In this volume Graham and Dodd devoted an entire chapter to distinctions between investment and speculation, in chief because of their view that "the failure properly to distingush between investment and speculation was in large measure responsible for the market excesses of 1928–1929 and the calamities that ensued."[23] It seems improbable that Scott was aware of this chapter when he was completing his work on the Restatement. The lack of interdisciplinary thinking and exchange was more pronounced then than now, although this study shows how inadequate the lines of communication remain to this day.

Graham and Dodd list the chief distinctions in common use at the time as follows:

Investment	*Speculation*
1. In bonds	In stocks
2. Outright purchases	Purchases on margin
3. For permanent holding	For a "quick turn"
4. For income	For profit
5. In safe securities	In risky issues

They then proceed to show the fallacy in each of these distinctions, presaging many of the principles of modern theory set forth in Appendix A. They reject the notion, advanced by an authority of the period, that all stocks are by their nature essentially and unavoidably speculative.[24] "It is logically unsound, furthermore, to deny investment rating to a strongly entrenched common stock merely because it possesses profit possibilities."[25] They reject the distinctions made between outright purchases and those made on margin.

> It should be obvious that buying a stock outright does not *ipso facto* make the transaction an investment. In truth the most speculative issues, *e.g.,* "penny mining stocks," *must* be purchased outright, since no one will lend money against them. Conversely, when the American public was urged during the war to buy Liberty Bonds with borrowed money, such purchases were nonetheless universally classed as investments.[26]

They point to the accepted practice of short-term investments in rejecting the notion that speculation is synonymous with a short-term holding. On the matter of income versus profit, they accept the notion that the purchase of small or nonyielding stocks (such as bank stocks in the early twentieth century) could for investment purposes be purchased on the expectation that steady growth in earnings and surplus would result in special distributions and increased value. It would be unsound, they argued, to call such an approach speculative, simply because expected earnings would be retained rather than paid out and realization of return would come through appreciation in market value rather than through dividend flow. As for safety versus risk, they rejected as unsound the notion that investment character inheres in an issue per se. "The price is frequently an essential element, so that a stock (and even a bond) may have investment merit at one price level but not at another."[27] They recognized the critical role of diversification in controlling risk and even anticipated the hedging possibilities that are only now becoming widely accepted:

> Furthermore, an investment might be justified in a group of issues, which would not be sufficiently safe if made in any one of them singly. In other words, diversification might be necessary to reduce the risk involved in the separate issues to the minimum consonant with the requirements of investment. (This would be true, for example, of a special type of investment policy centering upon the purchase of common stocks at well below liquidating values.)
>
> In our view it is also proper to consider as investment operations certain types of arbitrage and hedging commitments which involve the sale of one security against the purchase of another. In these operations the element of safety is provided by the com-

bination of purchase and sale. This is an extension of the ordinary concept of investment, but one which appears to the writers to be entirely logical.[28]

It is tantalizing to ponder the influence that Graham and Dodd might have had on the legal notion of prudence, had Scott been exposed to the full force of their logic and analysis. Since the Treatise was not published until 1939, it was entirely possible that he could have seen Graham and Dodd's work during the five years between publication of the Restatement and his Treatise. There is, however, no sign that these two streams of thought ever reached a confluence.

Regulatory Myopia

Despite the helpful messages from the Labor Department (regarding investments by pension funds) and the Treasury Department (regarding investments by private foundations), acceptance of the lessons of modern portfolio theory by regulators in positions to influence prudence standards is far from complete. The instinct to label, for all time and place, is apparently hard to resist, as hard (it seems) as it is easy for a regulator to *know* with certainty on which product or technique to affix the label "speculative." A brief review of recent actions taken by the FRB, the SEC, and the CFTC with respect to options and futures contracts illustrates the enduring fallacy of labels and the need for a comprehensive reinterpretation of the prudent man rule.

FRB on Trust Department Use of Options and Futures. In a letter dated January 11, 1983, the FRB's Division of Banking Supervision and Regulation instructed trust examination personnel at the Federal Reserve Banks on the use by trust institutions of options and financial futures contracts for fiduciary accounts.[29] Under the pluralistic bank regulatory scheme adopted by the United States, the guidelines apply directly to the examination of fiduciary activities of state bank trust departments and trust companies that are members of the Federal Reserve System and nonmember trust company subsidiaries of bank holding companies. However, as the authoritative opinion of the nation's central bank and chief bank regulator on the question of prudence, the letter can be expected to exert a strong impact on the investment practices of all those subject to some form of prudence standard and on those, such as judges, regulators, and lawyers, who must interpret and apply the precepts of prudence to the new options and financial futures products. Here, then, was an opportunity for the FRB to provide a modern interpretation of the traditional prudent man rule. It was an opportunity missed.

After acknowledging the greatly increased interest in options and financial futures among professional investment managers and the growing volume of trades, the letter begins by concluding that, under traditional state common-law formulations of the rule, options and futures contracts were considered improper. The rule required a trustee to invest for "preservation of the corpus of the trust's assets as well as for the production of reasonable income." Investments were to be tested one by one. "Any investment transaction involving a high degree of risk, or producing no established income yield, was considered *per se* speculative and therefore improper. Clearly included within this category were transactions such as margin purchases and short sales." Reasoning by analogy, the letter concludes that options and financial futures are similarly improper. No case support or other authority for these sweeping conclusions is furnished.

Modern portfolio theory is too widely understood and accepted to be ignored by the FRB. Instead, like a bitter pill, it is reluctantly swallowed but not quite digested.

> Under modern investment theories, however, the focus of investment strategy *may* involve the entire portfolio. *In theory,* particular securities or transactions may be individually risky or nonincome producing, yet have characteristics that result in greater safety and return for either portions of the assets or the portfolio as a whole. [Emphasis supplied.]

While acknowledging the question as one of state law, except for corporate employee benefit accounts subject to ERISA, the letter proceeds both generally and with detailed specification to define prudence with reference to options and financial futures.

> In summary, in spite of the broader range of what may or may not currently be held to be legal, it is believed that a minimal standard of "prudence" continues to apply. Therefore, it would appear that futures and options contracts, where permitted, should represent potential additional tools to be used as vehicles for reducing overall portfolio risk, or for increasing portfolio yield without subjecting the account's assets to unwarranted risk. In addition, contract transactions *at least* should be prudent in light of an account's entire portfolio and its investment objectives; and positions should never be taken solely in an attempt to generate trading profits based upon anticipated interest rate or market movements (speculation). [Emphasis supplied.]

Standing alone, this statement evinces a grudging acceptance of portfolio theory.[30] While hardly a clarion call to the states summoning forth a modern interpretation of the prudent man rule,[31] it seems in the main to avoid the labeling approach. It does affix the name "speculation" to positions taken to profit from anticipated changes in interest rates or other market movements. Of course, this is precisely what is done in the cash markets when the portfolio is rebalanced to favor debt (if interest rates are expected to fall) or equity (if stocks are expected to grow in favor). The goal is to profit from these anticipated moves. The underlying judgments are the same. Only the medium for trying to benefit from those judgments is different. Ought there to be so different a result in terms of prudence? To carry the point further, each equity purchase for a portfolio typically involves an attempt to generate profit through capital appreciation of the equity (as well as through dividends). To do so is not considered imprudent per se. Yet, intuitively one senses it is at least as difficult, and many would argue more difficult, to form a soundly based conviction that a single issuer's stock is underpriced than it is to believe that the stock market or interest rates are about to turn.

The FRB letter is not limited to the general proposition quoted above. Noting that every investment strategy must be "prudent," it proceeds to describe four contract strategies as having "the potential to be administered in a prudent manner" and in the process affixes the speculative label to all others. In its sweep and specificity, the letter rivals the Treatise and the Restatement in embracing the litmus test approach.[32]

The four potentially prudent startegies are (1) short hedges of existing securities positions, (2) anticipatory long hedges of investments to be made from cash to be received on a date certain, (3) covered call option writing, and (4) covered arbitrage starategies, but only where the benefits accrue regardless of whether rates move up or down.

Among the other strategies identified as speculative and, therefore, imprudent per se are uncovered call options (unlimited exposure), purchases of call options as original investments (not to hedge or ensure enhanced yield), writing of put options (potential for loss of trust corpus), purchases of stock index futures (not to hedge or ensure enhanced yield), writing of covered call options against portfolio securities hedged with index futures (if stock called away index future ceases to function as hedge), and use of options on futures to hedge futures positions (playing solely in derivative markets).

These are sweeping indictments. Such underlying analysis as the letter contains is harmful to the notions of prudence advanced in this study. Consider, for example, the reasoning offered to explain why the writing of put options deserves the speculative label:

> Although the risks involved in selling naked put options are theoretically similar in certain respects to writing covered call options, the writing or *sale* of put options involves the risk of a direct cash loss of principal or corpus—as opposed only to the "opportunity loss" associated with maintaining a covered call position. Since loss of corpus is to be strictly avoided under traditional trust investment principles, the sale of put options, whether naked or covered, should be regarded as primarily speculative, and therefore *not* a prudent strategy. Of course, the sale of a put would be permissible to close out a previously purchased put position for which the insurance feature is no longer needed.

It is highly formalistic, and economically unsound, to call the loss realized when stock worth $100 is called away from a fiduciary at $80 an "opportunity loss," while characterizing the loss realized when stock worth $80 is put to a fiduciary at $100 as a "direct cash loss of principal or corpus." Beyond the illogic of this position on its own terms, the premises are wrong as well. The analysis proceeds on the assumption that only the performance of a particular put or call, in isolation from everything else going on in the portfolio, is what matters. Whether the put is part of a carefully developed yield-enhancing strategy or not seems to be irrelevant; so too, apparently, is the care given to selecting the particular securities against which to write the put.

It is noteworthy that questions raised about the FRB letter prompted a brief clarification, dated December 2, 1983.[33] In response to concerns expressed about the degree to which the FRB's discussion was meant to prohibit the use of various instruments and strategies, little comfort was offered. Noting that guidelines, rather than "formal or inflexible rules" were intended, the letter observed that there were, as yet, no court decisions on the matter. Thus, "[i]t was certainly *conceivable* that acceptable strategies or transactions beyond those cited in the guidelines as having potentially prudent applications, may be demonstrated as analytically sound and appropriate for particular fiduciary accounts under carefully limited circumstances, provided, of course, that there is appropriate legal authorization." [Emphasis supplied.]

SEC on Mutual Fund Use of Options and Futures. Under Section 18 of the Investment Company Act of 1940 (1940 Act), investment companies are either forbidden or severely restrained from issuing "senior securities."[34]

The SEC views these prohibitions as intended by Congress to limit the speculative character of investment company holdings. Thus, a "senior security" for the investment company can be analogized to a leveraged investment for a fiduciary under the prudent man rule. Leverage is equated with excessive risk that is speculative and, therefore, forbidden.

Section 2(a)(36) of the 1940 Act includes in the definition of "senior security," "any bond, debenture, note or similar obligation or instrument constituting a security and evidencing indebtedness." The SEC has taken the position that the purchase or sale of futures and the sale of options, involving as they do a continuing obligation, constitute the issuance of "senior securities." However dubious this position may be, it has provided a basis for the SEC to define what it considers prudent and what it considers imprudent for regulated investment companies to do in using the financial futures and options markets.

The evolution of SEC thinking on the subject of financial futures and options is instructive. Its first approach, in 1972, was to subject all uses of futures and options contracts to the 300 percent asset coverage test, which would be applied to open- as well as closed-end funds.[35] The 1972 release established strict margin requirements as well. The rules applied to all futures contracts used by an investment company, without regard to the purpose to be served by the use and its expected impact on the whole portfolio.

The SEC's goal was to give effect to the 1940 Act's effort to limit the "speculative character of funds." Of course, futures and options on futures can be used speculatively, through the tremendous leverage they offer; they can also be used as hedges, offsetting other positions in the portfolio. The release failed to distinguish between these purposes. It simply curtailed all uses of futures by limiting them to 10 percent of a fund's assets, without distinguishing between the kinds of use that might be made of them.

The rule limiting investment in a futures contract to twice initial margin fails to take account of how the contract is intended to serve the portfolio. The limit serves as a ceiling on losses a fund can take on any futures contract. However, where the futures contract is serving to hedge portfolio securities (e.g., a short futures position in the Treasury bond futures contract to hedge the debt portion of the portfolio against an anticipated rise in interest rates), any "losses" caused by variation margin calls will be offset by gains in the debt portion of the portfolio. In the case of a contract serving to hedge, it is senseless to dictate that it be terminated at some arbitrary point. By failing to consider the purpose to be served by the product, the SEC wrote a rule that exhibits the fallacy of labeling products as intrinsically "speculative."

The SEC's next pronouncement on the subject came in an interpretative release issued in 1979.[36] In that release, the SEC reasserted that the purchase or sale of futures and options on futures, when used by regulated investment companies, *could* be found to be "senior securities"—on the grounds that present consideration was being received for future (contingent) obligations. At the same time, however, the SEC said that if the fund kept a segregated cash account equal to the *market value of the contract* no "senior security" would be found, presumably because there would then be no leverage.

Again the SEC used a per se rule to address the problem that futures contracts could be viewed as exposing an investment company's shareholders to "undue speculation." Without distinguishing between the very different potential uses of futures contracts, the SEC claimed simply that the segregated account requirement "will function as a practical limit on the amount of leverage which the investment company may undertake and on the potential increase in the speculative character of its outstanding common stock."[37]

While eliminating the possibility of leverage, the rule was equally effective in eliminating the chance to use the futures markets to hedge investments held in the portfolio. Imagine a fund with $120 million in its portfolio, of which $100 million is invested in equities. The fund manager, fearful of a market decline (but unwilling to incur the high transaction costs of shifting from equity to debt), seeks to hedge the fund's equity position by opening a short position in the Standard & Poor's (S&P) 500 futures market equal to $100 million. Initial margin for such a position would be in the range of 5 percent of the contract value, or $5 million, and Treasury bills could be used for the purpose. However, the SEC's requirement that the fund set up a segregated cash account equal to the underlying contract (i.e., $100 million) makes the hedge impossible.

Beginning in 1984, the SEC began to exhibit more sophistication in its approach to the dilemma of whether, and how, to permit investment companies to use the new financial futures and options products. Without surrendering its assertion of power to define, for investors holding more than 14.4 million accounts who have placed more than $370 billion in the hands of investment company managers,[38] what is prudent and therefore permissible under the 1940 Act and what is imprudent and hence prohibited, the SEC started to acknowledge differences between the hedging use and other uses. In a series of no-action letters commencing with Stein Roe Bond Fund, Inc., in January 1984,[39] the SEC staff permitted both open-end and closed-end funds to trade interest rate futures, stock index futures, options on stock index futures, and index options for hedging purposes. The most recent step in this progression occurred in August 1985 when a no-action letter authorized GMO Core Trust to purchase futures contracts for purposes other than hedging.[40]

Under its more lenient rules, however, segregation requirements remain, designed to assure that the possiblities for leverage are not being exploited. Thus, when a fund purchases a futures contract or writes a put option on a futures contract or index, it must segregate, solely to back up those positions, cash equivalents equal to the long futures or short put options positions held. When a fund writes a call option on a stock index future or stock index, if it is at- or out-of-the-money, stocks in the fund's portfolio equal in value to the aggregate exercise value of the options contracts are deemed to constitute "cover," and no segregation is required. If the call options are *in* the money when written, the fund must segregate cash equivalents equal in value to the amount by which the aggregate call option position is in the money.

While the SEC has shown a steady and substantial movement away from its earlier label-fixing tendencies, its rules still deprive regulated investment companies of the opportunity to use futures and options in a flexible way across the spectrum of possible deployments from what, in futures parlance, would be a pure "hedge" at one extreme to a pure "speculation" at the other. Of more fundamental concern, however, is the SEC's assertion of power under Section 18 of the 1940 Act. This section was intended by Congress to deal with leveraged *capital structures,* not leveraged portfolio investments. It is only by equating the two that the SEC puts itself into the business of defining what is and isn't prudent. This is a role the SEC doesn't fit well. Its successes are principally derived from disclosure-based regulation. Moreover, by persisting in the notion that a whole range of uses of futures and options are too speculative for investment companies, the SEC forces those seeking to offer such opportunities to the public to avoid regulation under the 1940 Act altogether. This feat can be accomplished by making the trading in futures, rather than investing in securities, the fund's primary business. This policy has two adverse effects. For funds able to escape 1940 Act jurisdiction, public investors lose its protections. For funds that want to operate *primarily* in the securities markets but add a broad range of futures and options products and strategies as well, public investors are denied access entirely because such a fund can now only operate outside of the jurisdiction of the 1940 Act.

CFTC on Commodity Pool Operators. The CFTC regulates commodity pool operators (CPOs), who are defined in the Commodity Exchange Act (CEA) to include those who organize and operate funds "for the purpose of trading in any commodity for future delivery."[41] CPOs must register with the CFTC, meet various rules regarding disclosure,[42] reporting,[43] and recordkeeping,[44] and comply with the reparation provisions of the CEA.[45] Under the CEA, securities are "commodities," so that one who trades in contracts calling for their future delivery is potentially a CPO. Acting under its exemptive powers,[46] and in response to the 1982 direction of the Senate Committee on Agriculture, Nutrition and Forestry[47] to exempt registered investment companies, banks, trust companies, and insurance companies that use futures as a hedge, the CFTC's Division of Trading and Markets has issued a series of interpretative letters to the effect that such entities, because they were otherwise regulated *and* not operated "for the purpose" of trading commodities interests, were not pools. More recently the CFTC adopted Rule 4.5, generally exempting such entities from registration as CPOs if they limit their use of futures to "bona fide hedging" purposes.

It was in this way that the CFTC found itself confronted with the dilemma of distinguishing between futures used to reduce or truncate portfolio risk and futures used for speculation. With the development of anticipatory hedging strategies for stock indices and bonds, where there was no fixed commitment to make an offsetting cash investment in the future, the CFTC recognized the difficulty of distinguishing between a long futures position opened to hedge an anticipated price move and one opened to seize the opportunity to profit from that move.

In its interpretative letter issued for the Stein Roe Bond Fund, Inc.,[48] the CFTC required the fund to represent that a substantial majority (i.e., 75 percent) of all anticipatory hedges would be completed by the actual purchase of the underlying securities (even though, at the time, circumstances might make such a purchase unwise). In two other interpretative letters, the CFTC took a different approach, requiring that sales of futures and the purchase of put options on futures (which, of course, to constitute hedges could only be opened against portfolio securities) would, over time, represent a substantial majority of the fund's use of futures and related options for all purposes. These quantitative limits were intended to evidence a lack of speculative use.

In Rule 4.5, the CFTC embraced the Stein Roe approach, requiring that a substantial majority of all anticipatory hedges be completed. Commentators objected strenuously to this solution when the rule was proposed. While appropriate to define a hedge in the case of physical commodities, where, for example, a sweater manufacturer might buy wool futures to protect himself against a price change in the commodity he needed for his business, it seemed inapposite for portfolio managers. In the financial setting, an anticipatory hedge is designed to obtain the benefits of a price movement, not necessarily to obtain the underlying securities. There is no sound basis for insisting on a completion test. In terms of portfolio management, it is arbitrary; indeed, where the price movement has been substantial, such that the manager's best judgment would call for a sale of the underlying securities (were they then owned), purchasing those securities simply to meet the completion test would be tantamount to compelling imprudence.

The fact is that whether a long futures position is opened as a hedge or as a speculation is too subjective and variable a matter to use as a pivot for regulation.

The foregoing review has sought to demonstrate both the virulence of the tendency to affix labels to investment products and techniques and its futility. Shown to be at odds with the economics of investing by Graham and Dodd in their first edition of *Security Analysis,* published in 1934, and repeatedly since that time as modern portfolio theory has evolved, the fallacy of labeling has endured in the law, imposing needless and costly restraints on fiduciary conduct.

Equivalences

As investment products grow in number, sophistication, and complexity, it becomes increasingly possible to achieve very similar investment goals with two or more products or otherwise in two or more ways. The significance of this fact for the constrained rule of prudence is simply that its treatment of particular types of products or techniques as imprudent is undermined if there are alternative means of accomplishing an objective that are not suspect under the labeling approach previously discussed. Legal distinctions grow increasingly attenuated and artificial, weakening the strength of the law and the respect accorded it by those affected.

Puts and Calls

The writing of call options against long stock positions is now recognized by most regulators, and certainly by the professional community of investment managers, as a conservative, income-enhancing technique for truncating risk. The call writer limits his opportunity for gain in a rising market to the strike price plus the premium received for the call, and in return reduces his risk of loss in a declining market by that premium. This strategy was not initially perceived to be conservative. In 1973, for example, the Comptroller of the Currency stated in a letter to national banks that all options transactions were speculative as a matter of law.[49] Not until the end of 1979 did the Comptroller acknowledge that, as investment tools, options are inherently neither prudent nor imprudent.

Other regulators have not moved to this neutral position. In particular, they resist acceptance of the writing of puts against cash or cash equivalents even though this strategy is essentially equivalent in economic purpose and result to that of covered call writing.[50] There is no reason for drawing such a fundamental line between these two analogous techniques for risk management. There are differences, to be sure. For example, while the call writer owns the underlying stock and is willing to part with it, the put writer holds cash equivalents, which he is willing to trade for the stock. The call writer is earning such dividend income as the stock yields while the put writer is receiving interest on the cash equivalents. But these differences are not significant in terms of prudence measurement.

Zeros, Treasury Bonds, and Futures

One of the more striking developments of the past decade has been the shift in bond portfolio management from a strictly buy-and-hold strategy, which had dominated investment styles for decades if not centuries, to the notion that bond portfolios can be actively managed to produce higher returns. Driven by disappointing results in the stock markets, unprecedented volatility among debt instruments arising from inflationary pressures of the 1970s, and demands for superior performance, financial intermediaries developed a variety of approaches to actively manage bonds.[51]

Just the notion of "trading" bonds for short-term profit due to a rise in market price raises red flags for fiduciaries trained on the Treatise and the Restatement. When consulted, legal advisers could flash only the palest of green lights after a futile search for helpful authority. They were forced back upon the idea that circumstances seem to have changed, justifying new approaches that, if adopted by enough fiduciaries, should some day work a redefinition of prudence. In the meantime, there was the comfort of knowing that other fiduciaries were moving to an active bond strategy.[52]

Fiduciaries who do pursue active bond management strategies provide useful illustrations of the equivalence phenomenon. Consider, for example, a fiduciary holding $10 million in thirty-year Treasury bonds. Careful study brings the fiduciary to the conclusion that interest rates will decline, signaling the desirability of increasing his exposure to thirty-year Treasury bonds, from $10 million to $20 million. Bonds with larger weighted average maturities are more sensitive to interest rate changes. When stated in present value terms, the weighted average maturity of a bond is called its "duration," a concept developed in 1938 by Frederick R. Macaulay to take into account not just the fixed maturity of a bond, but the timing of all elements of cash flow while the bond remained outstanding. Except for a zero-coupon bond, which has a duration equal to the years to fixed maturity, a bond's duration will always be less than that period. The higher its coupon, the shorter its duration, and correspondingly, the lower its price sensitivity to interest rate fluctuations.

Until the advent of coupon stripping (commenced in 1982) and the Chicago Board of Trade's Treasury bond futures market (commenced in 1977), the only way a fiduciary could accomplish the goal of increasing its exposure to thirty-year Treasury bonds was through borrowing (assuming no other available funds in the portfolio), a practice the constrained rule would not condone. Today, the fiduciary could meet the same goal in two alternative ways: one involving the use of zero-coupon bonds, the other involving the use of bond futures contracts.

From a handful of investment banking institutions, the fiduciary could buy thirty-year coupon-stripped Treasury bonds yielding, for example, 9 ½ percent, at about $7.7 per $100 face value. He would not have to buy $10 million face amount of stripped bonds, however, to create an exposure to interest rate fluctuations equivalent to holding $20 million in thirty-year Treasury bonds. Because the duration of the stripped bonds is thirty years, compared to a duration of ten years for a 9½ percent coupon thirty-year Treasury bond, only $3.3 million, or one-third of the face amount of the stripped bonds, would be necessary to achieve the desired duration and interest rate exposure. This would require a cash disbursement of only $254,000. The unused cash could remain invested in money market instruments. One could also buy stripped bonds of shorter maturity in a sufficient face amount to achieve an equivalent duration.

Alternatively, the fiduciary could purchase on the Chicago Board of Trade 120 bond futures contracts, each with a face value of $100,000, for a total face value of $12 million.[53] In terms of sensitivity to interest rate movement, this purchase would be equivalent to purchasing $10 million of 9½ percent coupon thirty-year Treasury bonds, except that in this case no cash disbursement would occur. The initial margin of 2 percent of the $12 million face value would amount to $240,000 and could be posted in Treasury bills without loss of yield.[54]

Among these three alternatives, the safest course for the fiduciary concerned about the law of prudence would be to buy the stripped bonds because there is no borrowing and no use of futures, a wasting asset[55] particularly suspect when used to "bet" on interest rate fluctuations rather than to hedge against them. Under the constrained rule it would be difficult to argue against the purchase of the stripped bond, since there is no risk of loss of nominal value if held to maturity and, as discussed, the rule demands little by way of attention to the risk of inflation.

For the fiduciary with an eye to marketplace prudence, the choice is different. Stripped bonds are popular with investors seeking to immunize a fixed future commitment from intervening market risk. As a result, they may trade at premiums that combined with the fee taken by the broker for stripping make them the most expensive of the three alternatives. In addition, they are the most illiquid. Between the remaining two choices, futures may have the edge due to lower transaction costs and greater liquidity, although this may not always be true. The point, however, is that the constrained rule makes no sense when one attempts to apply it to one or more equivalent techniques for achieving a particular investment objective, where some of those techniques are substantially more suspect under the rule than others. It should be noted that this analysis has ignored the default risk, which might differ among the three alternatives depending upon the financial intermediaries involved. The prudent fiduciary must consider this question carefully.

Other Equivalences

There are many other products and techniques that can serve as functional equivalences for one another. Stock index options and futures combined with Treasury bills can serve as the equivalent of a market portfolio of equities. Options and futures can be used by market timers with lower transaction costs and greater speed than deployments in the primary markets. Stock index futures can now be used as a surrogate for short selling, which (as demonstrated in Appendix A) can probably achieve a more efficient portfolio and reduce market risk overall.[56] Junk bonds, with high interest rates, can serve fiduciaries as a *safer* surrogate for an equity exposure in the same companies, capping the upside in exchange for a high promised yield and a claim against the assets senior to equity in the event of liquidation.[57] Viewed in this manner, junk bonds serve in a way somewhat analogously to an equity position on which a call has been written. Leverage accomplished through margin accounts to buy stock may be equivalent in many respects to the leverage achieved through the unmargined purchase of stock in companies with very high debt-to-equity ratios.[58]

It suffices here simply to note the existence of these equivalences and suggest that many more could be listed. The point is to illustrate the inadequacy of the constrained rule to take account of the growth in product development and the central tendency of professional managers to explore increasingly complex and diverse techniques for managing risk and lowering transaction costs.

Innovation

The constrained prudent man rule inhibits innovation by fiduciaries. As the public marketplace for securities grows increasingly efficient, efforts to outperform the market often lead along sparsely traveled paths, where pricing is less efficient and opportunities arise for those with special skills. Yet, prudence, in testing a particular investment product or technique used by a fiduciary, looks to see whether other fiduciaries have been following a similar strategy. As discussed previously, in *Chase v. Pevear* the court blessed investments because they were found in the portfolios of other fiduciaries, while declaring other investments to be imprudent because they were not shown to be in common use. The court apparently did not consider it relevant to discover why the challenged fiduciary was using these securities or why others were or were not using them. The lesson seems to be that prudence, like misery, loves company. Losses will not result in surcharge if enough different fiduciaries suffer from the same bad investment idea. The innovator, however, becomes a personal guarantor of success in that, regardless of the reasoning behind his path-breaking decision, the absence of other fiduciaries constitutes powerful evidence of imprudence.

The risks of going it alone have led legal advisers to counsel fiduciaries who would innovate on the importance of getting other fiduciaries to join in making the same kinds of investments. This advice is often resisted, because innovators are loath to share their good ideas.

The brief history of securities lending by Smith College illustrates the use of an innovative technique by a small institution to reap significant gains until that technique entered the mainstream of institutional practice and became dominated by big institutions trading in huge volume and with shrinking profit margins. Smith College was one of the earliest institutions to participate in securities lending transactions, which are described more fully in Chapter 4. As shown in Table 3.1, between 1972 and 1974, Smith's securities lending income grew in significance and then diminished over the later part of the decade. At its peak, in 1974, lending income was equal to almost one-quarter of Smith's entire investment income from its endowment.

The sharp decline in Smith's securities lending income beginning in 1975 was

Table 3.1 Smith College Securities Lending Program

Fiscal year ended June 30	Securities lending income
1972	$ 123,225
1973	344,185
1974	1,052,632
1975	473,256
1976	200,336
1977	53,907
1978	43,376
1979 and later years	0

Source: Records of Smith College

Table 3.2 Harvard University Securities Lending Program

Fiscal year ended June 30	Securities lending income
1974	$ 700,000
1975	800,000
1976	1,100,000
1977	1,100,000
1978	1,600,000
1979	2,300,000
1980	4,200,000
1981	4,200,000
1982	2,800,000
1983	2,000,000
1984	1,200,000
1985	900,000

Source: Records of Harvard Management Company

caused by the laws of supply and demand. It was no coincidence that Smith's profits from securities lending began to decline when larger institutions, including universities like Harvard and Princeton, began to make securities loans. In 1974, as shown in Table 3.2, Harvard earned less money from securities lending than did Smith, but as Harvard's securities lending program moved into high gear, its profits grew, more than doubling in the first four years (to 1978) and nearly tripling over the next two years (to 1980).

The larger endowments were forced to sacrifice profit margins for volume. What was once a lenders' market became dominated by large portfolios, among which borrowers could shop for the cheapest loan. Soon, the larger universities like Harvard were themselves being squeezed by even bigger lending portfolios that entered the market in the late 1970s as a result of regulatory and tax changes. Three new players came into the lending game: private foundations and mutual funds in 1978, as the result of changes in the Internal Revenue Code and regulatory interpretations,[59] and pension funds in 1981, as the result of a ruling by the Labor Department.[60] (See Table 3.3.)

This dramatic increase in the supply of securities available for lending was accompanied by only a small increase in borrowing demand by broker-dealers. The result was a sharp drop in profit margins on loan transactions and a preference among borrowers for dealing with the very large lending institutions. Smith College was simply squeezed out of the market in which it had been an innovator, and Harvard, as its declining income suggests, was adversely affected by the increase in large institutions eager to make loans. Indeed, Harvard's shrinking income since 1981 exactly matches the burgeoning use of securities lending by the largest among the nation's corporate pension plans.

Smith College, it would appear, was not restrained in its (then) innovative use of securities lending to earn significant extra returns with reasonable safety. In its boldness, Smith College was unusual. For institutions reluctant to challenge the "safety in numbers" rule of prudence, securities lending became an increasingly

Table 3.3 Percentage of Companies That Use Securities Lending

Plan assets	1980	1981	1982	1983	1984
Over $1 billion	2%	43%	37%	32%	39%
$501–1,000 million	0	33	32	40	31
$251– 500 million	1	22	37	31	30
$201– 250 million	0	29	27	20	19
$151– 200 million	0	15	23	27	22
$101– 150 million	0	14	14	6	6
$ 51– 100 million	1	4	8	10	12
$ 41– 50 million	0	0	5	4	3
$ 31– 40 million	1	3	5	7	3
$ 21– 30 million	1	1	2	4	5
$ 16– 20 million	2	0	2	2	3
$ 10– 15 million	0	0	2	6	7
Under $10 million	1	2	3	0	0

Source: 1985 Report on Large Corporate Pensions, Greenwich Associates, at 57

less profitable enterprise as the number of participants grew enough to provide that measure of safety. This will always be true to some degree, simply because of the laws of supply and demand.

Risk Theory

As noted in Appendix A, the economist's definition of risk differs from the colloquial meaning of the term, which is also the meaning accepted by the traditional prudent man rule. In common parlance, investments with uncertain prospects are considered "risky." And portfolios are either risky (i.e., speculative) or safe (i.e., prudent). The notion that different portfolios could choose within a wide range of risk levels, depending upon cash flow needs and other factors pertaining to purpose, was not accepted in the Treatise and Restatement. But in economics, risk is defined in terms of uncertainty of outcome. Thus, to take an extreme case to make the point, an investment with a very high probability of bankruptcy may be relatively less "risky" than one much "safer" in conventional parlance. The substantial body of evidence supporting the efficiency of markets points to a conclusion that the only way to increase return in an efficient portfolio is to increase its risk. This rule presumes a fair game.

Economists Richard Brealey and Stewart Myers have observed that, as recently as twenty years ago, a suggestion that security investment was fair in the sense that assets were accurately priced and higher returns were obtainable only through greater exposure to risk would generally have been regarded as bizarre. Today this theory is widely accepted in business schools and among fiduciaries and investment management professionals.[61] It is not, however, reflected in the Treatise or Restatement, nor has it found the sympathetic ear of a judge willing to value the practical realities of the marketplace more dearly than the abstract virtues of stare decisis.[62]

Many fiduciaries and their legal advisers would exhibit nervousness in explicitly fashioning a greater-than-market risk strategy in order to achieve higher returns than were promised by the market. However obvious and powerful this principle may appear to economists and professional investment managers, support for it in the authoritative literature of the law is missing. For a judge schooled in the constrained rule of prudence, taking more risk to earn *more* return, if things don't turn out well, is an invitation to surcharge. Until the economist's notions of risk are integrated into the legal rule of prudence, the restraining effects of that rule will remain.

The Venture Capital and Innovation Study prepared in 1984 for the Joint Economic Committee of the Congress reports that 63.5 percent of the venture capital firms consulted believed there was a bias among institutional investors against investing in small businesses, with the leading causes being a lack of institutional expertise in small business investing and the "excessive risk-adverse behavior of institutional investors."[63] While perhaps itself biased, this view lends some support to the idea that the prudent man rule exerts a restraining influence. More telling was the study's findings (a) that the liberalizing regulations issued by the Labor Department in June 1979 were a "major factor" in the surge of pension fund investment in venture capital after that date,[64] and (b) that the uncertainties of the federal prudent man rule contained in ERISA, including the possibility of being judged investment-by-investment, may have contributed to a shift toward greater risk aversion by pension fund fiduciaries from 1974, when ERISA was enacted, until the interpretative regulations of 1979.[65]

This nervousness of fiduciaries (and particularly their legal advisers) over risk theory stands in contrast to a different strategy where modern theory would counsel caution but the constrained rule remains untroubled. As many economists have pointed out, there is scant evidence that professional managers can produce on a sustained basis superior returns from managing stock portfolios of equivalent risk.[66] Yet, as this study's questionnaire results indicate,[67] fiduciaries have no prudential concerns over explicitly retaining managers to try to achieve superior performance and paying them substantial fees for the effort, whether or not successful.

The constrained rule stands at odds with other aspects of modern risk theory. For example, it disregards the risk of inflation. It's hard to imagine a fiduciary being surcharged for committing his entire portfolio to thirty-year Treasury bonds, even if it was reasonable to suppose that inflation would significantly erode the real value of the principal when repaid at maturity. However, unless the needs of the fund were exactly served by the income flow and return of principal in nominal terms, such a decision ought to be classified as imprudent.

Delegation

Perhaps in no other area is the constrained prudent man rule more laggard than with respect to delegation, and in no other area has so much progress been made to circumvent it.

Both the Treatise and Restatement advance the notion that "[a] trustee cannot properly delegate to another power to select investments."[68] Judicial declarations that a trustee may not delegate discretionary powers are commonplace.[69] Increasingly, however, delegation becomes unavoidable. The dramatic growth in new financial products and investment techniques recounted in Chapter 2 has made it difficult, even for fiduciaries whose business it is to invest money, to be expert across the wide spectrum of opportunities. As a practical matter, delegation is essential; were the Treatise and Restatement not blocking the way, the legal issue—like the business issue of which it is a part—would be not whether to delegate but how to delegate in the most effective way.

As noted in Chapter 1, impressive efforts to remove the legal barriers to delegation have been made through regulation,[70] statute,[71] and powerfully reasoned commentary.[72] The central theme of these efforts is to bring the question of delegation within the test of prudence—was it reasonable under all the circumstances—rather than to treat it (as the Treatise and Restatement do) as something apart from, and much more rigid than, the reasonableness standard that is the measure of prudence in other respects. However, it was not until 1961 that New York by statute authorized investment by fiduciaries in investment companies registered under the 1940 Act, leaving open and uncertain the legality of investments in other pooled vehicles. There remain in the statutes of New York and Connecticut governing investments by insurance companies a requirement that each investment be authorized or approved by the board of directors of the insurer or an appropriate committee of the board.[73] This requirement has caused uncertainty and concern among large insurance companies and has even given rise to artificial legal constructs involving superficial board ratification of decisions taken by management. As the funds under management and the variety of deployments grew, legal advisers, of necessity, gave these statutes broader readings than the plain meaning of the words and the absence of helpful judicial precedents would warrant. These readings were founded upon common sense and practical necessity; however, they still lack authoritative support from either the courts or the regulators.

In 1970 an incident involving the New York State Insurance Department illustrated the lingering potential for mischief that the constrained prudent man rule can have in the important area of delegation.

In December 1970, the New York State Insurance Department issued a seemingly innocuous three-paragraph informal opinion declaring illegal any "trading authorization" by which employee welfare fund trustees give discretionary stock trading power to a broker, bank, or other person or institution. In reaching that determination, the Department interpreted the New York insurance law[74] in light of the Treatise and the nineteenth century common-law rule against delegation to which the Treatise gave modern vitality. As previously discussed, this rule prohibits a trustee from delegating responsibilities involving the exercise of judgment and discretion.[75]

The opinion related to trusts under the Department's jurisdiction, so-called Taft-Hartley employee welfare and pension funds, which consist of those funds under the joint management of employers and employees. The opinion flew in the face of widespread practice among trustees of such funds to delegate discretion over investment selection to professional managers. A flurry of concern swept the financial community—a concern that started with the Taft-Hartley funds, but rippled beyond that relatively small segment to the wider investment management community. Could the informal opinion serve as legal precedent for other trusts, such as university endowments or non-Taft-Hartley pensions? The opinion challenged delegation practices that were considered a logical and, indeed, necessary response to the growth in size of pension and other institutional funds and the parallel development of an enormously varied and complex marketplace for the deployment of investment capital.

In the nonlegal world of fiduciaries responsible for investments, this economic climate offered a powerful case for delegation. The Department, however, turned to the Treatise rather than the marketplace to interpret a statute that simply charges trustees with overall responsibility for trust funds.

The Investment Counsel Association of America, concerned with the havoc that the Department's position could wreak, organized a committee to oppose the Department's opinion. Interested investment and legal counsel were contacted, meetings held, and a memorandum prepared for submission to the Department. A difficulty encountered by the group was that the Treatise's authoritative statements on the matter, replicated in the Restatement, made it hard to support with legal authorities the marketplace reality that delegation had to be legal because it was so transparently necessary. The memorandum submitted to the Department argued that the legality of a specific delegation, such as investment counsel authority over selection and disposition of securities, depends on many surrounding circumstances, including the existence of specific authority in the governing instrument, the nature and capabilities of the trustee, the size, purpose, and nature of the trust, and the arrangement between the investment counsel and the trustee in managing the trust.[76]

At the same time, committee members sent letters to the Department, urging it to revise and restate its position in the informal opinion. The committee also sent the Department proposed "Guidelines for Exercise of Investment Responsibilities by Trustees Subject to Section 37 of the Insurance Law."[77] These guidelines explicitly permitted a trust to provide for certain investment-related delegations and set forth procedures and limitations consonant with industry practice and with the unsettled but permissive "totality of circumstances" doctrine developed by the courts. With the addition of some restrictive language on the types of investment decisions that cannot be delegated at all,[78] the Department adopted the proposed guidelines.

What lessons can be drawn from this episode? First, with enough organized pressure, the law will respond to the needs of modern capitalism. Second, the dangers of antiquated rules linger and are capable of causing mischief in the marketplace, as was in fact to be the case as this episode continued.

Since the financial community and the Department ultimately agreed on what the law should be, their controversy appeared to be over. However, the source of that controversy—the informal opinion—would haunt New York jurisprudence a few years later. In *Trustees of Local 442 Pension Fund v. Schenck*,[79] the New York Appellate Division affirmed a finding of breach of fiduciary duty where the pension fund trustees delegated investment authority to a management company. The court relied entirely on the Department's "policy" as stated in its retracted 1970 informal opinion. Whether the facts of the *Local 442* case substantiated the result is not clear: The court apparently did not review those facts, but instead based its decision on the broad statement of law in the informal opinion. For example, the court said in dictum that the management company invested fund money in "highly speculative stocks," but it said nothing about whether the contractual arrangements provided for adequate supervision by the trustees or whether the allegedly speculative stocks fell into any of the prohibited categories of the Department's 1971 guidelines. Apparently unaware of these guidelines, the court mistook the 1970 informal opinion for the Department's current position and accepted that opinion as good law.

One could assign blame for the *Local 442* decision to the court or counsel for the losing side for failing to uncover the Department's position or to the Department, for ineptly stating New York law in its informal opinion. The deeper problem, however, lies in the fact that each decisional body took as its mission the articulation of the existing rules of the game—the stare decisis imperative of the common law—rather than the adoption of functional rules based on economic change—the evolutionary imperative of the common law that coexists in tension with the demands of stare decisis. Few areas of law are more ripe for the evolutionary approach than the regulation of fiduciaries in the rapidly changing world of investment management.

This episode suggests the need for a more economically rooted legal culture, one that takes its cues not from ancient doctrine or categorical rules but from the legitimate needs of the communities that must ultimately live by the law. It appears that in recent years the United States Supreme Court has moved increasingly toward this kind of culture.[80]

Any reappraisal of the anti-delegation rule must consider the historical context in which the rule developed and compare that setting with today's marketplace to see whether it continues to serve a useful role. As discussed more extensively in Chapter 2, the rule evolved in the nineteenth century with particular reference to trusts that irrevocably placed funds in the hands of a trustee for one or two generations. It was sensible to suppose, at that time, that the person chosen to serve could readily master the entire repertoire of available investment opportunities. What the law sought to assure was that the person selected to exercise judgment and discretion would in fact do so. Because there was no recognized need to turn to others for specialized skills, doing so could not be justified.

Today's marketplace is vastly different, as Chapter 2 seeks to document. Appreciation of the shifts can quickly be gained from Professor Robert Charles Clark's brilliant essay on the four stages of capitalism.[81] In that work, Clark identifies, as the first stage, the age of the entrepreneur—those owner-operators who in the nineteenth century created large business enterprises in corporate form for the first time in history. As these corporations increasingly provided access to the public markets with stock offerings in the early decades of the twentieth century, the entrepreneurial function was divided into ownership and control, ushering in the age of the professional business manager[82]—identified by Professor Clark as the second stage.

It was in the third stage that the restraints and conflicts between the traditional rule of prudence and the exigencies of the marketplace grew and were most sharply felt. As described by Professor Clark:

> The third stage of capitalism has been growing since the beginning of this century, and probably reached young adulthood in the 1960's. It is the age of the portfolio manager, and its characteristic institution is the institutional investor, or financial intermediary. As the second stage split entrepreneurship into ownership and control, and professionalized the latter, so the third stage split ownership into capital supplying and investment, and professionalized the investment function.

Professor Clark's fourth stage, which he sees now in its infancy, is called the age of the savings planner, an age in which capital supplying is being split into the possession of beneficial claims and the decision to save, with the savings-decision function being professionalized.

These four stages trace a process of increasingly refined delegation to capture the efficiencies of a vast increase in professionalism. Among financial intermediaries, this professionalism has grown not only in terms of the sheer quantity of those offering their services, but in the particularization of their skills. A glance at the range of mutual funds publicly available today illustrates the point. Whereas as recently as 1966, when the SEC's *Report on the Public Policy Implications of Investment Company Growth*[83] was completed, there were 379 mutual funds available, offering mainly three categories of investment objectives (common stock, balanced and bond, or bond and preferred stock),[84] by 1985 there were 1,858 mutual funds divided by the Investment Company Institute into fifteen broad categories (aggressive growth, growth, growth and income, precious metals, international, balanced, income, option/income, government, GNMA, corporate bond, long-term municipal bond, state municipals, money market, and limited maturity muni-bond).[85] Of course, within each category there are many variations. In 1966, one of the largest fund complexes, Fidelity Management and Research Company, offered twelve different mutual funds.[86] Today quotations for thirty-nine separate Fidelity funds are found in the financial press.

It is apparent that the anti-delegation rule had to yield to the greater efficiencies available through specialized management skills and product development—and yield it has. Unfortunately, the continuing existence of the anti-delegation rule in the Treatise and Restatement has riveted the attention of legal advisers on the matter of whether delegation is allowed. Lawyers should instead be focusing on the far more pertinent question of how to shape the rules of delegation in what Clark calls the "golden era of the financial intermediary" to maximize the gains available from specialization, consistent with an adequate level of customer protection against the potential for abuse in the exercise of that discretion. There are many open questions. What of the responsibility of fiduciaries for selecting and monitoring delegees or for the performance of those delegees; what of the delegees' duties to the fiduciaries who selected them and to the beneficiaries whose funds they manage; and what of the duties of the so-called investment management consultants[87] who may be employed by the fiduciaries to assist them in selecting and evaluating delegees and allocating fund assets? These issues deserve greater attention from scholars of law and finance than has until now been the case. Sweeping away the ancient doctrines against delegation can help to bring into focus the need for more sophisticated analysis of how best to allocate responsibility among the growing tiers of professionals who occupy the space between beneficiary and investment decision-maker.

NOTES

[1] *See* discussion in Chapter 1.

[2] H.M. Markowitz, *Portfolio Selection: Efficient Diversification of Investments* (1959) (an outgrowth of Markowitz, "Portfolio Selection," 7 J. Fin. 77 (1952)).

[3] 44 Fed. Reg. 37,221 (June 26, 1979).

[4] Treas. Reg. § 53.4944-1.

[5] In re Bank of New York, 364 N.Y.S.2d 164 (1974) (referred to herein as *Spitzer,* the name of the guardian ad litem involved in the case).

[6] For a commentary, in verse, on Justice Frankfurter's likening of due process to a Plimsoll Line, *see* Field, "Frankfurter, J., concurring . . .," 71 Harv. L. Rev. 77, 77 (1957).

[7] *See, e.g.,* Tinic & West, "Risk, Return and Equilibrium: A Revisit," J. Pol. Econ. (forthcoming), reporting on test results indicating that CAPM's two-parameter model is not supported

by the historical relationship between stock returns and systematic risk over the period from 1935 to 1982 and, further, suggesting that the test results are sensitive to the choice of the proxy for the "market portfolio."

[8]*Spitzer, supra* note 5, at 168.

[9]Interpretations of *Spitzer* vary. *Compare* Cary, Letter to the Editor, N.Y.L.J. (Feb. 24, 1975), at 4 *with* Lipton, "An Analysis: Prudent Man Test in Investments," N.Y.L.J. (Jan. 10, 1975) at 1. Langbein and Posner made heroic efforts to interpret the constrained rule more flexibly than the individual investment approach would warrant. The fact remains, however, that to date no reported case has been found to espouse their commendable theory. Langbein & Posner, "Market Funds and Trust Investment Law," 1976 A. B. F. Res. J. 1.

[10]44 Fed. Reg. 37,221, 37,224 (June 26, 1979).

[11]*See* discussion in B. Malkiel, *A Random Walk Down Wall Street* (4th ed. 1985) at 322; B. Malkiel & Firstenberg, *Managing Risk in An Uncertain Era* (1976) at 22. For a detailed review, written for lawyers, of evidence and theory bearing on the efficient market hypothesis, *see* Gordon & Kornhauser, "Efficient Markets, Costly Information, and Securities Research," 60 N.Y.U. L. Rev. 761 (1985).

[12]Blume & Keim, *Risk and Return Characteristics of Lower-Grade Bonds* (December 1984) (unpublished paper written for the Rodney L. White Center for Financial Research, The Wharton School, University of Pennsylvania).

[13]More systematic support is found in "Venture Capital and Innovation," A Study Prepared for Use of the Joint Economic Committee, December 28, 1984, S. Prt. 98-288 (98th Cong. 2d Sess.) at 34–5. Venture capital firms reported that about 50 percent of their portfolio investments were classified as "winners" (performing equal to or better than initial expectations), about 13 to 17 percent are "losers" (performing substantially below initial expectations), and the remainder are classified as "the living dead" (viable businesses but lacking sufficient potential to go public or merge upward).

[14]It is interesting to note that 70 percent of all questionnaire respondents thought that "venture capital pools" were permissible, while only 39 percent felt that way about "new and untried enterprises," which of course describes what venture capital pools invest in. It is quite likely that this difference in perception is grounded in the legal analysis offered in the text.

[15]*See* discussion in Chapter 4 at 133. Additionally, it should be noted that futures contracts are not, strictly speaking, "wasting assets" because each contract represents a firm commitment for the "delivery" at a certain date. But the short-term nature of the contracts and the prevalence of settlement of financial futures in cash rather than through actual delivery raise the danger that both futures and options may be considered "wasting assets."

[16]*Id.*

[17]*See* discussion in Chapter 1 at 12–13.

[18]*See* discussion in Chapter 1 at 18–19.

[19]Compact Edition (Oxford University Press 1971) at 2952.

[20]Headley, "Trust Investments," Tr. & Est. (October 1952) at 739, 740.

[21]3 Treatise § 227.6, at 1816.

[22]B. Graham & D. Dodd, *Security Analysis* (McGraw-Hill 1934).

[23]*Id.* at 50.

[24]*Id.* at 8 n.1.

[25]*Id.* at 51.

[26]*Id.* at 51.

[27]*Id.* at 55. In the 4th (and last) edition of *Security Analysis,* published in 1962, Graham put this point more broadly:

Strictly speaking, there can be no such thing as an "investment issue" in the absolute sense, *i.e.,* implying that it remains an investment regardless of price. In the case of high-grade bonds and preferred stocks, this point may not be important, for their prices are rarely so inflated as to introduce serious risk of loss of their principal. But in the common-stock field this risk may frequently be created by an undue advance in price—so much so, indeed, that

in our opinion the great majority of common stocks of strong companies must be considered speculative a good part of the time after a bull market is well under way, simply because their price is too high to warrant safety of principal in any intelligible sense of the phrase.
Security Analysis (4th ed. 1962) at 50.

[28]*Security Analysis* (1934) at 55.

[29]Fed. Banking L. Rep. (CCH) at ¶ 35,318.

[30]It is interesting to contrast this reluctant acceptance of portfolio theory with the Federal Reserve Board's more open embrace of the efficient market hypothesis in concluding that the use of variable margin requirements by regulators to moderate undue stock price fluctuations is a difficult undertaking with limited value. *A Review and Evaluation of Federal Margin Requirements, A Study by the Staff of the Board of Governors of the Federal Reserve System* (December 1984) at 14.

[31]A modern interpretation should begin by simply accepting both the language of *Harvard College v. Amory* and its plain meaning.

[32]*See* letter from Louis Margolis of Salomon Brothers Inc to Robert S. Plotkin of the Federal Reserve Board, dated April 25, 1983, objecting to the FRB letter, particularly with reference to its views on purchasing stock index futures, purchasing call options, and writing put options, and describing the FRB letter as "the legal list approach to investment regulation."

[33]Fed. Banking L. Rep. (CCH) at ¶ 35,320.

[34]Section 18(a), applying only to closed-end funds, permits the issuance of senior securities subject to a 300 percent asset coverage test. Section 18(f), applying only to open-end funds, prohibits the issuance of senior securities entirely (except to banks subject to the 300 percent asset test).

[35]Investment Company Act Release 7221 (June 9, 1972), Fed. Sec. L. Rep. (CCH) ¶ 51,301.

[36]Investment Company Act Release 10666 (April 18, 1979), Fed. Sec. L. Rep. (CCH) ¶ 48,525.

[37]*Id.* at 37,553–8.

[38]Investment Company Institute, 1985 Mutual Fund Fact Book at 7, 59.

[39]*Stein Roe Bond Fund, Inc.* (interest rate futures) [1984 Transfer Binder] Fed. Sec. L. Rep. (CCH) ¶ 77,614 (available January 17, 1984); *Pension Hedge Fund, Inc.* (index futures and options on index futures) [1984 Transfer Binder] Fed. Sec. L. Rep. (CCH) ¶ 77,615 (available January 20, 1984); *Z-Seven Fund, Inc.* (index futures, options on index futures and index options) [1984 Transfer Binder] Fed. Sec. L. Rep. (CCH) ¶ 77,664 (available May 21, 1984).

[40]*GMO Core Trust* (available August 19, 1985) (fund's investment objective was total return greater than S&P 500 Stock Index through investment in a broadly diversified and liquid portfolio; purchase of futures on S&P 500 Index intended to achieve diversity and liquidity and reduce brokerage costs more effectively than use of primary market). *See also Thomson McKinnon Investment Trust* (available August 23, 1985) (summarizing staff's position on use by investment companies of futures and options products).

[41]Commodity Exchange Act [hereinafter cited as CEA] § 2(a)(1)(A).

[42]CFTC Reg. 4.21.

[43]CFTC Reg. 4.22.

[44]CFTC Reg. 4.23.

[45]CEA, *supra* note 41, § 14.

[46]*Id.,* § 2(a)(1)(A).

[47]S. Rep. No. 384, 97th Cong., 2d Sess. 79–80 (1982).

[48]*Stein Roe Bond Fund, Inc.* [1982–84 Transfer Binder] Comm. Fut. L. Rep. (CCH) ¶ 21,906.

[49]Gordon, "Clothing the 'Naked' Put," Rev. Sec. Reg. 997 (January 9, 1981).

[50]*Id; see also* FRB letter, dated 11 January 1983, to trust examination personnel at Federal Reserve Banks, set forth in Fed. Banking L. Rep. at ¶ 35,318 and discussed in this Chapter at 89.

[51]*See* Wagner & Tito, "Definitive New Measures of Bond Performance . . . and Risk," Pen-

sion World 10 (May 1977); McEnally, "Duration as a Practical Tool for Bond Management," J. Portfolio Mgmt. 53 (Summer 1977). There are many different techniques for active bond management, clustered under the three major approaches: (1) seeking to exploit temporary imbalances in the bond market; (2) seeking to exploit mispricings of particular bonds; and (3) seeking to anticipate changes in interest rates on spreads between bond market segments.

[52]It is ironic that abandonment of the traditional buy-and-hold strategy for bonds in favor of trading on the basis of predicted interest rate changes occurred at about the same time as some managers first became impressed with the efficient market hypothesis and the case it made for the passive index fund approach to stock investing.

[53]Because bond futures contracts are specified on the basis of $100,000 face value per contract of fifteen-year or longer maturity 8 percent coupon Treasury bonds, while the cash instrument to be "cloned" in this example has a thirty-year maturity and a 9½ percent coupon, the face value of the contract would have to be adjusted by the "hedge-ratio"—a conversion factor designed to equate those instruments in terms of sensitivity to changes in interest rates. In this particular example, the "hedge-ratio" would equal 1.2, which multiplied by $10 million results in $12 million face value to be acquired in the futures markets.

[54]Variations within this alternative might be the use of the forward market for Treasury bonds maintained by some dealers and options on futures in Treasury bonds, which commenced trading on the Chicago Board of Trade in 1982. To keep the example simple, these variations are not developed in the text.

[55]See note 15 supra for a discussion of futures as "wasting assets."

[56]See discussion in Appendix A, Section A at 165–66.

[57]It is interesting to note that in their second edition of Security Analysis, published in 1940, Graham and Dodd recommend approaching "speculative senior issues" as if they were common stocks, but recognizing their limited claims, rather than to consider them as an inferior type of senior security. Security Analysis (McGraw-Hill 2d ed.) at 8.

[58]This point is elaborated in an unpublished paper written for this study by Professor Kose John of New York University's Graduate School of Business and its Salomon Brothers Center for the Study of Financial Institutions.

[59]Pub. L. No. 95-345, 92 Stat. 481 (August 15, 1978). There had been earlier private rulings (e.g., Knox College, December 14, 1977; Edna McConnell Clark Foundation, Inc., January 16, 1978), followed by Revenue Ruling 78-88, March 6, 1978, 1978-10 IRB 12, holding that securities lending did not give rise to unrelated business taxable income or to unrelated debt financed income. The legislation clarified additional uncertainties, not previously addressed by the Internal Revenue Service. The legislation specified that securities lending would not involve a sale or exchange in which gain or loss was recognized and that income derived therefrom by private foundations would constitute investment income under Section 4940(c)(2) of the Internal Revenue Code (thereby avoiding an "excess business holding" problem).

[60]Prohibited Transaction Exemption 81-6, 46 Fed. Reg. 7518 (January 23, 1981).

[61]R. Brealey & S. Myers, Principles of Corporate Finance (2d ed. 1984) at 281.

[62]Hamilton v. Nielsen, 678 F.2d 709 (7th Cir. 1982), appears to be the only reported case thus far to reveal the influence of portfolio theory. In dictum Judge Posner suggested that plaintiffs should have based their surcharge claim on portfolio theory.

[63]"Venture Capital and Innovation," A Study Prepared for Use of the Joint Economic Committee, 28 December 1984, S. Prt. 98-288, 98th Cong., 2d Sess. at 42–43.

[64]Id. at 8–9 and 73.

[65]Id. at 72.

[66]See note 11 supra.

[67]Eighty-eight percent of all questionnaire respondents expressed the belief that certain investment managers can consistently provide superior performance (Question 5), 87 percent believed it possible to select those managers (Question 6), and 89 percent believed that the prudent man rule does not obstruct arrangements for delegation (Question 2).

[68]Restatement (Second) of Trusts § 171 comment h; see also 2 Treatise § 171.2, at 1395 (3d ed. 1967).

[69]See cases cited in 2 Treatise (3d ed. 1967) § 171.2, at 1395 n.7.

[70]*See* notes 3 and 4 *supra.*

[71]*See* Uniform Management of Institutional Funds Act.

[72]*See* W. Cary & C. Bright, *The Developing Law of Endowment Funds: "The Law and the Lore" Revisited* (1974).

[73]New York Insurance Law, § 1411(a) (McKinney 1985); Conn. Gen. Stat. Ann. § 38-141a (West 1969).

[74]*See* New York Insurance Law § 4413(a) (McKinney 1985) ("The trustees of every employee welfare fund shall be responsible in a fiduciary capacity for all assets received, managed or disbursed by them, or under their authority, on behalf of such fund.")

[75]9 Monthly Bulletin, State of New York, Insurance Dep't 2 (Dec. 1970) ("It has been a common law rule of long standing . . . that a trustee . . . cannot delegate to others powers vested in him which would involve the exercise of judgment and discretion.") (citing Treatise, § 171.2, and cases).

[76]*See* Investment Counsel Association, Memorandum, Informal Opinion of Office of General Counsel of New York State Insurance Dep't 5 (March 30, 1971) (unpub. ms.) (citing cases).

[77]*See* attachment to Letter of Richard J. Cunningham to Roger W. Tompkins, Deputy Superintendent and General Counsel, New York Insurance Dep't (April 26, 1971).

[78]For example, the proposed guidelines had provided "that certain types of securities shall be excluded from the fund, such as puts, calls, straddles or stock options." Proposed Guidelines § II(1)(h). The Department added to that list "arbitrage, short sales and purchases on margin." State of New York Insurance Dep't, Circular Letter No. 3, Guidelines for the Exercise of Investment Responsibilities by Trustees of Employee Welfare and Pension Funds Subject to Article III-A of The New York State Insurance Law § 1(i) (August 11, 1971).

[79]56 A.D.2d 707 (4th Dep't 1977).

[80]*See, e.g.,* Easterbrook, "The Supreme Court 1983 Term—Foreword," 98 Harv. L. Rev. 4, 4–5 (1984) ("The Justices today are more sophisticated in economic reasoning, and they apply it in a more thoroughgoing way than at any other time in our history.").

[81]Clark, "The Four Stages of Capitalism: Reflections on Investment Management Treatises," 94 Harv. L. Rev. 561 (1981).

[82]*See* A.A. Berle & G.C. Means, *The Modern Corporation and Private Property* (1932).

[83]*SEC Report on Public Policy Implications of Investment Company Growth,* 89th Cong., 2d Sess., H.R. No. 2337 (December 2, 1966) [hereinafter cited as SEC Report].

[84]*Id.* at 45.

[85]Source: Investment Company Institute.

[86]SEC Report, *supra* note 83, at 48.

[87]*See* Chapter 2, *supra* at 72, for discussion of this relatively new type of professional.

CHAPTER 4

A Modern Paradigm of Prudence

The "Modern Paradigm" Defined

As the preceding chapters have shown, the economic assumptions embedded in the legal doctrine of prudence stand in irreconcilable opposition to those that follow from a survey of developments in the financial marketplace and in financial theory over the last fifty years. In short, the law's prudent man bears little resemblance today to prudent men or women in the real world, even those engaged in "safeguarding the property of others."

If the preceding chapters can be accepted as a fair presentation of the current state of the law on the one hand and financial theory and the marketplace for investments on the other, it becomes necessary to close the gap—to choose between the law's definition of prudence and the investment world's. It is the assertion of this study that to the extent that legal doctrine necessarily rests upon empirical premises, the law must develop in step with changes in those underlying premises. A modern interpretation of prudence, responsive to those changes, is needed. It should draw upon the broadest possible currents of change. And it should recognize that nothing useful can be said about an investment in the abstract; it can only be judged in terms of its impact on the whole portfolio and the purposes for which the portfolio is held. Yet it can be seen that the characteristic process of legal analysis continues to be the scrutiny of a given investment detached from the portfolio of which it is a part and the purposes to which it is dedicated, with the only exogenous point of reference being whether other fiduciaries used it too.

A modern paradigm for prudence, then, would shift the focus from the disembodied investment to the fiduciary, the portfolio, and its purpose. In light of the overarching principle, reaffirmed by the most soundly reasoned cases and recent legislative and administrative developments, that prudence is a test of conduct and not performance, the most promising vehicle for accomplishing that shift is a paradigm of prudence based above all on process. Neither the overall performance of the portfolio nor the performance of individual investments should be viewed as central to the inquiry. Prudence should be measured principally by the process through which investment strategies and tactics are developed, adopted, implemented, and monitored. Prudence is demonstrated by the process through which risk is managed rather than by the labeling of specific investment risks as either prudent or imprudent. Investment products and techniques are essentially neutral; none should be classified prudent or imprudent per se. It is the way in which they are used, and how decisions as to their use are made, that should be examined to determine whether the prudence standard has been met.

More specifically, for any investment product or technique employed by a fiduciary or any delegate selected by the fiduciary in connection with such employment (including pooled investment vehicles), the test of prudence is the care, diligence, and skill demonstrated by the fiduciary in considering all relevant factors bearing on an investment decision. If particular investment products or techniques are not imprudent per se, neither are they per se prudent for all purposes and at all times. Their use, without more, will not suffice. Prudence is not self-evident. Nor will it be enough to point to their use by other fiduciaries. What matters is not that others have used the product or technique (for whatever reasons), but the basis for its use by the fiduciary in question.

Among the relevant factors to be considered are at least the following:

1. The role the investment product or technique is intended to play in the total portfolio.

2. Whether that role is reasonably designed, as part of the total portfolio, to serve the purposes for which the portfolio is being held and invested, taking into account the risk of loss and opportunity for gain associated with the investment product or technique (including such factors as tax effects and informational costs of initiation, monitoring, and termination), the composition of the portfolio in terms of its diversification and systemic risk, and the minimum projected cash flows from income and capital gain over future periods compared with the maximum projected cash demands on the portfolio over those periods.

3. The competence of the fiduciary or the delegates selected by him to employ the product or technique.

4. If delegates are involved, the reasonableness of the terms and conditions of such delegation, taking into account the compensation structure, monitoring mechanisms, and provisions for termination.

If the test of prudence is to be found in the process by which investment choice is exercised, it follows that documents must be kept to record that process for future use in the event of challenge. In selecting investment products or techniques that are not conventional for fiduciaries, especially those that have traditionally been regarded as improper for trustees of personal trusts and estates, particular attention to careful documentation of all relevant factors bearing on the decision should be observed. For, despite the logic of the modern paradigm for prudence and its growing acceptance, one can anticipate that courts, confronted as they always are with specific cases in which plaintiffs have incurred substantial losses, may grow more conservative than theory would support.

It would be particularly important to document fully the reasons for the action taken, with a showing that in the reasonable judgment of the fiduciary the risks to the total portfolio have not been unreasonably increased and, under the circumstances, the portfolio would be more advantaged by using the investment product or technique than by following conventional investment strategies. This kind of showing ought to satisfy a judge that the duty of caution to which a fiduciary remains subject has been met.

Judging the prudence of a fiduciary's investments according to the quality of the surrounding decision-making process in no way disables one from concluding in any particular case that an investment was, in essence, "too risky." Indeed, determining the appropriateness of an investment in light of the needs of the particular portfolio is an essential element of any prudent investment process. What a process-oriented standard *does* emphatically reject, however, is the notion that types of investments can be labeled "prudent" or "imprudent" (as would a legal list) or even "probably prudent" or "probably imprudent" (as does the Treatise and the Restatement) in the abstract. Once we recognize that prudence always depends on the circumstances and that circumstances diverge so widely as not to be susceptible of generalization (either as between different classes of fiduciaries or, within classes of fiduciaries, from case to case), we necessarily leave behind the certainty of per se rules for the flexibility of case-by-case review. Admittedly, in doing so we exchange the arbitrariness of per se rules for the indeterminacy and unpredictability of a fact-bound standard. However, even with these vices the process-based paradigm seems most in harmony with the original conception of the prudent man rule found in the flexible and open-textured language of *Harvard College v. Amory*.

It is all the more ironic, then, that such progress as we have witnessed to date in moving toward the process test and its attendant receptivity to the best available economic wisdom has been achieved by moving away from the *Harvard College* standard. The Uniform Management of Institutional Funds Act of 1972 (UMIFA), the Employee Retirement Income Security Act of 1974 (ERISA), the Section 4944 regulations of the Internal Revenue Code, and the new California prudence standard each change the *Harvard College* language in an effort to signal their departure from the set of anachronisms that that language has come to represent. The resulting fragmentation leads to a preoccupation with the differences among the various tests, obscuring their true character as simply minor variations on a major theme. Circumstances vary infinitely but the analytical process—careful and reasoned consideration of the suitability of an investment for the particular portfolio, taking into account the best available wisdom concerning portfolio management—is always the same.

For this reason it seems fruitless to dwell on the differences between the private trust standard and the endowment standard, the endowment standard and the pension fund standard, and so forth. Prudence is best understood and analyzed as a unitary standard with a multitude of individual applications. Even the most prominent single departure from the classic prudence formula—the shift to a quasi-corporate "ordinary business care and prudence standard" found in UMIFA and the Section 4944 regulations—does not reflect a difference between endowments and personal trusts significant enough to warrant analyzing investment prudence differently. The origins of that language are rooted in the frustrations of draftsmen with the heavy baggage collected over the years by the traditional rule. On matters of corporate governance, the differences between private trusts and charitable institutions certainly do warrant different treatment. But on the issue of *investment* prudence, the "ordinary business care and prudence" formula invokes the business judgment rule in order to borrow the emphasis on process found in that doctrine. There is no reason why the standards governing other types of trustees should not borrow from the "corporate" standard for the same limited purpose.

It may be useful at this point to anticipate and address two likely objections to the process-oriented test. First, any process-based test is vulnerable to attack as empty of substantive content. Surely, the argument runs, it is possible to imagine some conduct that would be imprudent no matter how elaborate the surrounding decision-making process. For example, Scott suggests in the Treatise that a duty of caution is necessary in addition to the duties of care and skill because some investments are simply too risky for fiduciaries no matter how shrewdly decided upon.[1] Or, how can a strict process-oriented view generate a principled basis for criticizing a process based upon false premises, such as astrology, since an astrology-based decision-making process could easily be as thoroughly elaborated and internally consistent as any of the mainstream investment schools?

By emphasizing the importance of process, there is no intention to empty the reviewing function of all substantive content. In examining the prudence of a fiduciary's investment record, a court may be expected to scrutinize the substantive elements of the decisional process, not to substitute its judgments for those of the fiduciary, but to assure that some rational basis existed for the fiduciary's judgments.

More specifically, it is not the purpose of this study to endorse extreme risk-taking or to deny either the need for some limit (which would differ for each portfolio) on the appropriate overall risk level for a fiduciary or the need to make a value judgment about the soundness of a fiduciary's economic premises. The claim of this study is only to show the futility of answering those questions with broad generalizations or discrete categories. As previously discussed, any sound investment process must observe the traditional duty of caution by considering the suitability of an investment in light of the portfolio's risk tolerance. However, the traditional interpretation of that duty is markedly different from the duty of caution implicit in the process standard. That standard sets no presumptions about appropriate portfolio risk levels for the portfolios of fiduciaries generally or of any fiduciary in particular. Traditional readings of the duty of caution strongly suggest that trustees should choose securities having risk levels comfortably below that of the market. For example, Scott writes in the Treatise that a trustee need not invest only in government bonds because "[t]here are other securities which yield a higher return as to which the element of risk is sufficiently small so as to make them proper trust investments."[2]

Undoubtedly such notions underlie the anxieties of many trustees (especially those of philanthropic and educational institutions) about deliberately pursuing an above-market level of risk. To some, aggressive efforts to achieve levels of return significantly superior to that of the marketplace create discomfort; there is a sense in which the goal of excelling in this endeavor may be viewed as an unseemly, even immoral adventure in speculation destined to bring all concerned to grief. This Faustian vision of prudent investing assumes, falsely, the existence of "safe" investments yielding reasonable real returns. Further, it is inconsistent with the notion, implicit in the widespread legal duty of trustees with "special investment skills" to use those skills, that one responsible for the investment of another's funds should seek the most efficient use of those funds. Within reasonable limits established in light of the cash flow needs of a fund and its tolerance for volatility, efficiency may involve exposing the portfolio to higher than average risks to achieve higher than average returns or using unconventional products and techniques to achieve the same returns promised by more conventional means but at lower risk levels. The paradigm of prudence offered here is not intolerant of efforts to achieve superior investment results in these various ways. But neither is its emphasis on process intended to create a shield against accountability for the results of incompetence or irrationality.

The second objection to the process standard can be stated much more succinctly: A process-based theory that places a premium on creating a "paper trail" is a typical lawyer's solution. It creates more work for lawyers (who generate the paper) while leaving the merits unaddressed. The answer to this objection rests largely on common sense. A court that is appropriately suspicious and inquisitive about paper trails will be able to discern whether thorough documentation is merely a cosmetic device or a genuine record of diligent and informed deliberation. A court applying the modern paradigm of prudence would look beyond the mere existence of records in order to determine why an investment was made. If the record reveals incompetence, inattention to substantively relevant factors, or the absence of a reasonable basis for an investment decision in light of the portfolio's needs, the presence of a well-papered file should not insulate the fiduciary from liability.

In this respect the modern paradigm would extend the scope of the prudence inquiry beyond the facts considered relevant in the two leading decisions emphasizing process: *In Re Morgan Guaranty Trust Company of New York*[3] and *Stark v. United States Trust Company of New York*.[4] Both are relatively recent decisions applying New York law in the private trust context, and both have helped to reinforce the cardinal principle that prudence is a rule of conduct and not of performance by relying heavily on the existence of well-documented and systematic decisional processes in concluding that the defendants acted prudently. Indeed, in the *Stark* case, the performance of the challenged investments was disastrous: They dropped in value from about $940,000 to $93,000 within three years.[5]

A court applying the modern paradigm, while not necessarily reaching a different result, would probe the investment decision record for certain critical facts not revealed by the *Morgan* or *Stark* decisions. For example, the *Morgan* court describes in detail the existence of an elaborate decision-making process for stock investments and states that the stocks were thoroughly investigated, but does not explore the substance of the investment philosophy implemented by that process. The *Stark* decision, after a more searching inquiry, exposes and evaluates the content of the decision-making process regarding each of the three challenged common stock investments. The court, however, fails to set its inquiry in the framework of the overall portfolio. Indeed, the court makes passing references to the existence of other stocks in the portfolio[6] but never states the composition of that portfolio or even its total value. The modern paradigm, while by no means making modern portfolio theory a necessary element of investment prudence, would incorporate that economic model into the law to the minimal extent of requiring investments to make sense in light of the overall portfolio.

Some brief examples illustrating the substantive aspect of the prudence paradigm may add texture to the foregoing rebuttal. Consider first a small foundation with no source of income other than its $10 million endowment. Its charter makes clear the founder's goals of remaining in existence indefinitely and of grant-making in particular areas on a sustained basis, so that grantees chosen can rely on annual gifts for periods of at least five years. The board of trustees establishes an office and staff budgeted at $200,000 and proceeds to make grants totalling $800,000 per year with commitments extending forward at least five years. The investment committee is directed by the board to invest the endowment appropriately in light of the foundation's purpose and financial commitments, with an eye as well to the goal of preserving the purchasing power of the endowment.

With an impeccable record to document its decision, the committee commits the entire endowment to a well-diversified pool of small stocks,[7] reasoning from portfolio theory and practice that the only way to increase return in a diversified portfolio is to increase risk, that past performance of small stocks suggests that they may be an excellent medium for achieving higher returns and that diversification will protect the funds from incurring the unpriced risk that modern portfolio theory predicts will follow from more concentrated investing. Recognizing that small stocks pay meager dividends, inadequate alone to provide even one-half of the 10 percent return needed for cash flow, the committee accepts the necessity of selling securities to generate what is needed. While aware that small stocks have exhibited very high volatility (over the fifty-eight-year period since 1926 they had a standard deviation of 36.3 percent compared to 21.2 percent for the Standard & Poor's (S&P) composite index),[8] the committee fails to let the possible consequences of that fact, were small stocks to do badly over the short-term, influence its decision, which is based on historical results over the long-term.

Had the foundation commenced operations in 1969, deploying its $10 million endowment in small stocks and spending at the rate of $1 million per year, in five years the corpus would have dwindled to $1.75 million.[9] In light of its purpose and corresponding cash flow needs, this investment strategy would be imprudent under the modern paradigm, and no amount of "process" or careful record keeping to document it should change that conclusion. Nor should the fact that, had the foundation started just six years later in 1975, its corpus would have swelled to $38.10 million in five years despite the annual payout.[10]

Had the $10 million endowment been unnecessary to fund the institution's cash flow needs (as could be the case where a college is meeting cash flow out of tuition and annual giving from alumni), the legal conclusion might well have been different. The imprudence of the foundation's investment choice stems from its disregard of the reasonably foreseeable consequences of being forced to sell securities in a sustained down-market in order to meet fixed long-term obligations.

Now consider a college with cash flow needs that can be varied somewhat, income from tuition that can be increased without significant loss of student applications and annual giving by alumni that can be expected to increase. All income from its endowment has typically, and as a matter of policy rather than necessity, been applied to college operations, but contributes less than 5 percent of its cash flow. With ample documentation of its decision, the investment committee chooses to use Treasury bills to generate its small share of the cash flow, observing that the yield is assured and the investment is virtually riskless for the short-term investor because Treasury bills have never experienced a negative total return in nominal terms. Aware of the risk of inflation, the committee nonetheless chooses to ignore it, content with the sure knowledge that its strategy will preserve the size of the endowment in nominal terms while meeting the college's expected (but not indispensable) annual call on that fund for cash flow.

The reasonably foreseeable consequence of this strategy is a sharp erosion in the real value of the endowment. Pursued over the ten-year period from 1975 to 1984, for example, the cost of this strategy, which ignored the risk of inflation, would have been to cut the real value of the endowment by almost one-half. Of course, there are no cases declaring such a nominally conservative strategy imprudent. Under the modern paradigm, however, a court would be justified in giving special scrutiny to an investment approach that ignored the risk of inflation under circumstances where neither the broad purposes nor the specific cash flow needs of the institution compelled that result.

The Modern Paradigm in Action

With these points in mind, it remains to consider how a process-based paradigm would operate in the current financial environment.

As detailed in Chapter 2, the inflationary spiral of recent years fostered intense efforts by fiduciaries to find new investment products and techniques to enhance, or at least maintain, the purchasing power of their portfolios. At the same time that fiduciaries were confronted with the peril of high inflation, they were being accosted by increasing economic evidence that the principal U.S. capital markets were remarkably efficient, rendering quixotic the quest for superior performance.

In the U.S. publicly traded markets, economists were suggesting that skill, industry, and foresight yield little or no marginal utility over mindlessly (but cheaply) tracking the market. Faced with these challenges, fiduciaries turned to unconventional products and techniques, many of which lay outside the traditional ring of prudence. The notion was that precisely that skill, industry, and foresight that was perhaps becoming less useful in the highly efficient public markets was increasingly rewarded in the more imperfect markets selected for asset deployment.

Another set of challenges and opportunities arose in the late 1970s as a result of the highly volatile interest rates of that period. Hedging against interest rate fluctuations became a pressing concern for all institutional investors and spurred the growth of strategies involving complicated new instruments such as financial futures and options. Of course, these markets had long been considered "off limits" to fiduciaries and the terrain was foreign to them. The knowledge and sophistication required to compass these derivative markets make them a fruitful source of illustrations of the process-oriented values of careful monitoring and documentation.

It may be helpful, in seeking to illustrate the elements of a sound investment process meeting the requirements of this modern paradigm of prudence, to focus attention on some of the less conventional products and techniques to which fiduciaries have turned in recent years. This choice to emphasize unconventional products and techniques should not be taken to imply either that superior returns are not worth pursuing in the more developed markets (such as heavily traded common stocks) or that traditional investment arenas do not present important process issues. Rather, unconventional and suspect investments, because of their presumptive imprudence in the minds of many, present a more demanding test of the thesis that almost any investment could be prudent under some circumstances if undertaken pursuant to a sound process.

Accordingly, this section seeks to illustrate and amplify the foregoing observations through specific applications of the process paradigm in the context of securities lending, real estate, venture capital, options and futures, and repurchase agreements. Each of these investment products and techniques lends itself both to general application of the process paradigm and to illustration of some specific problem in prudent investing today. The final illustrations of the paradigm appear in a discussion of two recent judicial decisions that serve as good examples of the shortcomings of the law's present notions of prudence.

In using the less conventional products and techniques discussed below, there is no intention to recommend their use by fiduciaries. Indeed, none of what follows should be taken as investment advice in either a specific or general sense. The illustrations are intended only to help the reader in understanding the new legal standard of prudence being advanced.

Securities Lending

At least since the 1930s (when the Securities Exchange Act of 1934 required that short sales be settled by delivery of borrowed securities), broker-dealers have been regularly in the market for borrowed securities. Until the 1960s, securities lending was done between broker-dealers as an accommodation. With trading volume increases in the 1960s and early 1970s, demand for securities loans increased. Charges began to be imposed on loans and then, in the early 1970s, broker-dealers began turning to institutional holders to meet the growing demand for security loans. Commercial banks also increased their borrowing. Securities were borrowed to cover securities fails (securities sold but not available for delivery), short sales, and option and arbitrage positions.

Here, then, was an entirely new investment technique available to fiduciaries. As the earlier analysis of Smith College's experience in securities lending revealed, returns sufficient to warrant the effort, at least for a smaller institution, might only occur until the technique became so widely accepted that the supply of loans from lending institutions exceeded the demand for them. For the first fiduciary to innovate in this new area, what should the record show to demonstrate that the prudence standard had been met? At a minimum, the record should reveal that each of the following issues had been examined thoroughly in light of the basic factor analysis previously set out as the test of prudence in its modern setting.

The Role of Securities Lending in the Total Portfolio. The key aspect of this technique (as with repurchase and reverse repurchase agreements and many other short-term investment strategies) is that, for a fee, the fiduciary permits others to use available portfolio assets, without materially impairing the ability of the fiduciary to sell, purchase, or otherwise manage those assets as if the securities loan had not been made. If this condition can be met, securities lending offers the prospect of incremental gain without any opportunity cost (other than through different short-term investment strategies). If the condition cannot be met, the technique raises an important issue of opportunity cost that may make its use harder to justify.

The Risk of Loss/Opportunity for Gain. Securities lending is conducted through open-ended loan agreements, which may be terminated on short notice by either party. On average, loans are outstanding for two to three days and are usually callable on five days' notice. The lender lends one or more securities from its portfolio to the borrower and contemporaneously receives back collateral at least equal to the value of the securities loaned. The lender receives from the borrower all payments (e.g., dividends or interest) in respect of the loaned securities made during the period of the loan, so that the lender continues to enjoy all the economic benefits (and to bear all the risks) of the loaned securities. The collateral is continuously adjusted ("marked to market") to reflect changes in the value of the collateral, so that the lender is at all times fully secured. In the early years of institutional securities lending, the lender would invest the cash collateral in highly liquid short-term securities and be entitled to retain all of the interest earned as its loan fee. As supply swelled to meet, and then exceed, demand, a portion of the interest was rebated to the borrower. Alternatively, if Treasury bonds or letters of credit were delivered as collateral, the borrower simply paid the lender a loan fee.

The gain side of this analysis commenced with a consideration of the gross fees expected to be paid, which would turn on the level of lending activity reasonably anticipated. However, in addition, it was necessary to reach a net figure, determined by deducting the informational cost of gaining the competence to understand and initiate a securities lending program, the cost of managing the program, the tax, if any, on loan fees, the custodial charges involved in establishing the loans, holding the collateral, adding to or subtracting from it under the "marking to market" requirement, and terminating the loans and finder's fees, if any.

For tax-exempt portfolios, there was substantial uncertainty as to whether the fee income and even the dividend and interest equivalency payments for the securities loaned were taxable as "unrelated business income." Although more remote, there was even concern expressed by some tax advisers that the loan would be treated for tax purposes as a "sale" of inventory held for sale in the ordinary course of the "business of securities lending" by the tax-exempt fund, thereby subjecting the "gain" on such "sale" to tax at ordinary corporate tax rates. Securities lending is one example (among many) of the critical importance of considering one's tax position in choosing between one kind of investment product or technique and another.

It was not until 1978 that all of these tax issues were favorably resolved by specific legislation.[11] Fiduciaries who engaged in securities lending before the tax uncertainties were clarified typically did so on the basis of judgment informed by expert advice—both financial and legal. On the basis of some experts' advice, fiduciaries were able to conclude from a "worst case" scenario that even if a tax were imposed the program would generate incremental income net of the tax and other costs. In other cases, particularly where the expert saw the possibility of a tax on the loaned security's unrealized appreciation, based on the "sale from inventory" theory, the worst case scenario could easily result in a substantial net loss.

Suppose a fiduciary for a tax-exempt fund simply ignored the question of tax entirely. Suppose further that, after three years of successful operation, the Internal Revenue Service assessed taxes that in the aggregate caused a substantial loss for the portfolio, net of all gains achieved through the securities lending program. Did the fiduciary meet the test of prudence? The answer, absent some extraordinary circumstance, is no. Next to assuring the safe custody of the portfolio, for the fiduciary of a tax-exempt fund nothing is more basic than preserving the tax-exempt treatment of the fund's income except in cases where an explicit decision is made to accept taxable income because the net expected returns warrant doing so.

Suppose the same substantial loss due to tax liabilities, but in this case the fiduciary instituted the program only after a careful review of the tax questions and in reliance upon the written advice of counsel, reasonably believed by the fiduciary to be reliable, to the effect that, although the issue was not free from doubt, in counsel's opinion no tax would be imposed. Here the answer should be yes to the question of whether the test of prudence was met. The record reveals careful analysis of the tax risk and reasonable reliance on an expert's advice. A fiduciary is no more a guarantor of the opinions expressed by experts than he is of a portfolio's performance. The fact that a legal expert turns out to be wrong should not subject the fiduciary to liability where reliance was reasonably placed. Treatment of reliance on legal advice should be no different than treatment of reliance on the expert investment advice of managers or employees.

So much for the gain side. The risk of loss side of the analysis commenced with the recognition that both the securities loaned and the equivalent payments had to be highly secure from any risk of loss attributable to the loan. At 2 to 3 percent of the value of the securities loaned before deducting expenses, the return was obviously not calibrated against any material credit risk. The principal concern related to the borrower's financial condition. As with any extension of credit there are risks of delay in recovery or even loss of rights in the collateral should the borrower fail. If bankruptcy proceedings for the borrower commenced before the loan was called and, if necessary, the collateral applied to satisfy the loan, the "automatic stay" resulting from that proceeding, which puts a "freeze" on all the borrower's property, would bar the lender from using the collateral to pay off the loan, even though this is precisely what the loan agreement authorizes him to do. Eventually the lender should be permitted by the court to proceed in this way, but the delay could be lengthy and there is no assurance that the time value of the delay would be recouped. This problem could be exacerbated if (contrary to normal practice) the cash collateral had been placed in longer-term debt instruments that would be sensitive to interest rate fluctuations.

A further problem would arise if there had been additions to the collateral under the "mark to market" requirement within four months of the bankruptcy. Those additions would constitute "preferences" under the bankruptcy law,[12] entitling the borrower (or its trustee) to recover them for the benefit of all creditors.

What these risks meant to the prudent investor was simply that security loans ought not to be made on the assurance that the collateral would take care of things if the borrower went "belly up." Instead, the loans should be made only to high credit borrowers, their credit standing should be continuously monitored, and the loans should be called immediately if there were any delay in marking to market or other sign of trouble.

Other, more obvious, concerns needed to be addressed as well. Because of the relative complexity of the securities lending transaction, it was important for the arrangement to be carefully spelled out in an agreement. Because the collateral was intended to give the lender status as a fully *secured* creditor, it was also essential that the creditor establish that legal position by taking possession of the collateral and policing the marks to market to see that at all times the collateral had a value at least equal to the market value of the securities on loan. It was the failure to assure safe custody and possession of the securities "purchased" in repo transactions that caused substantial losses to the New York school districts dealing with the now defunct Lion Capital firm.[13]

As applied to these risks, the prudence standard would not require that they be entirely eliminated. It would entail diligence in coming to understand and manage them. As the volume of securities lending and those eager to become lenders increased, intermediaries began offering services designed to relieve fiduciaries of the anxieties these risks imposed. Banks offered, for a fee, to manage a lending program for the fiduciary and indemnify the portfolio against loss. In lieu of collateral, borrowers would sometimes provide bank letters of credit, which were not subject to the infirmities of collateral in the event of a borrower's bankruptcy. These developments multiplied the options available to the fiduciary seeking to control risk.

Competence. As this discussion suggests, a securities lending program requires expertise. A fiduciary not only must gain sufficient knowledge to understand all the elements of the lending transaction; he must have, or retain others who have, the competence and time to manage a program effectively. This is perhaps the most important precept of prudence. However attractive a particular investment product or technique may appear, a fiduciary ought not to use it unless after careful scrutiny he has a solidly based belief that he (or a delegate chosen by him to carry it out) has the requisite competence to do it well. Securities lending, like many other unconventional investment strategies, is not for all fiduciaries. The ancient advice to cobblers about "sticking to your last"[14] bears mention here. Prudence does not compel a fiduciary to employ any particular product or technique. That standard does, however, demand of a fiduciary that he answer the question of competence before embarking on any new course of investment activity—not just general ability in the field of portfolio management, but specialized competence in the particular activity to be undertaken.

While a fiduciary ought not to be liable for loss resulting from the unanticipated bankruptcy of a borrower, a contrary conclusion would be the likely result if, through a failure to appreciate the significance of possessing the collateral or obtaining timely marks to market, the fiduciary incurred losses due to not having a secured claim to collateral equal to the market value of the securities on loan.

Documentation. It should be now well understood that the prudence standard creates a powerful need for a written record to document diligence and informed deliberation in the decision-making process. This is no less true for securities lending than for any other course of action. Indeed, given the complexities of this activity, the need for careful documentation is probably greater than would be the case for more conventional products and techniques.

It is worth noting that in 1985 the Federal Financial Institutions Examination Council saw fit to issue policy guidelines for financial institutions engaged in the lending of securities, whether for their own accounts or on behalf of others.[15] The council is composed of senior representatives of the various bank regulatory agencies. Their policy focuses on prudent controls for securities lending programs, covering such areas as record keeping, collateral management and control, credit analysis and selection of securities borrowers, the establishment of credit and concentration limits, and the need for written securities lending agreements. It was prompted by heightened regulatory sensitivity to the potential for problems due to the recent bankruptcies of several securities brokers who were recognized to be the primary borrowers of securities. While coming more than fifteen years after institutions began actively to engage in securities lending, the policy statement is a useful model of how some of the important issues involved in a lending program might be addressed to meet the need for documentation.

Real Estate

Real estate accounts for over 50 percent of the nation's total wealth.[16] As a medium of investment, it offers important opportunities for diversification of investment risk. The absence of large, central markets, the diffusion of purchase and sale transactions across the country, and the vast diversity of product distinguish this medium of investment from the more uniform tendencies of the large, publicly traded stock and bond markets. Within the real estate market there is ample opportunity for diversification by, for example, location, type of project, and financial position chosen.

Beyond the advantages of diversification, real estate has been a unique source of both the stable income of a bond portfolio *and* the inflation protection of a real asset. The rental income from a diversified portfolio of real estate interests has historically been a stable income source similar to that of a bond portfolio. The underlying market value of real estate, however, is influenced by quite different factors—replacement construction costs for one—that have often proven sensitive to inflation. Equity positions in shopping centers have been particularly good inflation-hedged investments. Leveraged with fixed-rate mortgages and tied to strong retail businesses through net leases paying fixed and percentage rents (the latter tied to gross sales) and passing on to the lessees the cost of common area maintenace, real estate taxes, and the like, shopping center investments can not only hedge the inflation risk, but profit substantially from an inflationary environment.

These attributes of real estate make it an attractive medium for some fiduciaries, particularly ones seeking to replicate in their portfolios as close an approximation of the "market" prescribed by the capital asset pricing model (CAPM) as possible.

Over the past five- and ten-year periods, real estate has shown substantially higher returns than long-term high-grade corporate bonds with apparently much lower volatility.[17] Indeed, the returns come close to those achieved by a diversified portfolio of stocks (the S&P 500) and are about the same as a balanced portfolio of stocks and bonds, but with far lower volatility. Table 4.1 shows the annualized rates of return and standard deviations of return for the pooled real estate funds offered to pension funds and other institutional investors by Prudential Life Insurance Company, The Equitable Life Assurance Society of the United States, and Morgan Guaranty Trust Company of New York over the five- and ten-year

Table 4.1

	5 Years to 3/31/85		10 Years to 3/31/85	
	Rate of return	Standard deviation	Rate of return	Standard deviation
Equitable	13.91	3.14	12.79	2.57
Prudential	12.97	2.47	14.85	3.47
Morgan Guaranty	19.57	5.87	18.15	9.17
S&P 500	17.88	15.26	13.49	14.71
Salomon Bros. LTHG Bonds	14.77	18.49	8.09	15.19
Consumer Price Index	5.86	1.95	7.29	2.00

Source: Rogers, Casey & Barksdale, Inc.

periods ended March 31, 1985 and the comparable numbers for the S&P 500 Index, the Salomon Brothers Long-Term High-Grade Corporate Bond Index, ninety-day Treasury bills, and the Consumer Price Index.[18]

A study of real estate returns over a longer period, from 1947 to 1982, by Roger G. Ibbotson and Laurence B. Siegel, generally confirms the overall return behavior of real estate presented in Table 4.1.[19] Over that period a general index of real estate total returns for unleveraged real estate increased seventeenfold, representing a compound annual rate of return of 8.3 percent.[20] Leveraged real estate equities would show even higher rates of return.

For the fiduciary considering a commitment to real estate, the prudence standard requires (as in the case of securities lending) that (i) the role of real estate in the total portfolio, (ii) the risk of loss/opportunity for gain, and (iii) the matter of competence and the related one of delegation each be carefully addressed and documented. A look at some of the questions raised may help in illuminating the process by which investment decisions in this field should be made.

The Role of Real Estate in the Total Portfolio. The preceding discussion of real estate as an investment medium would provide the basis for developing a cogent argument for committing some portion of the portfolio to this asset. Thus, the objectives of such a program might include a long-term rate of return competitive with a diversified portfolio of stocks and bonds, less volatility than either stocks or bonds, inflation protection, and, perhaps most important, diversification. The record should contain appropriate evidence that these objectives are feasible.

Although Federal Housing Administration mortgages have achieved these goals, it isn't at all clear that such an investment, or an investment in today's burgeoning mortgage securities markets (where mortgages are essentially pooled and readily marketable securities backed by those pools issued in public offerings), would accomplish the objectives of inflation protection and diversification, in the sense that they would not covary with the dominant trends of the U.S. equity and debt markets. To achieve these objectives it would probably be necessary to invest in an ownership position with respect to income-producing properties or properties held for development, where, albeit at generally greater risk than obtains when the position is taken after the development and lease-up phases are complete, it is possible to participate in the enhancement of real estate values through the development process. The insurance and bank managed real estate funds included in Table 4.1 offer this type of real estate investment, as do a growing number of other real estate pools targeted for pension funds and other institutional investors.

Real estate is often claimed to provide a good hedge against inflation. After the decade of the 1970s, in which historically high levels of inflation prevailed, together with disappointing returns in both the equity and fixed-income markets and a contrasting increase in the value of selected real assets, many institutional investors turned to real estate as a promising alternative in an inflationary environment. However, lower levels of inflation will correspondingly lower the relative advantage of a real estate portfolio over stocks and bonds. And the extent to which real estate is effective as an inflation hedge varies significantly with the structure of the particular investment.

The absence of covariance between real estate and stocks or bonds makes it a particularly good way to enhance the efficiency of a portfolio. Studies have shown that real estate returns having positive expected returns have a negative correlation with stock returns and either negative or only a small positive correlation with Treasury bills and corporate bonds.[21] Without sacrificing expected returns, real risk to the portfolio can be significantly reduced by including real estate in the portfolio.[22]

The portion of a portfolio to be committed to real estate should be carefully established. A major factor in this decision would be the fact that, with the exception of publicly traded real estate pools such as real estate investment trusts (REITs) and the recently developed mortgage securities markets, real estate investments are relatively illiquid. If, due to cash flow needs, one were forced to sell a real estate investment quickly, one would not expect to do well. Real estate markets are far less efficient than large public-traded debt and equity markets. It takes patience to invest and likewise to disinvest. Therefore, the prudent fiduciary must be sure that the anticipated cash flow demands on its portfolio can be met without a hasty sale of its real estate holdings.[23]

The Risk of Loss/Opportunity for Gain. Because real estate markets are highly imperfect, there are enhanced opportunities for gain as well as greater risks of loss than typically obtain in the publicly traded debt and equity markets. Real estate investing is difficult, time-consuming, and costly. There are no central markets where participants come together in a regulated setting to trade. Pricing inefficiencies are more likely to exist. Adding to this element of riskiness is the need to achieve geographical diversification in a real estate portfolio, for the ability to obtain specialized knowledge about particular properties becomes increasingly difficult as the investor moves farther and farther away from the local real estate markets he knows best. Identifying those in remote places who have the best information can be very difficult as well as costly, with the chances of becoming a victim rather than a beneficiary of the pricing inefficiencies so common to real estate increasing directly with the distance.

There is no "market index" fund for real estate that can be used with the certainty and low cost that any of the many publicly available index mutual funds provides for corporate equities. These factors place the highest premium on skill, industry, and foresight; they require that the fiduciary weigh carefully the informational costs involved in satisfying this need. In that regard, a fiduciary should recognize that real estate is a specialized field where general knowledgeability about investments is not enough. A demonstrated track record in the use of financial instruments, for example, is not readily transferable to real estate. The matter of competence, then, is critical to achieving a favorable mix of high gain potential with low risk of loss.

Other elements of risk peculiar to real estate include its cyclical nature, as measured by office vacancy rates, housing starts, and commercial and industrial building space,[24] and the common use of property appraisals to support investment decisions. As illuminated in congressional hearings on the demise of REITs in the mid-1970s,[25] even in the absence of fraudulent inflations, appraisals are frequently wrong or, through inexperience or poor judgment, are accorded greater weight than they deserve or in other ways misapplied to the investment in question.[26]

In considering a commitment to real estate, the fiduciary must decide across the broad spectrum of possibilities where to position himself in terms of risk and reward. Broad categories such as real estate equities and mortgages fail to convey the many alternative positions that can be achieved through structuring within those classes. Probably the greatest risk to the investor occurs in financing the development phase of a real estate project: At this point there are the multiple risks of construction (e.g., cost escalation and delay) and lease-up. Returns should reflect these risks, although that may depend on how the project is financed.

There are a range of possibilities. At one extreme, in the case of an office building, for example, the investor might purchase the land and finance the whole development, selecting a contractor to do the building and a leasing agent to sign up tenants. This would be an equity investment, without leverage. At the other extreme, the investor might be solely a lender at fixed interest to the project, making a mortgage loan to the project owner, either at the time of land acquisition, commencement of construction, completion of construction, or completion of lease-up. Between these extremes lie an almost infinite variety of arrangements by which an investor can achieve his desired risk level and cash flow needs, while taking into account his tax status and the desires of other parties to the transaction. Looking more closely at some of the typical arrangements may be useful, not only for purposes of a risk/reward analysis but to illustrate the difficulty of meaningfully applying the traditional prudence standard in this area.

Investment in unimproved land is an accepted medium for achieving returns through appreciation in land values over time.[27] It is also a first step in seeking enhanced returns through the development process. Raw land is typically a nonproductive asset, in that no current income is generated and carrying costs, such as real estate tax (if applicable), liability insurance, fencing, and the like, must be incurred. For these reasons the traditional prudence standard would hold such investments to be imprudent.[28] While, as mentioned previously, nonproductive assets may be wrong for personal trusts, where income beneficiaries as well as remaindermen have conflicting claims on the corpus, they are not wrong because of their imprudence as an investment but because of their inappropriateness to the purposes of the trust. In seeming to equate these very different matters by labeling particular investment products or techniques "imprudent" if they were considered unsuitable to a trust having the dual purpose of serving a life beneficiary dependent on steady cash flow and a distant remainderman, the Treatise and the Restatement disserved fiduciaries. For trusts or other forms of endowment that lack a bifurcated purpose, investment in raw land can be analyzed on its own merits, *as an investment,* and considered as part of a portfolio. Indeed, even in the case of a dual purpose personal trust, raw land might fit in a portfolio constructed to give the life beneficiary his fair share through other high income-generating investments.

The traditional view of raw land becomes even harder to sustain when one considers that a first mortgage on land (appropriately appraised) would avoid suspicion under traditional prudence standards. The label "first mortgage" puts the investment in a nonsuspect category under the Restatement both because the principal is adequately secured and it is generating income.[29] This is true even though land loans of this sort often involve the mortgagee's funding of interest to be paid back to him.

In the real world of risk, the investor as mortgagee has fixed his potential for gain by the interest rate charged while remaining exposed to the inflation risk, the real interest rate risk, and some risk of loss due to default, depending upon the size of the owner's equity, the reliability of the appraisal, the carrying costs, and the range of unpredictable events, such as a zoning change and demographic shifts, that can importantly affect future land values. What the investor has lost, in avoiding an equity investment in the land, is the considerable potential for growth, particularly in an inflationary period.

The same analysis would apply to a first mortgage loan during the development stage. Here too the upside is usually capped by fixed interest, which is funded by the mortgage lender. The risks of inflation and interest rate fluctuation are reduced, because the loan is typically of shorter duration. The risks of loss due to default multiply, however, because of the uncertainties of construction, including the cost of materials and of labor, as well as the pace of building to completion. Beyond the construction phase, there are the risks of lease-up, upon the success of which the permanent mortgagee will often condition his loan. In terms of the traditional prudence standard, this is a "new and untried enterprise," lacking a stable record of earnings or growth. This is always the case in real estate developments. As land is developed, it becomes a specific business enterprise—be it an office building, shopping center, hotel, or warehouse—that remains untested until completed and exposed to customer demand.

Despite the high risks associated with construction lending,[30] the first mortgage construction lender would not be suspect under the traditional prudence standard while the owner of the development would risk having his investment labeled imprudent. The "new and untried enterprise" would not be viewed as belonging to the lender, because he hadn't invested *in it,* just loaned to it. There is no logic to this difference in approach. The superficial sense of safety implied by a first mortgage position may be undermined by any number of risk factors that affect the overall project and those committed to it in one form or another. Where an investor and a developer "joint venture" a particular development project, it may well be appropriate for the investor to have a senior position to the developer, but notions of prudence should not compel that seniority be expressed in the traditional trappings of a "first mortgage."

There are many possibilities. The parties may simply allocate cash flow first to the investor until his capital and a suitable interest rate have been returned. Rather than deploy his assets to cover the whole cost of the project, the investor might use leverage by bringing in a commercial lender or first mortgagee. His senior position vis-à-vis the developer might then be expressed as a second mortgage, which unfortunately bears the label "imprudent" under the Restatement.[31]

Alternatively, the investor might issue an unqualified "hell or high water" take-out commitment to the first mortgagee, giving that lender, in effect, a put at maturity of the construction loan or at any earlier point should the loan get in to default. An essentially equivalent technique would be to guarantee the first mortgage note. If the investor's position took the form of a partnership interest, the first mortgagee might be similarly comforted by a contingent commitment from the investor to respond to partnership calls for additional equity in the event of cost overruns or other needs.

All of these techniques have the same general purpose of achieving the benefits of leverage at reduced cost by using the investor's funds (as in a second mortgage loan) or credit (as in a "put" or guarantee) to lower the risk of loss to the construction lender and (as a result) the cost of borrowing.

One problem with labeling is that functional equivalences may be treated differently under the prudence standard (as illustrated in Chapter 3). While second mortgages are labeled suspect as involving less than prime security and a guarantee may be viewed as a form of leverage, which, as noted previously, is highly suspect as an investment tool for fiduciaries,[32] a take-out commitment for the first mortgage is simply not covered by the Restatement, and for that reason, not presumptively imprudent. While it may seem rather silly to suggest that a court couldn't delve sufficiently beneath the surface of the take-out to recognize its leveraging features, the point is that labels often become a substitute for analysis. The legal list approach that once prevailed so widely in American trust law (and was not repealed in New York until 1970) illustrates the point on a grander scale.[33]

The true nature of a second mortgage position depends upon a range of factors, including the size of the first mortgage relative to appraised value and its debt service demands, the equity supporting the second mortgage, the extent to which the obligor (the partnership or developer as general partner) is liable on the second mortgage, and the credit standing of that obligation.

Another point should be made. Under traditional notions of prudence, investments in partnerships are improper.[34] This illustrates the fallacy of labeling at its most piquant. The investor's decision to provide (i) all of the funds necessary to a development project, (ii) some of the funds, with the balance coming from a commercial lender, or (iii) none of the funds, with a take-out, guarantee, or partnership call agreement providing the needed cushion for the commercial lender depends critically on such questions as how the remainder of the investor's portfolio is then deployed, the after-tax effects of these different approaches, and the interest rate environment at the time. The risk of leverage to the investor turns on whether the commercial lender has access to the investor's credit to cover a loss in excess of the value (in a distress sale, to be sure) of the property, as would be the case in a guarantee or take-out, or does not have such access, as would typically be the case if the investor was a limited partner with no call obligation or the commercial loan was made on a nonrecourse basis.

Similarly, the wisdom of investing as a partner depends critically on whether it is done as a limited partner, in which case the status is very much akin to that of a stockholder in terms of being shielded from liability for debts of the enterprise, or as a general partner, where exposure is unlimited, not only for the general partner's own acts and those of the enterprise but for the acts of other general partners as well.

This simple analysis, and the striking differences in risk exposure that turn on the circumstances of each case, go unrecognized by the blanket prohibitions against leveraged or partnership investments often found in traditional interpretations of the prudence doctrine.[35]

Real estate provides a particularly good example of how important tax effects can be in assessing the true risk-adjusted return expectations of a particular investment. For the fiduciary of tax-exempt funds, the risk of incurring an unnecessary tax on income derived, for example, from "debt-financed property" or a "trade or business" is often present in real estate investing. A more subtle but no less real "tax" on the returns of the tax-exempt fund occurs when it makes an investment whose returns include tax benefits of no use to the fund. Prudence requires an understanding of these risks and either their avoidance through careful structuring or an explicit reckoning of the after-tax returns in relation to comparable investments promising tax-free returns.

A detailed analysis of tax issues would be out of place in this study, but an example or two may help to make the general point more clearly. If a tax-exempt fund were to invest as a limited partner in a partnership organized to acquire improved real estate, any mortgage on that real estate, whether securing recourse or nonrecourse debt of the partnership, would result in the fund's investment being treated as "debt-financed property" under the Internal Revenue Code and a portion of the income earned on that investment being subject to tax at corporate rates. If the investment vehicle used were a corporation, no tax on equity returns to the tax-exempt fund would be assessed, but the corporation would itself be taxed, unlike the partnership, which is a "pass-through" vehicle not subject to taxation. The corporate tax would have the effect of an indirect levy on the fund's equity in the corporation. The desired leverage could be accomplished without a direct or indirect tax to the fund, however, by structuring the fund's investment in the partnership as a second mortgage. Of course, this change would alter the relationship between the fund and the other partners, perhaps in ways that were unacceptable. These matters would have to be negotiated. The point is simply that tax effects are of major significance, requiring expertise and some creativity to address in economically efficient ways for all concerned.

Depreciation and other tax deductions illustrate the same point. Tax-exempt investors, deriving no benefit from tax deductions, should avoid becoming a purchaser of them. Through careful structuring, depreciation and other tax deductions can be "sold" to taxable investors in a position to derive maximum benefits from them. Thus, generally, it is more efficient for taxable investors to own depreciable real estate improvements and tax-exempt investors to lend against them. On the other hand it is inefficient for land, which is not depreciable, to be owned by a taxable entity. If, instead, the land is purchased by a tax-exempt investor and leased to the taxable entity, that entity can deduct fully its lease payments, thereby enabling it to pay more to the tax-exempt investor financing the land than would have been possible had it purchased the land outright with a mortgage loan from the tax-exempt investor (where only the interest would be deductible by the taxable entity).

Competence and the Related Question of Delegation. Because real estate investing is so specialized, it seems obvious that specialized competence must be found to manage it successfully. Finding the requisite expertise isn't easy. It has been estimated that there are over 100 advisers on stock and bond investing for each one offering real estate services to retirement plans.

If the size of one's commitment to real estate is large enough, it becomes feasible to develop an "in-house" capacity. Banks and insurance companies, in acting as trustees, can readily draw on their real estate expertise to manage institutional funds committed to real estate investments under their care. Other institutions, as well, have developed an in-house capacity to make real estate investments. The Ford Foundation did so in the late 1960s and throughout the decade of the 1970s. Columbia University has long managed its own extensive real estate holdings in New York City and used its expertise to make other real estate investments as well.

The advantages of an in-house capacity include lower cost, avoidance of conflicts of interest (since employees can be expected to devote themselves full-time and with undivided loyalty to their employer), ease of supervision, and the flexibility of being able to change employees quickly as circumstances warrant. A variation on this mode of operation would involve supplementing an in-house capacity with outside advisers, whose recommendations were reviewed and approved by the employees.[36] Most real estate advisers, however, prefer to function with discretion, and, indeed, the demands for quick decision-making in real estate provide practical support for this mode of operation when independent advisers are engaged. It comes as no surprise, then, to discover that most real estate expertise offered to institutional funds is available only through real estate investment pools, where the managers exercise full discretion over the deployment of pool assets, within such policies and guidelines as they may have imposed on themselves in their offering materials and the investment contracts defining the relationship between investor and manager. In short, except in the case of particularly large funds, where in-house management is a feasible alternative, to gain competence in real estate investing delegation is generally necessary. In this regard, real estate illustrates another point of restraint and conflict between the traditional trust standard and the realities of modern money management. Because the anti-delegation rule was explored in earlier chapters, it will suffice here simply to observe the necessity for delegation in order to achieve the level of competence in real estate investing that the modern paradigm of prudence requires.

The logic for holding real estate assets in a portfolio is strong. It functions well as a hedge against inflation. In addition, with real estate comprising over half of all the wealth in the United States, its claim to some share of the "market" that should be held to avoid diversifiable risk is clear. Given the economic basis for investing in real estate and the necessity to delegate in order to invest well, the aged notions against delegation should yield. It ought not be necessary, as some lawyers have tried to do in the past,[37] to treat a pooled investment medium such as a mutual fund or REIT as a separate business enterprise, an investment that entails no more of a delegation than investing in IBM. This sort of analysis at best is strained; it fails to deal directly with the problem. Delegation ought to be incorporated in the prudent man standard, as one of the permissible techniques for obtaining the competence necessary to carry out a particular investment strategy. As noted in Chapter 1, this has been done in UMIFA, ERISA, and the Section 4944 regulations.[38] However, these statutory and regulating standards provide little guidance to a fiduciary seeking to address this matter. The important questions of prudence, beyond determining whether to delegate, involve how to make a wise selection, how best to structure the compensation so that the delegee's interests and those of the fund are aligned, how to provide for termination of the arrangement, and what the level of monitoring ought to be.

Venture Capital

"Venture capital" is the term applied to investments in "new and untried enterprises" that are "lacking a stable record of growth," to use the Restatement's description of two sorts of investment situated beyond the limits of prudence, as traditionally conceived. The venture capital industry has mushroomed since the 1969 to 1977 period, when the assets committed to this medium of investment remained static at about $2.5 billion.[39] Today there are estimated to be over 500 firms active in the field managing over $16 billion in assets, of which the largest source is pension funds.[40]

Success stories seem to abound in the venture capital field. However, hard performance data is not readily available.[41] What can be gleaned from reliable sources suggests that the high expectations of venture capital firms are supported by the past experience of some firms, particularly those willing to share their performance with prospective investors and financial intermediaries. However, a note of caution should be sounded here. Because so much of venture capital is privately conducted, beyond the systematic scrutiny of analysts or the investing public, failures in this field are unlikely to be as visible as successes. Reported results are likely to contain a positive bias of uncertain dimension.

Venture capital specialists offer to prospective clients expected returns in the range of 25 to 30 percent per year over the seven- to ten-year maturation cycle typical in venture capital funds. In a study entitled "Venture Capital and Innovation" prepared for the Joint Economic Committee of the Congress,[42] aggregate data for the brief three-year period of 1982 to 1984 were collected. While obviously not representative of any particular firm's experience or even the collective experience of many firms over the full maturation cycle for a fund, the data support the notion that some venture capital firms can do well for their investors. Over the 1982 to 1984 period, this study shows that independent venture capital firms increased the value of their portfolios by 31 percent per year.[43] Using data gathered from its own survey of independent firms, the consulting firm of Cambridge Associates reports that over longer periods average annual returns have been in the range of 15 to 35 percent, with some below 10 percent and others as high as 70 percent.[44] Over shorter periods venture capital can exhibit wide swings above and (of late) below the market. In 1985, for example, two widely followed surrogates for venture capital, T. Rowe Price's New Horizon Fund and Hambrecht and Quist's Technology Index, were significantly outdistanced by the S&P 500.[45]

Critical to the success of those funds that have succeeded (and it should be emphasized, not all funds have succeeded) are two principles drawn from economic literature. Because business failures among the start-up enterprises in which managers of venture capital invest are bound to occur, diversification within a fund becomes essential. Through a spreading of the risk across a good number of new business ventures, the near certainty that some will fail does not preclude a large success for the fund overall. This rationale draws on a second economic truth. Assuming reasonably skilled managers, it is just as certain that some of the start-ups will succeed as it is that some will fail. Those that succeed return entrepreneurial rents to the venture capital fund that typically compensate well for the risks undertaken.

The venture capital market is relatively untouched by arguments supporting the efficient market hypothesis (which as we have seen are under attack even in the case of our highly liquid and heavily traded exchange-listed equities).[46] That market is, and will no doubt remain, inefficient. The rewards available to those possessed of skill, industry, and foresight in this specialized area are generous, as the records demonstrate. In this sense, venture capital is similar to real estate. Because the markets are not publicly scrutinized or traded or subject to legal requirements for disclosure in any way comparable to what the SEC requires for public companies, less skilled and knowledgeable investors cannot readily benefit from the investment decisions of those more skilled and knowledgeable. Indeed, when a successful venture capital investment is made, the cycle typically involves the entry of public investors only upon the issuer's initial public offering, at which point, or soon thereafter, the venture capitalist sells his position to the less skilled and knowledgeable public investors, usually at a high premium over his cost.

As discussed previously, the traditional constrained view of prudence would seem to rule out venture capital on several counts.[47] Despite general agreement on this point among lawyers, over the past twenty years a growing number of fiduciaries subject to the prudence standard (in one form or another) have made investments in venture capital funds. For bank trustees managing pooled personal trust funds, where the standard was most constrained and exposure to surcharge the greatest, the investments were made by the bank in order to compete effectively, so persuasive was the economic evidence that some portion of a portfolio should be allocated to this market. Banks that took this risk did so with the knowledge that they were self-insurers against a likely surcharge if things turned out badly.

Under the modern paradigm of prudence advanced in this study, there would be no labeling of venture capital as presumptively prudent or imprudent. The initial questions to be addressed, as suggested by the factor analysis, would be its place in the portfolio and the risk/reward equation. Other questions of particular importance to venture capital would include (a) the business experience and investment record of those proposing to manage the funds allocated to venture capital—in short, the matter of competence; (b) the extent of delegation involved (is there any review of investment decisions; how long will the delegation last); (c) the compensation scheme; and (d) limitations on withdrawal, change of manager, and sale of interest.

As stressed previously, the key to asset deployment of any kind is having the competence to undertake it. Most fiduciaries seeking to deploy portfolio funds in venture capital do so through venture capital pools, because, typically, the fiduciaries lack the special expertise required, the most capable managers in the field are available only in the pool mode, and the necessary diversification can readily be achieved in this way.[48]

There is, however, another kind of competence that must be exercised before proceeding with a commitment to venture capital. Indeed, it is required in any case of delegation, regardless of the purpose—competence in effecting the contract of delegation itself. For venture capital, this contract.typically takes the form of a limited partnership agreement and, if the managers choose not to function in their capacity as general partners, a management agreement between the partnership and the managers. Much the same structure would apply for a pooled fund dedicated to such specialized endeavors as risk arbitrage, leveraged buyouts, trading in financial or physical commodity futures, and hedging in and among securities, options, and futures.

While under the modern paradigm, delegation is not only tolerated, but encouraged or even compelled, where competence is otherwise lacking, the terms and conditions of delegation, in the particular circumstances that justify it, become all important. In this case a special competence is needed by a fiduciary—a competence not traditionally delegated to others.[49] It requires an understanding of the variables to be negotiated and some judgment about what is important. To illustrate this point, it is useful to discuss briefly some of the more important issues that a fiduciary ought to weigh carefully in defining the terms of delegation to managers of a venture capital fund. The effort is not to be definitive, either in mentioning the whole "laundry list" of important issues or discussing any of them exhaustively. It is simply to illuminate the range and complexity of issues involved in establishing a sound relationship for venture capital investing through delegation.

Bell Cows. The earlier in the life of a venture capital fund that a fiduciary "circles" the investment, the more negotiating leverage he has in shaping the terms of delegation. If he is first, a so-called bell cow,[50] allowing his name to be used by the promoters as a signal to other potential investors that the project looks sound, he achieves maximum leverage. By tagging along toward the end of a successful offering, he foregoes substantial leverage and may be required to take the deal "as is" or not at all. Thus, once again, real world prudence (capturing the benefits of being first) is at odds with prudence seen through the lens of courts and commentary (only when other fiduciaries have regularly done it will its prudence be established).[51]

Managerial Commitment. Because a venture capital fund takes approximately seven to ten years to realize its full potential and is particularly dependent on the quality of management in achieving that fecund state, not only must the investor accept a gestation period, but the managers should remain on the job for that span of time, highly committed to achieving the superior results originally promised. Creating appropriate incentives—often in the form of some combination of sticks and carrots—becomes a rich area for ingenuity and negotiation. Will the managers devote all their time to the fund? If not, how much? Will they agree not to start other funds or engage in other advisory activities until this fund is fully invested? If there are other funds, will this one get first call on deals? Suppose key managers retire, become disabled, or quit? Can compensation be scheduled to assure a keen level of managerial interest throughout the life of the fund?

Compensation. Venture capital funds typically involve a base fee payable currently throughout the life of the fund to cover the managers' salaries and expenses and an incentive fee—calculated as a percentage of total return—to create the high motivation looked for in this field. Arrangements tend to favor the managers or the investors, depending upon how popular venture capital is at the time. In the mid-1970s, very few institutional investors had an appetite for this mode of investment. As a result those institutions willing to invest could demand compensation structures calculated to attract and hold the attention and allegiance of the managers. In the early 1980s, the pendulum swung, institutional money available for venture capital swelled, and as a result compensation arrangements increasingly favored the managers.

What, then, are some of the variables? They include the size of the base and incentive fees and whether the incentive fee should be payable on any return or only on the return in excess of some minimum (the "hurdle rate"). The theory is that the promoters promised an expected return of, say, 25 percent per year with the risk-free rate at 8 percent per year. The investor ought not to pay an incentive fee for performance no better than that which could be achieved at no risk of capital loss through the use of Treasury bills. While hurdle rates were common in the mid-1970s, they all but disappeared in the early 1980s as the market shifted in favor of those selling their skills.

Another idea worth considering is to vary the incentive fee with performance. As the return to investors increases over some hurdle rate, so too does the share allocated to the managers.

Will interim distributions to the managers be made, and, if so, out of only realized or both realized and unrealized appreciation? In either case, to protect the fund against large gains in the early years followed by losses in the later ones, a pay-back mechanism is needed, supported by a good credit.

It is interesting to note that for compensation arrangements typical in venture capital funds used by institutional investors the standards of fairness and prudence imposed on registered investment advisers and investment companies by Congress and the SEC have been utterly ignored. Thus, for registered investment advisers managing the assets of investment companies on an incentive fee basis, the law requires that compensation *increase and decrease* proportionately with investment performance in relation to the investment record of an appropriate index of securities prices.[52] Such symmetry is virtually unknown among venture capital funds offered privately to institutional investors, who by definition are capable of figuring out for themselves what a fair fee is and then negotiating to obtain it. As noted previously, the closest thing to symmetry in the private world of venture capital was the use of hurdle rates in the mid- to late 1970s, before venture capital captured the imagination of so many fiduciaries seeking ways to beat the poorly performing public stock markets.

Fiduciaries are enjoined by the prudence standard—especially its modern paradigm—from entering into a delegation in which the fee is excessive or in other ways unfair to them. Modern theory would suggest the wisdom of evaluating, and even compensating, venture capital managers on the basis of how they perform, not in comparison to the S&P 500 or any other broad-based market index, but in comparison to other managers operating in essentially the same medium, with the same risks and over the same time periods. While such data might be hard to obtain, it would not be impossible and could be highly informative. At this writing, however, there does not appear to be much call for such data by fiduciaries or much use made of it in constructing incentive fee formulas. It is interesting and, indeed, rather puzzling that the earlier mentioned Venture Capital and Innovation Study for the Joint Economic Committee (including the General Accounting Office study and other investigations underpinning it) makes no mention of fees or fee structures at all, even to inform the reader whether the performance numbers are gross or net of the fees.

Conflicts of Interest. Should managers be allowed to co-invest or make follow-on investments, either personally or on behalf of another fund? Should their personal investments be limited to public companies? If co-investing is permitted, should both acquisitions and dispositions be made only at the same time and on the same basis as the fund? What about fund investments in issuers with which the managers have an affiliation or in which they have a prior investment? These are all sticky issues deserving of close attention.

Withdrawals, Transfers, and Terminations. While the right to withdraw might appear to make the delegation less questionable, it is generally undesirable both for the managers and for the other investors to allow withdrawals to occur at any time. If optimum performance typically requires approximately eight years, the fund can be badly served by withdrawals along the way. Transfers pose less difficult issues. Termination of the fund, with a liquidating distribution, is an unusual, and often costly, step to be taken only in extremis. What events, beyond death or resignation of the managers, would meet this test is an issue for negotiation.

These points illustrate the rich complexity of delegation in the venture capital field. Equally complex and yet different are the possible terms of delegation for other forms of investment, such as real estate, risk arbitrage, and commodity and financial futures trading, to mention only a few. The lesson for prudence is that delegation itself requires of the fiduciary a level of competence sufficient to understand the nature of the business, the range of variables, and how best to select among those variables to serve the interests of his trust.

Options and Futures

In *Harvard College v. Amory,* Justice Putnam defined prudence principally by declaring what it could not be. Prudence became the opposite of speculation. As previously discussed, this is the core distinction that emerges from a review of the cases. Rather than develop this notion by reference to the use of investment products, however, the cases following *Harvard College* commenced a process of labeling certain products and techniques as speculative. The "speculator" became known by the tools of his trade. Nowhere is this tendency more pronounced than for options and futures.[53] They are, in a sense, "unproductive assets," in that they have no predictable yield. They may be viewed as "wasting assets." As different types of delayed delivery contracts, in which one party (in the case of an option) or both parties (in the case of a future) agree to exchange specified property on a specified date in the future at a price established in the present, they waste away to nothing upon the expiration of the time period. Immediately before expiration, they may, or may not, have value depending upon how the market value for the underlying property has changed over the life of the option or future. Viewed in isolation, they appear to be relatively short-term "bets" on the price movement of particular underlying assets, such as wheat, corn, pork bellies, or more recently, foreign currencies, stocks and stock indices, and various debt obligations. Short-term "bets" smack of gambling. The labels "wasting" and "unproductive" suggest high risk.

Of course, the history of the options and futures markets lends support to the notion that these products deserve the speculative label. Options and futures were well-known in the eighteenth and nineteenth centuries, both here and in England, under the term "time operations," which embraced all transactions made without possession of the underlying security, all agreements to buy or sell securities at a future date, and all options to do the same. Viewed as a pernicious form of gambling, "time operations" were declared illegal in England in 1737 and in New York in 1812. Although the English law lasted until 1860 and the New York one until 1858, both were much honored in the breach because time operations were, in fact, important aspects of early securities trading. These questionable origins, however, have lingered in the collective memory of the marketplace.[54]

It was not until 1973 that securities exchanges began to trade options on individual stocks. Before then options had been traded in the over-the-counter market, but they were not standardized, nor was there an insurance system in place to give comfort that the writers of puts and calls could honor their obligations. In part because of these substantive factors and in part because of the long shadow cast by the Treatise and the Restatement, these markets were, in fact, almost exclusively the domain of the professional trader and others acting for their own accounts rather than as fiduciaries.

In the case of futures,[55] trading on organized exchanges has existed since the

1860s. The exchanges developed standardized contracts and clearinghouses for verification, margining, and providing clearing funds to assure performance. From the outset, the economic purposes served by futures were risk transfer and price identification.

For the grower of wheat, the futures market in his product became important both to identify in advance the price at which he could expect to sell his crop and, if he chose, to assure a sale at that price by writing a fixed-price contract for future delivery of a product he did not then have to sell—in other words, selling short. In so doing, the wheat grower was said to be "hedging." The price of wheat tended to vary over time. The grower was willing to give up the additional profit from a possible rise in the price of wheat to avoid a loss should the price decline. The other party to the grower's futures contract might be another hedger. For example, a bread producer, equally risk-adverse, might seek to fix the price of flour for the coming year, in order to set his other variable costs and establish a price for his finished product. Alternatively, the other party might want the risk that the wheat producer is seeking to avoid, because of the potential for profit should he gauge accurately the direction in which the price of wheat would move. Those seeking profits in the futures market came to be known as "speculators."

In the world of futures, the labels were preaffixed. Since those subject to the prudent man standard were neither growers nor users of commodities, they would automatically be characterized as "speculators" were they to enter the futures markets. However appropriate as a means of describing non-hedgers in the futures markets, this term, without more, put futures trading beyond the limits of a constrained prudent man rule.

Other terminology used in the futures markets compounds the problem. The futures exchange clearinghouses require investors to post initial and variation "margins." The level of initial margin, which is in the nature of a good-faith deposit assuring performance, varies depending upon whether the position to be margined is viewed by the Commodity Futures Trading Commission (CFTC) as "hedged" or "speculative." Of course, as noted in the Restatement, "trading on margin" was something prudent investors did not do. "Margin" in the securities markets refers to the investor's down payment for the purchase of a stock, with the balance of the purchase price being loaned by the broker or other lender to consummate the transaction. No credit is extended when initial margin is posted to open a futures position. However, there is leverage, often a large amount of it. Thus, for example, an initial margin of $3,000 for a hedging account and $6,000 for a speculative one will suffice to purchase or sell a $100,000 contract in the S&P 500 stock index.[56]

Given this history, it is not surprising that options and futures came to be viewed as essentially imprudent per se. However, over the past decade there have been vast changes in these markets and in the general understanding of how they can be used by institutional investors to limit and manage risk. It is, therefore, a tribute to the power and longevity of the Treatise's influence that the use of options and futures is still, today, considered either precluded or of questionable legality under the prudent man rule by some 35 percent of those institutions responding to the questionnaire that is part of this study (Questionnaire).[57]

In the following discussion, techniques for using options and futures are examined to show how harmful to modern portfolio management the label "speculative" can be when affixed to these products. Specifically, the examples seek to prove that what may appear to be "imprudent" in isolation can be prudent when properly understood and considered in the context of the overall portfolio. Taking the analysis a step further, through the possible uses of these products it will be shown that attempting to define prudence as the absence of speculation is at best mischievous and, at worst, could condemn the fiduciary to marketplace imprudence.

Hedging Debt Securities. A fiduciary with long-term bonds might sell interest rate futures contracts as an offset against the effect of expected increases in interest rates. Such a step would be particularly desirable to stabilize the effective return on those bonds, if it were likely that they might have to be sold over, say, the next two years to generate cash flow. While giving up any increase in bond value from a reduction in interest rates over the next two years, the fiduciary would have protected his portfolio against decreases in bond value should rates increase.

Similarly, a fiduciary with short-term bonds might purchase interest rate futures contracts as a hedge against an expected reduction in interest rates, instead of switching immediately to longer term bonds. As the short-term bonds matured, the long futures position could be closed out as the longer term bonds were acquired.

Many observers have analogized these strategies to the purchase of insurance, with the premium being the cost of the derivative instrument, the asset insured being the present value of the debt held or to be acquired, and the term of insurance being the duration of the derivative instrument.

There are, to be sure, transaction costs associated with futures positions. Additionally, there are risks, whether the futures are being used to hedge debt securities or for other purposes discussed in the following sections. The soundness of using futures depends upon their value to the fund measured against the costs and risks involved. It is in establishing this equation that the test of prudence should be sought. In the case of futures used to hedge debt securities, of course, the techniques are intended to *reduce* the overall risk of the portfolio, not increase it.

This is not the place to dwell at length on the risks of using futures. It may be helpful, however, to mention the principal ones. Basis risk exists because the correlation between changes in prices of futures contracts and of the securities being hedged is only approximate.[58] It is influenced by a range of factors, including variations in market demand for futures and for debt securities and differences between the financial instruments being hedged and the instruments underlying the standard futures contracts available in the marketplace.

Another risk arises out of the high degree of leverage resulting from the low-margin deposits required. The futures exchanges limit the amount of fluctuation permitted in futures contract prices in a single trading day. Once that daily limit is reached, no more trades may be made on that day at a price beyond the limit. One result of the limit rule is to moderate price movements. Another result, however, may be to block the liquidation of an unfavorable position. Indeed, futures contract prices have occasionally moved to the daily limit for several consecutive trading days with little or no trading, thereby preventing prompt liquidation of futures positions, with consequent loss. Of course, assuming a reasonably good correlation, the use of interest rate futures to hedge portfolio securities in such a volatile setting should result in offsetting increases in the value of those portfolio securities.

On the positive side, studies show that the financial futures and options markets exhibit better trading efficiency than the cash markets.[59] Because contracts in these markets normally do not involve delivery of the underlying security (in the case of stock index futures and options on stock indices settlements *must* be in cash), the significant costs of physical delivery are eliminated. In addition, the futures and options markets tend to be highly liquid, assuring fast completion of transactions.

Hedging Equity Securities. Stock index options or futures can be used in ways similar to interest rate futures to anticipate changes in the underlying equity markets. For example, a fiduciary anticipating receipt of additional funds for management over the next year and worried that the market may be about to commence a significant advance could purchase a call option on the stocks he planned to buy or simply purchase a call option on a stock index or open a long position on a stock index future, thereby hedging, to the extent of the correlation, the future investment of those funds. Alternatively, the fiduciary might borrow in anticipation of receipt of the additional funds and purchase the underlying equities directly. This approach would likely be more cumbersome and costly.

If the fiduciary anticipates having to sell equities over the next year to meet funding requirements and foresees a market decline, he can protect against that possibility by buying put options on the stocks he plans to sell or a put option on a stock index or by opening a short position on a stock index future. Low transaction costs, speed, and avoidance of market impact may make this a preferable strategy than simply selling the equities, although that is obviously another way to achieve the same goal.

These same techniques can be used to establish, maintain, and alter a portfolio balance between debt, equity, and cash equivalents and even among different types of debt or equity. They can be used as more efficient ways of timing the market. For these uses it strains the term to call them "hedges."[60] They are techniques for adjusting or managing risk. Risk management (as can be seen from the review of economic teaching in Appendix A) ought to be the major goal of a fiduciary. If risk management involves the balancing and rebalancing of a portfolio in light of anticipated changes in the debt and equity markets, and it surely does, then a fiduciary is plainly permitted, perhaps expected, and in time may be compelled by the modern paradigm of prudence, to understand the alternative ways of managing risk that are available to him, evaluate them, and make reasoned selections to carry out his judgments.

Equivalences. With the advent of the financial futures and options markets, the fiduciary now can easily hedge a portfolio of securities against interest rate volatility or the systemic risk of the equity markets. Not to do so exposes the portfolio to unnecessary risk, not unlike the risk exposure incurred by the pure "speculator" in a futures market. Yet none would suggest that the fiduciary, as a matter of prudence, ought to maintain such hedges at all times. But neither should prudence preclude the use of financial futures or options as an alternative means of capturing the expected returns (and exposure to risk) of the debt or equity markets.

Consider, for example, the technique of using Treasury bills and stock options in combination to achieve the leverage feature of options with the safety of a riskless asset. Used in a ratio of 90:10, this strategy gives the investor significant opportunity for profit if the price of the underlying equities selected for the purchase of call options (or the market if index options are used)'rises while avoiding the substantial losses that would result from a broad-based downturn in the equity markets, if a full commitment to equities had been made.[61]

Alternatively, one might use stock index futures as a substitute for a stock index fund. The leverage available from the stock index futures (initial margin of $6,000 controlling a contract worth $100,000 of the S&P 500) would enable the fund's assets to be invested in Treasury bills. Whether this technique for achieving full market exposure to the S&P 500 is preferable to an index fund would depend on many factors, including, for example, the relationship between returns on the Treasury bills and dividend returns on an index fund, the respective transaction costs involved (including, in particular, the aggregate cost of rolling over the futures position every one to three months), and the matter of liquidity.

Option Writing. Call options can be written (i.e., sold) against specific stocks held in the portfolio. Similarly, put options can be written against portfolio cash. If the purchase of call and put options is analogous to buying insurance, then option writing is analogous to selling a form of insurance to others. For a premium, the call writer agrees to sell stock at a fixed price. If the stock rises above the exercise price, the writer has the stock called away, with the result that he loses the benefit of the rise in price, cushioned, however, by the premium. If the stock falls below the exercise price, of course, the option lapses, with the premium serving as an offset to the decrease in the stock's value. The put option functions in a similar way. These strategies tend to stabilize portfolio returns, trading upside potential for the reality of premium income. The products themselves, viewed in isolation, would in the past have been labelled speculative and therefore imprudent. When examined in the context of the portfolio overall, they are seen as tools to reduce volatility.[62]

Arbitrage. As noted previously, a fiduciary seeking to invest in the S&P 500 can either buy an S&P 500 index fund or place the funds in cash equivalents and buy S&P 500 stock index futures contracts, using the cash equivalents as initial margin. Returns from these strategies should be similar. Thus, the futures should sell at a premium to the index equal to the yield on cash equivalents less the dividend yield on the S&P 500 over the life of the futures contract. In fact, the S&P 500 futures contract has been substantially underpriced for extended periods of time.[63] When this phenomenon occurs, a fiduciary might reasonably move from holding the index fund to holding the futures contract, if analysis of transaction costs indicated that a significantly enhanced *net* return (e.g., at least 2 percent) could be earned by the switch.

Under the modern paradigm of prudence, what factors should the fiduciary consider? Investment risks would involve the amount of dividends foregone compared with the amount of interest earned on the cash equivalents. While interest rate risk can be handled by matching the cash equivalent maturities to the expiration of the futures contract, the marking to market process (in a down market) could reduce the yield because variation margin earns no return. Another risk is the actual price realized on the sale of the index fund, which may vary from what is expected. Careful understanding, evaluation, and mitigation (where possible) of these risks is what prudence demands. While "arbitrage" may appear to be outside the circle of prudence as drawn by the Treatise and the Restatement, this strategy, if properly understood, ought to be accepted for what it is—a means of achieving higher expected return at the same risk. While certainly not compelled for the prudent fiduciary, it is a strategy appropriate for study and possible implementation once the risks and rewards have been thoroughly evaluated.

Other forms of arbitrage combining very low risk with incremental returns in the range of 2 to 3 percent per year can be effected through the use of stock options. Looked at as separate steps, in isolation, traditional notions of prudence would surely be violated. Once the strategy is understood, however, the separate steps involved become acceptable as part of an appropriate strategy to add modest incremental income at low risk.

Consider, for example, a reverse conversion.[64] This is a covered arbitrage strategy using optionable stock held in a portfolio and intended to increase short-term income without interfering with the longer term management of the portfolio. It entails (a) the sale of shares of an optionable stock and, concurrently, the purchase of a call option and sale of a put option on the same stock, having identical expiration dates (that may range from one to six months) and identical exercise prices (which would be essentially the same as the price at which the stock was sold), (b) the investment of all net proceeds (i.e., the stock sale proceeds plus the premium for the put less the cost of the call and the transaction costs) in cash equivalents, and (c) the repurchase of the stock at the end of the option period, either through exercise of the call (if the price of the stock had risen) or acceptance of the put (if the price of the stock had fallen). Although the strategy involves a sale of stock, the put and call options together constitute a synthetic substitute, so that the portfolio remains exposed to the opportunity for gain and risk of loss associated with the stock. Excluded, however, are dividends and voting rights. The strategy would only make sense when the interest earned from the net proceeds invested in cash equivalents exceeds by, say, 2 or 3 percent per year, the sum of any trading loss in reacquiring the stock, all dividends foregone, and other fees and expenses of executing the strategy.

Another short-term arbitrage strategy could employ forward conversions to capture the benefits offered to shareholders of issuers encouraging the reinvestment of dividends in the issuer's stock by offering that stock at a significant discount from market. A fiduciary could temporarily acquire stock for the purpose of effecting this arbitrage without exposure to the risks of owning it by, concurrently with its purchase, selling a call option and buying a put option on the same stock, having identical expiration dates, and identical exercise prices. To accomplish this strategy, the shares purchased through the dividend reinvestment must be sold short over the one-to-five day "smoothing" period during which the market price for reinvestment of dividends is fixed by the issuer. The objective is to sell the shares at the same market price as that which applied to their purchase. If successful, the profit will equal the discount before expenses.

These strategies and others like them are complicated. They involve risks of various sorts. Prudence requires a thorough understanding of how the transactions work, what is required to make them worth undertaking, what the risks are, and how to address them so that they become tolerable in light of the prospects for return. These strategies are designed for incremental returns on a portfolio already deployed. They involve no leverage. Under a modern paradigm of prudence, they could be acceptable tools for adding to return if the competence necessary to evaluate and use them was demonstrable on the record and the costs of gaining that competence were fully accounted for in the risk/reward analysis.

Trading in Futures. Under the modern paradigm of prudence, which breaks the absolute linkage between speculation and imprudence, "speculative" trading of a diversified portfolio of futures and forward contracts, including, for example, currencies, money market instruments, stock indices, precious and industrial metals, energy products, grains, and other commodities, would not automatically be excluded. Analysis of the opportunities and risks would proceed just as it would for other proposed deployments.

It is useful to look at a hypothetical set of facts, drawn, however, from actual performance records, to give some texture to the analysis a fiduciary might undertake in exploring a commitment to futures and forward contract trading. As in any deployment of assets, demonstrated competence in the particular investment medium is essential. Suppose the fiduciary lacks this expertise himself and so elects to consider investing with others through a commodity futures pool, which typically takes the form of a limited partnership. He finds a manager with a ten-year composite performance record beginning in 1975 of 32 percent per year, compounded. This record, which is net of all fees and commissions, compares favorably with the S&P 500 index for the same period, which showed a compound annual return of 14.9 percent. In considering this record of competence, the fiduciary takes note of the fact that performance results of managers of stocks and bonds are typically reported without deducting management fees (a fact making the standard comparison with the S&P 500 inaccurate). For the five-year period ending in 1984, the pool's compound annual rate of return is 27 percent compared to 16.2 percent for the S&P 500. In only one of the ten years, 1983, was there a loss. Noting that the return in 1975 was 145 percent, the fiduciary inquires about 1973 and 1974, aware that starting dates, when selected by managers, can often conceal as much (or more) than they reveal. In this case, however, the manager welcomes the question. The returns were even higher.

The manager's goal is superior performance while limiting risk and offering diversification from investments in securities and real estate. The trading method uses technical trend analysis and money management principles that have been applied continuously throughout the ten-year period. The manager attributes his success principally to three factors: First, the trading method uses complex technical systems to vigorously analyze individual markets and assess overall risk while employing leverage conservatively. Second, there is a high degree of liquidity in the futures markets traded by the manager compared to the cash stock and bond markets, a significant factor for technical trading. For example, the total dollar value of trading in currencies is estimated to be some 50 to 100 times the dollar volume of trading in all shares on the New York Stock Exchange, and the dollar volume of trading in bond, bill, and stock index futures substantially exceeds the dollar volume of trading in the respective cash markets. Third, many other participants in the futures markets are not seeking profits from futures trading but rather are hedging their physical inventories or future requirements—in effect seeking a form of price insurance that professional traders provide when the circumstances are considered by them to be attractive. Many others are unsophisticated. The hedging function, of course, has no strong analog in the securities markets.

The manager believes, on the basis of experience, that profit potential does not depend on favorable general economic conditions, but is to some extent correlated with volatility. He emphasizes the diversification of the firm's trading. Currently, he monitors about fifty and trades thirty-five separate futures markets. He points out that the firm enjoys substantial interest income, due to the fact that, unlike margin accounts for securities trading, commodity exchanges and brokers permit trading accounts to use interest-bearing obligations such as Treasury bills, rather than cash, as initial margin. Approximately 85 to 90 percent of the pool's assets are invested in these obligations at all times. Only 15 to 30 percent of the pool's assets are deposited on margin at any time. The manager has over $200 million under management, with an additional $20 million of his own funds included in the pool. His staff numbers thirty, with thirteen experienced senior-level professionals to constantly monitor the pool's positions. Over $5 million has been spent on research to develop the programs.

Of course, there are risks. Futures trading is volatile. Trading positions are highly leveraged and small price movements can cause an immediate and substantial loss to the investor. In addition, daily limits imposed by commodity exchanges can cause illiquidity, if high volatility moves the daily limit for several consecutive days with little or no trading, a situation that has been known to occur in some markets. In addition, the fiduciary notes that he cannot liquidate his investment in the pool whenever he chooses. Redemptions are permitted only at the end of a month on fifteen days' notice. There is no market for the limited partnership interests and transfers can be made only with the manager's consent.

Depending on the tolerance of his fund for risk, the composition of the balance of the fund, his minimum cash flow needs, and his willingness to sustain loss, the fiduciary might reasonably proceed with an investment of a limited portion of the portfolio on the basis of this analysis. However, aware of the possibility that the manager's performance might be just plain luck,[65] he looks for data on overall performance by commodity pool operators, as they are somewhat flamboyantly known in the trade. Statistics on the eighty-four public funds active during the nine-year period from 1975 through 1983 have recently been compiled by Scott H. Irwin and B. Wade Brorsen.[66] Overall, 65 percent of the funds had negative returns for the period and 35 percent were positive. If an investor randomly selected a fund, the probability of selecting a profitable one was slightly better than one chance in three. However, the aggregate compound annual return for all funds averaged 15.2 percent,[67] meaning that a few of the funds were very profitable. Indeed, if the four most profitable funds were excluded from the sample, aggregate compound annual returns for the remaining eighty funds averaged −14.3 percent. The standard deviation of the funds' performance averaged 25.1 percent.

In analyzing these results relative to those of the manager he is considering, the fiduciary would want to see if the differences could be explained in terms other than luck. In examining the funds, he discovers that none were as broadly diversified across different futures markets as the manager's pool; furthermore, the four best performing public funds of the eighty-four included in the sample were significantly more diversified than the remainder.

Another salient fact that turned up in the Irwin and Brorsen study relates to the annual operating costs of public futures funds. As a percentage of average annual equity, commission costs for twenty funds averaged 10.7 percent, with a range of 6 to 27.8 percent. Management, incentive, and administrative costs averaged 8.5 percent of average annual equity with a range of 0.7 to 23.8 percent. Thus, total annual operating costs averaged 19.2 percent.

Analysis of these numbers reveals that the high levels of commission costs were primarily due to the public funds' paying close to retail commission rates, often to affiliates. In contrast, the private fund manager under consideration is unaffiliated with any futures broker, negotiates hard for reduced rates, and has succeeded in keeping them in the range of 2 to 8 percent per year of average annual equity. While his management, incentive, and administration fees were high, in the range of 10 percent of average annual equity, over 5 percent was attributable to incentive fees (at the rate of 20 percent of new profit) payable only on account of the superior performance achieved.

The most important finding of the Irwin and Brorsen study, at least for the prudent man rule, relates to the potential role of futures funds in a portfolio of financial assets. Over the nine-year period of the study, it was found that by adding public futures funds to a portfolio otherwise composed of Treasury bills, Treasury bonds, and stocks, the portfolio risk for the same expected return was reduced by 18 percent at the lower end of the efficient frontier to 30 percent at the higher end. The beneficial portfolio effect of public funds was due to the correlation between high rates of inflation and public futures funds, bills, bonds, and stocks. Thus, while the public futures funds had the largest standard deviation of returns (21.2 percent) compared with 14.9 percent for stocks, 15.6 percent for bonds, and 3.3 percent for bills, those funds were positively correlated with inflation and negatively correlated with the other three investments, all of which were negatively correlated with inflation. Thus, adding public futures funds to the portfolio smoothed real return variation by offsetting the fluctuation of returns on bills, bonds, and stocks.

These findings provide a splendid example of how investment products and techniques that in isolation appear to carry undue risk can be deployed in a portfolio to reduce overall risk.

The matter of competence, generally a crucial factor in the modern paradigm of prudence, is especially important in the more esoteric markets for derivative securities, such as futures and options. Not only must the fiduciary or his delegate understand the nature of the transactions in which he proposes to engage and their inherent risks, but he must understand too the risks posed by those with whom he must deal. For example, although regulations of the CFTC and the futures exchanges are intended to eliminate the credit risk of doing business with futures commission merchants, the recent failure of Volume Investors Corporation revealed a gap in this protection. Volume Investors was a clearing member firm on COMEX and other exchanges. It was forced to default on large margin calls by the COMEX Clearing Association in March 1985 when a two-day gold price surge caused three of its customers holding large short positions to default on Volume's margin calls to them. Volume went into receivership and the funds of about 100 nondefaulting customers, in segregated accounts with the firm, went to cover Volume's obligations to the COMEX Clearing Association.

In this way many investors learned for the first time that the clearing association's guarantee only covered the other side of transactions in which Volume and its customers were engaged (some $9 million of such losses were made good by the association) and that prudence required an assessment of the financial strength not only of the futures commission merchant itself but of its other customers.[68] This risk, although not widely understood, could upon due inquiry have been discovered by a careful investor. For fiduciaries the lesson of Volume Investors is simply that one must strive to understand the risks—all of them—that surround a particular investment strategy and then find ways to address them. Of course, the kind of risk exposed in the Volume Investors case is probably not priced in the market. Ways should be found to eliminate that sort of risk because one is not compensated for undertaking it.[69]

Repurchase Agreements

Repurchase agreements (repos) constitute the contractual framework by which short-term funds are borrowed or loaned, with the loans being secured by U.S. government securities or other types of money market instruments. The lender "purchases" the securities under an agreement obligating him to resell them to the "borrower," who is obligated to repurchase them, either on a fixed date or at any time at the option of either party. The repurchase price is fixed above the purchase price, the spread representing compensation for the use of the funds.

The Board of Governors of the Federal Reserve System (FRB) has used repos since 1917 to effect short-term changes in the level of bank reserves. With the advent of high real rates of interest and increasingly sophisticated cash management techniques, repos have grown in use by all manner of money market participants. Because the length of the agreement is negotiable, repos can be tailored to achieve incremental returns on temporarily idle cash while still assuring that cash flow needs will be met.

A number of financial reverses over the past several years have involved repos, tending to give them a bad name. Much could be written about these events. For the purposes of this study, two of these financial reverses are briefly discussed to illustrate the obvious but frequently forgotten point that a fiduciary should not undertake *any* investment strategy, however commonplace or straightforward, unless he or his chosen delegates have the competence necessary to understand and use that strategy well. To proceed without the requisite competence is to act imprudently.

The New York State Dormitory Authority. When Lombard-Wall, Inc., a dealer in government securities, filed for protection from its creditors under Chapter 11 of the Federal Bankruptcy Code (Bankruptcy Code) in August 1982, the New York State Dormitory Authority (Authority) had some $305 million, or 60 percent of its portfolio, invested with that firm. With $55 million of its claims unsecured, the Authority was Lombard-Wall's largest unsecured creditor.

The Authority invested virtually all of its idle cash under repos with Lombard-Wall. Since it was "purchasing" U.S. government securities, it apparently considered the transactions to be as riskless as if it were purchasing those securities with no strings attached. In its report on the $17.5 million loss ultimately realized by the Authority in its repo transactions with Lombard-Wall, the New York Senate Committee on Investigations and Taxation reached the blunt conclusion that the employees responsible for the investments were "incompetent."[70] They apparently failed to appreciate the nature of a repo transaction, which in various important ways differs from the purchase of, for example, Treasury bills.

Before the ruling by Judge Ryan of the Bankruptcy Court for the Southern District of New York that repos were to be treated as "secured lending transactions" under the Bankruptcy Code,[71] some parties to these transactions operated under the assumption that they constituted true sales of the underlying government securities, so that the "purchaser" would own those securities free and clear of any possible claim by the seller or its trustee in bankruptcy. Most of those operating on the "sale" assumption were nonetheless aware of the possibility that the transaction might be viewed as a secured loan, in which event the government securities would not have been sold but only pledged to secure the loan. They would remain the property of the pledgor (Lombard-Wall in this case), subject to order of a bankruptcy judge in the event of the pledgor's bankruptcy. Against this possibility, most investors made sure that they, or their agents, had physical possession of the government securities so that, if the "sale" theory were rejected, at least they would be in the posture of a secured creditor. In addition, they took care to check the creditworthiness of the other party to the repo before doing business with him, to monitor the other party's financial standing during the life of the repo, and to assure that marks to market were made to keep the value of the government securities in balance with the funds loaned.

The Authority, however, took none of these precautions, apparently because the employees responsible had no comprehension of the transactions in which they were engaged. Thus, for example, the government securities "purchased" by the Authority were permitted to be held by Lombard-Wall's custodian. Even if the employees could not be faulted for assuming the sale theory to be valid, they violated the most basic standard of prudence in failing to assure safe custody of the Authority's assets either in their hands or the hands of custodians acting for the Authority. When Lombard-Wall went bankrupt, the securities in question were pooled for the benefit of *all* its creditors.

In addition, the Authority employees permitted the value of the government securities to be reported at par rather than market value. The result of this error in comprehending the nature of a repo was to eliminate the benefits intended to be provided by the obligation to "mark to market." As bond values declined, the market value (but not the par value) of the collateral declined below the level necessary to provide adequate coverage for the loan. No marks to market were made because the reports never showed the gap between market and par. Finally, a substantial portion of the investments were made without any written agreement whatsoever.

The Authority employees are not, strictly speaking, subject to the prudent man rule. Had they been, their failure to comprehend the nature of the repo transactions in which they were engaged would unquestionably constitute imprudence, under the modern paradigm as well as under older interpretations of the rule.

The New York State School Districts and Municipalities. When in May 1984 the Lion Capital Group and RTD Securities, Inc., two government securities trading firms, filed for protection from creditors under the Bankruptcy Code, some seventy-three New York State school districts and municipalities had approximately $95 million in jeopardy with these firms under repos. Despite the warning provided by the 1982 failure of Lombard-Wall and the Authority's loss of $17.5 million, the school districts and municipalities, with few exceptions, invested in a manner strikingly similar to the Authority. Thus, they did not take delivery of the government securities "sold" to them. Instead, they accepted assurances from Lion Capital that the securities were being held for them by Bradford Trust Company. Bradford Trust, it turns out, denied holding the securities for the investors, claiming instead that it holds them as collateral for business loans made to Lion Capital.[72]

It is worth mentioning that not all agencies of state and local government that engaged in repos did so without comprehending what they were about. The New York City Housing Development Corporation, with $130 million in repos with Lombard-Wall at the time of its failure, recovered its entire investment in timely fashion, apparently due to well-drawn written agreements under which a perfected security interest in the government securities was achieved.[73]

The lesson here is a simple one that nevertheless bears frequent repetition, particularly as the tools for management of risk grow in number and complexity. In whatever medium the fiduciary selects to deploy funds, he must have, or retain others who have, the demonstrable competence to comprehend and work within that medium.

As in the case of security lending, the Federal Financial Institutions Examination Council in 1985 issued policy guidelines for engaging in repos, intended to help depository institutions avoid the adverse consequences of a possible bankruptcy by the counterparties to these transactions.[74] Coming too late to help the Authority or the other New York agencies that suffered repo losses, the guidelines are a good example of what prudence would expect of one about to embark on an investment program involving this product.

First Alabama Bank of Montgomery, N.A. v. Martin *and* Chase v. Pevear *Revisited*

This section revisits two recent cases strongly criticized in Chapter 1 and Appendix B for using the constrained prudent man rule—*First Alabama Bank of Montgomery, N.A. v. Martin*[75] and *Chase v. Pevear*[76]—in order to suggest how the facts of those cases might have been analyzed by a court applying a process-based paradigm.

The object of this exercise is not literally to "decide" those cases; that would be both presumptuous and unsound, given that one must rely on the necessarily incomplete and selective rendition of the facts provided in the reported decisions. Instead, taking the facts as given, this section contrasts the questions that a court applying the process paradigm would ask with those actually considered by the courts that decided the cases.

Plaintiffs in the *Martin* case, a class action, were the beneficiaries of almost 1,250 individual trusts invested by defendant trustee, a bank, in two common trust funds. The Supreme Court of Alabama affirmed the trial court's surcharge of the trustee for imprudence in the purchase of debentures issued by six REITs for one of the common trust funds, a bond fund, and of seventeen common stocks for the other, an equity fund. The supreme court also affirmed the lower court's finding that the sale of five other common stocks at the bottom of the market was imprudent even though their purchase was not.

As discussed in more detail in Chapter 1, the court conceived its task as the determination of whether each one of the challenged investments was, in isolation, a proper trust investment. In reaching its decision that the bank "failed to fulfill its primary responsibility, which was to provide for the safety of the trust's principal,"[77] the court cited with approval a brief article that appeared in *Trusts and Estates,* the trust law practitioners' magazine, in 1952:

> The difference between speculation and investment is well described by Dr. Headley.... [O]ne who buys common stocks with the idea of selling them on the market for higher prices is speculating. One who is making a prudent investment examines the stocks' intrinsic values and purchases them for a long-term investment.[78]

However, nothing appears in the reported facts to suggest that the bank had purchased the stocks as "short-term" investments. Instead, the trust investment officer who made the investments in 1971 and 1972 testified that his philosophy at the time was to seek out undervalued securities rather than the then extremely high-priced "favorite 50" and to buy stock "in the growth cycle of a company and not after it has matured."[79] The court considered the lower court's finding of imprudence to be "strengthen[ed]" by the officer's testimony that he sought out undervalued securities.[80]

How would the analysis have differed if the Alabama court had employed the process paradigm? At a minimum, the court would have asked the following questions:

1. What role were the investments intended to play in the overall portfolio? Did they contribute to diversification by industry, location, risk, and sensitivity to inflation? What did the total portfolio contain, and what was the performance of the overall portfolio in relation to the market?

2. What were the portfolio's requirements for return, both in the form of regular income and long-term growth of principal, and its tolerance for volatility?

3. What opportunities for gain and risks of loss did the investments present, and were those opportunities and risks consistent with the portfolio characteristics described in response to point 2 above?

4. How sound was the process that led to the investment? Did the trustee understand the opportunities and risks involved and systematically analyze them in light of the needs of the whole portfolio? Were the trustee's tools for measuring risk and return reasonable in light of the state of knowledge about investments at the time?

It is one measure of the extent of difference between the Alabama court's definition of prudence and the modern paradigm's that the reported decision in *Martin* fails to provide most of the facts that would be necessary to answer these questions. The court nowhere indicates the total size of the two common trust funds, the nature of the other investments in the funds, their overall performance, or that of the market. It is possible to deduce from the court's statement that the six REIT debentures comprised 23 percent of the bond fund when purchased, that the total amount of that fund at the time was about $11.5 million.[81] The debentures declined 47 percent in value, resulting in a loss (and a surcharge) of $1,226,798. In the case of the stocks, the only numerical information provided is the total surcharge for losses: $1,426,354.88.

Instead of considering the needs of the types of trusts involved and then weighing the soundness of the trustee's investment philosophy in light of those needs, the court occupied itself with determining whether each of the challenged investments was "safe." While very early in the opinion the court describes testimony as to overall portfolio philosophy ("the essential investment purpose of the bond fund was to produce income and the essential investment purposes of the equity fund were the appreciation of equity and the production of income"),[82] that centrally important testimony is never referred to again. Nor did the court consider the importance to the remaindermen of attempting to preserve the real value of the principal against erosion by inflation. And instead of analyzing the investments on their merits, the court disapproved each one because it failed some universal litmus test of safety. In the case of the REIT debentures, the court relied in part on the testimony of the plaintiff's expert witness, who cited a multi-factor test for the safety of debt investments and opined that all six REITs failed the test because they had not existed for the seven- to ten-year period necessary for analyzing a firm's record under the test.[83] In the case of the stocks, the court looked to similar litmus tests such as S&P ratings or a seven-factor test that testimony revealed would have branded twenty-five of the thirty stocks in the Dow Jones industrial average as unsafe.[84] A process-based analysis, on the other hand, would uphold the investments if their risk/return characteristics were reasonable when measured against other available investments and the needs of the portfolio.

As discussed in Chapter 1, the *Chase v. Pevear*[85] decision, written by Justice Braucher of the Massachusetts Supreme Judicial Court, displays a far more sophisticated analysis of investment prudence than does the *Martin* case. In reviewing the lower court's surcharge of the trustee of a large personal trust for about $95,000 in investment losses, Justice Braucher specifically rejected the notion of identifying prudent investments by litmus tests such as S&P ratings, minimum periods of "seasoning," or certain lines of business.[86] Unfortunately, the court's principal guidepost in affirming the surcharge as to some investments and reversing it as to others appears to have been the equally mechanical test of whether that investment was widely held by other trustees and financial institutions.

As with the *Martin* case, many of the factual elements of prudence analysis under a process standard go completely undiscussed in the court's opinion. The opinion reveals that the entire portfolio dropped in value from $2 million at the end of 1972 to $1.24 million at the end of 1974.[87] Thus, as in the *Martin* case, the *Chase* decision grew out of the market slump of 1973 to 1974. Of the seven challenged investments that produced total losses of about $95,000, four of them (representing less than 4 percent of the entire portfolio) were debentures or common stock of firms in the housing industry. The other three investments were common stock of Penn Central and the Meredith Corporation and debentures of W.T. Grant Company. The opinion does not reveal what percentage those three investments comprised of the overall portfolio.[88] Aside from the mention of some testimony that housing industry investments were considered promising at the time of purchase[89] and of a finding by a master that an investment of 4 percent of the portfolio in the housing industry was not itself imprudent,[90] the opinion reveals no consideration of whether the challenged investments were wise in light of the overall portfolio. There is no discussion of the composition of the rest of the portfolio, the trust's needs for income and growth of principal, or, most important, of the trustee's decision-making process. Further, despite the court's repeated reliance on the number of "financial institutions" and common trust funds that held particular investments, the court never considers why those investments were held by the others, how they meshed with other investments in the other portfolios, and whether those other institutions and funds presented portfolio characteristics and fund objectives similar to those of the particular trust fund at issue.

Under the process standard, the fact that other fiduciaries had made the same or similar investments would not be a central factor to consider. As supporting evidence of prudence, however, this fact could be adduced, but only if the inquiry proceeded well beyond the existence of the investment to determine why it had been made. Similarly, the fact that a particular investment was not held by other fiduciaries should not be determinative in judging prudence. The central inquiry remains rooted in the analysis of why the investment was made by the fiduciary whose behavior is being questioned. The absence of the same or similar investments by other fiduciaries could have secondary or supporting value, but only if enough information was collected to support a conclusion that others similarly situated avoided the investment out of a belief that to hold it would be imprudent.

NOTES

[1] 1 A. W. Scott, *Law of Trusts* § 227.3, at 1811 (3d ed. 1967) [hereinafter cited as Treatise]. *See also* Restatement (Second) of Trusts § 227(a) comment e (1959) [hereinafter cited as Restatement].

[2] *See* 1 Treatise, *supra* note 1, § 227.3, at 1812.

[3] 396 N.Y.S.2d 781 (Surr. 1977); *see* discussion in Chapter 1 at 21.

[4] 445 F. Supp. 670 (S.D.N.Y. 1978); *see* discussion in Chapter 1 at 21.

[5] *Id.* at 672.

[6] *See id.* at 672, 682.

[7] *See* discussion in Chapter 2 commencing at 75.

[8] *Id.*

[9] Ibbotson-Sinquefield, *Stocks, Bonds, Bills and Inflation: The Past and the Future.* For the five years 1969 to 1973, the average annual compound return for the Ibbotson-Sinquefield small stock portfolio was −12.3 percent.

[10] *Id.* For the five years 1975 to 1979, the average annual compound return for the Ibbotson-Sinquefield small stock portfolio was +39.8 percent.

[11] Pub. L. No. 95-345, 92 Stat. 481 (August 15, 1978). There had been earlier private rulings (e.g., *Knox College,* December 14, 1977; *Edna McConnell Clark Foundation, Inc.,* January 16, 1978), followed by Revenue Ruling 78-88, March 6, 1978, 1978-10 IRB 12, holding that securities lending did not give rise to unrelated business taxable income or to unrelated debt financed income. The legislation clarified additional uncertainties, not previously addressed by the Internal Revenue Service. The legislation specified that securities lending would not involve a sale or exchange in which gain or loss was recognized and that income derived therefrom by private foundations would constitute investment income under Section 4940(c) (2) of the Internal Revenue Code (thereby avoiding an "excess business holding" problem).

[12] A "preference" under the Bankruptcy Code of 1978 is a transfer of property of a debtor to a creditor on account of a pre-existing debt where the transfer is (i) made by the debtor while insolvent, (ii) within the four-month period immediately prior to commencement of a bankruptcy proceeding, and (iii) has the effect of enabling the creditor to get a greater percentage of his debt than some other creditor of the same class.

[13] *See* discussion commencing at 141 *infra.*

[14] The adage is attributed to Pliny in J. W. Norton-Kyshe, ed., *Dictionary of Legal Quotations* (1904) at 173 n.4.

[15] *See* Federal Financial Institutions Examination Council, *Supervisory Policy on Securities Lending,* Banking Circular No. 196, 1984–85 Fed. Banking L. Rep. (CCH) ¶ 86,248 at 90,773 (May 7, 1985).

[16] Ibbotson, Siegel, & Love, "World Wealth: U. S. and Foreign Market Values and Returns," J. Portfolio Mgmt. (Fall 1985) at 6.

[17] Some would argue that the lower standard deviation for real estate returns may be attributable to the fact that the yearly returns are typically calculated on the basis of appraisals rather than actual purchases and sales. This argument may be weakened by the fact that appraisals are often based upon the actual sale prices of comparable real estate.

[18] Data furnished by Rogers, Casey & Barksdale, Inc.

[19] Ibbotson & Siegel, *Real Estate Returns: A Comparison With Other Investments* (forthcoming) [hereinafter cited as Real Estate Returns].

[20] *Id.* at 1, 18, and Table 3, at 25.

[21] Ibbotson & Siegel, *Real Estate Returns, supra* note 19; *Stocks, Bonds, Bills and Inflation: Quarterly Service* 20–40 (4th Quarter 1984) (Ibbotson Assocs. Chicago, Ill.); Zerbst & Cambon, "Real Estate: Historical Returns and Risks," J. Portfolio Mgmt. 5–20 (Spring 1984). However, some would suggest that the absence of a covariance between real estate and stocks and bonds may simply be a statistical artifact, derived from the difference in determining value (appraisals for real estate and actual arm's length transactions for stocks and bonds).

[22] Irwin & Landa, "The Use of Real Estate, Futures and Gold as Portfolio Assets," J. Portfolio Mgmt. (Summer 1986) (forthcoming).

[23]Differences in marketability and valuation techniques between real estate and such highly marketable securities as stocks and bonds make comparisons, particularly of standard deviations, difficult. Ibbotson and Siegel suggest these factors lower the apparent risk (the standard deviation of returns) of real estate relative to its true risk. *See* Real Estate Returns, *supra* note 19, at 15.

[24]*See* Federal Deposit Insurance Corporation, Notice of Public Hearing on Proposed Amendment to Agency Regulations, 50 Fed. Reg. 23963 (1985), charts 1, 2, 3 at 23970–72. This notice contains a useful analysis of the risks posed to banks from real estate investment. Drawing on a number of economic studies, it reaches the conclusion that real estate-related activities are riskier than a bank's traditional activities and have sufficient covariance with those activities to increase bank risk overall.

[25]*Real Estate Investment Trusts and the Effect They Have Had and May Be Expected to Have on the Banking System: Hearings Before the Senate Committee on Banking, Housing and Urban Affairs* 94th Cong., 2d Sess. 297 (1976).

[26]For example, appraisals may be based on a gross sales price, without considering selling expense, taxes, or the present value of the future sale. They may be based on a "when completed and occupied on a fully stabilized basis," for a project still under construction.

[27]Burton Malkiel, in his classic *A Random Walk Down Wall Street* (4th ed. 1985) at 282, makes the point with the following quote from Henry George, more than 100 years ago: "Go, get yourself a piece of ground, and hold possession. . . . You need do nothing more. You may sit down and smoke your pipe; you may lie around like the lazzaroni of Naples or the leperos of Mexico; you may go up in a balloon, or down a hole in the ground and without doing one stroke of work, without adding one iota to the wealth of the community, in ten years you will be rich."

[28]*See* 1 Treatise, *supra* note 1 § 240; Restatement, *supra* note 1 § 240 and commentary. *But see* Treasury Regulations promulgated under Section 4944.

[29]*See* Restatement, *supra* note 1 § 227(a) comment f.

[30]In the REIT debacle of the 1970s, it was the construction mortgage REITs that experienced the most failures.

[31]*See* Restatement, *supra* note 1 § 227(a) comment h ("Ordinarily second or other junior mortgages are not proper trust investments.").

[32]*See, e.g.,* Restatement, *supra* note 1 § 227(a) comment f (including margin purchases of stock among a list of improper trust investments).

[33]*See* G. G. Bogert & G. T. Bogert, *Trusts and Trustees* (2d ed. rev. 1980) § 613, at 55. New York (which adopted its first legal list statute in 1889, *see* Note, "Trust Fund Investment in New York: The Prudent Man Rule and Diversification of Investments," 47 N.Y.U. L. Rev. 527, 530 (1972)) was one of the last states to drop the legal list approach to prudence in favor of the prudent man rule. Its legal list standard was repealed on May 1, 1970. Ch. 321, L. 1970.

[34]Such an investment would also be suspect under the traditional prohibition on the conduct of a business by a fiduciary. *See* Restatement, *supra* note 1 § 227(a) comment f ("employment of trust property in the carrying on of trade or business" is improper); *see also* 1 Treatise, *supra* note 1 § 227.6.

[35]*See* notes 29 and 31, *supra.*

[36]Princeton University has successfully pursued this mode of operation in the commercial development of the University's land holdings to the south of its campus and along Route 1.

[37]As recently as the mid-1970s, New York law firms were struggling to find a satisfactory analytical route around the non-delegation rule in order to permit bank trustees to invest in publicly traded REITs. Aware of the need to enact a specific law in 1961 to relieve doubts about the legality of investing in mutual funds, lawyers appreciated the negative implications of this law for other pooled investment vehicles and sought—without much success—some distinguishing features in the business of REITs to lift them out of the mutual fund precedent.

[38]*See* discussion in Chapter 1 at 38–39.

[39]GAO Report to Senator Lloyd Bentsen, Joint Economic Committee: "Government-Industry Cooperation Can Enhance the Venture Capital Process" (August 12, 1982) at 5.

[40]Venture Economics, Inc., *Annual Report for National Venture Capital Association on Funds Raised and Investment Activity in 1984* 3, 17 (September 1985) at 3, 17.

[41]A unique exception to this general statement is American Research and Development Company (ARD), founded in 1946 and operated publicly until its acquisition by Textron in 1972. Emphasizing start-ups and early stage financings in the technology field, it represented a significant portion of all assets committed to venture capital in the decades of the 1950s and 1960s. ARD's twenty-five-year average annual compound return was 16.7 percent, compared to 12.7 percent for the S&P 500, its twenty-five-year cumulative return was 4,784.8 percent compared to 1,862.8 percent for the S&P 500 and its standard deviation was 58.1 compared to 17.1 for the S&P 500. If its biggest success, Digital Equipment Corporation, is excluded from the calculation, ARD's twenty-five-year average annual compound return drops to 7.7 percent, significantly below the comparable figure of 12.7 percent for the S&P 500. Cambridge Associates, *Venture Capital Investment* (1983) at B-4, Table 11.

[42]"Venture Capital and Innovation," A Study Prepared for the Use of the Joint Economic Committee, December 28, 1984, S. Prt. 98-288 (98th Cong., 2d Sess.).

[43]*Id.* at 36–7. Small business investment companies reported a compound growth of 19 percent per annum for the 1982 to 1984 period and firms owned by major corporations reported a compound growth rate of only 4.2 percent for the same period. These reports were collected in a written survey mailed to 565 venture capital firms (including seventy-seven corporate firms), 267 of which returned usable responses.

[44]Cambridge Associates, *Venture Capital Investment, Executive Summary* (1985) and *Venture Capital Investment* (1983). The 1985 report states that "[i]n general, the distribution of returns between partnerships and within successful partnerships is highly skewed, with many partnerships holding marginal or even losing investments and a few major winners more than carrying the whole."

[45]For 1985 the S&P 500 was up 26.3 percent (without income reinvested) compared to increases in the New Horizon Fund of 18.4 percent and in the Hambrecht and Quist Technology Index of 10.7 percent.

[46]*See* Appendix A, Section E; Rohrer, "Who says you can't beat the market?" *Institutional Investor* 141 (July 1985); Rosenberg, Reid, & Lanstein, "Persuasive Evidence of Market Inefficiency," J. Portfolio Mgmt. 9 (Spring 1985); "Some 'Efficient-Market' Scholars Decide It's Possible to Beat the Averages After All," Wall St. J., 31 December 1985, at 11.

[47]For example, venture capital enterprises are new and untried, and lack a stable record of growth. If the investment is made through a fund, the fiduciary must be prepared for the near certainty of failure for one or more of the start-up enterprises in which the fund invests, thus raising difficulties under the "item-by-item" test of prudence. Further, investments in a fund may be viewed as an unlawful delegation. Washington State's 1984 amendment of its legislation governing investments by trustees to explicitly permit limited investment in "new, unproven, untried . . . enterprises . . ." underscores the point. *See* Wash. Rev. Code § 11.100.023.

[48]There can be substantial economic advantages to carrying out a commitment to venture capital internally, but the legal strain resulting from the traditional prudence standard as applied to this mode of operation increases. *See* discussion in Chapter 3 commencing at 85.

[49]This may be changing. *See* discussion of investment management consultants in Chapter 2, commencing at 72.

[50]Animal metaphors abound in the world of investments. Some who have followed what looked to be a bell-cow and lived to regret their sheeplike behavior, prefer to use the term Judas goat to describe such a leader.

[51]*See* discussion in Chapter 3 commencing at 98.

[52]*See generally* Investment Company Act Release No. 7113 (Investment Advisers Act Release No. 315) (April 19, 1972). Congress passed the Business Development Act of 1980, which allows registered investment advisers to venture capital pools to receive incentive compensation of up to 20 percent of gains realized, without requiring symmetry, but subject to a maze of burdensome requirements that in the aggregate sharply reduce the utility of this effort by the Congress and the SEC to accept the marketplace definition of fair compensation in the specialized

field of venture capital. In 1985, the SEC exempted investment advisers to large investors from the prohibition against compensation tied to capital gain or capital appreciation and from the requirement that incentive compensation formulas be symmetrical. Investment Advisers Act Release No. 996 (November 14, 1985).

[53]The discussion that follows assumes on the part of the reader a general familiarity with these products and the terminology employed in their use.

[54]*See* unpublished paper entitled "Speculative Stock Transactions: A Historical Note for the 'Prudent Man' Study," prepared for this study in September 1985 by Peter Eisenstadt. *See* Dos Passos, *A Treatise on the Law of Stock-Brokers and Stock Exchanges* (New York 1905) Vol, I, at 475–82, 488–92. Questionable origins aside, recent events contribute to the lingering suspicions of these markets. *See, e.g.,* the allegations of price manipulations in silver futures by the Hunt family of Texas in 1979 and 1980 and *Business Week's* cover story (August 1985) on "The Casino Society," featuring futures and options as among the most prominent games to be played. And see statement of James Sterngold in note 57 *infra.*

[55]This term is intended to include all products presently subject to the jurisdiction of the Commodity Futures Trading Commission, including options on commodities and options on futures.

[56]Merrick & Figlewski, *An Introduction to Financial Futures,* Occasional Paper 1984 No. 6 (New York University) 16. This is an excellent primer on the subject.

[57]The arithmetic average of all responding institutions who answered either "precluded" or "questionable" to questions 14(a) through (m), inclusive. In his column on "Futures/Options" in the *New York Times* (November 25, 1985 at D5), James Sterngold concludes: "Just the mention of options has long had the ability to scare corporate treasurers. Right or wrong, options carry a reputation of being the tool of a gambler, not of a prudent investor."

[58]The "basis" is the difference between the futures market price and the cash market price of the underlying good or security being hedged. Changes in the basis over time create basis risk.

[59]FRB, CFTC, SEC, *A Study of the Effects on the Economy of Trading in Futures and Options* (December 1984) [hereinafter cited as Futures and Options Study] II-32; Kling, *Futures Markets and Transactions Costs* (Washington: Board of Governors of the Federal Reserve System, March 1984).

[60]Futures and Options Study, *supra* note 59, at II-23.

[61]*See generally* L. McMillan, *Options as a Strategic Investment* Ch. 25 (1980).

[62]For an enlightening, sophisticated discussion of the multiple uses of options as equivalents of, or in combination with, the underlying securities, *see* Black, "Fact and Fantasy in the Use of Options," Fin. Analysts J. 36 (July–August 1975).

[63]Explanations for this effect vary. The most plausible holds that, because institutions are the primary holders of index funds, there is a shortage of arbitragers buying long futures against sales of index funds, because institutions have legal and organizational constraints operating against such a switch and others cannot readily "short" the S&P 500. In addition, since the futures markets are far more efficient for carrying out a bearish strategy, there are times when the stock index futures exchanges attract those with a disproportionately negative outlook, compared to those concurrently operating in the underlying stock market. These phenomena in combination could account for the lower than expected premiums for the S&P 500 stock index contract.

[64]For a detailed explanation of conversions and reverse conversions, *see Report of the Special Study of Options Markets to the Securities and Exchange Commission* 148 (1978).

[65]Malkiel's coin-tosser example well illustrates this possibility. Malkiel, *Random Walk Down Wall Street* 168–69 (4th ed. Norton 1985). *Compare* Buffett's example of Omaha-based orangutans tossing coins. Buffett, "Up the Inefficient Market (Graham & Dodd Is Alive and Well in Wall Street)," *Barron's* 11 (February 25, 1985).

[66]Irwin & Brorsen, "Public Futures Funds," J. Futures Markets 462–85 (Fall 1985). Statistics on private funds are not available.

[67]The returns are net of all fees and commissions and are calculated on the basis of a log-weighted average.

[68]*See generally* Corcoran, "Ten Cautionary Rules for Institutional Investors," *Intermarket* 58 (Jan. 1986).

[69]Andrea Corcoran, Director of the CFTC's Division of Trading and Markets, suggests that an institution large enough to establish its own futures commission merchant or clearing affiliate should consider that option. *Id.* at 60.

[70]"Millions at Risk," *A Report on The Investment Procedures of Authorities and Public Benefit Corporations,* New York State Senate Committee on Investigations and Taxation 4 (January 12, 1983) [hereinafter cited as Senate Report].

[71]Lombard-Wall Incorporated v. Bankers Trust Company, 23 BR 165 (1982).

[72]*See generally Gambling with Public Funds, The Lion Capital Bankruptcy and Its Implications for Government Investment Practices,* New York State Assembly Committee on Ways and Means (March 1985). More recently it was reported that a federal bankruptcy judge had approved a settlement in the Lion Capital Group bankruptcy proceeding that would give the school districts and municipalities about 73 cents on the dollar in respect of their claims. "Judge Clears Plan for 34 Cities Schools to Get $29 Million From Lion Capital," Wall St. J. 4 (Sept. 6, 1985).

[73]Senate Report, *supra* note 70, at 25.

[74]Federal Financial Institutions Examination Council, *Interagency Supervisory Policy Statement Regarding Repurchase Agreements of Depository Institutions With Securities Dealers and Others* (November 29, 1985), 50 Fed. Reg. 49,764 (December 4, 1985). This Policy Statement has been adopted or proposed for adoption by all of its constituent agencies.

[75]425 So. 2d 415 (Ala.), *cert. denied,* 461 U. S. 938 (1983).

[76]419 N.E.2d 1358 (Mass. 1981).

[77]425 So. 2d at 427.

[78]*Id.* at 427.

[79]*Id.* at 421.

[80]*Id.* at 428.

[81]*Id.* at 422.

[82]*Id.* at 419.

[83]*Id.* at 422.

[84]*Id.* at 419–21.

[85]419 N.E.2d 1358 (Mass. 1981).

[86]*Id.* at 1366.

[87]*Id.* at 1362.

[88]*Id.* at 1367.

[89]*Id.* at 1362.

[90]*Id.* at 1367.

CHAPTER 5

Conclusions and Recommendations

Summary of Conclusions

As Regards the Law of Prudence:

1. The prudent man standard has triumphed over the legal list approach for practically all fiduciaries managing other people's money in the United States, whether for Employee Retirement Income Security Act of 1974 (ERISA)-governed pension funds or personal trusts or endowments of one kind or another.

2. The promise of flexibility conveyed by the prudent man standard has failed in application, due primarily to interpretations rendered by judges and commentators more receptive to the legal principle of stare decisis than to the evolving economic principles that increasingly inform investment management. Neither the Treatise, the Restatement, nor any modern case (save one[1]) uncovered in this study explicitly interprets the prudent man standard in light of modern economic precepts.

3. The model of prudence elaborated in the Treatise and the Restatement, while remaining virtually constant for fifty years, has shaped the legal understanding of the duties of investment management, not only for trustees of personal trusts but for other fiduciaries as well. Today these documents continue to exert a powerfully constraining influence over the attitudes and behavior of fiduciaries and the legal opinions of lawyers and judges.

4. The powerfully stabilizing effect of these authoritative commentaries on the common law of prudence was augmented by the complexity of modern portfolio theory, the alternative financial model on which a new paradigm of prudence could be based, and changes in other institutions of trust law that acceptance of this model would entail. These changes would include making diversification mandatory, absent an unusual showing by the trustee, such as some special insight, and using a "total return" scheme, rather than income and capital gain, to allocate investment returns between life beneficiaries and remaindermen.

5. While some modern cases show a tendency to uphold the prudence of investment decisions that are conventional in both their choice of product and technique, as long as the fiduciary can provide a record of diligence and informed deliberation,[2] others find imprudence in defiance of widely accepted economic theory,[3] or anchor their conclusions in the superficial logic that, if other trustees did it, it must be prudent.[4]

6. The New York Court of Appeals in its 1869 decision in *King v. Talbot* ruled that investments in common stock were per se imprudent. Since then, with the notable exception of the Supreme Court of Alabama in *First Alabama Bank of Montgomery, N. A. v. Martin* (which seemed to accord such treatment to real estate investment trusts (REITs)), no court has ruled particular investment products or techniques to be imprudent per se under the prudent man standard. The tendency to label remains strong, however, among regulators as well as judges. There is good reason to believe that a fiduciary could be held liable for losses resulting from the use of a product or technique sufficiently innovative that one could not point to similar use by others, despite a record of informed deliberation.

7. Significant progress toward adapting the prudent man standard to modern economic theory has been made, but almost entirely through legislative and regulatory initiatives in selected areas, such as the Labor Department's interpretation of prudence under ERISA, the Internal Revenue Service's regulations under Section 4944 of the Internal Revenue Code, the Uniform Management of Institutional Funds Act of 1972 (UMIFA), and California's new prudent man standard. How courts will interpret these efforts to bridge the gap between law and economics remains to be seen.

As Regards the Perception of Prudence Among Fiduciaries: The major findings of the survey of fiduciaries (as summarized in the Introduction) bear repeating here.

1. A significant number of fiduciaries believe that the law precludes certain investment opportunities that they would otherwise seek to pursue in what they believe to be the proper discharge of their duties.

2. Many new or unconventional investment products and techniques are considered either legally precluded or questionable by a significant number of fiduciaries.

3. Although some less conventional investments (such as venture capital, real estate, and foreign equities) have gained acceptance in the portfolios of most respondents, others (such as options, futures, and index funds) are not used by most of the respondents.

4. Significant differences exist among groups of fiduciaries regarding the extent of perceived constraint. The spectrum of opinion corresponds to what would be predicted by the relevant legal standards: Bank trust departments, subject in their management of personal trust assets to the most rigid version of the prudent man rule, report the most constraint; at the opposite extreme, corporate pension fund sponsors, subject to ERISA, the most liberal version of the prudence standard, report the least; educational and philanthropic endowments, subject to standards of intermediate liberality, are roughly in the middle.

5. Delegation of investment authority, a major legal stumbling block before statutory and regulatory reforms over the last fifteen years, is both widespread and apparently unproblematic for the great majority of fiduciaries other than bank trust departments. A significant proportion of those nonbank fiduciaries have retained consultants to assist in selecting investment managers.

6. Developments in financial theory over the last two-and-a-half decades have made a distinct but not overwhelming impression on the attitudes of fiduciaries. For example, while fiduciaries appear to concur with most financial economists that markets are so efficient that it is extremely difficult to achieve consistent superior performance, most fiduciaries believe it possible to best the market and worthwhile to try. Further, although modern portfolio theory has significantly influenced the measurement of portfolio risk by fiduciaries, the most popular investment strategy remains portfolio theory's precursor, value-oriented fundamental analysis.

As Regards the Lessons of History:

1. A survey of the changing marketplace for investments since 1830, the year *Harvard College v. Amory* was decided, reveals a circular journey from Judge Putnam's awareness in 1830 that risk was pervasive ("Do what you will, the capital is at hazard") through a long period in which "safe" investments were thought to exist and fiduciaries expected to find them, often with the help of labels affixed to specific products by commentators, courts, and legislatures, to the present era, in which safety as an investment concept has become an anachronism, emptied of meaning by a growing awareness that uncertainty is the central factor at work in the marketplace and that the management of risk, rather than its avoidance, is the primary task of the fiduciary.

2. Growth in the size and complexity of the marketplace, particularly since World War II, has been accompanied by (a) remarkable improvements in financial reporting and in the fairness of the trading markets, as insider trading increasingly became an unacceptable practice, and (b) the growth in professionalism among fiduciaries and other financial intermediaries, including security analysts, investment managers, broker-dealers, and investment management consultants. In the face of these changes, marketplace prudence often compels a fiduciary to delegate management responsibilities to specialists.

As Regards the Implications of Economics for Prudence:

1. In the publicly traded capital markets, security prices in the main are efficient, in the sense that most information material to investment choice is rapidly and cheaply made available to investors and rapidly reflected in security prices. The more a market is scrutinized and used, the higher its level of pricing efficiency. The converse is also true. Opportunities for superior performance through skill, industry, and foresight increase as the pricing efficiency of particular markets decreases. The more conventional the product or the more plausible the strategy, the less likely it is that above-average results can be achieved. Accordingly, because the prudence standard was not intended to be intolerant of those seeking superior performance, it must be defined to accommodate the innovator who proceeds alone but with diligence and informed deliberation.

2. By holding a well-diversified portfolio, it is possible to remove issuer-specific risks, leaving only the systemic risk of the particular market for which the securities in the portfolio are a proxy. The lesson for prudence is that the standard should be applied to the portfolio as a whole, rather than, as suggested in the case of *Spitzer,*[5] to each security in the portfolio. The volatility of each individual security is only important in its impact on the volatility of the whole portfolio and should be so tested in evaluating the prudence of holding it. Therefore, it is meaningless to discuss in the abstract the prudence of a "type" of investment, such as stock in a new and untried enterprise, or of a technique, such as the writing of put options.

3. While risk continues to be viewed as the possibility of capital loss, the symmetry of security return distributions permits risk to be better understood as the variability of expected returns around a mean. All investors are assumed to be risk-averse and, accordingly, to pay more for an investment with less variance of possible return around an expected return than for one with more variance. Paying more for an expected return is another way of saying the yield on an investment with less variance is lower than the yield on an investment with more variance. This, in combination with the immediately preceding paragraph, leads to the widely accepted thesis that the higher the systematic or undiversifiable risk, the higher the expected returns. For prudence, the implications are that efforts to equate "speculation" with imprudence and to distinguish it from "investment," except perhaps at the marginal extremes, are doomed to failure. Since higher expected returns can only come from exposure to higher risks, the choice of risk depends critically on one's time horizon, one's cash flow needs, and one's tolerance for volatility. There is a broad, indeed nearly infinite, spectrum of possibilities in establishing economically defensible risk levels. Across that spectrum, it is not possible to find some Plimsoll line[6] where speculation commences, nor is it socially useful for courts or other governmental bodies to try.

4. Despite major advances in understanding how financial markets operate and the validity of the important implications for investment behavior summarized in the preceding paragraphs, uncertainties remain. Neither the capital asset pricing model (CAPM) nor any of the other asset pricing models commands universal acceptance as an explanation of the expected return of assets.[7] Greater understanding, while creating a widely accepted framework for analysis of market behavior, has produced many models (with each having some validity) and more complexity overall. Although the most actively traded markets in the United States display a general efficiency, anomalies (e.g., the small firm effect, the low P/E effect, and the January effect) continue to be uncovered, creating uncertainty as to whether they result from an inability to measure risk properly or are true market inefficiencies. Whether, and to what extent, the various equilibrium models for explaining expected return rest on the efficiency of markets is unclear. And, despite the central importance of the "market portfolio" to portfolio theory, its composition remains unclear because of many open questions as to what to include in the pool of "all risky assets" for which it is a surrogate. (For example, is the pool limited to assets in the domestic economy or does it include foreign assets, and if so, which ones?) For the fiduciary, the lesson is that there are no entirely satisfactory formulae to guide investment behavior within the accepted framework of portfolio theory. As informed by that theory, prudence will tolerate many alternative strategies while dictating none.

5. Although ex post it can be observed that some investment managers have achieved consistently superior performance, economics offers no system for identifying them, ex ante. In particular, despite its broad appeal to those diligently seeking the best managers, past superior performance is not a reliable predictor of future superior performance.

6. In measuring a manager's performance and comparing it with the performance of others, the levels of risk assumed in the manager's portfolio and in those with which it is being compared should be taken into account. Doing so is difficult, however, because of the number of different asset pricing models available to establish a benchmark for measuring risk and comparing performance.

The Modern Paradigm of Prudence

The foregoing conclusions demonstrate that the traditional legal doctrine of prudence and the economic assumptions on which that doctrine rests stand irreconcilably opposed to notions of prudence drawn from the marketplace and financial theory. The law's prudent man bears little resemblance to prudent men and women engaged in the real world of investment, even those engaged in "safeguarding the property of others."

The law must be brought up-to-date. A modern interpretation of prudence is needed to reconcile these differences. It should draw upon the broadest possible currents of change. It should recognize the important and established principle of finance economics that nothing useful can be said about an investment in the abstract; it can only be judged in terms of its impact on the whole portfolio and the purposes for which the portfolio is held.

A modern paradigm for prudence, then, would shift the focus from the disembodied investment to the fiduciary, the portfolio, and its purpose. In light of the overarching principle, reaffirmed by the most soundly reasoned cases and recent legislative and administrative developments, that prudence is a test of conduct and not performance, the soundest vehicle for accomplishing that shift is a paradigm of prudence based above all on process. Neither the overall performance of the portfolio nor the performance of individual investments should be viewed as central to the inquiry. Prudence should be measured principally by the process through which investment strategies and tactics are developed, adopted, implemented, and monitored. Prudence is demonstrated by the process through which risk is managed rather than by the labeling of specific investment risks as either prudent or imprudent. Investment products and techniques are essentially neutral; none should be classified prudent or imprudent per se. It is the way in which they are used, and how decisions as to their use are made, that should be examined to determine whether the prudence standard has been met.

More specifically, for any investment product or technique employed by a fiduciary or any delegate selected by the fiduciary in connection with such employment (including pooled investment vehicles), the test of prudence is the care, diligence, and skill demonstrated by the fiduciary in considering all relevant factors

bearing on that decision. If particular investment products or technique
imprudent per se, neither are they per se prudent for all purposes and at
Their use, without more, will not suffice. Prudence is not self-evident. Nor will it
be enough to point to their use by other fiduciaries. What matters is not that others have used the product or technique (for whatever reasons), but the basis for
its use by the fiduciary in question.

Among the relevant factors to be considered are at least the following:

1. The role the investment product or technique is intended to play in the total
portfolio.

2. Whether that role is reasonably designed, as part of the total portfolio, to
serve the purposes for which the portfolio is being held and invested, taking
into account the risk of loss and opportunity for gain associated with the
investment product or technique (including such factors as tax effects and
informational costs of initiation, monitoring, and termination), the composition of the portfolio in terms of its diversification and systemic risk, and the
minimum projected cash flows from income and capital gain over future periods compared with the maximum projected cash demands on the portfolio
over those periods.

3. The competence of the fiduciary or the delegates selected by him to employ
the product or technique.

4. If delegates are involved, the reasonableness of the terms and conditions of
such delegation, taking into account the compensation structure, monitoring
mechanisms, and provisions for termination.

If the test of prudence is to be found in the process by which investment choice
is exercised, it follows that documents must be kept to record that process for
future use in the event of challenge.

Judging the prudence of a fiduciary's investments according to the quality of
the surrounding decision-making process in no way disables one from concluding
in any particular case that an investment was, in essence, "too risky." The process-based paradigm developed in this study requires more than just procedures
and a paper trail to show that they were followed. By emphasizing the importance
of process, there is no intention to empty the reviewing function of all substantive
content. Process should not be allowed to paper over incompetence or irrationality. The prudence standard has long embraced a duty of caution, which the
modern paradigm advanced in this study does nothing to disturb. In examining
the prudence of a fiduciary's investment record, a court may be expected to scrutinize the substantive elements of the decision-making process, not to substitute
its judgments for those of the fiduciary, but to assure that some rational basis for
the fiduciary's judgments existed.

Recommendations Regarding the Restatement

It has been the dual goal of this study to identify the gap between legal and marketplace notions of prudence and to bridge that gap by offering a modern paradigm of prudence. In seeking to explain why the law has been outpaced by eco-

nomic advances and marketplace shifts, case law and commentary have led back to the Treatise and the Restatement. As Professor Jeffrey Gordon concludes in Appendix B, Scott's teachings on investment management by trustees, while remaining virtually constant over a fifty-year period, have shaped the legal understanding of the duties of investment management. This has been true not only for trustees of personal trusts but for other fiduciaries as well. Indeed, as demonstrated in Chapters 1 and 3 and in the results of this study's questionnaire (Questionnaire), Scott's work continues to exert a powerfully constraining influence over the attitudes and behavior of fiduciaries, the legal opinions of lawyers and judges, and the approach to regulation by some government agencies.

This study recommends that the American Law Institute undertake a new restatement of the law of fund management by fiduciaries, which would elaborate and refine the principles of prudence advanced here, superseding (to the extent inconsistent with) the corresponding portions of the Restatement.

Although the Second Restatement is now more than a quarter of a century old, having been completed in 1959, and perhaps worthy of reexamination throughout, this recommendation is limited to the more urgent need to update the much older portions of the Restatement that relate to investment management, spinning them off into a separate restatement addressed not only to trustees in the formal sense of the term but to fiduciaries of all types who are subject to some version of the prudent man rule, whether judicially evolved or statutorily defined, and if the latter, whether at the state or federal level.

The cluster of sections contained in the Restatement that would be separated for review and updating as a new restatement of the law of fund management by fiduciaries is drawn from Chapter 7 of the Restatement, The Administration of the Trust, and would include at least Section 171 (Duty Not to Delegate), Section 174 (Duty to Exercise Reasonable Care and Skill), Section 175 (Duty to Take and Keep Control), Section 176 (Duty to Preserve the Trust Property), Section 181 (Duty to Make the Trust Property Productive), Section 182 (Duty to Pay Income to Beneficiary), Section 213 (Balancing Losses Against Gains), Section 225 (Liability for Acts of Agents), Section 227 (Investments Which a Trustee Can Properly Make), Section 228 (Distribution of Risk of Loss), Section 229 (Amount Which May Be Lent on Mortgage), Section 230 (Duty to Dispose of Improper Investments), Section 231 (Investments Subsequently Becoming Improper), Section 232 (Impartiality Between Successive Beneficiaries), Section 239 (Wasting Property), and Section 240 (Unproductive Property).

The impact that modern portfolio theory would have on the need to diversify (Section 228) and the allocation of returns as between income beneficiaries and remaindermen in the case of personal trusts (Section 232) bears emphasis. As Professor Gordon notes in Appendix B, acceptance of portfolio theory would probably impose a general duty to diversify (as in ERISA) except upon a strong showing of special insight by the fiduciary, thus altering the rule in those jurisdictions, such as New York, where diversification remains optional. And, again as developed by Professor Gordon in Appendix B, portfolio theory calls for the development of a total return allocation scheme, which would entail revision to the Uniform Principal and Income Act.

The case for undertaking a separate project to develop a new restatement of the law of fund management, rather than simply waiting for the day when the Restatement can be re-examined in its entirety, rests principally on three factors. The first, as this study has sought to show, is simply that the law is laggard in its approach to assessing the prudence of investment decision-making by fiduciaries. The second factor, also argued by this study, is the continuing obstacle that the Restatement presents to those who would bring the law into line with marketplace notions of prudence. The third factor is the issue's importance. More than $1,384 billion is today under the management of fiduciaries subject to some version of the prudent man rule.[8] Trends for the future point toward a steady increase in that percentage. Thus, it matters across a wide spectrum of individuals and institutions that the law is laggard. And it matters, too, that the Restatement is an obstacle to a more rapid legal evolution. With the obstacle removed, acceptance of a modern paradigm of prudence could become more firmly established. Beyond this need there is a major opportunity for the American Law Institute to elaborate and texture the prudence standard for fiduciary conduct in fund management, providing important guidance in many areas, such as delegation, exoneration, and standards for judging the soundness of economic premises, where virtually none exists today.

It is beyond the scope of this study to make specific recommendations regarding the affected sections of the Restatement. However, a recommendation is in order regarding the "black letter" rule itself. As previously indicated, to avoid the constraining influence of the Treatise and the Restatement, there have been several legislative and regulatory efforts to use distinguishing words and phrases that help to disengage modern expressions of the rule from the Treatise's legacy. The "ordinary business care and prudence" standard used in the Section 4944 regulations and UMIFA and the lengthy definition recently adopted in California are examples of this tendency. It is this study's recommendation that these and other variations be addressed in the new restatement of fund management as variations on a single theme. A black letter rule should express that theme in a simple, short statement of the type found in *Harvard College* or the Restatement itself (it being not the black letter rule but the commentary that has been the chief source of the Restatement's constraining influence).

NOTES

[1]Hamilton v. Nielsen, 678 F.2d 709 (7th Cir. 1982).

[2]In re Bank of N.Y., 364 N.Y.S. 2d 164 (1974); In re Morgan Guar. Trust Co. of N.Y., 396 N.Y.S.2d 781 (1977); Stark v. United States Trust Co. of N.Y., 445 F. Supp. 670 (S.D.N.Y. 1978).

[3]First Ala. Bank of Montgomery, N.A. v. Martin, 425 So. 2d 415 (Ala. 1983).

[4]Chase v. Pevear, 419 N.E.2d 1358 (Mass. 1981).

[5]In re Bank of N.Y., 364 N.Y.S.2d 164 (1974).

[6]For a commentary, in verse, on Justice Frankfurter's likening of due process to a Plimsoll line, *see* Field, "Frankfurter, J. Concurring," 71 Harv. L. Rev. 77, 77 (1957).

[7]*See, e.g.,* Tinic & West, "Risk, Return and Equilibrium: A Revisit," J. Pol. Econ. (forthcoming), reporting on test results indicating that CAPM's two-parameter model is not supported by historical relationship between stock returns and systematic risk over period from 1935 to 1982 and, further, suggesting that the test results are sensitive to the choice of the proxy for the "market portfolio."

[8]The sum of the estimated value of assets held by (*i*) pension funds subject to ERISA; (*ii*) personal trust funds managed by banks and trust companies; (*iii*) endowment funds of all universities, colleges, and other educational institutions; and *(iv)* endowment funds of all private foundations, derived from the sources indicated:

		Billions
i.	pension funds subject to ERISA	$1,000
	Source: R. A. Ippolito, *Pensions, Economics, and Public Policy (1986)* Table 1-1, at 5	
ii.	personal trust funds managed by FDIC-insured banks with trust powers and nonfederally insured trust companies affiliated with bank holding companies	295.6
	Source: Federal Financial Institutions Examination Council, *Trust Assets of Banks and Trust Companies* 1984 (Tentative)	
iii.	endowment funds of universities, colleges, and other educational institutions	25.5
	Source: "NACUBO 1984 Comparative Performance Study," *Business Officer* (April 1985) at 23	
iv.	endowment funds of private foundations	63.1
	Source: *The Foundation Directory* (10th ed. 1985) at xv	
		$1,384.2

This sum is somewhat understated because it proved impossible to obtain a good estimate of the size of funds held by individually managed personal trusts, religious organizations, and charitable or other nonprofit institutions not specifically covered above.

APPENDIX A

The Lessons of Modern Portfolio Theory

Edwin J. Elton and Martin J. Gruber

The purpose of this essay is to present an overview of some of the lessons of modern portfolio theory and capital asset pricing theory for a fiduciary subject to the prudent man rule. It is not concerned with the concept of prudence as interpreted by law, rather it is concerned with what modern portfolio and investment theory implies is prudent.

Fortunately or unfortunately, there is at this time no universally accepted doctrine in finance. Instead there are many theories, some perhaps better than others, but each with its own following. Often these competing theories give the fiduciary the same message, but sometimes they give conflicting messages. This essay attempts to point out similarities and differences where appropriate and finally to draw any common conclusions that exist.

This essay is divided into eight sections. Section A introduces some of the concepts and terminology that are necessary to understand later sections. In Section B the general theory of portfolio analysis is examined. Section C introduces the basic concept of an asset pricing model (a model for explaining expected return) and discusses those lessons that can be learned from it. In Section D, other modern theories of asset pricing and their implications for prudence are examined. Section E deals with investment principles when securities are priced efficiently. If all securities are priced as they should be, what choices remain for the prudent investor? Section F treats a set of economic principles that should apply under the prudent man rule, regardless of which of the previous theories is accepted. Section G deals with the selection of managers and the management process. Finally, Section H draws and summarizes some general conclusions from the other sections.

Among these conclusions are:

1. Diversification pays.

2. Special characteristics of the investor should be reflected in the composition of the investor's portfolio.

3. The riskiness of an asset can only be judged in terms of the overall portfolio.

4. The only way to increase expected return on a well-run portfolio is by increasing risk.

5. Investment performance should not be judged over a short period of time (e.g., one year or less).

6. Short selling, borrowing, options and futures are not per se improper; they can serve useful functions consistent with prudence.

A. Introduction

All of modern portfolio theory is concerned with the properties of returns from alternative investment vehicles. The concept of return is always defined in terms of cash flow to the investor plus change in market value. To be more precise, the "rate of return" on a security over a particular period is the change in price of the security plus any cash flow that accrues to the holder of the security over the period, divided by the original price of the security. The concept of rate of return does not change in considering different types of assets. For stocks, return consists of both dividends and capital gains, while for bonds it is interest paid plus the change in price, each divided by the price at the beginning of the measurement period. The problems of portfolio theory are complex because future returns, which can rarely be known with certainty, must be estimated. In fact, a risky or stochastic variable must be estimated. If we represent what might happen in the future by what has happened in the past, the distribution of returns for various securities would look like the frequency distributions in Figure A.1.

There are a huge number of financial instruments and alternative physical investments from which a potential investor can choose, and each would have its returns described by a frequency distribution like that in Figure A.1. It is difficult to make decisions in terms of such distributions or to picture combinations of them. Distributions such as these can be summarized by certain characteristics.

Figure A.1 Basic Series: Total Annual Returns 1926–1984

SERIES	GEOMETRIC MEAN	ARITHMETIC MEAN	STANDARD DEVIATION	DISTRIBUTION
COMMON STOCKS	9.5%	11.7%	21.2%	
SMALL STOCKS	12.4	18.2	36.3	
LONG TERM CORPORATE BONDS	4.4	4.6	7.6	
LONG TERM GOVERNMENT BONDS	3.7	3.9	7.5	
U.S. TREASURY BILLS	3.3	3.4	3.3	
INFLATION	3.0	3.2	4.9	

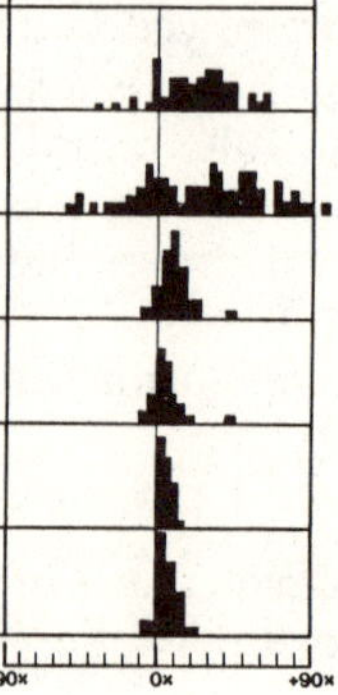

For most purposes, it is sufficient to produce two metrics to describe the probability distribution of returns: a measure of central tendency and a measure of dispersion.

The most widely used measure of central tendency is the mean or expected value. The concept of the mean or average return is very familiar. Everyone is accustomed to think in terms of batting averages in baseball or the average time per lap in racing, but an average is insufficient to convey all the information needed to understand the distribution of returns. It does not convey the likelihood of departures from the average outcome—the dispersion of outcomes around the average. It brings to mind the familiar story of the mathematician who drowned in a stream with an average depth of three inches! The most commonly used measure of dispersion is the variance, or its square root, the standard deviation. The variance is equal to the average squared deviation from the mean.

Returning to Figure A.1, it can be seen that common stocks have had a higher average (arithmetic mean) return than long-term government bonds (11.7 percent versus 3.9 percent), but they also have a higher standard deviation of return (21.4 percent versus 7.5 percent). The latter can be seen because the distribution is more spread out (fatter).

Throughout most of this chapter when discussing investment decisions, the concern is with both the expected value of returns and the standard deviation of returns. It is not at all controversial to assume that investors like higher levels of expected return. It is also well accepted that most individuals and institutions prefer to avoid risk (in the sense of requiring more expected return to compensate for an increase in risk).

Summarizing a distribution of returns by two measures allows ready computation of the distribution of returns of multiple assets. To get some idea of historical returns and standard deviations, Figure A.1 presents the mean return and standard deviation of return for a number of assets over the period of 1926 to 1984.[1] Over the historical period of more than fifty years common equities earned more than twice the return of bonds. However, the standard deviation of return for equities was also considerably higher. To gain some appreciation of this higher variability, recall from mathematics that two-thirds of the time an outcome should be within plus or minus one standard deviation of the mean.[2] Correspondingly, one-third of the time the outcome should be beyond one standard deviation. The mean return for common stocks plus or minus a standard deviation is −9.5 percent to 32.9 percent. Thus, one-third of the time common equity returns should be less than −9.5 percent or more than 32.9 percent.

Figure A.1 illustrates a central theme of this appendix: To increase the average or expected return on a portfolio, more risk must be incurred. While this point is made on the basis of stronger theoretical grounds subsequently, a quick glance at Figure A.1 shows that securities with higher standard deviations tend to have higher expected returns.

Perhaps a point that is often neglected in discussions of prudence should be made. Assume that a fiduciary has thought through the goals of the fund the fiduciary manages and has decided that, given the cash flow needs of the fund, it should be entirely invested in stocks. This was done recognizing both the higher expected return on stocks and the higher risk. Assume also that common equities declined in value over the next two years. Does this mean that the decision was incorrect? No. There must always be a differentiation made between ex ante and ex post returns. Investments are chosen based on an *expected* distribution of returns. Over any short to intermediate period, actual outcomes will differ from expectations. Over longer periods, expectations should be more accurate. The performance of managers over a short period should not be judged.

As discussed in more detail in following sections, taxes should affect the optimal investment decision. For those investors who are taxed at high rates, investments subject to partial or full tax exemption are especially appropriate. Conversely, investors in low or zero tax brackets should underinvest in or avoid tax-advantaged investments. Because part of the return on these investments is the tax savings, they are less attractive to those who cannot take advantage of this element of return. Thus, taxes are an important element that should affect the investment decision.

Transaction costs are another element that affects the return stream. There are very different transaction costs across different investment alternatives. Government bills have very low transaction costs. Private placement debt, on the other hand, has relatively high transaction costs, as do venture capital and real estate. Transaction costs can affect the best way of obtaining a goal. For example, consider the problem of holding a well-diversified portfolio. With only a small amount to invest this can be accomplished, by buying a few shares in each of a number of assets. Because buying a few shares involves large transaction costs, this is a very costly procedure. An alternative way of holding a well-diversified portfolio is to buy a mutual fund. Although there are additional transaction costs in such a purchase (e.g., a management fee), this may be a less costly alternative.

To gain more insight into how a fiduciary should behave, the lessons of modern portfolio theory must be examined.

B. Mean-Variance Analysis

The tenets of mean-variance analysis are rather simple: Investors prefer high to low return and low to high risk. Given a choice of a 10 percent return versus a 5 percent return with the same degree of certainty, investors would take the 10 percent return. Investors require compensation for taking increased amounts of risk. Given the chance to engage in a gamble with a 50 percent chance of paying $200 and a 50 percent chance of paying zero, an investor will pay less than $100 to take the gamble. How much less than $100 the investor will pay depends on the degree of risk aversion the investor exhibits. (This concept is discussed later.) The important point is not that an investor never takes risks, but that an investor accepts more risk only to obtain a higher expected payoff.

Under mean-variance analysis the important properties of any investment can be summarized in terms of a measure of expected return and a measure of dispersion around expected return, which has already been expressed as the standard deviation or variance. When looking at the characteristics of portfolios, it is possible to find that the expected return of the portfolio is simply a weighted average of the expected return of the individual securities that comprise it, where the weights are the fraction invested in each security. However, the risk (standard deviation) of the portfolio is in general less than a weighted average of the risks of the individual securities. In fact, portfolio risk is always less unless the securities have outcomes that vary exactly together (are perfectly correlated). If there is some degree of independence in the outcomes from different investments (the best outcome on one investment does not always happen when the best outcome

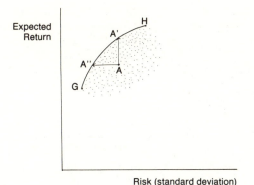

Figure A.2 The Efficient Frontier

on another investment is realized), then diversification lowers overall risk. This risk reduction is one of the few free lunches in economics. The extent of the free lunch depends on how closely the two securities move together (the extent of correlation between their returns).

In considering portfolios of several assets, a set of possibilities like those displayed in Figure A.2 must be examined. Note the solid black boundary drawn in the diagram. Recognizing nonsatiation and risk aversion as investor attributes, portfolios on this curve can be seen to dominate any of the securities or portfolios not on this curve. For example, consider point A. Clearly an investor would prefer portfolio A' since it has more return than A for the same risk. Similarly the investor would prefer A" to A since it has the same return but less risk. By repeating this for all points in the diagram, it is possible to trace out the boundary curve or "efficient frontier" as outlined. The efficient frontier starts at point G, the global minimum variance portfolio, and extends upward and to the right to point H, the maximum return portfolio. Point G is in general a very well-diversified portfolio, while point H could be a single security. Any investor should choose a portfolio somewhere along the shaded curve. This portfolio dominates all interior points. Exactly where on the curve an investor chooses to operate depends on that investor's personal risk-return trade-off.

Before continuing, two modifications to the efficient frontier must be discussed: What happens when short selling is added, and what happens when lending and borrowing are added?

1. Short Selling

The ability to short sell has two effects on the efficient frontier. As shown in Figure A.3, the frontier probably shifts up and to the left, and it continues to the right.[3] The ability to short sell securities creates a new set of possible investments. A security sold short produces a positive return when a security has a large decrease in price and a negative return when its price increases. It potentially improves the efficient frontier (moves it up and to the left) because the ability to short sell doubles the number of possible investments (each stock can be held long or short). Since investors are free not to short sell, the introduction of the ability to short sell cannot make investors worse off (move the efficient frontier down and to the right). If it never pays to short sell, the worst that can happen is that the efficient

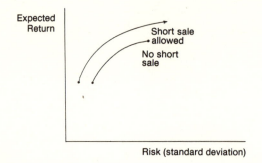

Figure A.3 The Efficient Frontier with and without Short Sales

frontier is unchanged. Without short sales all investors can do is not hold securities that they believe do poorly. With short sales, an opportunity is created that is expected to have almost the opposite characteristics of the investment when purchased. With short sales it is possible, in a sense, to disinvest in poor investments (hold them in negative amounts) and hence gain if they do poorly. If it ever pays to short sell any security, the efficient frontier is shifted up and to the left. This is an example of the old economic adage that a decision-maker cannot be worse off by being given additional choices and the decision-maker may well be better off. In addition, short sales allow the investor to decrease or eliminate market risk. As later discussed at greater length, in a large, well-diversified portfolio, unique risk is eliminated and only market risk remains. Short sales allow the reduction of market risk to very low levels. As just discussed, the return on a short sale is the opposite of the return on a long purchase. About 35 percent of the return on a security is market related. If the market increases, the market return on securities held long is positive. In contrast, for securities held short the return is negative. If the market decreases the opposite occurs. Thus, the addition of short positions operates as a hedging mechanism, reducing the market exposure of a portfolio.

The extension of the efficient frontier to the right arises from the tendency of a very large amount of short selling to increase the risk and return on the portfolio. This increase in risk is easy to understand. Short sales can involve unlimited loss.

The lesson to be learned from this is that short sales can increase the possible level of return for any level of risk. Short sales can be abused and positions taken that are too extreme. However, short selling per se is not bad. Like any other investment strategy, it can be used prudently or imprudently.

2. Lending and Borrowing

It is necessary to introduce the concept of lending and borrowing. To be realistic, assume that the investor's borrowing rate is above the lending rate. Combinations of lending or borrowing with a portfolio of risky assets lie along a straight line. With lending and borrowing the efficient frontier looks like Figure A.4. Notice that for all investors, except for those whose risk-return trade-offs cause them to hold portfolios between portfolios L and B, the ability to lend and borrow improves their opportunities. The ability to lend (putting part of the funds in government securities) is hardly controversial. The borrowing part may be more controversial. Note from Figure A.4 that by choosing point X rather than point Y the investor earns the same return with less risk. Borrowing and buying a less risky

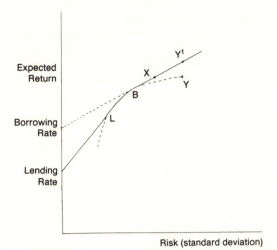

Figure A.4 The Efficient Frontier with Differential Lending and Borrowing Rates

portfolio can give higher returns and less risk than buying a more risky portfolio. Comparing Y' and Y in Figure A.4 shows that it is possible to achieve a higher expected return at the same risk level by borrowing. Of course, borrowing, like short sales or almost any financial mechanism, can be abused. It can be used to take extreme and imprudent risk positions. On the other hand, it can be used to enhance performance. Rejecting borrowing entirely would throw out positive opportunities. For example, consider an investor wishing to have a portfolio with higher expected return than offered by Portfolio B (e.g., the expected return of Y). This investor would have the same expected return and less risk by buying portfolio B and borrowing than by buying Portfolio Y, which does not involve borrowing.

Returning to the concept of the efficient frontier, it is necessary to delve further into the subject of prudent investing. The solid curve in Figure A.4 represents the efficient frontier. An investor should never hold a security or portfolio that lies below that frontier. Because all single securities except the riskless asset lie below the frontier, there is almost never a situation where a single security is efficient. All efficient portfolios are well diversified. The benefits of diversification are achieved with a surprisingly small number of securities.

To get an idea of the impact of the number of securities held on portfolio risk, consider Table A.1, which shows what happens on average to the variance of a randomly selected portfolio of common stocks when the number of stocks is changed.

Note that in the move from one to two securities, risk is reduced by 42 percent; in the move from one to six securities, it is reduced by 71 percent, and in the move from one to twenty securities, it is reduced by 81 percent. There is still a payoff from further diversification because a twenty-stock portfolio contains 21 percent more risk than a 100-stock portfolio and a 100-stock portfolio contains 5 percent more risk than a 1000-stock portfolio. These results refer to a randomly selected portfolio. With consideration of the risk characteristics, the effect of diversification might be even greater. Of course, diversification is constrained by transaction costs. Given the small size of transaction costs for many types of securities, extensive diversification should be rewarded.

Table A.1 Effect of Diversification

Number of securities	Portfolio variance (total risk) percent	Portfolio variances as a percent of a one stock portfolio
1	46.619	100.00
2	26.839	57.57
4	16.948	36.35
6	13.651	29.28
8	12.003	25.75
10	11.014	23.63
12	10.354	22.21
14	9.883	21.20
16	9.530	20.44
18	9.256	19.85
20	9.036	19.38
25	8.640	18.53
30	8.376	17.97
35	8.188	17.56
40	8.047	17.26
45	7.937	17.03
50	7.849	16.84
75	7.585	16.27
100	7.453	15.99
125	7.374	15.82
150	7.321	15.70
175	7.284	15.62
200	7.255	15.56
250	7.216	15.48
300	7.190	15.42
350	7.171	15.38
400	7.157	15.35
450	7.146	15.33
500	7.137	15.31
600	7.124	15.28
700	7.114	15.26
800	7.107	15.24
900	7.102	15.23
1000	7.097	15.22
Infinity	7.058	15.14

Source: Ibbotson Associates, *Stock, Bills, and Inflation: 1985 Yearbook* (1985).

Another lesson to be learned from mean-variance analysis is the need to focus on the overall portfolio rather than on one asset at a time. Reexamine Figure A.2. Many of the dots lying below the efficient frontier represent individual assets. The efficient frontier represents a series of portfolios of assets. It follows that nobody should hold single assets (except perhaps the riskless asset). Single assets are dominated by the efficient frontier. Of course a portfolio on the efficient frontier contains a collection of single assets. An asset might appear undesirable if viewed in isolation, yet have a very desirable impact on a portfolio. For example, an asset might have a high variance and only an average return (compared to the other assets in a portfolio), yet be a very desirable addition to a portfolio because it is not correlated (does not move together) with the remaining assets in the portfolio. An asset must always be judged in terms of its impact on a portfolio, rather than in isolation.

Drawing on this general theory of portfolio analysis, economists have sought to develop methods of pricing risky assets, both individually and as part of a portfolio.

C. The Simplest Notion of Equilibrium—The Standard Capital Asset Pricing Model

The most widely used model to explain asset prices is known as the standard capital asset pricing model (CAPM). Developed independently by three well-known financial economists, it is often referred to as the Sharpe-Lintner-Mossin capital asset pricing model in honor of its discoverers. While alternative models that explain why expected returns differ across assets have been produced in recent years (discussed in later sections of this appendix), the standard CAPM still plays a central role in the financial community.

1. Underlying Assumptions

The CAPM is a model that describes how investors should behave and how prices and returns at which markets clear are set. Before discussing the model in more detail, it is worthwhile specifying the assumptions underlying the CAPM.

The first assumption behind the CAPM is that there are no transaction costs. There is no cost (friction) of buying or selling any asset. If transaction costs were present, the expected return from owning any asset and the desirability of owning it would be a function of whether or not the investor already owned it. Thus, to include transaction costs in the model adds a great deal of complexity. While transaction costs may be large enough to play a role in the decision-making process of the small investor or in affecting the alternative investments that are close substitutes (as discussed in the previous and later sections of this appendix), they are sufficiently small for enough (large) investors that they should have only a minor effect on equilibrium prices.

The second assumption behind the CAPM is that assets are infinitely divisible. This means that investors could take any position in an investment, regardless of the size of their wealth. For example, they can buy $1 of IBM stock. While this is not strictly true for the small investor, given the opportunity to hold commingled funds and mutual funds it is not an unrealistic assumption.

The third assumption is the absence of personal income tax.[4] This means, for example, that the individual is indifferent to the form (dividends or capital gains) in which the return on the investment is received. This is a realistic assumption for pension and other tax-exempt funds.

The fourth assumption is that an individual's or institution's purchases or sales cannot affect the price of a stock. This is analogous to the assumption of perfect competition. While no single investor can affect prices by an individual action, investors in total determine prices by their actions.

The fifth assumption is that investors are expected to make decisions solely in terms of expected value and dispersion of possible outcomes around expected value (standard deviation)—that they are only concerned with the mean and variance of return. (This is discussed in greater detail throughout this appendix.)

The sixth assumption is that unlimited short sales are allowed. The individual investor can sell short any amount of any shares.

The seventh assumption is that of unlimited lending and borrowing at the riskless rate. The investor can lend or borrow any amount of funds desired at a rate of interest equal to the rate for riskless securities.

The eighth and ninth assumptions deal with the homogeneity of expectations. First, investors are assumed to be concerned only with the mean and variance of returns (or prices) over a single period, and all investors are assumed to define the relevant period in exactly the same manner. Second, all investors are assumed to have identical expectations with respect to the inputs necessary to the portfolio decision. These inputs are expected returns, the variance of returns, and the correlation matrix representing the correlation structure between all pairs of stocks.

The tenth assumption is that all assets are marketable. All assets, including human capital, can be sold and bought on the market.[5]

These ten assumptions obviously do not hold in the real world. The reader should be and is undoubtedly uncomfortable about these assumptions, probably more uncomfortable than he or she is about the fact that many of the design features of the modern car were derived by a physicist under the assumption of a frictionless environment. Yet the model derived under these assumptions, like the physicist's theorem of frictionless movement, sheds light on how the real world operates. Furthermore, by making the assumptions explicit at this stage, the theory can later be modified in the interest of greater realism (as is done later in this appendix).

2. The Standard Capital Asset Pricing Model and What It Implies

If all of the assumptions behind the standard CAPM are accepted, it is possible to arrive at an equilibrium relationship.[6] This relationship expresses the expected return on any asset or portfolio as the sum of two terms. The first term is the compensation the investor would require for giving up the use of funds in an environment that is riskless in nominal terms—called the riskless rate of interest and usually approximated by the rate of return on thirty-day Treasury bills. The second term is the compensation investors require for bearing risk. It is equal to the excess return on the market portfolio (the expected rate of return on the market portfolio minus the riskless rate) times the sensitivity of the security or portfolio to the return on the market. This latter term is usually called beta.[7] This can be expressed as:

expected return on asset i = riskless rate of return +
$$\beta_i \times (\text{expected rate of return on market portfolio} - \text{riskless rate of return})$$

Some of the terms require more explanation. The market portfolio represents the aggregate of all risky assets—literally all assets with the exception of the riskless asset.[8] Thus, if IBM represents one percent of all risky assets it represents one percent of the market portfolio.

The beta for any security or portfolio is a measure of how sensitive the return on that security or portfolio is to the return on the market portfolio. If a stock

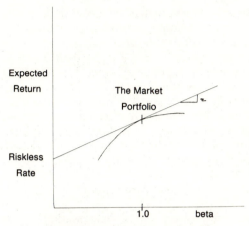

Figure A.5 The Security Market Line

had a beta of two and the market return increased by one percent, the return on the stock could be expected to increase by 2 percent.

This relationship is generally known as the security market line. It represents a concrete notion of equilibrium. The expected return for all securities and portfolios is described by this relationship, which plots as a straight line in expected return-beta space as depicted in Figure A.5.

Notice that expected return increases linearly with beta. More insight can be gained by realizing that the risk of any stock (its standard deviation) can be divided into two parts—that due to the market and that not due to the market. The market risk of any security is equal to the product of the sensitivity to the market of a security (its beta) and the risk (standard deviation) of the market. The risk of a security not due to the market is often called its residual risk. This can be represented as:[9]

$$
\begin{array}{ccc}
\text{total risk on} & = & \text{the market risk} & + & \text{the residual risk} \\
\text{security } i & & \text{of security } i & & \text{of security } i
\end{array}
$$

As increasingly diversified portfolios are held, the residual risks on individual stocks tend to cancel each other out and only market risk is left. Thus, a second set of terminology has arisen. The risk associated with the market is called nondiversifiable risk, and the residual risk is called diversifiable risk. The latter terminology is appropriate, since nonmarket risk tends to go to zero for highly diversified portfolios. The economic intuition behind the security market line is that reward is gained only for bearing market risk (beta), because reward should not be gained for bearing risk that can be diversified away. Thus, if the investor holds a portfolio with residual risk he or she is taking a risk for which no compensation is received.

In fact, it follows from the standard CAPM that the only portfolio of risky assets that any individual or institution should hold is the market portfolio. The residual risk on the market portfolio is exactly zero, and no other portfolio exists that has zero residual risk. Since the standard CAPM implies that nonmarket risk is not compensated, it should be eliminated. However, there still exists the problem of wanting less risk or more risk than is contained in the market portfolio. The level of risk can be adjusted by simply combining the market portfolio with lending or borrowing to obtain the desired level of risk.

For example, if an investor desires less risk than is inherent in the market portfolio, the investor might place one-half of the funds in the market and one-half of the funds in Treasury bills. If the investor desires more risk, the investor borrows and places his original capital plus the borrowed capital in the market portfolio. This conclusion is so important it has been given a name in the literature—the *two mutual fund theorem.* It says that all investors can form an optimal portfolio by mixing two mutual funds—the market portfolio and a fund holding the riskless asset. The proportions in which they are mixed is determined by the investor's risk-return preference.

Some of the lessons of the standard CAPM are:

1. An investor is rewarded for taking beta (market) risk, but not for other kinds of risk.

2. The only portfolio of risky assets any investor should hold is the market portfolio.

3. Each investor should adjust his or her overall portfolio to the desired risk-return preference by lending or borrowing.

3. Implications for Investment Behavior

Before discussing the implications for prudence, one caveat is in order. There is one major problem in implementing the standard CAPM, even if belief in it is complete: identifying the market portfolio. This is important enough to merit a separate section, which is discussed shortly. Assume for now that the market portfolio has been identified and can be held at tolerable cost.

a. Holding the Market Portfolio. One of the strongest implications of a strict interpretation of the standard CAPM is that all investors should hold the market portfolio. This is a passive strategy. It not only involves no forecasting of security or asset performance, it implies that spending money on such forecasting is foolhardy.

Perhaps a slightly less strict interpretation would say that any deviation from holding the market portfolio requires justification. If a security or class of securities were perceived as being out of equilibrium (offering a return above that specified by the security market line), then an action in deviating from the market portfolio might be defended. The investor, however, would have to be able to specify that the deviations were sufficient to cover:

1. The extra transaction costs involved in deviation from the market.

2. The diversifiable risk incurred in deviating from the market portfolio.

3. The costs of analysis incurred in finding the "underpriced" securities.

b. Leverage Is Permissible. Under the CAPM, the only way to increase return is to increase risk. If an investor wants more return than is expected from the market portfolio he or she must incur more risk. If a higher risk return position is warranted by the objectives of the investor, the only efficient way to get there is to borrow to increase the investment in the market portfolio. Trying to increase return by deviating from the market portfolio (buying more high beta-stock) is inefficient, for deviations from the market portfolio introduce residual (diversifiable) risk. Residual risk does not increase expected return. The implications of the CAPM cannot be accepted without accepting leverage as a viable investment strategy.

c. Potential for Negative Results. The believer in the standard CAPM must keep in mind that this is an expected value theory. Realistically, expectations are met only in the long run. In the short run there is nothing unusual about returns deviating from what is expected. Thus, the theory should only describe what happens over very long periods of time. Over short periods, the theory won't describe reality. For example, holding a high-beta (e.g., leveraged) portfolio should produce high returns over a long period of time, but over short periods it may produce low or even negative returns. The explanation for this is easy to see. High-beta portfolios give high expected (long run) returns because they are riskier. If they always (over every time period) gave higher returns they would not be riskier. If an investor cannot bear adverse outcomes in the short run that investor should not be following a high-beta strategy.

4. Problems With the Market Portfolio

Until now, the assumption has been that the market portfolio was easily identifiable. In fact, according to the CAPM, the market portfolio should include all risky assets, each in proportion to the share it claims of the aggregate of all risky assets. This makes the market portfolio difficult to identify and has other major implications for investor behavior.[10]

Under the tenets of the standard CAPM, no investor should be criticized for holding a particular type of risky investment; in fact, depending on the circumstances, an investor might be criticized for not holding it. As an example, consider so called junk bonds. These bonds are low rated but have higher yields. When viewed in isolation, the bond of an issuer that might go bankrupt could be considered an imprudent investment. However, if the tenets of the CAPM are accepted, the residual risks are diversified away and the extra return promised by junk bonds provides the correct level of compensation for the risks involved. It is important to stress that the theory *cannot* be interpreted two ways. If an equilibrium model holds, then all assets should be purchased. If an equilibrium model is acted on, eliminating securities with a probability of bankruptcy from the portfolio requires as much justification as trying to pick winners. Once again, transaction costs, the cost of bearing diversifiable risk, and the cost of analysis must be covered.

If the use of a passive portfolio is supported on the basis of general equilibrium models, the widest possible interpretation of a market portfolio must be supported. Holding an index fund (market portfolio) of common stocks without the inclusion of debt instruments is not consistent with equilibrium theory. Indeed, a correct passive portfolio must theoretically include the full range of risky assets, including such items as commodities, junk bonds, small stocks, real estate, and collectibles.

If a class of assets is left out of a portfolio, the burden of proof for leaving it out should rest on the investor. Since the managed portfolio should replicate the market portfolio of all risky assets, the more important (the larger the total dollar value of) a type of asset excluded from the portfolio, the more harm is done by excluding it. As a practical matter, types of assets might be reasonably excluded because of large transaction costs, which include the costs resulting from illiquidity.

An index fund of stocks might be part of a market portfolio, but it should be *only* a part. Even when considering the universe of stocks, care must be taken. Most index funds attempt to duplicate some market index—typically one like the Standard & Poor (S&P) index, which only includes large stocks. This is inappropriate because all stocks, including over-the-counter stocks, should be included. There are differences in the performance of large stocks and small stocks. There are differences in the performance of established enterprises and new ventures. These differences cannot be ignored. The theory calls for the inclusion of all stocks, including those that may have traditionally been thought of as highly risky.

There is one other point that should be made in this section. Even under the standard CAPM and its implication of holding the market portfolio, a little thought will show that the assets held in the "market" portfolio might vary from investor to investor. Take the case of a pension fund administrator for a steel company. If a major asset of that fund is the future payment stream coming from the steel company, then a disproportionate amount of the fund's wealth is sensitive to the economic performance of the steel industry and hence the performance of steel stocks. It would be desirable for the common stocks held by this fund to include no steel stocks. In fact, it is possible to go further and argue that the fund should be underweight (hold less than market weights) in other stocks that move closely with the fortunes of the steel industry (perhaps other metal stocks or auto stocks). Considerations such as these have been discussed in the literature of financial economics, and conclusions like those described above have been reached.[11]

It may seem from the foregoing discussion that the practical problems with assembling the market portfolio are so numerous (such as the liquidity problems associated with holding art and other collectibles) as to render the effort futile. This conclusion exaggerates the importance of the difficulties in achieving a true "market" portfolio. Even if whole categories of assets (such as collectibles) are excluded for practical reasons, a large fund should still be able reasonably to approximate the market portfolio.

D. Other Equilibrium Models—Implications for Other Passive Portfolios

In the last section, one model for explaining why expected returns differ across assets was discussed. A large number of alternative models have been proposed for explaining why expected returns differ across assets.

Furthermore, there is empirical evidence that suggests that these alternatives may be more descriptive of reality than the standard CAPM. In this section, these alternative models are discussed, along with the optimal portfolio strategy they lead to and the implications these investment strategies have for prudence.

Alternatives to the standard CAPM are of two types. One type is derived by continuing the CAPM's assumption that investors are only concerned with the mean and variance of return, but relaxing one or more of its other assumptions. The second type, known as arbitrage pricing theory (APT), proceeds from assumptions about what factors affect returns. It does not require that investors be mean-variance maximizers.

1. Equilibrium Models Based on Assumption That Investors Use Mean-Variance Anaylsis

As discussed previously, the standard CAPM rests on ten assumptions, one of which is that investors are concerned only with mean and variance of returns. What distinguishes alternative models is a relaxation of one or more of those other nine assumptions. For example, the effect of taxes or of inflation may be taken into account.

a. The Zero Beta Capital Asset Pricing model. The most popular alternative to the standard CAPM is the so-called zero-beta CAPM. One of the assumptions that bothers people about the standard CAPM is that investors can not only lend, but also borrow, at the same riskless rate of interest. Investors can purchase Treasury bills, an instrument generally assumed to be riskless. Likewise, investors can buy federally insured certificates of deposit from major financial intermediaries. While these instruments may have some default risk, this risk is so small that assuming them to be riskless is reasonable. However, investors cannot borrow at the same rate as the federal government or large commercial banks. Thus, an assumption of an ability to borrow and lend at the same riskless rate is probably sufficiently unrealistic as to affect asset pricing. Figure A.6 depicts the investor's choice when there is a differential lending and borrowing rate.

The efficient frontier becomes A L B C. The market portofolio is on the efficient frontier, lying on the curved portion between L and B. However, unlike the standard capital asset pricing model the *market portfolio is no longer optimal for all investors.* Investors may find portfolios along the line segment A L more desirable. These would be obtained by putting part of a fund in the riskless asset and part in risky portofolio L, which would have a beta lower than one. Portfolios composed solely of risky assets and lying on the curved segment GL would be inferior. Thus, it is preferable to obtain lower risk by mixing a reasonably risky portfolio L with the riskless asset rather than by placing 100 percent of the fund in a low-risk portfolio. Whether or not a portfolio lies on GL may be difficult to determine. However an investor who knowingly chooses such a portfolio would be impru-

Figure A.6 The Investor's Choice with Differential Lending and Borrowing Rates

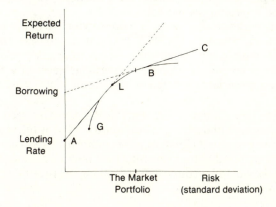

dent, since a higher return could be obtained for the same risk by mixing L and A. A particularly interesting portfolio is G. G is the least risky portfolio of risky assets available. However, if it is possible to lend at the riskless rate (and buying Treasury bills is clearly possible), it is imprudent to invest even in the least risky portfolio of risky assets, because the same expected return can be achieved at a lower level of risk by lending.

Another feasible set of risky portfolios is that lying on the segment LB. One of these portfolios is the market protfolio, but there are other risky portfolios on this segment. The most risky portfolio that can be held is B. An investor desiring to hold a portfolio along the line segment BC would invest the whole fund, plus an additional amount obtained by borrowing, in risky portfolio B. Thus, with differential lending and borrowing rates three posibilities can be observed:

1. Investors putting part of their fund in L and the remainder in a riskless asset.

2. Investors putting 100 percent of their fund in a risky portfolio.

3. Investors borrowing and putting more than 100 percent of their fund in portfolio B.

Investing 100 percent of an investor's money in a market portfolio of risky assets has often been suggested as the only appropriate strategy. This conclusion rests on the unrealistic assumptions underlying the standard CAPM. Relaxing the assumptions invalidates this prescription. This is obviously the case when lending and borrowing rates are different. A similar result follows when other assumptions are relaxed, as discussed in subsequent sections. Thus, authors advocating an investment strategy of 100 percent in the market portfolio as the only prudent investment must defend either the assumptions underlying the standard CAPM or its descriptive power! This presciption is not robust to slight changes in assumptions.

If Figure A.6 is a reasonable representation of how investors act, then expected returns on assets should be determined by the zero-beta CAPM.[12] This same CAPM results from an assumption of differential lending and borrowing rates or an assumption of lending at the riskless rate but borrowing being prohibited or an assumption of neither lending nor borrowing at the riskless rate.[13]

The reason for the term "zero beta" should now be clearer to readers. If the zero-beta CAPM holds, the expected return on any asset depends on the expected return on a portfolio uncorrelated with the market (the zero-beta portfolio) and the expected return on the market.

Empirical evidence on balance is more supportive of the zero-beta form of the CAPM than the standard CAPM.[14] Investment advisers probably use the zero beta CAPM most often to aid them in spotting underpriced securities. Thus, empirical evidence would support the reasonableness of a wide variety of portfolios being appropriate for different investors subject to the prudence standard.[15]

b. The After-Tax Capital Asset Pricing Model. The second most frequently relaxed assumption underlying the standard CAPM is the assumption that investors make decisions on the basis of pre-tax returns. If cash flows from all potential investments are taxed at the same rate, then making decisions on the basis of pre-tax cash flows would be equivalent to making decisions on the basis of post-tax cash flows, and the standard CAPM would not have to be modified even though taxes are paid on investment returns. However, differential taxation of investment cash flows is a prominent feature of the tax law. For example, capital gains are taxed at a different rate than dividend income. Likewise, municipal bonds are taxed at more favorable rates than government bonds. Even for tax-exempt funds, there are differences. If a tax-exempt fund borrows to invest, the leveraged returns are taxed at ordinary corporate rates.

The tax feature that has been incorporated into the after-tax CAPM is the differential taxation of capital gains and ordinary income. It should be pointed out that not all researchers accept the importance of this distinction. Differential taxation of capital gains and ordinary income has clearly been a feature of the U. S. tax system over much of its history. What is important, however, is the effective rate paid on these two streams. Some researchers have argued that dividend income allows greater write-offs of interest expense, thus lowering the effective tax rate.[16] If it is lowered sufficiently, then the rate on ordinary income and capital gains could be essentially the same, and looking at pre-tax returns would be approriate. Although some observers make this argument and some empirical evidence supports it, the bulk of the evidence is in favor of an effective differential in the taxation of ordinary and capital gains income.[17]

One implication of the after-tax CAPM being the appropriate description of reality is that once again it is no longer optimal for all investors to hold the market portfolio. The deviations from the market portfolio depend on the investor's tax bracket relative to the tax bracket affecting market prices. If the investor's tax bracket is greater than the bracket that determines market prices, then a portfolio with more than market representation in low-dividend-paying stocks and less than market representation in high-dividend stocks is preferred. In the same manner, if the investor's tax bracket is less than the bracket determining market prices, a portfolio with more than market representation in high-dividend-paying stocks and less than market representation in low-dividend stocks is the preferred portfolio.

It may seem that there are so many possibilities that no portfolio of risky assets can be deemed imprudent. As noted earlier, this is not the case. A portfolio composed solely of risky assets on the efficient frontier would nonetheless be inferior to a portfolio involving lending with higher return and the same risk or the same return at lower risk. In addition, the earlier analysis clarifies the reasoning behind certain investment strategies. For example, because of the way differential tax rates affect the pricing of assets, a fiduciary for a tax-exempt fund seeking to use primarily low-dividend stocks should have the burden of showing that:

1. The fiduciary had a special ability to select undervalued low-dividend stocks.

2. This special ability was likely to produce extra returns that more than compensate for the benefits that high-dividend-paying stocks offer to tax-exempt funds.

3. The special ability to select undervalued stocks was not transferable to those paying high dividends.

c. Inflation-Adjusted CAPMs. A number of CAPMs assume that inflation affects the equilibrium of expected return on securities. The underlying assumption of these models is that asset returns are differentially affected by inflation. Once again, the important element is that inflation affects securities differently. This causes inflation to be an important consideration. If inflation had a constant effect on all securities or if the effect of inflation on an individual security varied randomly across securities, then inflation need not be explicitly incorporated in the equilibrium asset pricing model.

If inflation is important, then investors should hold efficient portfolios where returns are defined in real terms rather than in nominal terms. Since the rate of inflation is uncertain, nominally riskless assets are risky in real terms. In the U.S. economy there is no asset whose return is adjusted by inflation and therefore riskless in real terms. Thus, in the U.S. economy there are no riskless assets in real terms.[18]

Without a riskless asset, a wide range of portfolios is reasonable to hold from an investor's point of view. The zero-beta form of the CAPM in real terms should explain expected returns. Very little can be said about the characteristics of efficient portfolios other than that they are widely diversified; the market portfolio is one candidate, but so too are the other risky portfolios lying between L and B in Figure A.6. The major point to keep in mind is that given the existence of uncertain inflation, the set of portfolios that a prudent investor might hold includes a wide range of highly diversified portfolios with the market portfolio remaining as one (but by no means the only) possible candidate.

d. Nontraded Assets and the CAPM. Some assets are not traded. The most notable of these is human capital. In this society, an investor cannot buy or sell another's right to future income. Thus, human capital is nontradable. A second example is a home. Homes, of course, are clearly tradable. However, most individuals do not trade their homes to rebalance their portfolios. Thus, investors may, in essence, be treating their homes as nontradable. The effect of nontradable assets is that each individual's portfolio should be custom designed. A portfolio should have underrepresentation of assets that are highly correlated with nontraded assets. For example, a steel executive whose income is highly affected by the performance of the steel industry should hold fewer assets whose performance is also affected by the steel industry than should the average investor. If nontraded assets are important, custom design of portfolios is necessary.

e. Other CAPM Models. There are a number of other CAPM models. Some allow for the inclusion of other assets, such as assets with returns denominated in currency other than the investor's home currency.[19] Other nonstandard CAPMs incorporate the effect of some investors having an effect on price when they trade, and some are derived from an assumption that investors consider more than the mean and variance of the distribution of returns in making portfolio decisions.[20] These models bear some resemblance to arbitrage pricing theory models, but they differ in that they are derived from, and the form of the model is determined by, consideration of formal utility theory rather than by consideration of the return generating process. The main implication of these models is that holding the market portfolio is no longer an optimal strategy for all investors. Rather, investors choose from a wide range of optimum portfolios. These portfolios cannot be specifically characterized as were prior models. Thus, a more detailed discussion of each is unwarranted.

2. Non-Mean-Variance Equilibrium Models

Each of the models dicussed previously relies on the assumption that investors are mean-variance maximizers. There is an alternative to this class of models. The alternative theory is called arbitrage pricing theory (APT). The name "arbitrage pricing theory" arises from the assumption that investors will arbitrage away any differences in the expected return on assets that have the same risks. Of course, the same assumption underlies the standard CAPM. The basic assumption of APT is not that investors are mean-variance maximizers, but rather that returns are affected by systematic influences that can be specified. The relationship between these systematic influences and the return on any asset over time is called the return generating process.[21] Examples of such systematic influences might be changes in oil prices or interest rates or steel prices. Not all of those influences are priced (i.e., offset expected or equilibirum returns). Part of APT consists of specifying those influences in the return generating process that are priced.[22]

What are the implications of APT for investment theory? First, there is a distinction between priced factors and unpriced factors. The return on a security is likely to be affected by both factors that are general to all securities and factors that are only important to a subset of securities. The effect of the general factors is unlikely to be eliminated in a large portfolio. Thus, these factors affect the expected return on all assets. The effect of factors that only affect a subset of securities is likely to be eliminated in a large portfolio. Thus, sensitivity to these factors does not result in higher expected return. As a concrete example, suppose that seven factors affecting the economy can be identified. Four of the factors are pervasive and, therefore, affect expected return (are priced) because they cannot be eliminated through diversification. Three of the factors are not pervasive in their influence because they affect only some segments of the economy. Since these risk factors can be diversified away, they do not affect expected return (are unpriced).

The separation of priced factors from unpriced factors is an important concept for investor behavior. Assume there is a steel factor that is not pervasive enough throughout the economy to be priced. An investment manager who concentrated on selecting steel companies would bear the extra risk of this factor without earning any additional expected return. Such a strategy would be detrimental unless the manager could demonstrate two things: *first,* sufficient expertise in selecting steel stocks to more than compensate for the extra risk, and *second,* the nontransferability of this expertise to a broader range of securities.

Constructing a portfolio that is sensitive to priced factors involves a different consideration. Since sensitivity to priced factors involves extra return, the choice of sensitivity to priced factors is a risk-return trade-off. The choice is neither good nor bad per se but depends on the goals (risk-return preferences) of the fiduciary making the choice.

There is a third issue that can be analyzed in the APT framework. This is the effect of other income on the choice of an optimal portfolio. Assume the investor has other income besides the income from the investment portfolio. Furthermore, assume this income is related to factors that affect a security's returns. Then the risk on the combination of the other income and the investment portfolio is reduced if the sensitivity of the investment portfolio to factors that also affect other income is lowered.

Arbitrage Pricing Theory is the newest widely acknowledged theory in finance.[23] The lessons to be learned from it are:

1. A portfolio may have to be constructed to take account of the risk of several systematic influences in addition to market movement. If these systematic risks are priced, an investor will be compensated for taking them, just as the CAPM suggests one is compensated for assuming greater market risk.

2. Risk may have to be measured by sensitivity to each of those systematic influences.

3. The market portfolio may play no unique role as a model for judging performance or as a benchmark passive strategy.

However, the theory is so new that the relevant influences have not yet been discovered. At this time, only these broad implications can be outlined.

E. Efficient Market Theory

Each of the models discussed thus far can be viewed as being consistent with the notion of fair prices existing in the market or of the market being efficient. A more detailed discussion of what "efficient markets" really are and what they imply for the prudent investor follows.

A great deal of research has attempted to show that security markets are informationally efficient. The basic concept is that information is impounded so quickly into the share price that by the time the investor can take advantage of the information it is already reflected in the share price. Consider the following example. Assume the firm announces earnings of $3 when analysts had been expecting $1. This is clearly good news. The expectation is that share prices rise in order to reflect this news. In an informationally efficient market, before an investor could place the order, the share price would have already risen to an unbiased estimate of its final price after adjusting for the earnings announcement. In an informationally efficient market, the share price of an individual security might rise or fall after the initial adjustment as the analysts evaluate the meaning of the unexpected high earnings. If the higher earnings reflected a change in the basic earning power of the company, then the stock price might rise further as analysts receive additional information that would support this interpretation. If the earnings are extraordinary earnings (perhaps associated with the sale of an asset), then the stock price should fall as analysts learn that the earnings surprise is a one-time phenomenon. However, in an informationally efficient market, buying a large number of similar companies with unexpected earnings surprises does not lead to excess returns.

The concept of efficiency is closely related to the concept of a fair game. If the securities market is a fair game, then there is no way to use information available at any point in time to make a profit beyond that which is consistent with the risk inherent in the security.

This discussion may seem either intuitively obvious or completely unappealing. To further clarify the discussion, some conditions under which it would not be correct must be specified. Assume that an investor has information that is *not* incorporated in the stock price when he buys but which will be incorporated soon thereafter. For example, suppose a government employee in charge of military contracts is about to approve a large contract for a small and previously unused supplier of butter to the army. This contract will result in a huge increase in profits for the company, but the market has assessed the probability of the company getting it as very small. Thus, only a fraction of the potential profits are incorporated in price. The procurement officer could make a much larger return than the equilibrium return for this company by purchasing its stock. The fair game model would not hold with respect to the procurement officer. Thus, if the information available to an investor is not incorporated in price, the fair game model does not hold with respect to that information.

The informational efficiency literature has been divided into three groups depending on the information with respect to which the market is efficient. These groups are called weak form, semi-strong form, and strong form. For weak-form tests, the information set is the past history of stock prices and past trading volume. For semi-strong form-tests, the information set is one or more pieces of publicly available information. Finally, for strong-form tests, the information set is all information, whether public or not, that is at the disposal of any group of investors.

To test any fair game model, an estimate of expected returns is required. There have been many choices. For some tests, the actual return in the preceding period is used as an estimate of expected return. In other cases, the estimate of expected return is implied from some model. The most commonly used model is the standard CAPM discussed previously. However, other models have been used.

The evidence on informational efficiency is discussed throughout and no additional detailed discussion is necessary.[24] However, some general conclusions should be presented. Most evidence shows that there is a very small correlation between past returns and future returns.[25] Tests that have examined whether the small amount of information in past returns can be used to earn abnormal profits have been negative.[26] Thus, researchers feel that markets are weak-form efficient. The evidence on strong-form efficiency looks primarily at the effects of insider trading. Insiders are clearly privy to nonpublic information. It should be expected that such information leads to excess returns. However, taking advantage of this information is illegal. Evidence supports the notion that insiders make excess returns and, accordingly, that markets are not strong-form efficient.[27] Evidence on semi-strong-form efficiency is mixed. By and large, new information seems to be fully incorporated in share price within a day or two of the announcement.[28] However, for the market to be truly informationally efficient, the impact of information should be immediate. This does not seem to be the case. Some abnormalities or inefficiencies that seem to be present are discussed later.

1. Implications of the Efficiency Literature

Consider for the moment the impact of an earnings surprise. Assume that the evidence is that earnings surprises are rapidly and unbiasedly incorporated in share price. What is left for the fiduciary to do? There are two aspects of the evaluation process for which there is little or no empirical evidence. First, are there some analysts that better predict earnings surprises and second, can some analysts better estimate the impact of an earnings surprise?

Prospective earnings surprises lead to a favorable impact on share price on average. However, after an earnings surprise some firms' prices decline rather than rise. Excess profits could be made if it were possible by superior analysis both to predict earnings surprises and separate out those firms whose shares will rise rapidly upon announcement of such a surprise. However, there are very few tests concerning the ability to forecast surprises or concerning the ability to better analyze the impact of announcements on earnings.[29] There is one recent study, Dimson and Marsh [9], that does indicate that analysts may be able to identify stocks that will outperform a passive strategy, although this study does not focus on the predicition of earnings.

2. Implications of Completely Efficient Markets

Assume that markets are completely efficient in the sense that information is rapidly incorporated in share price. analysts have no ability to forecast surprises, and they do not have any special ability differentially to analyze the impact of new information. What, then, is the role of investment managers?

First some misconceptions must be discussed. It is often stated that in an efficient market the only appropriate strategy is to hold the market portfolio. This does not logically follow. Holding the market portfolio is one implication of the standard CAPM. Yet market efficiency is also perfectly consistent with any of the other equilibrium models. For example, efficiency of the market would be consistent with the zero-beta form of the CAPM. As discussed previously, assuming the zero-beta CAPM holds does not imply that investors should hold the market portfolio. If taxes are important, then investors should tilt their portfolios to take advantage of their relative tax status. If one owns nontraded assets, portfolios should be designed to underinvest in assets highly correlated with the nontraded assets. In short, the appropriate investment strategy discussed in the sections on equilibrium models is unchanged by the concept of informational efficiency.

However, market efficiency does not require that any of the equilibrium models discussed previously holds.[30] What is the appropriate investment strategy if an investor is unwilling to accept any of the equilibrium models discussed earlier? Without an equilibrium model there is no necessary relationship between expected return and risk. Without an explicit tradeoff between risk and return, the appropriate strategy is simply to reduce risk. If no estimates of the risk of individual securities are made, then equal investment in each security is appropriate. If estimates of the risk structure are made, then a strategy to minimize risk is the appropriate passive strategy, and all that can be strongly asserted is that the portfolio should be well diversified.

3. Evidence of Market Inefficiencies

Research over the last five years has produced a growing body of evidence that even one of the most efficient markets (the New York Stock Exchange) has inefficiencies.[31] One of the most often quoted inefficiencies is the size effect.[32] It has been well documented that, after adjusting for risk, small firms have higher realized returns than large firms. A number of authors have attempted to explain the small-firm effect by arguing that the risk for small firms was underestimated or by explaining it in terms of some other missing factor. However, to date no satisfactory explanation exists for the small-firm inefficiency.

Another inefficiency that has received attention is the P/E effect.[33] Once again, after adjusting for risk, low P/E firms give higher returns than high P/E firms.

There is a high correlation between firm size and P/E, so that the small-firm effect and the P/E effect may be similar phenomena. However, once again no satisfactory explanation exists. Because size and P/E are easily observed, it is surprising that any information contained in these variables is not already incorporated in share price.[34]

Another inefficency is known as the January effect. A great deal of literature has been produced that supplies evidence that securities yield high excess returns for the entire month of January. Recently this phenomenon has been tied in with the small-firm effect. For example, Keim [19] presents evidence that about 25 percent of the size effect occurs during the first five trading days in January. A natural explanation for this might be tax-loss selling. Roll [26] presents this position and suggests that the phenomenon is larger for small firms since these firms are unlikely to be held by large institutions. Reinganum [25] shows that the small firms tend to produce larger returns for the first five days in January whether they showed capital loss or capital gains over the previous period. This would seem to invalidate the tax loss hypothesis. This view gets further support from Berges, McConnell, and Schlarbaum [3], who find a small-firm January effect in Canada but the effect is present both before and after the introduction of a capital gains tax.

Some other inefficiencies are less surprising. There is growing evidence that analyst forecasts contain valuable information.[35] There is evidence that certain analysts seem to be able to forecast earnings or returns above what could be explained by chance. Forecasts by internal analysts employed by fiduciaries are, of course, not widely available to the investing public. Thus, inefficiency with respect to these estimates is more difficult to eliminate than that due to widely available information such as firm size, and one could thus expect this effect to be more persistent.

The inefficiencies discussed above are a subset of those that have been documented. Over time, many will disappear as more accurate measures of risk are developed. However, new inefficiencies are likely to be discovered. The important point is not merely to identify those inefficiencies that have been discovered but rather to recognize that inefficiencies exist and are likely to continue. In the early years of the efficient market literature, adherents argued that markets were so efficient that hiring professional managers was a waste of resources. While this literature is a welcome caution on how much professional management can add to value, current evidence would indicate that active management can, in some cases, add sufficient return to justify its cost.

In summary, the state of the efficient market literature would seem to suggest that while markets are almost efficient, anomalies exist. The concept of a totally efficient market for all assets suggests a completely passive strategy on the part of the investor. Exceptions from efficiency suggest that investors can and perhaps should in some cases deviate from a passive strategy, but they must be able to document the reason for and process of this deviation. (This is discussed further in Section G.)

F. Other Considerations in Portfolio Management

In preceding sections, standard portfolio theory, general equilibrium theory, and efficient market theory are discussed. Here, some topics that are important in the investment area but that do not fall into any of the earlier categories are discussed.

1. The Importance of the Investor's Horizon

Consider a pure discount or zero-coupon bond. The only cash flow to the investor in this instrument is the cash flow at maturity, which incorporates both return of principal and interest. Without intermediate cash flows, there is no risk of reinvestment. Examples of pure discount instruments include Treasury bills and stripped government bonds (e.g., Tigers and Cats). An investor whose horizon exactly matches the maturity of the pure discount instrument has zero risk (ignoring the risk of default). An investor with any other horizon bears interest rate risk. This is a dramatic example of the effect of the investor's horizon on the riskiness of an investment strategy. The same effect can be seen with other strategies. For example, over long periods common equities have outperformed bonds as an investment strategy. However, the month-to-month and year-to-year variability of common equity is substantially higher than bonds. Thus, any investor with a long horizon should favor equities relative to an investor with a shorter horizon.

2. Importance of Risk Preference

Various equilibrium models and the passive strategies to which they led were previously discussed. Except in the extreme case of the standard CAPM, a number of alternative portfolios of risky assets are potentially optimal for a fiduciary. When a number of portfolios are on the efficient frontier, modern investment theory posits that the choice among them depends only on the fiduciary's risk-return preference. Without an analysis of the fiduciary's risk preferences, the choice among the portfolios cannot be made. The point is not that explicit guidance can be given, but rather that an optimum portfolio does exist, and its makeup depends on the fiduciary's risk-return tradeoff. Thus, except in the case where the standard CAPM is accepted as the appropriate model for all asset pricing, some evidence of an analysis of the investor's risk preference should be present.

3. Effect of Maximum Loss

A number of investment programs have a specific minimum cash need. Returns above the stated cash requirements are useful but are not as important as the ability to meet the scheduled cash need. In other words, there is an asymmetry in the outcomes. Failure to meet the demand for cash is extremely serious while extra returns, although beneficial, have less value. This kind of asymmetric reward should be incorporated in the investment strategy. It can be incorporated in a number of ways. It might be reflected in a two-portfolio strategy. Here, the first portfolio would contain assets of low risk and of a size sufficient to meet the target return. The second portfolio would be more aggressive, designed to provide extra return. A second alternative is to construct one aggressive portfolio but to also buy a put against it.[36] The put would have an exercise price equal to the amount of money necessary to be put aside in order to meet the target. The active portfolio would not have any special characteristics that would identify it as useful for meeting the target return.

4. The Effect of Illiquidity

A number of investment alternatives are not easily sold. Privately placed real estate is an example. Many mortgage loans or loans with equity kickers would be other examples. The characteristic of most illiquid investments is that they offer a higher return than corresponding liquid investments. For a portfolio with no immediate cash needs, investments like these may well be preferred given the additional return they offer. However, if the fund has cash needs or can have unanticipated cash needs, then some provision to accomodate such needs is necessary. Thus, the prudent investor must explicitly examine potential needs for cash withdrawal. Furthermore, the amount invested in illiquid investments must be related to the potential cash needs of the portfolio.

5. Judging Securities and Techniques by Their Purpose

Securities can be used in combination to generate a portfolio that has all the characteristics of a portfolio composed of very different securities. The simplest example is artificial options. It is well known that any arbitrary portfolio of common equities can be combined with Treasury bills in such a way that the combination has the same characteristics as owning the underlying stock portfolio plus a put option on that portfolio. The creation of artificial puts involves a shift from equities to Treasury bills as stock prices decline and a shift from Treasury bills to equities as stock prices rise. This dynamic portfolio adjustment causes the combination of an equity portfolio and a portfolio of Treasury bills to replicate the return pattern of the equity portfolio plus a put option on that portfolio. The construction of an artificial put involves continual adjustment of the bond stock mix in a predetermined manner. The underlying point is that the reasonableness of any investment decision should be judged in terms of the purpose sought to be achieved in the context of overall portfolio management. If the decision to hold Treasury bills with a particular stock portfolio is based on the idea of combining a risky portfolio with the "floor" that a put option creates, its prudence must be tested on how well that goal is achieved rather than on the merits of just holding Treasury bills and the risky portfolio.

6. Dominated Securities

A prudent investor should not hold a dominated security. The simplest example of a dominated security is a nongovernment bond having a lower yield than a government bond obtainable at the same price and with the same maturity yet with no special characteristics such as an advantageous tax status. Government bills are considered to be free of default risk. A number of banks offer C.D.s at much lower rates of interest than can be obtained on a government bill with the same maturity. These instruments are riskier than government debt. A prudent investor does not invest at lower interest rates when higher interest rates are available in less or equally risky instruments. While this is the most obvious example of dominated securities, other examples exist.

Many funds try to earn extra return by making timing decisions on when to invest in various categories of securities. The most common of these is the bond stock mix. A manager switches between bonds and stocks in anticipation of changes in the relative performance of these instruments. To market time in this manner an investor incurs the cost of buying and selling the securities. There is an alternative way to carry out a market timing strategy. This involves taking positions in futures. For example, assume an investor wished to increase equity exposure relative to debt exposure. This can be accomplished by purchasing equity futures and selling debt futures. Futures transactions are considerably cheaper than transactions in the underlying security.[37] If the portfolio is highly correlated with a portfolio for which futures exist, then timing by futures dominates timing by changing the underlying securities held in the portfolio. Even if an investor's portfolio is very different than the portfolio for which futures exist, timing by futures may be preferred. There is an added risk when the portfolio differs from the portfolio on which futures are written. This risk is one of adverse changes in the relative performance of the actual portfolio invested in and the portfolio against which futures are written. The choice of timing method depends on an evaluation of this added risk compared with the savings in transaction costs through use of futures.

G. Portfolio Strategy Development and Implementation

One of the most difficult aspects of portfolio management is the selection of a strategy and one or more managers appropriate to effect it. This entire appendix has been, in part, concerned with this issue—it is now time to reexamine it.

The investment process should start with a set of goals. Vague intentions such as "I want to maximize return and not take much risk" are no longer sufficient. The concern must be with managing both risk and return. Return can be decreased, and risk increased, through imprudent management. But given prudent management, the only way to increase expected return is through bearing more risk. The amount of risk that an account can bear and the tradeoff between risk and return that a fund sponsor will take must be thoroughly analyzed. Courts must realize that minimizing risk is not the only defensible strategy and that in fact, as discussed earlier, minimizing the risk on the portfolio of risky assets may be an imprudent strategy. Placing 100 percent of funds in Treasury bills is safe in terms of the default risk, but there is an opportunity cost in foregone returns as well as the risk of inflation. If any bad outcome is taken as a sign of imprudent management, then all managers are forced to take low-risk, low-return strategies. Obviously the other extreme of adopting a high-risk, high-return strategy is not appropriate for most investors. Even a long-term investor with small intermediate cash flow needs has to be alert to the danger of gambling ruin in the short run. Fiduciaries should always be concerned with balancing risk and return.

The fiduciary must formulate a set of goals delineated, at the very least, in terms of risk and return. The goals should, at a minimum, also specify constraints on liquidity as appropriate for anticipated cash outflows and consider the tax implications of any investment policy.

Once goals are established, an appropriate passive strategy should be formulated to meet these goals. A considerable amount of time has already been spent discussing passive portfolios. While slavishly following a passive strategy is not advocated, an appropriate passive strategy serves as a benchmark to help select managers or management philosophies and as a way of monitoring performance over time.

While the selection of an optimal passive portfolio is not easy, and in fact there is probably not a single, truly optimal passive portfolio for any fiduciary, the selection of an appropriate passive portfolio, consistent with goals and circumstances of a fiduciary's situation, places the rest of the investment process in its proper perspective.

To select the passive portfolio, the fiduciary must examine his goals in terms of risk and return, special liquidity needs, special tax treatment, the economic circumstances that determine flows into and out of the fund, and beliefs about the behavior of security markets. Once a passive portfolio is determined, deviations from that passive portfolio—active management—can be examined. As a general rule deriving from modern portfolio theory, the more the fiduciary chooses to vary from the passive portfolio strategy, the more evidence is needed of ability and economic rationale.

To illustrate this, concentrate for a monment on the common stock portion of a portfolio and assume that there are no special attributes of the fiduciary and that the standard CAPM is accepted as a reasonable model for describing expected returns so that a widely diversified (market) portfolio of common stocks is appropriate. If the fiduciary decides simply to hire one manager to hold an index fund of common stocks, the decision becomes very simple. Expertise in running index funds at a low management fee is all that is required. Even here some discretion is called for. Different managers attempt to approximate the market portfolio in different ways (e.g., by holding a smaller number of stocks than is contained in the market portfolio), the idea being to decrease transaction costs while nearly replicating the market portfolio. In selecting such a manager, the fiduciary needs to know how the manager intends to replicate the market portfolio and to see the manager's track record of how well this has been done. In addition, the fiduciary needs to examine transaction costs. The final choice among alternative managers involves the tradeoff between one performance attribute (how well the portfolio traces the market portfolio) and two sets of costs (management fees and transaction costs within the portfolio).

What about the fiduciary who decides to deviate from the passive strategy? At the very least, the fiduciary needs some evidence that:

1. The investment strategy to be followed by the manager is consistent with the tenets of modern portfolio theory.

2. The manager has, in fact, followed the strategy he or she professes to follow.

3. The manager's past performance has been successful.

4. The costs of deviating from a passive strategy are reasonably expected to be more than met by gains.

In addition, the manager's performance must be continually tracked once hired to ensure that the above outlined points are met.

A few examples of how these rules might apply should be examined. Assume that a pension fund fiduciary selects a manager who specializes in constructing a portfolio of high technology stocks. There are two extreme cases to consider: first, where the fiduciary gives the manager all funds that are intended to be invested in equities, and second, where the high technology manager is given only the amount of funds that under the passive portfolio would be invested in high technology stocks. Start with the latter case. There is beginning to be some evidence in the literature of financial economics that analysts can outperform random selection.[38] However, in hiring a manager for the high technology sector of the portfolio, the fund sponsor should require evidence that the manager hired can outperform random selection. In this case, the evidence should first take the form of examining the process used by the manager to select stocks. What special skills does the manager profess to have that allows the manager to pick winners? Is it superior technological knowledge of the industries and the process involved, superior knowledge of the market place for new products, or something else? The fiduciary should then attempt to see if the manager actually has these special skills (e.g., does the staff possess the qualifications necessary to implement the strategy). Next, the fiduciary should look at the historical record of the manager. Has this manager been successful in managing portfolios of this type in the past? Here it is important to measure the manager against the appropriate benchmark. For a manager of high technology stocks, the appropriate benchmark is the population of high technology stocks, not the S&P 500. If a wider group of stocks is used as a benchmark, the manager of high technology stocks might look good (or poor) over a period of years because high technology stock did well (or poorly) over those years. If the manager is hired to replicate the high technology component of a passive portfolio, the relevant question is whether the manager outperformed that component.

Finally, if the manager outperforms a passive component, the fiduciary must ensure that the extra performance was sufficient to compensate for the extra diversifiable risk that was involved, the extra transaction costs involved in actively managing this segment of the portfolio, and the management fee that would have to be paid.

If the manager is hired, performance must be monitored over time. The more the manager deviates from the high technology component of the passive portfolio, the more closely he or she should be monitored. If the manager does not deviate from the high technology component of the passive portfolio, the management should be questioned. The fiduciary is paying an active management fee. If all the fiduciary is getting is passive management, then too much is being paid for the service.

If the fiduciary is getting active management, then underperforming the high technology portions of the passive portfolio over a short to intermediate period of time, from one to three years, is not necessarily evidence of poor management. Engaging in any active management usually results in increased risk over a passive strategy. This means that bad outcomes can occur. If they did not, the strategy would not be riskier. What must be monitored is whether the manager is following the strategy he or she purported to follow and whether the manager has maintained the ability to follow that strategy. While the question of capacity should always be tracked along with performance, obviously the longer the period of inferior performance, the closer should be the scrutiny of the manager.

What about the case where all common stock funds are given to the active high technology stock manager for investment? In this case a greater burden of showing prudence is placed on the fiduciary. Placing all funds in one sector or type of stock means that the manager bears a large amount of diversifiable risk, for which there is no compensation paid. To bear such risk requires solid reasons why a commensurate increase in return can be expected. While this is not the same as the case of holding a single asset discussed earlier, it is somewhat analogous. A portfolio concentrated in one sector of the market is likely to lie below the efficient frontier because it is not well diversified. If all assets are placed in such a nondiversified portfolio, strong evidence of an ability to produce superior performance must be produced.

Look at another case of active management, the case of a dividend rollover scheme (buy before a stock goes ex-dividend and sell afterward) offered to a tax-free institution.[39] It is well documented that the price of a stock should and does fall by less than the amount of the dividend when the stock goes ex-dividend. Tax-free institutions are theoretically in a position to take advantage of this phenomenon. In fact, in the absence of transaction costs, this would clearly be a profitable strategy for a tax-free or a low-tax institution to follow. Theory would seem to be on the side of this strategy. However, a moment's reflection quickly reveals that, at least in part, offsetting the gain from the tax-dividend behavior of common stocks is the high turnover and thus the large amount of transaction costs that are incurred. Here the key question becomes whether or not the ex-dividend gain is sufficient to offset the transaction cost of getting into and out of the stocks. The sponsor considering such a strategy should require:

1. Evidence as to the size of the ex-dividend drop in price relative to the dividend.

2. Evidence as to the level of transaction costs that have been incurred on accounts like this.

3. An exact specification of the trading rule that will be used.

4. Evidence of past performance of the trading rule on other accounts similarly managed.

If the technique appears promising given its past performance and the fiduciary commits funds to a manager to carry out the technique, the fiduciary must be careful to monitor performance. Once again, over a short period, the rule may not work well. For example, in a period when the stock market is going down, it would not be expected to work well at all.

Similar arguments can be made with any deviations from a passive portfolio. The more extreme the deviation, the more cogent must be the arguments for following it (both in terms of theory and empirical evidence), and the more closely the implementation of strategy and performance must be monitored.

Actually, the previous discussion applies equally well to a fiduciary hiring an active manager or to a fiduciary actively managing all or part of the portfolio directly. One more lesson should be mentioned for the fiduciary who hires several managers. It is the fiduciary's obligation to monitor the entire portfolio (the sum of all managers' portfolios) to make sure that active management fees are not being paid for passive management. To the extent that the actions of individual managers are not coordinated they can cancel each other out, with the total portfolio coming to resemble an index fund, albeit an index fund on which large active fees are paid.

H. Conclusions

This essay has reviewed several alternative theories of asset pricing, each of which has a significant number of adherents in the financial community and also a healthy number of detractors. There are certain lessons for the fiduciary, however, that are shared by all of these theories and therefore survive as widely accepted tenets of modern portfolio theory. It seems appropriate to review them here:

1. Diversification pays.

All of the modern theories of portfolio analysis and capital asset pricing stress the need for diversification both across and within different types of assets. While moving away from the concept of the market portfolio, the point must be stressed that even with special characteristics or special knowledge the portfolio held should be widely diversified.

Equlibrium theory suggests that all types of assets should be represented in a portfolio. While it is necessary to be careful of non-traded assets and the transaction costs associated with them, all assets should be considered as appropriate candidates for a portfolio.

2. Special characteristics or knowledge can justify tilting the widely diversified portfolio in certain directions.

For example, a pension fund whose inflow depends on the fortunes of the steel industry should tilt away from assets whose returns are positively correlated with the performance of the steel industry. As a second example, tax-free funds generally should not tilt against high-income securities. The exception to this would be if the investment manager had special ability to invest in the securities of the type that should be underinvested in, and this special ability was not transferable.

A well-founded belief in the ability to select undervalued securities or types of assets should lead to a diversified portfolio tilted in favor of these securities or types of assets.

3. The more tilting that is done, the greater the burden of proof on the fiduciary.

The greater the tilting, the more nondiversifiable risk is added. In addition, greater tilting requires added transaction costs. The expected payoff must be large enough to compensate for bearing nondiversifiable risk and for added transaction costs and management fees. Satisfactory evidence must be offered in terms of economic rationale and empirical evidence that the additional risk and costs are justified.

4. The risk of buying an asset or continuing to hold an asset can only be judged in terms of the impact of that asset on the portfolio.

No asset or investment technique is risky or not risky in isolation. The asset must be looked at as a member of a diversified portfolio and the technique in the context of its purpose with reference to that portfolio. A striking example of this is a short sale. There is a possibility of an unlimited loss with a short sale. Thus in isolation, a short sale is an extremely risky investment technique. However, in a portfolio a short sale may reduce risk. The only way to eliminate market-related risk is to short sell some securities. Short sales in a portfolio with a net long position normally reduce the risk of the portfolio.

5. The only way to increase the return of an efficient portfolio is to increase its risk. A manager must be judged in terms of both the risk and the return. Placing total emphasis on risk would force all managers to hold the risk-free asset and to give up returns.

6. Selecting a risky portfolio often means poor performance on a yearly basis. Common stock has historically outperformed bonds on a long-term basis.

However, the odds are substantial that in any one year returns on common stock will be negative.

7. Short selling and borrowing should not necessarily be considered improper. While both can be used to take extreme risk positions, they can equally well be used to increase the risk-return opportunities available to a fiduciary.

8. Do not invest in dominated securities or portfolios. There are several types of securites or portfolios that are dominated. Corporate bonds or bank obligations may yield less than government bonds of similar maturity. Portfolios that have higher risk for the same return or other portfolios should also be avoided.

9. Risk depends on the investor's horizon. A ten-year pure discount instrument is risky for a one-year holding period but riskless in terms of meeting a known obligation at the end of ten years.

BIBLIOGRAPHY

1. Banz, R. "The Relationship Between Return and Market Value of Common Stock." *Journal of Financial Economics* 9 (1981): 3–8.
2. Basu, S. "The Relationship Between Earnings Yield Market Value and the Return for NYSE Common Stock: Further Evidence." *Journal of Finance* 32 (1977): 663.
3. Bergess, A., J. J. McConnell, and G. G. Schlarbaum. "An Investigation of the Turn-of-the-Year Effect, the Small Firm Effect, and the Tax-Loss-Selling-Pressure Hypothesis in Canadian Stock Returns," manuscript (Purdue University, West Lafayette, Indiana 1982).
4. Black, F. "Capital Market Equilibrium with Restricted Borrowing." *Journal of Business* 45 (1972): 444–55.
5. ———. "International Capital Market Equilibrium With Investment Barriers." *Journal of Financial Economics* (1974): 337–52.
6. ———, M. Jensen, and M. Scholes. "The Capital Asset Pricing Model: Some Empirical Tests." In Jensen (ed.), *Studies in the Theory of Capital Markets* (New York: Praeger 1972).
7. ———, and M. Scholes. "The Effects of Dividend Yield and Dividend Policy on Common Stock Prices and Returns." *Journal of Financial Economics* 1 (1974): 1–22.
8. Brennan, M. "Capital Market Equilibrium With Divergent Borrowing and Lending Rates." *Journal of Financial and Quantitative Analysis* 6 (1971): 1197–205.
9. Dimson and Marsh. "An Analysis of Brokers and Analysts Unpublished Forecast of U.K. Stock Returns." *Journal of Finance* 39 (1984): 1257–93.
10. Elton, Edwin and M. Gruber. "Marginal Stockholder Tax Rates and the Clientele Effect." *Review of Economics and Statistics* 52 (1968): 68–74.
11. ———. *Modern Portfolio Theory and Investment Analysis.* 2d ed. (John Wiley, New York 1981).
12. ———, and M. Gultekin. "The Usefulness of Estimates of Analysts Earnings." *Journal of Financial And Quantitative Analysis* (1984).
13. ———. "Risk Reduction and Portfolio Size: An Analytical Solution." *Journal of Business* 50 (1977): 415–37.
14. Fama, E. and J. Macbeth. "Tests of the Multiperiod Two-Parameter Model." *Journal of Financial Economics* (1974): 43–66.
15. Granger, C. "A Survey of Empirical Studies on Capital Markets." In Elton and Gruber (eds.) *International Captial Markets* (Amsterdam: North Holland 1975).
16. Grauer, F., R. Litzenberger, and R. Stehle. "Sharing Rules and Equilibrium in an International Capital Market Under Uncertainty." *Journal of Finance Economics* 3 (1976): 233–56.

17. Ibbotson and Sinquefield. "Stocks, Bonds, Bills and Inflation: The Past and the Future." Working paper (Financial Analysts Research Foundation, University of Virginia 1982).
18. Jaffe, J. "Special Information and Insider Trading." *Journal of Business* 47 (1974): 1027–42.
19. Keim, D. B. "Size Related Anomalies and Stock Return Seasonality: Further Empirical Evidence." *Journal of Financial Economics* 12 (1983).
20. Kraus, A., and B. Litzenberger. "Market Equilibrium in a Multiperiod State Preference Model With Logarithmic Utility." *Journal of Finance* 30 (1973): 1213–27.
21. Lindenberg, E. "Capital Market Equilibrium With Price Affecting Institutional Investors." In Elton and Gruber (eds.) *Portfolio Theory 25 Years Later* (Amsterdam: North Holland 1979).
22. Litzenberger, R. and K. Ramaswamy. "The Effect of Personal Taxes and Dividends on Capital Asset Prices: Theory and Empirical Evidence." *Journal of Financial Economics* 8 (1979): 163–95.
23. ———. "The Effects of Dividends on Common Stock Prices: Tax Effects or Information Effects?" *Journal of Finance* 37 (1977): 333–64.
24. Miller, M. and M. Scholes. "Dividend and Taxes." *Journal of Financial Economics* 6 (1977): 333–64.
25. Reinganum, M. "The Anomalous Stock Market Behavior of Small Firms in January: Empirical Tests for Tax Loss Selling Effect." *Journal of Financial Economics* 12 (1983).
26. Roll, R. "The Turn of the Year Effect and the Return Premium of Small Firms." *Journal of Portfolio Management* (1982).
27. ———. "A Possible Explanation of the Small Firm Effect." *Journal of Finance* 36 (1981): 879–88.
28. ———. "Critique of the Asset Pricing Theory's Tests; Part I: On Past and Potential Testability of the Theory." *Journal of Financial Economics* 4 (1977): 129–76
29. Solnik, B. "The Advantages of Domestic and International Diversification." In Elton and Gruber (eds.) *International Capital Markets* (Amsterdam: North Holland 1975).
30. Tinic, S. M., and R. W. West. "Risk and Return January vs. the Rest of the Year." *Journal of Financial Economics* 13 (1984).

NOTES

[1]*See* Ibbotson & Sinquefield [17].

[2]This assumes returns have a normal distribution.

[3]*See* Elton & Gruber [11], Chapter 3, for a more detailed and mathematical explanation of the statements made in this section.

[4]The major results of the model would hold if income tax and capital gains taxes were of equal size. The more realistic case where the rates differ is discussed in a later section of this appendix.

[5]*See* e.g., [6].

[6]In a later section of this chapter a discussion of efficient markets is presented. The assumptions behind the CAPM are a lot stricter (less realistic) than the assumptions behind efficient markets. Markets can be efficient without the CAPM model holding. If all the assumptions of the CAPM hold and the model is held perfectly at all points in time, then markets would be efficient. However, markets can be efficient even if the CAPM did not provide an adequate description of returns.

[7]This is usually written as an equation as follows:

$$E(R_i) = R_F + \beta_i(E(R_m) - R_F)$$

Where:

$E(R_i)$ = the expected return on any asset or portfolio.

$E(R_m)$ = the expected return on the market portfolio of all risky assets

R_F = the riskless rate of interest, e.g., usually the thirty-day Treasury bill rate.

β_i = the sensitivity of the return of asset i to the return on the market portfolio.

For a detailed derivation of this relationship see Elton & Gruber [11], Chapter 4.

[8]Whether the aggregate of all risky assets includes only the assets in one economy or all assets throughout the world is still an open question. The resolution of this question depends on how freely the investors in any one economy can purchase the assets in another economy. If investors in the U. S. economy can easily purchase assets in foreign economies, then, it could be expected that an integrated capital market and the market portfolio would consist of all assets, both domestic and foreign. If, on the other hand, there are restrictions on investors in the U. S. economy purchasing assets in foreign economies, the expectation would be that capital markets would be segmented, with the market portfolio consisting only of assets in the domestic economy.

$$\sigma_i^2 = \beta_i^2 \sigma_m^2 + \sigma_{ei}^2$$

Where:

σ_i^2 = the variance of the return on stock i.

σ_m^2 = the variance of the return on the market portfolio

σ_{ei}^2 = the variance of stock i not explained by the market—the nonmarket or residual risk of stock i.

[10]Roll [25] has expressed doubt that the market portfolio can now or ever will be correctly identified.

[11]For example, see [5], [20], and [21].

[12]Zero-beta CAPM:

$$\overline{R_i} = \overline{R_z} + \beta_i(\overline{R_m} - \overline{R_z})$$

Where:

$\overline{R_i}$ = the expected return on asset i.

$\overline{R_z}$ = the expected return on a portfolio whose return is independent of the market.

β_i = a measure of the responsiveness of asset i to changes in the return on the market portfolio.

[13]See Black [4] for the original proof. See Elton & Gruber [11], p. 304 for an intutive proof.

[14]See Black, Jensen, & Scholes [7] and Fama & MacBeth [14].

[15]See Black [4] and Brennan [8].

[16]See Miller & Scholes [24].

[17]See Black & Scholes [7], Litzenberger & Ramaswamy [22], and Elton & Gruber [10].

[18]Over long periods of time, short-term Treasury bills have produced rates of return equal to or slightly above the rate of inflation. However, over shorter time spans, Treasury bills frequently give returns below or above inflation. Of course, Treasury bills are not riskless in real terms.

[19]See Grauser, Litzenberger, & Stehle [15] or Solnik [29].

[20]See Kraus & Litzenberger [20] and Lindenberg [21].

[21]This can be represented as:

$$\begin{bmatrix} \text{Return on} \\ \text{stock } i \end{bmatrix} = \begin{bmatrix} \text{Constant} \end{bmatrix} + \begin{bmatrix} \text{Return due to} \\ \text{influence 1} \end{bmatrix} + \begin{bmatrix} \text{Return due to} \\ \text{influence 2} \end{bmatrix}$$

$$+ \begin{bmatrix} \text{Return due to} \\ \text{influence 3} \end{bmatrix} + \begin{bmatrix} \text{Random error} \end{bmatrix}$$

The above expression can be written more succinctly in equation form as follows:

$$R_{it} = a_i + \beta_{i1}I_{1t} + \beta_{i2}I_{2t} + \beta_{i3}I_{3t} + \cdots + e_{it}$$

[22]This can be expressed in equation form as:

$$\overline{R}_i = C + \beta_{i1}\lambda_1 + \beta_{i2}\lambda_2 + \beta_{i3}\lambda_3$$

[23]Of course, new models and variations on older ones continue to appear.

[24]Any standard text has a detailed discussion, e.g., Elton & Gruber [11], Chapter 15.

[25]An excellent survey is in Granger [16].

[26]See Granger [16].

[27]See Jaffee [18] and associated bibliography.

[28]See Elton & Gruber [11], Chapter 15 and the references contained therein.

[29]See Elton & Gruber [11] for an estimate of the amount of information needed to earn excess returns.

[30]A debate exists as to whether market efficiency is a necessary condition for any equilibrium model to hold. In its strictest sense for any equilibrium model to hold exactly at every moment of time and over any infinitessimally small instant in time, market efficiency is necessary. However, informational inefficiencies can exist and an equilibrium model can still provide an excellent description of returns over meaningful horizons. For example, if information takes a day or two to be reflected in market prices, markets are not perfectly efficient over that time interval, but a CAPM or other equilibrium model could still be an excellent description of expected returns for the investor with a six-month or longer horizon.

[31]In this section these inefficiencies are discussed.

[32]See Banz [1], Roll [27], and Reinganum [25].

[33]See Basu [2].

[34]An alternative explanation for the small firm and low P/E effects is that markets are efficient and the tests used to detect these apparent inefficiencies are inaccurate. There is also evidence that the results on the validity of the CAPM may be interrelated with the small firm effect, see Tinic & West [30].

[35]See Dimson & Marsh [9].

[36]A "put" is an option contract. Consider a six-month American put on General Motors stock at $80. The purchaser of the put can sell the stock at a price of $80 to the writer of the put option. This sale is at the purchaser's option and he can exercise the option at any time over the six months. The purchaser need never exercise the option and will not if the price of the stock is above $80. Thus, the minimum value the purchaser can end up with is $80 minus the cost of the put.

[37]In the fifth report to Congress on the effect of the absence of fixed rates on commissions published, see the SEC, May 26, 1977, p. 4: One-way transaction costs for an institutional trade are estimated at .47 percent per transaction or roughly one percent round trip. Futures transaction costs are less than .003 percent per trade.

[38]See, e.g., Dimson & Marsh [9]. This article also contains an excellent review of previous articles in this area.

[39]The discussion here centers on a pure dividend rollover scheme. Other variations of this scheme involve changing the timing of purchases and sales to take advantage of rollover.

APPENDIX B

The Puzzling Survival of the Constrained Prudent Man Rule

Jeffrey N. Gordon[1]

By now, attacks on the traditional understanding of the prudent man rule are commonplace.[2] Legal academics have sought to replace the "constrained" rule, based on a narrow conception of risk and safety, with an "unconstrained" rule that would permit a financial fiduciary to define "prudence" in light of the insights of contemporary economics. In particular, "modern portfolio theory" is presented as a superior account of risk and safety and thus a better guide to prudent investment.[3] The more general point is that an appropriate rule should embody sufficient flexibility to allow fiduciaries to adapt to the prevailing theories of markets and investments as held by prudent investors.

Nevertheless the traditional prudent man rule, the constrained rule, still lives on. A series of recent court decisions[4] and even administrative rulings[5] suggest that the traditional trust law notions of what counts as "prudence" have great staying power. Perhaps even more importantly, the constrained rule continues to influence the behavior of financial fiduciaries, many of whom report (in responses to the questionnaire in this study [Questionnaire]) that they are blocked from pursuing what they regard as optimum investment decisions.[6] As this volume demonstrates, the constrained rule discourages trustees (and other fiduciaries) from many investments and investment techniques now regularly employed by prudent investors: start-up enterprises, venture capital pools, many kinds of real estate-based investments, foreign stocks, short-selling of equity securities, and options and futures, for example. Some of these investments permit greater diversification across the investment spectrum.[7] Others, such as futures and options, are means of lowering the risks from volatile stock prices and interest rates.[8] Thus, because of the received understanding of the rule, trust beneficiaries are denied sophisticated investment management that could raise returns and lower risks. This is a strange role for a rule aimed at beneficiary protection.

This essay operates on three levels. Its main thrust is to account for a puzzle in the history of the law: how a rule founded on the adaptable wit of the prudent man has become a hindrance to sound fiduciary investment management. In so doing it presents the case for an unconstrained rule, told in terms of portfolio theory and in discourse suitable for adoption by a common-law court. The temptation is to think that mere survival demonstrates a rule's virtue; but if courts come to understand why the constrained rule has unnaturally persisted, they may be more receptive to the argument for its unconstraining.

Second, this essay also attempts to understand common-law processes of change in the context of the institutions of trust law. What *does* account for the survival of the constrained prudent man rule? The answer is a complicated one, in which at least two distinct elements have figured significantly: First is Prof. Scott's authoritative work, his Treatise and the Restatement of Trusts for which he was reporter, which has inhibited the customary common law process of reinterpretation and change. Second is the particular difficulty for the courts in receiving complicated social science theory that apparently entails wide-sweeping doctrinal change.

Finally, on a third level, the paper is a substantive examination of certain investment management doctrines of traditional trust law in light of modern portfolio theory. It turns out that the only significant clash between portfolio theory and trust doctrine arises in the allocation of returns between life beneficiaries and remaindermen. Statutory formulas allocate "income" (interest and cash dividends) to the former and "principal" (including capital gains and losses) to the latter. This is inconsistent with portfolio theory, which analyzes investment performance in terms of "total returns," dividends (or interest), and capital gains or losses during the relevant holding period. After canvassing several alternatives, the essay proposes an approach based on the "adjusted real yield" of the portfolio and calls for further investigation of the economic and legal specifics by a collaborative team of financial economists and lawyers. The fruits of this work could be embodied in uniform statutes or model trust clauses.

Of course, as discussed in Chapter 1 of this study, criticism of the constrained prudent man rule of private trust law has found a warmer reception in the statutory and regulatory arenas occupied by other classes of fiduciaries, such as the trustees of educational and philanthropic endowments and of pension funds. These other modern versions of the prudent man rule—the Uniform Management of Institutional Funds Act of 1972 (UMIFA), the regulations under Section 4944 of the Internal Revenue Code, and the Employee Retirement Income Security Act of 1974 (ERISA) and the regulations promulgated thereunder—each vary the traditional language of the constrained rule in order to distance themselves from its reach.

However, as discussed in Chapter 1 and Appendix C, the constrained rule, although a creature of trust law and a direct source of authority only for the trustees of private trusts, influences the behavior of all financial fiduciaries. It is currently the best developed body of law governing funds management by fiduciaries. It provides answers and analogies. Therefore, unlike the rest of this study, this essay attends almost exclusively to the prudent man rule of private trust law in order to understand why that body of doctrine, so potent in its influence on all financial fiduciaries, has proved so inordinately resistant to change.

A. The Rule and its Constrained Formulation

1. The Original Formulation

The original formulation of the prudent man rule, which has been adopted virtually verbatim by statute in 40 states,[9] is a model of flexibility. There were two key elements to the rule as stated in *Harvard College v. Amory*. First there was a substantive standard of safe investment. The trustee was to acquire investments appropriate for "permanent disposition" of his own funds, not for "speculation." The court realized that absolute safety of investment was impossible ("Do what you will, the capital is at hazard"[10]), but required within the limits of permanent disposition that the trustee consider the factors of safety and income. Second, there was a process standard. In making investment judgments, the trustee was to govern himself by the prevailing standard of how prudent men handled their own affairs.

2. The Restatement, the Treatise, and the Constrained Rule

The modern understanding of the prudent man rule was shaped by that great figure in the law of trusts, the late Harvard professor Austin Wakeman Scott. Scott was the reporter of the first and second Restatements of Trusts (Restatement), completed in 1935 and 1959, respectively, and the author of the leading Treatise on trusts, *Scott on Trusts* (Treatise), the first edition of which was published in 1939 and which has gone through two subsequent editions since, the last in 1967.[11] So closely are the Restatement and the Treatise allied that the system of section numbering appears identical. Scott's work has played a pivotal role in the legal understanding of the trustee's investment management duties. Most cases in the area, and other commentators, cite as authoritative either the Treatise or the Restatement (or rely on a formulation derived therefrom). Moreover, Scott's teachings on investment management by trustees have remained virtually unmodified over a fifty-year period. In particular, the relevant sections and comments of the second Restatement are virtually identical to those of the first Restatement[12] and continue to be regarded as authoritative today.

This essay proposes to read the Treatise and the Restatement on investment management as Scott's attempt to interpret and apply the *Harvard College* formulation through more specific rules and examples. However useful initially, these rules and examples no longer conform to the best understanding of prudent investment strategy and thus unwisely constrain trustees. To some extent Scott set forth rules that were more constraining, and less flexible, than *Harvard College* required. However, the far more serious problem is that no one has carried forward Scott's project of providing the "better view" in the law of trusts.[13] In a sense Scott has become "Scott," too authoritative to revise. Since the last edition of the Treatise and the second Restatement there has been an explosion of theoretical and empirical work by financial economists leading to new conceptions of investor and market behavior.[14] None of this is reflected in "Scott" and indeed contradicts much of what "Scott" states. This critique provides notes toward a revision that it is hoped Scott himself would have embraced.

Three key decisions in the Treatise and the Restatement transformed the flexible standard of *Harvard College* into what has become the constrained prudent man rule. First, Scott altered the rule to require a more conservative benchmark of prudence than *Harvard College*. Instead of the prudence of persons seeking "permanent disposition of their funds," Scott prescribes the prudence of one seeking primarily the "preservation of the estate."[15] An investment strategy designed to preserve principal presumably is more cautious than one aimed at "permanent disposition," which could include a buy-and-hold portfolio of common stocks at a higher level of risk and expected return. Moreover, in inflationary times, a mandate to "preserve the estate" becomes confounding; to preserve the estate in nominal terms may well defeat the testator's objective of transferring wealth to the next generation, but to preserve the estate in real terms requires investing that may risk the loss of principal.

Second, for the making of investment judgments, instead of a standard based on how prudent men conduct their own affairs, Scott prescribed the far more constraining test of "men who are safeguarding property for others."[16] Thus instead of the "prudent man" test, there is the "prudent trustee" test.[17] The implication is that a trustee should use especially safe means to attain the desired level of investment safety, rather than ordinarily prudent means.[18] So, for example, even taking the debatable point that preservation of capital ought to be the trustee's primary goal, Scott tells us that a prudent *trustee* may not pursue this goal in ways acceptable to a prudent *investor*. The result is to confuse the setting of appropriately safe investment objectives with the process of investing. This creates a particular problem for a financial model like portfolio theory, in which investments (and investment techniques) in service of greater safety may nevertheless appear risky viewed in isolation.

The final and most serious element of constraint was that in separating "prudence" from "speculation," Scott helped establish hard and fast rules that now stymie the trustee's ability to adapt, as per the *Harvard College* formulation, to "the circumstances then prevailing." On the forbidden list are, for example, margin purchases of securities, "speculative" stock, discount bonds, securities in new and untried enterprises, and second mortgages.[19] "Speculative stock" seems to refer to all companies except those "with regular earnings and paying regular dividends which may reasonably be expected to continue."[20]

The effect of the constrained prudent man rule is thus to inhibit trustee investment in investment vehicles and instruments that did not exist a generation ago, which prudent persons now believe enhance effective trust fund management, but which seem arguably analogous to forbidden investments. It may be difficult for a trustee to participate in a venture capital pool, even one that invests across a wide spectrum, because of the ukase against "new and untried enterprises." Or a trustee may be unable to participate in certain real estate investment pools, because the form of the investment looks subordinated (like the forbidden second mortgage), even though a permissible first mortgage construction loan in fact may present much greater risk.[21] Similarly, a trustee may be forced to divest, or may be excluded from acquiring initially, "discount bonds" (oftentimes known today as "junk bonds"), even though a well-diversified pool of such investments may provide greater return for the risk than gilt-edged bonds.[22]

Alternately, a trustee may be unable to use options to hedge against adverse stock market movements because of the sense that a Scott-influenced court would regard such instruments as "speculative." This is so even though appropriate use of options may provide at much lower cost the same economic protection of strategies that are legally unassailable.[23] Similarly, futures look "speculative" (and involve purchase "on margin"), even though, as discussed above, appropriate futures transactions can lower exposure to fluctuating interest rates.[24]

How is it that the modern trustee should be found in such a position? If the constrained prudent man rule is indeed obsolete, why has it persisted? At least part of the answer lies in the stabilizing influence that authoritative commentary can have on the development of the common law. (Indeed, this influence places particular obligation on the sponsors of commentary that makes claims of authority, such as Restatements, to update their work in light of relevant change.) This influence arises from at least two sources: the effect on the judges and the effect on potential litigants.

3. The Influence of Authority on Common Law Change

Although there are many theories about the common-law tradition, most rest on the willingness and capacity of judges to interpret precedent in light of change.[25] Cases rarely state their own black letter law. The "holding" of a case is bound up with complicated facts. Indeed, much of legal education is spent in showing students how factual distinctions may alter an outcome, the extent to which "the law" is deeply embedded in "the facts." Thus, a court that believes that circumstances have changed or that it has a deeper understanding of the policies to be served can frequently alter governing legal standard without overruling precedent.[26] Interpretations, when derived from cases, can be distinguished, narrowed, broadened, as may seem appropriate to the analysis. By contrast an authoritative commentary exerts a powerfully stabilizing effect on the common law precisely because it purports to crystallize cases into clear legal rules.[27] The commentary's implicit claim is to set forth the rules that are properly derived from the cases. The rules stand as an abstract set of instructions, divorced from the factual context that gives them shading and "open texture."[28] These rules are much harder for a court to negotiate than a line of precedent. With cases one can hearken to the underlying principles that might have led to a particular decision. A treatise, and particularly a Restatement, frequently suggest the law is simply "there" to be applied.[29]

Another reason for commentary's impact may be its role in judicial opinion writing. Judges presumably want to justify their decisions through a cogent analysis of the applicable law. But even an energetic judge, aided by the most energetic law clerks, would face an impossible workload if required to synthesize from scratch complex bodies of law for every opinion. Rather than rely on the account of the law provided by one of the parties, a judge is likely to turn to a disinterested source. The authoritative commentary provides precision and analytic refinement.[30] Reliance on it serves in appearance, and perhaps in fact, the judicial virtues of consistency and coherence.[31] Even if reversed, the judge is in some sense beyond reproach.

An authoritative commentary also derives its influence from its effect on potential litigants. At the simplest level, the ability of courts to change the law is constrained by the willingness of litigants to press suits first to judgment and then to authoritative appellate decisions. Litigation is also the means by which parties attempt to persuade judges that a particular rule is unfair, or obsolete. Even if a particular challenge fails, a steady drumbeat of litigation may have a cumulative effect. Important distinctions and qualifications may begin to emerge that eventually will lead to a new rule.

Litigants are presumably significantly influenced by the calculus of probable outcome. Parties often bring suits and refuse settlement offers before adjudication because of the expectation of gain. Particularly in trust investment, the calculus of litigation is likely to be an economic one: will the payoff from a more efficient investment rule justify the costs of the litigation. One of the most significant elements in this process is the subjective assessments by the parties as to likely outcome. An authoritative commentary changes the calculus not only because it may change the probability of a particular outcome, but also because it reduces the extent to which parties may disagree as to the probable outcome. This makes litigation to challenge the established rule less likely and in turn reinforces the authority of the commentary.[32]

It may be useful to illustrate the point. Imagine that a particular group of beneficiaries feels that management of their trusts is hampered by a narrow conception of prudence that bars investment of part of the portfolio in a promising venture capital pool. Assume that a successful declaratory judgment action would increase the net present value of each beneficiary's interest in his trust by $100,000. With a given line of cases on "speculation" (but no authoritative commentary), the beneficiaries, receiving different legal advice, may assess their chances of success as ranging from 35 percent to 65 percent. If litigation fees are $50,000, some beneficiaries will regard the expected return of maintaining litigation as positive and thus will press the court to reexamine its view of speculation. (The expected return will vary from $35,000 to $65,000, so a beneficiary assessing the chances of success as greater than 50 percent will expect a gain even after the assumed $50,000 litigation costs.)[33]

An authoritative commentary may change this picture radically. First, it may reduce the chances of success significantly because of the stabilizing effects discussed above. For example, because of Scott's criticism of investment in new and untried enterprise, the probability of judicial confirmation of the prudence of a venture capital pool is less than otherwise. Second, an authoritative commentary reduces the variation in individual estimates of success, again because of the stabilizing effect. All parties to a dispute are likely to be in closer agreement as to probable outcomes. Both of these factors reduce the chance of litigation, by requiring a much higher potential pay-off to justify the litigation and by reducing the likelihood of maverick estimates of success.[34]

Authoritative commentary may also influence litigants in the conduct of a lawsuit. Expecting the judge to be influenced by commentary, the parties will shape their factual presentations in light of the categories that the commentary sets forth. In anticipation of a possible lawsuit parties may try to shape their behavior so as to be able to adduce the facts made legally important. The particular influence of Scott in trust law, as opposed to authorities in other fields, may thus derive in significant part from the premeditation with which trust parties can establish "the facts." Unlike an accident giving rise to a tort action, for example, investment management strategy is presumably the result of conscious design, particularly where a professional trustee is involved. If authoritative commentary announces the ground rules, "the facts" can be preplanned. With rare exception, the facts (and theories) presented in any lawsuit will have been tailored to the commentary's fashion. If so, and if the potential litigants are risk averse, the rules and categories of authoritative commentary may be self-reinforcing.

The effects of an authoritative commentary are powerfully evident in the case of Scott. As discussed below, it is striking to see the way some contemporary courts, citing the Restatement, the Treatise, or other authority derived therefrom, have hauled professional trustees over the coals for investment policies that few financial economists would find exceptionable.[35] Equally remarkable is the relative paucity of modern cases raising the question of investment prudence.[36]

4. The Cases Reinterpreted

How might things be different if Scott were suddenly regarded as obsolete on investment management? The core distinction of the prudent man rule, as derived from the cases, is the distinction between prudence and speculation. The claim in this book is only that what counts as prudent must be understood in light of the best current understanding of markets and investor behavior. The insight that seems to underlie the Restatement and the Treatise, and subsequent judicial analysis, is a particular idea of safety: that only if each investment is "safe," measured in isolation, will the collection of assets, the portfolio, be safe. The central idea of portfolio theory is that the risk of a portfolio is dramatically distinct from the risk of particular investments contained in the portfolio. The risk of a portfolio is a function principally of the interrelation of its component investments. Thus, the trustee can use securities and instruments that would be highly risky if viewed in isolation to assemble a portfolio that is nevertheless "safe." Indeed, this portfolio may earn a significantly higher return than one constructed on earlier notions of safety.[37]

This portfolio theory approach certainly justifies inclusion in the portfolio of an appropriate amount of stocks thought to be risky.[38] It also justifies the use of financial instruments that, though highly volatile in themselves, may be deployed in a way to lower portfolio risk or to attain a portfolio of a particular risk at a lower cost.[39]

What is remarkable is that in applying this contemporary vision to the distinction between "prudence" and "speculation" a court need not overrule any of the cases on which Scott relies; it needs only to reinterpret them in light of a different conception of market and investor behavior.[40] For example, consider the cases that support one of Scott's pivotal assertions, that a trustee may not "properly purchase speculative shares of stock."[41] In *Kimball v. Reding,*[42] the trustee invested one-third of a $3000 fund in the stock of a start-up railroad. To be sure, on the court's theory the stock was "speculative." However, even on a portfolio theory approach, the investment of so large a percentage of the portfolio in a single security of this type would almost surely be regarded as imprudent speculation, because it made the *portfolio* too risky for a trustee.

The same analysis applies to the other cited cases. In *Matter of Cady,*[43] the trustee invested half of a $25,000 fund in oil and automobile stocks, solely on a stock broker's recommendation. The trustee had earlier made substantial investments in the stocks for his own account, and there was some suggestion that he had initially purchased the trust stock for his own account as well. The court characterized the stocks, which were unlisted on any market, as "wild cat" stocks and "wild speculation." In *St. Germaine's Adm'r v. Tuttle,*[44] Scott's last case on speculative stocks, the trustee invested more than one-third of an $8,000 fund in a company owned by his family, of which the trustee was an officer, director, and shareholder, and which was heavily in debt at the time of the investment. The results of none of these cases would change on a portfolio theory approach, which would regard concentration of a trusteed portfolio in a single security as very likely exposing the portfolio to unacceptable risk.

To emphasize the point, turn to the cases that underpin Scott's rule against investments in new and untried enterprises. In *Matter of McDowell,*[45] the trustee had invested one-half of a $124,000 fund in bonds of three railroads, two water companies, and a lumber company. All of these ventures had been organized shortly before the trustee's purchase, and some of them had not yet commenced to do business. In *Cornet v. Cornet,*[46] the objectionable new venture investments consisted of bonds in a Mexican water company and Mississippi River bridge company representing nearly one-half of a $25,000 fund. In *Randolph v. East Birmingham Land Co.,*[47] the trustee exchanged the sole trust asset, certain real estate, for one-half of the shares of a sham land development company under an agreement that let the promoters sell off all their shares. In the case *In re Hurlbut's Executor,*[48] the investment consisted of more than two-thirds of a $12,000 fund in the bonds of a start-up shipping company. None of these cases would come out differently under a modern portfolio theory approach of prudent investment. In each case the portion of the portfolio devoted to risky investments rendered the portfolio too risky in light of the substantive standard of safety appropriate for the trustee.[49]

In a process familiar to the common law lawyer, Scott derived his rules defining "prudence" from a process of connecting up the points represented by the decided cases, using as his lens the understanding available to him. Scott did not have the conceptual framework to distinguish effectively between "some" risk, which he obviously thought appropriate, and "too much risk."[50] Portfolio theory has given us that framework, one that permits us to redraw the line of "prudence" to fit more precisely the objectives of trustee investment management. The problem is that the authority of Scott's work has hindered what would otherwise be a natural development in the common law: the re-analysis of prior case law in light of what we believe to be a better understanding of markets and investments. Indeed, one of Scott's cases cited against new ventures could well serve as a linchpin for such re-analysis. In *Appeal of Dickinson,*[51] the questioned investment was stock in the then-expanding Union Pacific Railroad. The trustee made two purchases, the first amounting to approximately 20 percent of a $16,000 fund, the second adding another 15 percent. Despite the investment in a new venture, the court surcharged the trustee for the second purchase only, finding that the trustee was not justified "in investing in such stock as this was *so large a proportional part of the property.*"[52] The case thus turns on the risk added to the trust estate by such a disproportionately large investment in the railroad stock, not the risk of the stock per se. The court's intuition could be read into a more general portfolio theory approach.[53]

5. The Distorting Impact of the Treatise and the Restatement

The influence of the Treatise and the Restatement, however, have distorted the development of the law. Scott extracted his rules against speculative investment from cases which, certainly from the perspective of this essay, and probably from Scott's, would seem egregious. Recent cases purporting to rely on those rules have applied them to situations, which measured by the cases Scott cites, are relatively unproblematic, and which from the perspective of portfolio theory are virtually unexceptionable. For example, in *Chase v. Pevear*[54] (discussed in Chapter 1), the trustee was put to the test, in an appeal of a surcharge, of justifying investments of approximately 4 percent of portfolio assets in four publicly listed companies in the housing industry. For two of the investments, surcharge was sustained on the grounds that the trustee failed to sell soon enough. The court thus seems to have assumed that the trustee should have outguessed the market in foreseeing the decline of the value of those investments. For other investments (including Penn Central), the critical fact that persuaded the court against a surcharge on the basis of "unseasoning" or other assertions of speculation was the widespread holding of the stock by other financial institutions. The court did not consider the relative proportion of these investments to the trust as a whole, or other portfolio investments.

In *First Alabama Bank of Montgomery v. Martin*[55] (also discussed in Chapter 1), a bank trustee was surcharged for including in a well-diversified common trust fund seventeen publicly traded stocks and the bonds of six real estate investment trusts (REITs), which the court regarded as not meeting certain fixed criteria for safety. The court adopted a security-by-security approach on standards of company size, market capitalization, credit rating, and seasoning that would exclude most publicly traded securities. The court seemed indifferent to the proportion of the challenged investments in the portfolio or the make-up of the portfolio as a whole. The court also sustained a surcharge for the trustee's sale of other securities at what in hindsight was the bottom of the 1970s bear market, thus assuming special prescience by the trustee.

In a more complicated case, *Estate of McCredy,*[56] the trustee invested 6 percent of the portfolio in three common stocks deemed risky by the court, which examined them in isolation. Among the stocks it regarded as too risky (in the 1960s) for purchase under the prudent man rule was Chrysler Corporation, "'a businessman's risk stock' in a cyclical industry."[57] The trustee was not surcharged for the investments, but only because the test was not the prudent man rule. Instead, the court deferred to the testator's approval of the trustee's "personal investment philosophy," one that looked for appreciation of principal rather than dividends only.

In *Steiner v. Hawaiian Trust Co.,*[58] the trustee was surcharged for an $1100 investment from a fund of $107,000 in a "speculative" sugar company stock. Finally, in a case more problematic on diversification grounds, *Matter of Will of Newhoff,*[59] trustees were surcharged for investments in real estate investment trusts simply because they were not seasoned securities with a long earnings history. The court cited approvingly *First Alabama Bank.*[60]

Even cases that are generally viewed as protecting trustees demonstrate the distorting effects of a constrained rule. In the cases *In re Morgan Guaranty*[61] and *Stark v. U.S. Trust Co.,*[62] the courts rejected surcharge claims respecting particular equity securities, principally on the ground of the "prudent process" of the formal review, research, and decision-making of the professional trustees.[63] In both cases the court considered each challenged security in isolation, without regard for the relation of a security to the portfolio as a whole. Indeed, it is not possible to determine from the opinions what percentage of the portfolio was represented by any security. The courts' approach, unhinged from any substantive standard, invites analysis of paper trails rather than investment rationales and may well encourage expensive formal procedures that do not contribute to beneficiary welfare.[64]

The approach of these courts to "prudent investment" is remarkable in several respects. No consideration was given in the courts' opinions to portfolio theory rationales for the trustees' behavior, even though the theory has been an acceptable basis for investing among many investment managers since the late 1960s and a commonplace of legal academic discussion since the early 1970s.[65] Indeed, there is some evidence that sophisticated lawyers would not even consider making a portfolio theory argument to a court.[66] By contrast, in other areas of the law, certain claims of modern finance theory have rapidly been absorbed into the judicial reasoning process.[67]

The question remains: Why should the Restatement and the Treatise have had such a profound and persistent influence on the law of investment management. Certainly the first Restatement of Contracts and Williston's Treatise, for example, while influential, have not been treated with comparable judicial deference.[68]

At least one additional factor seems significant in accounting for their influence and thus the persistence of the constrained rule: the difficult process of judicial reception of a complex social science model. The discussion now turns to that issue.[69]

B. The Shift to a Portfolio Theory Model

The previous section has tried to account for the rigidity of judicial interpretations of the prudent man rule in terms of an historical anomaly—the happenstance career of Professor Scott. There is, however, another set of factors that may help account for past rigidity and be a continuing basis for rigidity in the future. These relate to the very complexity of the portfolio theory that underlies the claim for an unconstrained rule, the problems of monitoring conduct under such a rule, and the widespread changes in other institutions of trust law that acceptance of the model would entail.

1. Receiving a New Model

The claim of proponents of an unconstrained rule is that it is more "efficient"—that an unconstrained but prudent trustee can produce superior results for the beneficiaries: higher returns at a particular level of risk or lower risk for a particular level of returns. These gains derive both from the portfolio theory approach to investment management and from transactions costs savings through use of financial instruments such as financial futures and options in the implementation of an investment strategy. Moreover, the proponents say, the rule itself contemplates deference to good-faith prudent investing. Both of these claims, efficiency and flexibility, frequently find a receptive hearing in the courts—why not in this particular case? One answer may lie in a kind of vicious circle: That the most significant efficiencies of the unconstrained rule become evident only after one understands the portfolio theory model, but until courts understand the efficiency claims they will have little motivation to assimilate such a relatively complicated financial model. This point may become clearer through a comparison of the judicial response to an efficiency claim in a situation also laden with fiduciary duties, namely interested director contracts.

As Professor Marsh tells us, in 1880 there was a clear rule regarding the enforceability of contracts between a corporation and one of its directors (or between corporations with interlocking directors): Such contracts were voidable at the instance of the corporation or its shareholders, regardless of the fairness of the transaction. The rule "appeared to be impregnable. . . . It was stated in ringing terms by virtually every decided case, with arguments which seemed irrefutable, and it was sanctioned by age."[70] Nevertheless, as he continues, "[t]hirty years later this principle was dead."[71] The new judicial rule held these contracts enforceable upon full disclosure and ratification by disinterested directors and fairness of the contract in question.[72] The change appears to have occurred without clear judicial articulation of its basis. Yet such contracts became increasingly widespread and it seems that the advantages of a rule change had become apparent to all.[73] In a contemporary analytic framework, it can be said that the courts realized that the relaxed rule permitted the parties to save on transaction costs, in particular, search costs:[74] Buyer and seller could use their corporate connection to find one another more readily and to gain quick access to reliable information regarding reputation, capacity, and credit-worthiness. Given the opportunities for litigation and other shareholder action in response to egregious abuses, the relaxed rule provided a net benefit to the corporation. In short, the relaxed rule appeared to be more efficient.[75] Herein lies a puzzle. The relationship between a corporation and its directors have been described in judicial opinions in terms of fiduciary duties and trustee obligations drawn from the law of private trusts. Yet why should potential efficiencies lead to a new rule in director contracts (indeed, in the face of palpable conflicts of interest), but not in the case of the prudent man rule?

a. Understanding the Gains. There are at least two significant differences in the two cases. First, and most important, the potential gains from a relaxed director contracts rule are easier to understand than the gains from an unconstrained prudent man rule. In the director contracts case a court can readily perceive the transaction costs avoided by a mutually advantageous bargain between a connected buyer and seller. This is an intuition that would come naturally to the persons of affairs typically appointed to the bench. Thus the relaxed director contracts rule is an easy case to understand on the "policy" grounds that courts frequently adopt.

By contrast, the efficiencies in the prudent man rule case are less obvious. To appreciate the gains deriving from an unconstrained rule requires acceptance of a new financial model, in which the risk of an investment is measured in the context of a portfolio, not in isolation. Indeed, the very definition of "efficiency"—maximum expected return for a given level of risk—is a model-related concept. In an important sense, the gains exist only if the model is believed.[76] To be sure, courts inevitably employ some economic model in deciding investment prudence cases.[77] But given the complexity of the modern portfolio model it is not surprising that judicial acceptance should be slow.[78]

An additional factor in this pattern of judicial response is the previously noted unwillingness, or inability, of counsel to argue the gains from an unconstrained rule to the courts in surcharge cases.[79] Litigation frequently serves as the means by which parties attempt to educate and lobby courts. The tenets of portfolio theory have been a recognized branch of finance theory since the late 1960s and have been argued successfully to courts and administrative bodies in other contexts.[80] Nevertheless, not one of the reported surcharge cases in the 1970s or 1980s seems to have been argued on portfolio theory grounds, even where such an argument should have been decisive.[81] In such circumstances it is not surprising that a court did not adopt a portfolio theory approach sua sponte.[82]

b. Confining the Costs of Unconstraining. Apart from the difficulty in understanding the potential gains, there is a second obstacle to judicial acceptance of the unconstrained rule: whether the costs of such flexibility can be confined. Even if there are potential gains from an unconstrained rule, will the costs make such a rule inefficient? The question of these costs can be put more formally: Can the grant of discretion carried by an unconstrained rule be monitored so that incompetent or faithless performance will be adequately deterred?

Once again the comparison to the relaxed director contracts rule is useful. As to such contracts certain private parties obviously have an interest in monitoring against unfair dealings—for example, disinterested directors and shareholders. A prior approval process for such contracts curtails some abuses. There is a substantive standard that, although somewhat vague ("fairness"), sets parameters for ex post settling up through a shareholder derivative suit. Of course, the monitoring of interested director contracts is imperfect, but shareholder losses are unlikely to be catastrophic. In short, it is easy to assert that the gains of the relaxed rule will outweigh the costs of flexibility.

By contrast, the monitoring of performance under an unconstrained prudent man rule is more problematic. There are, of course, difficult questions of the capacity and adequacy of beneficiary monitoring.[83] More serious, however, is that the portfolio theory model complicates the determination of "prudence," both as a matter of theory among financial economists and as a matter of proof to the court (or other trier of fact). The standards from Scott's commentary for determining whether an investment was "prudent" had the virtue of relative ease of application: If a common stock, did it pay dividends and for how long? How long had the enterprise been in business? Did the security exceed the debt?[84] A portfolio theorist, on the other hand, would argue that few, if any, investments are imprudent per se. The question is, given the other portfolio components, did the investment make the portfolio as a whole imprudent. In particular, courts will be called upon to evaluate complicated strategies, not simply specific investments viewed in isolation. Instead of referring to a list of imprudent investments in the Restatement, a court will have to evaluate often conflicting expert testimony. A court may worry that "portfolio theory" might serve as a smokescreen for trustee incompetence.[85] Moreover, the cost to beneficiaries of a complicated investment strategy gone awry through mishandling is probably more serious than the loss to shareholders of a contractual overreaching by a director.

c. Understanding a New Model. What looks like flexibility—the absence of a list that separates the permissible from impermissible investments—is inherent to portfolio theory and necessary for an unconstrained rule. Merely because portfolio theory offers no mechanical tests for evaluating trustee conduct, however, does not justify a court's rejecting it to follow a rule based on an inferior theory of investment management. Moreover, the unconstrained rule allows less discretion than initially appears. The appropriate risk parameters for the particular trust funds significantly limit trustee investment behavior. A trustee will have no more discretion under an unconstrained rule to adopt a too-risky investment strategy than, under the present rule, to buy a too-risky security.

The general point is this: on occasion courts seem amenable to efficiency claims where assessments of gains and costs require only an incremental advance in the court's understanding of the situation. Acceptance of an unconstrained rule, and modern portfolio theory, requires more than an incremental change; rather, a new way of understanding investments and investment strategies, a complicated new model.[86] Before one understands the model, the gains of an unconstrained rule seem chimerical but the costs real. After one understands the model, the gains are real and the costs manageable. But the model is sufficiently complex that the first steps toward judicial assimilation may be difficult.

2. Trust Law Institutions

In addition to raising difficult issues about evaluating gains and costs, adoption of an unconstrained prudent man rule on portfolio theory grounds would challenge the durability of some important institutions in trust law. A sense of these further implications may have led courts away from accepting the theory and counsel away from pressing it. Courts may think that the stability of trust law is more important than, for example, torts or contracts, because of its intergenerational reach. Settled rules, even if obsolete, may be deemed to have greater value. This attitude may be reinforced as to trustee investment management because of the settlor's ability to contract around many such rules.[87] The worry about portfolio theory's reach is a red herring in some areas; in others, not.

a. The Trustee's Duty of Caution. A frequent criticism of an unconstrained prudent man rule is that it would establish too permissive a standard for the evaluation of trustee behavior. The particular claim is that an unconstrained rule amounts to a business judgment rule for trustees, which would result in virtual liability insulation for the trustee's investment decisions.[88] Properly understood, however, an unconstrained rule still includes a duty of caution.

The claim of permissiveness misunderstands the different premises of the business judgment rule and unconstrained prudent man rule. The business judgment rule can be understood only in light of the particular duties of a corporate director: A director, disinterested, who exercises reasonable care in informing himself about a particular business decision and who rationally believes the decision to be in the corporation's best interests, cannot be held liable if the decision turns out badly.[89] The trustee's duties, however, are different from the director's. In addition to a duty of reasonable care, and loyalty, the trustee owes a duty of caution.[90] This duty requires the trustee to assure an appropriate risk level in light of the needs of the trust. Nothing in portfolio theory erodes the trustee's obligation to invest with due caution; indeed, it puts that duty on firmer ground.

A comparison of the situation of the parties to be protected by a director or a trustee liability rule—shareholders and trust beneficiaries—shows that the two are situated quite differently. Since well-chosen risks frequently yield greater returns, most shareholders would not want a director liability rule that discouraged risk-taking. This is particularly so since shareholders can select firms on the basis of particular risks and the skill of management in risk-taking. Of particular importance is that shareholders can hold diversified portfolios of securities to reduce the risk to which they are exposed.[91] Finally, shareholders can monitor the performance of managers and dispose of those whose performance is substandard by casting their votes with an insurgent in a proxy battle, selling into a hostile takeover, or simply selling off their investment.[92] Thus, from a shareholder perspective it makes sense to protect the corporate director from liability for a disinterested business decision that rationally—but wrongly—assessed the risks and rewards.

On the other hand, a rule that encouraged a high degree of trustee risk-taking is not well-suited to trust beneficiary interests, on at least two grounds. First is the monitoring problem. Beneficiaries do not generally select the trustee (the settlor who did is probably dead), and even if they (or their representatives) have sufficient financial sophistication to identify poor risk-taking, they may find it burdensome to remove the trustee. Restrictions in the trust instrument and the problems of collective action by the beneficiaries probably make such action difficult. Unlike the corporate context, an outside trustee is unlikely to mount a campaign to persuade beneficiaries to substitute it as trustee.

The more serious objection is the limited ability of beneficiaries to diversify their trust holdings. The typical beneficiary may have a large portion of his wealth tied up in the trust. (This may be especially the case for minor, or unborn, remaindermen.) If so, he will be unable to diversify against a trust portfolio that is exposed to a high degree of risk. Thus no matter how wisely the trustee has selected the risks, this beneficiary will regard the portfolio as too risky for his interests.

Thus, on a portfolio theory analysis, trust law appropriately imposes a "duty of caution" on the trustee. Insofar as the business judgment rule takes no account of risk-taking (except in the limited sense that the risk must be rational in light of the expected return[93]), it is not an appropriate trust law standard. The insight of portfolio theory makes it clear that the duty of caution comes into play in the selection of the appropriate portfolio risk level, not as a bar to reasonable means of investing in light of the allowed risk.

b. Anti-Netting Rule. Another trust law institution that some claim is put into question by a portfolio theory approach is the rule against "balancing losses against gains."[94] Because portfolio theory looks at the performance of the portfolio as a whole, the argument is that the standard trust law anti-netting rule must be discarded.[95] In fact, the rule is not inconsistent with portfolio theory. The rule pertains to balancing losses arising from one or more *breaches of trust* against gains from any source. The implication of portfolio theory is only that whether a particular investment amounts to a breach of trust should be judged in light of the risk it adds to the portfolio, not in isolation. Thus the purchase of a particular security or instrument whose returns are volatile when viewed in isolation is not necessarily a breach of trust.

On the other hand, a misapplied anti-netting principle would make portfolio theory impossible to use. For the very essence of a portfolio strategy is a plan of diversification such that "losses" will be balanced out by "gains" in a way that makes the overall portfolio less risky and overall returns more dependable. Indeed, as discussed in Appendix A, a riskless portfolio would be one in which two securities had negative covariance of minus 1: any loss would be balanced out by a gain. Moreover, it is a rational portfolio strategy to include some securities whose expected returns may be negative, if, for example, in unusually difficult economic times their returns are positive and can balance out losses on the rest of the portfolio.

A case like *In re Bank of New York (Spitzer)*[96] illustrates how an anti-netting rule might be applied in light of a portfolio conception of prudent investment. The court is surely right in saying that an overall increase in the value of a portfolio should not "insulate the trustee from responsibility for imprudence with respect to individual investments for which it would otherwise be surcharged."[97] To hold otherwise would be to immunize a trustee in a rising market and perhaps to encourage unwarranted risk-taking in the attempt to recoup from errors. Even on a portfolio approach, particular investments may be imprudent. The key issue is the means for determining the prudence of particular investments. Few investments are imprudent per se, if the determination of prudence is portfolio-based.[98]

c. Optional Diversification. One area of established trust doctrine that would change upon acceptance of a portfolio theory paradigm is the optional diversification principle. The prevailing notion is that the trustee ordinarily must "distribute the risk of loss" by "reasonable diversification."[99] On the other hand, some jurisdictions, in particular New York, specifically reject the idea that prudence requires diversification.[100] The concept of diversification at issue in traditional analysis is a simple one: the advisability of putting eggs in several baskets. The justification for not requiring diversification is Andrew Carnegie's: "Put all your eggs in one basket and watch the basket."[101] A court that accepts portfolio theory is likely to regard diversification as mandatory except upon a showing of special insight by the trustee or some other unusual showing.[102] Portfolio theory's claim is not merely that diversification avoids the risk of loss, but rather that it increases expected return at the chosen risk level.

The diversification principle has this powerful advantage: It would provide a solid basis for decisions that now tenuously rest on other grounds. For example, in *Matter of Newhoff*,[103] the trustee of three family trusts had invested more than 50 percent of the principal of each trust in REITs that subsequently plummeted in value. Because New York does not require diversification, the only ground for surcharge was a finding that the particular investments were imprudent when made. The New York court was thus obliged to say that a newly formed REIT investing in construction and development mortgages was virtually per se imprudent as a trust investment. Thus, despite its frequent repetition and ostensible invocation of *Harvard College* and the prudent man rule, the *Newhoff* court in effect put REITs on a negative legal list. A portfolio approach would have led to the same result without the doctrinal embarrassment.

Acceptance of the diversification principle is not without complication. Courts may have to develop more precise standards for appropriate diversification. This will require courts to reflect upon the differences between "passively managed" portfolios, which follow a pure diversification strategy at the desired risk level, and for "actively managed portfolios," which combine diversification with the search for undervalued securities.[104]

d. Principal and Income. Perhaps the most important trust law institution put into question by acceptance of an unconstrained rule on portfolio theory grounds relates to the proper allocation of investment return. No principle in the law of trusts seems more settled than the rule that income beneficiaries receive ordinary cash dividends from common stock ownership and remaindermen receive capital gains if the stock is sold.[105] All the skirmishing is on the edges: for example, the allocation of extraordinary cash dividends[106] or of stock dividends.[107] Acceptance of portfolio theory, however, is profoundly inconsistent with the basic rule. The economic models on which portfolio theory relies all calculate investment returns on "total return" during a specific period, that is, cash flow (dividends and interest) plus gain (or loss).[108] The analysis of "covariance," or comovement among securities returns, which provides the basis for determining the amount of risk a particular security adds to a portfolio, depends upon this total return definition.

A division of a firm's return between "income" and "capital gain" is highly artificial from the viewpoint of financial economics. Imagine two firms, *A* and *B*. For each $100 of shareholders' equity each earns $10. *A*, thinking its primary business has reached a no-growth steady state, pays out all earnings as dividends. *B*, thinking its business provides additional investment opportunities, reinvests all earnings, which leads to an increase in its share price. Each is providing comparable economic return to its shareholders, just in different form. Indeed, a realization of capital gains on *B* stock provides income in a tax-favored form and may provide additional incentives for *B* to search for additional opportunities that earn at least a 10 percent return. A trustee holding *A*, however, must pay out all dividends to income beneficiaries (even if, because of inflation, the purchasing power of the remainder interest, the *A* stock in the portfolio, is meanwhile depreciating).[109] A trustee holding *B* can pay out nothing to income beneficiaries (even if the remainder interest is increasing in value because of *B*'s decision to reinvest earnings that would otherwise be available to an income beneficiary).

To assure some fairness between income beneficiaries and remaindermen, the trustee may have to adopt an investment policy that mixes *A* and *B*. Alternatively, present law apparently allows the trustee to refuse to hold *B*.[110] The result in either case will be a portfolio that is not optimally diversified—that has not been assembled with the objective of producing the greatest expected returns for the risk. It is easy to see why systematic exclusion of companies with low dividends but high reinvestment rates upsets a diversification scheme, but there is no assurance that a portfolio that emphasizes balance between high and low dividend paying securities will be well-diversified otherwise. The point is that the allocation of total returns between "income" and "principle" forced by settled trust law is profoundly inconsistent with the portfolio theory paradigm.[111]

There is a solution, of course, that has been adopted by many endowments and could be adapted to private trusts.[112] It would be possible to tally portfolio results on a "total return" basis but set standards for allocation of return between income and remainder interests based on assumptions regarding normalized annual returns. Such a solution is theoretically correct but might present practical problems in trust administration, because of the inevitable conflicts among income beneficiaries and remaindermen over appropriate assumptions.[113] Thus a particularly useful follow-up project if the paradigm of prudence offered in Chapter 4 of this study is adopted would be a revision of the Uniform Principal and Income Act to work out the practical details of a total return allocation scheme.[114]

Toward that revision it might be useful to set forth some preliminary analysis. In the drafting of a standard provision for trusts that do not contain an explicit substitute, the starting point must be certain assumptions about the customary intent of the settlor.[115] What can we infer from the settlor's general instructions that income from certain property should go to certain people now alive and that the principal should go to others who may or may not be alive, or indeed, who may be charitable institutions rather than individuals? We might infer that the settlor's main object is a continuous income stream to the life beneficiaries, but how should that stream be fashioned and who should bear the assorted risks of financial returns? In particular we should focus on the stability in real terms both of *payouts,* because of the settlor's likely desire to provide a consistent level of support, and of *corpus,* because stable payouts ultimately depend upon the corpus and because of the settlor's presumed desire to transfer wealth dynastically.

There are perhaps five separate approaches to the allocation of total trust returns that bear scrutiny: prudent trustee payout, fixed nominal payout, fixed real payout, fixed portfolio percentage payout and payout of yield above maintenance of fixed real corpus.

1. PRUDENT TRUSTEE PAYOUT. One way to handle the allocation problem is to remit it to the discretion of the trustee, under a "prudence" standard. Depending on portfolio performance and inflation-related changes in expenses faced by the life beneficiaries, the trustee could determine the appropriate allocation of returns. This approach, however, will inevitably put the trustee in the very diffi-

cult position of balancing (or trading off) the interests of life beneficiaries and remaindermen.

The closest analogy in current trust law practice appears to be clauses that permit the trustee discretion to allocate receipts or expenses to either principal or income. There is some doubt over the effectiveness of such clauses. The influence of the traditional allocation rules has led some courts to construe such clauses narrowly, as limited to situations of doubt under state law.[116] In one leading case, *In re Clarenbach's Will*,[117] the court rejected the trustee's use of such a clause to allocate to income half the capital gain realized on the sale of stock. A more substantive objection is that such clauses do not provide the trustee with a standard for exercising discretion.

An alternative model for prudent trustee payout is the invasion of principal clause, which permits the trustee to spend principal for life beneficiaries where appropriate. But such broad discretion misunderstands the allocation problem. In general, invasion of principal clauses seem best suited for unforseeable circumstances of beneficiary need, where special flexibility is necessary, rather for than forseeable problems of allocation. These should be addressed more specifically by the settlor. Reliance on continual trustee discretion is likely to embarrass both the life beneficiary, who may be put in the position of special pleading, and the trustee, who must consider the remainder interest (and potential future surcharge claims).[118] Thus if there is to be any sort of trustee discretion in the allocation question, it must be confined to the narrowest possible range.[119]

2. FIXED NOMINAL PAYOUT. A fixed nominal payout approach contemplates that the life beneficiary will receive a constant stream of income that neither increases to reflect inflation nor decreases to reflect portfolio losses.[120] The payout is an annuity fixed in nominal terms. One immediate question is how to fix the amount of the payout. Presumably the payout will be geared to some assumption about long term nominal yield of the portfolio.[121] Such an assumption could be set by statute, subject to change by the settlor, or the statute could require the settlor to provide the desired percentage (or actual dollar payout).[122] There are two principal strategies the settlor could adopt in setting the payout, based on the particular inflation assumption. The settlor could assign a payout based on a zero (or minimal) inflation rate, on the grounds that the portfolio will virtually always earn this nominal amount, so that the corpus will not be depleted to make the payout. This all but guarantees the certainty of income flow to the life beneficiaries and the existence of a remainder interest. There are many problems, however. If the zero inflation assumption is incorrect, the life beneficiaries are faced with steadily declining real income. Elements of return which represents a compensation for inflation, such as higher nominal interest rates, inure to the remaindermen. Moreover, irrespective of inflation, the remaindermen receive all growth in the value of the portfolio. For these reasons this strategy is likely on average to favor remaindermen.

The other strategy for the settlor is to set a payout based on a significant inflation assumption, so as to assure at least a certain real income payout for the life beneficiaries. This too has problems. Such a strategy will overcompensate the life beneficiaries in the early years, and if the inflation assumption is too high, or if the increase in nominal returns is less than the increase in inflation, the strategy will lead to significant deterioration of the corpus. Such deterioration puts at risk the provision of a continuous income stream to the life beneficiaries and certainly jeopardizes the remainder interest. Thus, although the nominal fixed income approach is formally a solution to the problem of return allocation, the settlor seems forced to choose between two unappetizing strategies.[123]

3. FIXED REAL PAYOUT. The fixed real payout approach contemplates that the life beneficiaries will receive a stream of income that is adjusted according to some inflation measure.[124] The payout is an annuity fixed in real terms. To set the payout requires an assumption about the long term sustainable real yield on a particular portfolio. This requires three assumptions: as to long term nominal returns (like the fixed nominal payout approach), as to the extent to which increases in inflation are matched by increases in portfolio returns, and as to the variability of real returns. The uncertainty associated with particularly the latter two assumptions is likely to force the settlor to set the payout at the rate which favors the remaindermen. For example, if inflation depresses real returns from particular financial instruments—for example, common stocks during the 1972–1981 period—the yield of a portfolio that contains such instruments may be depressed in real terms. A payout set without regard to this possibility may lead to deterioration of the corpus in real terms. This in turn would jeopardize the future payout to the life beneficiaries and the remainder interest. The response of the settlor is likely to be a very conservative assumption about sustainable real payouts that in most cases will favor the remaindermen.

A similar point could be made about the effect of the third assumption, the variability of real returns. It may well by that long run average real returns are indeed constant across different inflationary (and other economic) conditions but highly variable over short periods of time.[125] Forcing the payout of the average rate could lead to deterioration of corpus from a kind of "gambler's ruin": the need to make the payout in lean years will reduce the corpus, making it harder to catch up even in good years. Once again the inclination of the settlor will be to account for this risk by setting the payout at a rate which is likely to favor the remaindermen.

Another way to consider the problem of fixed payouts, either in nominal or real terms, is to look at the market for annuities. If the settlor's objectives could be addressed merely by guaranteeing a certain income stream, then the solution would be the purchase of annuity contracts for the life beneficiaries, the balance of the corpus to be held in trust for the remaindermen. Such purchases, however, are not regularly directed as part of the trust disposition. The fixed nominal annuity obviously does not address the problem of inflation. More interesting is the fixed real annuity. Such instruments do not appear to be a regular part of the annuity market. The likely reason is that they would be very expensive, because of risks associated with the issuing insurance company's ability to maintain constant real return—the risks associated with assumptions two and three above. In other words, the insurance company is in a similar position to that of the remaindermen. The insurance company will set a price (require a corpus) for a specific fixed real payout that will assure its ability to meet its payment obligation while earning a profit at the end (assuring against depletion of the corpus).[126] But the price—the ratio of guaranteed fixed real payout per dollar of premium—appears to be so high that settlors do not use such instruments. This suggests that settlors would not favor a fixed real payout approach as a solution to the total return problem. To guarantee a specific fixed real payout carries too high a price in terms of low real return assumptions that on average will favor the remaindermen.

The analysis so far suggests that fixed payout approaches, nominal or real, are not satisfactory, because the need to generate the fixed payout will lead the settlor to lower the payout requirement to avoid deterioration of the corpus. On average such an approach will favor the remainder interest. In other words, assuring absolute stability of payouts is not desirable because the corresponding necessity to maintain stability of corpus will then reduce the allowable payout. Another way of putting this argument is to say that for settlors who highly prefer fixed payouts, nominal or fixed, for their life beneficiaries, the Uniform Principal and Income Act is not particularly important. They can instruct trustees to enter into private contracts for such payouts with private insurers, who will most certainly use a total return approach in computing the price they will charge. That settlors do not commonly make such arrangements suggests that their objectives are more complex: relatively stable real payouts; relatively stable corpus, in a process which shares some of the fruits of portfolio growth with the life beneficiaries. Thus we turn to approaches that vary payout.

4. FIXED PORTFOLIO PERCENTAGE PAYOUT. A fixed portfolio percentage approach contemplates that the life beneficiaries will periodically receive a payout of a certain percentage of the current value of the portfolio.[127] Thus the payout will vary depending on the fluctuating value of the portfolio, even though the payout percentage remains constant. Presumably the percentage will set in light of assumptions about sustainable long term nominal and real returns on the portfolio. This approach raises questions about the stability of the payouts and the corpus, particularly because of the risks of inflation and other factors bearing on portfolio returns. If the payout percentage is set too high, the corpus is subject to deterioration and the payouts will become smaller. This leads toward strategies that on average favor the remainder interest, as discussed above. But the real problem is that the fixed portfolio percentage approach does not focus on the important variables—real payouts and real corpus—but on a third variable—the percentage payout—which seems to bear only incidental (and variable) relationship to them.

5. PAYOUT OF ADJUSTED REAL YIELD, a/k/a PAYOUT OF YIELD ABOVE FIXED REAL CORPUS. An adjusted real yield approach contemplates that the life beneficiaries will receive payouts geared to the real yield of the portfolio. The payout is based on total portfolio returns for the period (income and capital gains) after correcting for any loss in the real value of the corpus, whether from inflation or capital loss.[128] This approach requires no assumptions about long term portfolio yields or the rate of inflation. Preservation of the corpus follows automatically from this approach, which protects the life beneficiary's income stream and the remainder interest. The problem, of course, is that stability of the corpus comes at the expense of a stable income stream, in nominal or real terms, to the life beneficiaries. This problem is particularly acute because of the requirement that the value of the corpus be held constant taking into account capital losses. It is easy to imagine periods in which the total real returns on a well-managed portfolio were quite minimal, if not negative.

How can this income stability problem be addressed? One way is to set a tentative payout assumption based on long term average real yields and construct a "stabilization" account that reflects surpluses or shortfalls. In years of higher-than-average returns the account would accumulate funds that would cover payouts for leaner years. The account could be bounded above and below: At a certain point the payout assumption would change to reflect accumulated higher or lower returns.[129] Thus the adjusted real yield approach suggested here is based on real portfolio yields, but would use a stabilization fund to smooth out variability in actual payouts.

Although there are many technical financial and legal problems, such an approach seems closest to effectuating the settlor's objectives of a steady real income stream that nevertheless admits of some variation. It seems almost certain that this approach will produce higher average sustainable real payouts for the life beneficiaries than either fixed payout approach. If the stabilization account is properly conceived, the life beneficiaries, and the remainder interest, can be protected against dramatic shifts. The approach will also underscore that the proper emphasis for trustee investment management is to produce a steady stream of real returns while managing the inevitable flux of market conditions.

a. Financial Problems. Now let us turn briefly to some of the technical financial problems. The first set of questions relate to establishment of the benchmark real yield expectation. Two matters are at issue: first, the identification of the appropriate benchmark trusteed portfolio (which could conceivably change over time); second, the computation of real yields on this portfolio. One would want to know, for example, the composition of the portfolio that provided the most stable real returns over particular time periods and the extent of the trade-off between increased real returns and additional risk. The second major set of questions relate to the stabilization account. What is the appropriate lower bound (i.e., negative surplus) to avoid the "gambler's ruin" problem of quickly deteriorating corpus; how sharply should the payout assumption be reduced after that point? Similarly, what is the appropriate upper bound (and changed payout assumption) to avoid unfair diversion of return to the remaindermen?

All of these questions are peculiarly empirical and peculiarly suitable for analysis in the first instance by financial economists, not lawyers. Thus this essay's recommendation is that a suitable authoritative body—the National Conference of Commissioners on Uniform State Law or the American Law Institute, for example—retain an appropriate team of financial economists to work through some of these problems. Their work could lead to specific numbers that might become statutory assumptions in the absence of contrary provision by the settlor, or to a procedure for determining the correct numbers. For example, it may turn out that the best way to set the payout assumption is by a moving average of certain nominal yields.

In the end there may even be a modest role for trustee discretion, in the event of dramatically changed conditions outside of forseeable investment cycles.

b. Legal Problems. Let us briefly flag at least some of the legal problems obviously raised by an adjusted real yield approach. If this approach to the total returns allocation question seems attractive, then these, and perhaps other legal questions, will require greater scrutiny. There appear to be two sets of problems: first, federal tax issues; second, state trusts, estates, and future interests issues.

i. Federal Tax. The federal tax questions arise out of the issue of whether the payout under the adjusted real yield approach is consistent with the various concepts of "income" used for the taxation of trust income and for the taxation of estate and gift transfers. The traditional distinction of "principal and income" has been utilized in developing the tax rules. A new approach to allocation under state law or as settlor-crafted provisions in trust instruments raises questions about the continued "fit" of the tax rules. These questions are very knotty; this paper proposes only to identify some of them.

As to the taxation of trust income: Although a trust is a tax-paying entity, it is treated as a mere conduit for "income required to be distributed."[130] Moreover, such "income" is taxable to the beneficiaries whether or not actually distributed.[131] Will the use of reserve funds in the adjusted real yield approach jeopardize the deductibility of distributed income for the trust? Will it result in tax liability for beneficiaries on income not yet received? The Code directs us to look to the state law of trusts for the definition of "income."[132] The regulations indicate that "[t]he determination of whether trust income is required to be distributed currently depends upon the terms of the trust instrument and the applicable local law."[133] Shouldn't this mean that a state statutory change to modify the allocation formula—thus modifying the law of trusts—would sufficiently address any potential problem? In the absence of such change, is there any problem with settlor-crafted provisions based on adjusted real yield?[134]

Another serious question is the impact of the adjusted real yield approach on the marital deduction for bequests and gifts made in trust by a spouse. Once again, just a brief sketch: To qualify for the deduction, a bequest (or gift) in trust must provide the spouse recipient with the equivalent of absolute ownership or, at the very least, the right to receive "all income" from the property during the recipient's life.[135] The question is whether the payout under the adjusted real yield approach meets the statutory "all income" requirement. The regulations say that this income requirement is satisfied if the recipient is treated substantially as a life beneficiary under the law of trusts.[136] So once again, a state statutory change in allocation should be a relatively clear way to avoid federal estate and gift tax problems. On the other hand, the regulations also suggest that a settlor-crafted allocation formula adopting the adjusted real yield approach would not necessarily jeopardize the marital deduction:

> Provisions granting adminstrative powers to the trustee will not have the effect of disqualifying an interest passing in trust unless the grant of powers evidences the intention to deprive the surviving spouse of the beneficial enjoyment required by the statute. . . . Among the powers which if subject to reasonable limitations will not disqualify the interest passing in trust are the power to determine the allocation or apportionment of receipts and disbursements between income and corpus[.][137]

It may well be that clarification from the Internal Revenue Service would be necessary to provide comfort, particularly for settlor-crafted provisions.[138]

ii. State Trusts, Estates, and Future Interests.   The first state law problem is the applicability of various common law and statutory limitations on "accumulation" of trust income. The accumulation problem arguably arises when trust "income" (conventionally, interest and dividends) exceeds the payout amount. This could easily happen under the adjusted real yield approach, for part of the interest on fixed income securities might well be retained to hold constant the real value of the corpus.[139] The accumulation problem is two-fold: first, is the accumulation permissible even if consistent with the settlor's intent in light of common law or statutory rules against perpetuities?[140] Second, does the accumulation represent a withholding of funds due the life beneficiary, in derogation of the settlor's intent?[141]

Obviously a statutory change in the allocation formula could address these accumulation limitations directly. But even without statutory change one could argue, following Restatement (Second) of Property, that any retention of funds under the adjusted real yield approach is not an "accumulation," because it is "merely in the course of judicious management of the trust."[142] In other words, because the approach is a means of managing the trust so as to produce a relatively stable real income stream to the life beneficiaries, it raises none of the policy concerns that have given rise to the doctrines against accumulation.

Another legal question raised by the adjusted real yield approach is what happens to any surplus in the stabilization account upon the life beneficiary's death. It would seem that the surplus should properly go to the remaindermen. On the assumption that any deficit in the stabilization account would not have to be covered by the life beneficiary's estate—and thus would reduce the corpus—some rough symmetry suggest that any surplus should inure to the remaindermen. This also seems consistent with the settlor's intention: to provide the life beneficiary with a steady income stream *during his life,* with the corpus passing to a successor designated by the settlor. The surplus account is simply part of a mechanism for assuring that steady real income stream, not an unconditional property interest of the life beneficiary.

iii. Retroactivity.   The final legal problem, a policy question as well, is whether statutory adoption of an adjusted real yield allocation formula should be retroactive. Should trusts that contain general "principal and income" language become subject to the new allocation formula? One useful comparison is to significant statutory changes to the trustee's investment management powers, such as a change from a legal list to a prudent man rule. Such changes generally apply retroactively, even without specific legislative declaration to this effect.[143] The only exception seems to be if the trust instrument contains "specific directions . . . which unalterably prescribe the investments to be made."[144] This seems sound. Statutory change is presumably based on what is believed to be a better understanding of markets and investments; why deny the benefits to trusts already in existence and to their beneficiaries?

A similar argument could be made for retroactive application of a revised allocation statute. What motivates the change, after all, is the desire to employ a superior means of investment management: an unconstrained prudent man rule. In general, better investment management should not lead to a conflict between beneficiaries and remaindermen; it increases the value of the trust to both sets of interests. The problem seems more ticklish, however, because the revised allocation formula will more directly reallocate between interested parties. On a total return approach, gains that traditionally have gone to remaindermen may go to income beneficiaries. On the other hand, if something like the adjusted real yield proposal is adopted, what previously had been regarded as income may go to remaindermen. The disruption of settled expectations is likely to be a short term phenomenon, particularly as it becomes clear that no set of interests is favored. Moreover, reflection upon the trustee's current ability to manipulate allocation through adjustment of the portfolio's holdings may further undercut any objection against retroactivity. Thus, unless the trust instrument contains an allocation clause that expressly changes the customary "principal and income" division,[145] adoption of a new allocation formula should apply retroactively. Any new statute should so state.

C. Conclusion

The persistence of the constrained prudent man rule may not be a puzzle after all. The constrained rule derives principally from authoritative commentary that has remained virtually unchanged over a fifty year period. An alternative, unconstrained rule rests on a sophisticated economic model whose conclusions slowly percolate through the bar. Acceptance of the model may require further change in an area of the law where innovations come slowly. This is not to justify legal standards that contradict our best understanding, only to explain why an obsolete rule has persisted, and in so explaining, hasten the process of change.

NOTES

[1] Associate Professor of Law, New York University. Professor Gordon would like to acknowledge additional financial support provided by the Filomen D'Agostino and Max E. Greenberg Research Fund of New York University School of Law, the able research assistance of Michael Shenberg, N.Y.U. '85 and Chris Cambria, N.Y.U. '86, and the extended comments of James Jacobs, Jack Johnston, Lewis Kornhauser, Jessica Lane, John Langbein, William Nelson, John Peschel, Ricky Revesz, and Larry White (none of whom bears responsibility for remaining errors).

[2] Among the most useful articles are: Note, "The Regulation of Risky Investments," 83 Harv. L. Rev. 603 (1970); "Regulating Risk-Taking by Mutual Funds," 82 Yale L.J. 1305 (1973); Johnston, "Prudence in Trust Investment," 8 Mich. J. L. Ref. 491 (1975); Note, "Fiduciary Standards and the Prudent Man Rule Under the Employment Income Security Act of 1974," 88 Harv. L. Rev. 960 (1975); Note, "Trustee Investment Powers: Imprudent Application of the Prudent Man Rule," 50 Notre Dame Law. 519 (1975); Langbein & Posner, "Market Funds and Trust Investment Law," 1976 A.B.F. Research J. 1 (1976) (particularly influential); H. Bines, "Modern Portfolio Theory and Investment Management Law: Refinement of Legal Doctrine," 76 Colum. L. Rev. 721 (1976). For a very good overview of the current understanding of portfolio theory and its limits, see Elton & Gruber, *The Lessons of Modern Portfolio Theory,* Appendix A, *supra; see also* Gordon & Kornhauser, "Efficient Markets, Costly Information, and Securities Research," 60 N.Y.U. L. Rev. 761 (1985).

[3] Portfolio theory can be understood as making the following claims: Investors care about the risk and return of assets; indeed, they prefer the greatest return for the least risk and insist on being compensated in proportion to the risk. The risk from owning any particular asset can be lowered if the investor also owns other assets the returns on which respond to different firm-specific and general economic factors. In a familiar simple example, the risk from owning stock in an umbrella manufacturer is lower if the investor also owns stock in a suntan lotion manufacturer, for abnormally sunny (or rainy) weather will enhance one firm's profits even while it hurts the other firm. This generalizes to the broader claim that the risk from owning any particular asset is best measured in terms of the risk that the asset adds to a well diversified portfolio of assets.

Three results follow. First, in making investment decisions an investor should look to the risk and return on his portfolio. Second, an asset that is very risky if viewed in isolation may not be particularly risky when viewed from this portfolio perspective. In the example, it is simply misleading to add that the umbrella manufacturer's stock is "risky" if it turns out that that portfolio produced by adding the suntan lotion manufacturer's stock yields very stable returns. Third, because of the competition to assemble "efficient" portfolios (greatest return for least risk), investors will be compensated for bearing only that risk which cannot be eliminated through diversification. In the example, the market returns on suntan lotion manufacturer stock will be geared not to the firm's variable earnings viewed in isoloation, but to the risk that cannot be eliminated by holding the stock in combination with the umbrella manufacturer's stock. Thus an investor holding only the suntan lotion manufacturer's stock ordinarily takes on additional risk without the compensation of greater expected returns.

The sources cited in note 2 *supra* provide a more elaborate, and mathematically formal, account of portfolio theory.

[4]See text accompanying notes 54–64 *infra*.

[5]*See* Fed. Res. Bd., "Trust Dep't Use of Options and Futures Contracts," 3 Fed. Banking L. Rep. (CCH) ¶ 35,318 (Jan. 1983); *see also* Comptroller's Handbook for National Trust Examiners D-2 (Aug. 1978) (labeling as "usually speculative" and thus improper for trust fund investment, e.g., options, venture companies, warrants) subsequently withdrawn (1979) to avoid conflict with regulations under Employee Retirement Income Security Act of 1974, but with a caveat that personal trusts are subject to local law. For a discussion of the grudging evolution of the SEC's policies see Chapter 3 *supra*.

[6]The Questionnaire, discussed in the Introduction and in Appendix C, demonstrates that many bank trust departments, endowments, and foundations regard themselves as significantly constrained by current legal standards of prudence in their investment practices. The majority of all respondents stated that the following investments and techniques were either legally precluded or questionable for them: commodity futures, short selling, margin purchases, and certain uses of options. The bank trust departments and the foundations were particularly leery of futures, options, and other innovative instruments and techniques. Nearly two-thirds of the bank trust departments stated that investment in new and untried enterprises or venture capital pools were either legally precluded or questionable. More generally, nearly two-thirds of the banks reported that they were "sometimes" precluded by the applicable standard of prudence from investment opportunities they would otherwise pursue.

The wariness of these financial fiduciaries is not surprising in light of the wary legal advice that many of them apparently receive. A 1978 report on innovative investment strategies by the Committee on Investments by Fiduciaries of the American Bar Association Section on Real Estate, Probate, and Trust Law repeatedly emphasizes the risks associated with instruments or strategies that lack adequate seasoning or judicial support. "Current Investment Questions and the Prudent Man Rule," 13 Real Prop., Prob. and Tr. J. 650, 654, 657, 662, 670–71 (1978).

[7]See the discussion in Chapter 4 of the diversification added by real estate investments. A similar point could be made concerning investments in foreign companies, which may be subject to different economic factors than U.S. firms.

For a more specific account of the benefits of diversification in increasing portfolio returns for a given level of risk, see the discussion of portfolio theory in Appendix A and the thumbnail sketch in note 3 *supra*.

[8]See Chapter 4 for a discussion of the ways in which futures and options can hedge the risk associated with equity and debt securities respectively.

For a discussion of how futures may be used in a portfolio, see J. Merrick & S. Figlewski, "An Introduction to Financial Futures," NYU Occasional Papers (1984). For a discussion regarding use of options (and futures), see FRB, CFTC, SEC, *A Study of the Effects on the Economy of Trading in Futures and Options* (1984).

[9]G. Bogert & G. Bogert, *Trusts and Trustees* § 613 (2d ed. rev. 1980). Up until the early 1940s most states required trustees to select investments from a "legal list" of supposedly the safest investments, primarily limited to government bonds, mortgages, and occasionally fixed income securities of the most stable companies. The Depression showed that virtually no instrument was immune from default or payment moratorium. See Chapter 2 *supra*.

[10]26 Mass. (9 Pick.) 446, 461 (1830).

[11]Scott produced editions in 1939, 1956, and 1967. Scott updated the third edition with pocketparts until a few years before his death in 1981. The publisher has continued the updates. Scott's *Law of Trusts* is hereinafter cited as "the Treatise," with reference to the cited edition. Parallel citations to each edition are given where appropriate to demonstrate consistency.

[12]The most critical sections are § 213 (Balancing Losses Against Gains), § 227 (Investments Which a Trustee Can Properly Make), and § 228 (Distribution of Risk of Loss). The Restatement

(First) of Trusts is hereinafter referred to as "first Restatement" and the Restatement (Second) as "second Restatement."

[13]Many would regard Scott as a modernizer in the investment management area, citing, in particular, his endorsement of common stocks as prudent investments (depending on the stock). See Restatement (First) of Trusts § 227 comment f; Treatise (1st ed. 1939), § 227.11, at pp. 1219–22. At times Scott reflects awareness of the need for flexibility in defining prudence, see, e.g., Restatement (Second) of Trusts § 227 comment e (adding statement that "It is impossible to lay down a hard-and-fast rule as to what is a prudent investment[.]"), despite the investment rules elsewhere presented as per se and immutable. Particularly the third edition of the Treatise reflects awareness of the problem: "When a certain investment is held in one case to be improper, the courts are likely to treat the case as a precedent holding that no investment of that type is proper. . . . Undoubtedly in recent years there has been a more scientific study of investments, but the results of this study are not always reflected in the cases." 3 Treatise (3d ed. 1967), § 227, at pp. 1808–09.

[14]See note 65 infra. In addition, major legislation transformed securities markets from the Depression and pre-Depression financial environment against which the first Restatement was written. See Securities Act of 1933, 15 U.S.C. § 77a et seq.; Securities Exchange Act of 1934, 15 U.S.C. § 78a et seq.; Trust Indenture Act of 1939, 15 U.S.C. § 77aaa et seq.; Investment Company Act of 1940, 15 U.S.C. § 80a-1 et seq. See generally J. Seligman, The Transformation of Wall Street (1982).

[15]Restatement (First) and (Second) of Trusts § 227; 2 Treatise (1st ed. 1939), § 227, at p. 1197; 3 Treatise (2d ed. 1956), § 227, at p. 1660; 3 Treatise (3d ed. 1967), § 227, at pp. 1805–06.

[16]2 Treatise (1st ed. 1939), § 227, at p. 1198; 3 Treatise (2d ed. 1956), § 227, at p. 1661; 3 Treatise (3d ed. 1967), § 227, at p. 1806 (approving of this distinction as made in In re Estate of Cook, 171 A. 730 (Del. 1934)).

[17]Why Scott moved away from a "prudent investor" standard to a "prudent trustee" standard is unclear. At the time of the first Restatement, most states were "legal list" states. The Restatement formulation suggests an attempt at compromise between the "liberal" Massachusetts rule and the conservative rule followed elsewhere. Scott is criticized for this "prudent investor"/"prudent trustee" distinction by a leading member of the Massachusetts trusts and estates bar. See Shattuck, "The Development of the Prudent Man Rule for Fiduciary Investment in the United States in the Twentieth Century," 12 Ohio St. L.J. 491, 515 (1951) ("There is no warrant for that distinction under the language of Harvard College v. Amory, and there are no logical reasons for it if all the words of the Prudent Man Rule are given full effect, but there is nevertheless a constant temptation, backed by British precedent, to fall into that error.").

This point serves to illustrate Scott's influence in comparison to other treatise writers. The first edition of G. Bogert, Trusts and Trustees, the other important modern trust law treatise, was published in 1935, preceding Scott's first edition by four years. Bogert described the prudent man rule as requiring the trustee to "display the same care and judgment that would be shown by an ordinarily able businessman in managing his own affairs for the purpose of accomplishing ends similar to those of the trust." 3 G. Bogert, Trusts and Trustees (1st ed. 1935), § 612, at pp. 1940–41. Not only does Bogert focus on how a prudent man conducts his own affairs, but also clearly declares that conduct is to be fashioned in light of the ends of the trust. With Bogert's view as a starting point, it would be easier to distinguish between safety as an investment objective as opposed to an artificial constraint on investment techniques. This is a distinction that tends to be blurred by a "prudent trustee" test. Scott's view has prevailed, however, as is conceded in the most recent edition of Bogert's treatise. G. Bogert & G. Bogert, Trusts and Trustees (2d ed. rev. 1980), § 612, at pp. 14–15.

[18]The Restatement states that the trustee should make "only such investments as a prudent man would make of his own property having primarily in mind the preservation of the estate and the amount and regularity of the income to be derived." Restatement (First) and (Second) of Trusts § 227(a). This establishes the investment objective (a certain level of safety) and the process of investing (that of a prudent man which such goals for himself). This is confused by the overlay of the Treatise, see text and accompanying notes 16–17 supra, which suggests that

the trustee must use "safe" means to attain this goal of safety, as opposed to the appropriate means.

[19]Restatement (First) and (Second) of Trusts § 227, comment f; 2 Treatise (1st ed. 1939), § 227.6, at pp. 1206–08; 3 Treatise (2d ed. 1956), § 227.6, at pp. 1670–72; 3 Treatise (3d ed. 1967), § 227.6, at pp. 1816–17.

[20]Restatement (First) of Trusts § 227, comment f; Restatement (Second) of Trusts § 227, comment m.

[21]See Chapter 4 supra.

[22]See, e.g., Blume & Keim, Risk and Return Characteristics of Lower-Grade Bonds (Working Paper, Wharton School 1984).

[23]To take a simple example: A trustee who believed that a particular stock would soon decline in price could sell the stock without legal objection, even though selling a call option on the stock might well provide equivalent protection at lower cost. See note 8 supra. A slightly more complicated example involves the use of a "protective put" option, which gives the holder the option to sell (or "put") the stock to the seller. In this way a trustee could also "immunize" the portfolio (in whole or in part) against anticipated downward price movements, again without a possibly more costly (but legally unobjectionable) sale of the underlying stocks. See Pozen, "The Purchase of Protective Puts by Financial Institutions," Fin. Analysts J. (July–August 1978).

A still more complicated example is a "90/10 Treasury bill/option strategy," under which 90 percent of the assets earmarked for the strategy are invested in Treasury bills and the remaining 10 percent are used to purchase puts and calls on individual stocks or stock indices. This combines the leveraged profit potential of options with the safety of Treasury bills, in a way that significantly limits exposure to adverse stock market movements. "Accordingly, even though it involves the speculative purchase of options, a 90/10 strategy is conservative, involving relatively low risk exposure. Its major advantage over S&P 500 stock returns [a legally unobjectionable investment] is that it avoids substantial losses during bear markets." FRB, CFTC, SEC, A Study of the Effects on the Economy of Trading in Futures and Options App. IV-A 9 (1984). See also L. McMillan, Options as a Strategic Investment, ch. 25 (1980). See also Chapter 3 supra.

[24]See note 8, supra; see also Chapter 3 supra (discussing equivalences).

[25]See, e.g., O. Holmes, The Common Law (Howe ed. 1963); K. Llewellyn, Jurisprudence: Realism in Theory and Practice (1962). Some recent work in the law and economics literature debates the necessary role of judges in improving the law. Compare Rubin, "Why is the Common Law Efficient?" 6 J. Legal Stud. 51 (1977) (litigants challenge inefficient rules, which mutate) with Cooter & Kornhauser, "Can Litigation Improve the Law Without the Help of Judges?" 9 J. Legal Stud. 139 (1980) (only modest improvement from litigation effect alone). See note 34 infra.

For an interesting account of how a major commentator can help persuade courts of the desirability of change, see Waters, "The Property in the Promise: A Study of the Third Party Beneficiary Rule," 98 Harv. L. Rev. 1111, 1148–72 (1985).

[26]Ronald Dworkin has developed a metaphor of law as a chain novel that illustrates this point powerfully. In Dworkin's metaphor, each successive author is obligated to "continue" the chain, rather than "starting over"—to integrate prior legal experience in deciding the next case rather than discarding it. See "How Law is Like Literature" in R. Dworkin, A Matter of Principle (1985), discussed in Lane, "The Poetics of Legal Interpretation" (forthcoming Columbia L. Rev. 1986). It is much harder to integrate a Restatement that has crystallized prior cases into now-obsolete rules than to reinterpret the cases themselves.

[27]Indeed, Professor Gilmore describes the movement beginning in the 1920s to "restate" the law as the legal establishment's attempt to refute the charges of the legal realists that the case method gave judges vast discretion to decide cases according to their prejudices. Gilmore, "Legal Realism: Its Cause and Cure," 70 Yale L.J. 1037 (1961); G. Gilmore, The Death of Contract 59, 67 (1974). The draftsmen believed and intended that the abstraction of cases into common-law rules would constrain the law. For a critique of Gilmore and a discussion of the role of the restatement movement in the history of American law reform, see Crystal, "Codification and the Rise of the Restatement Movement," 54 Wash. L. Rev. 239 (1979); see also L. Friedman, A History of American Law 582 (1973) (criticizing restatements as conservatizing). One obvious question, addressed in subsequent parts of this paper, is what other factors made the Restatement of Trusts

and the Treatise a more powerful influence on the law of trust management than, for example, the first Restatement of Contracts on the question of the enforceability of a gratuitous promise. *See* G. Gilmore, *supra,* at 59–76.

[28]*See* Gordley, "European Codes and American Restatements: Some Difficulties," 81 Colum. L. Rev. 140, 149, 153–56 (1981) (discussing problems of uncertainty and clarity); *see also* Clark, "The Restatement of the Law of Contract," 42 Yale L.J. 643, 646 (1933) (criticizing Restatement of Contracts as "attempting to force a black letter sentence [to] do what it can never do—state pages of history and policy and honest study and deliberation"). For a general critique of the project of "restating" the law, *see* H. Hart & A. Sacks, *The Legal Process* 758–66 (tent. ed. 1958).

Those who draft restatements (or write authoritative treatises) are not unaware of these problems, however. Corbin criticized Williston for excessive reliance on theory unresponsive to the actual facts. Corbin, Book Review, 30 Yale L. J. 773 (1921); Corbin, Book Review, 29 Yale L. J. 942 (1920). Restatement (Second) of Contracts has been described as shifting from "rules" to "standards" in the processes of contract formation and interpretation. Speidel, *Restatement Second:* Omitted Terms and Contract Method, 67 Corn. L. Rev. 785 (1982).

On the other hand, authoritative commentary may help clarify—and stabilize—parties' legal entitlements, facilitating planning and bargaining.

[29]In this regard it is interesting to note the efforts of the Massachusetts courts, which had 100 years' experience in applying the prudent man rule before the first Restatement, to avoid fixed rules about "prudence." Two analyses of the cases contemporaneous with the first Restatement indicate that the courts had preserved much greater flexibility than the commentator. *See* J. Robinson & H. Robinson, "Trustee's Investments in Massachusetts," 14 B.U.L. Rev. 88 (1934); Walker, "The Investment of Trust Funds Under the So-Called 'Massachusetts Rule,'" 13 Conn. B. J. 237 (1939); *see also* Shattuck, "The Massachusetts Prudent Man in Trust Investments," 25 B.U.L. Rev. 307 (1945).

[30]*See, e.g.,* Speidel, *Restatement Second:* Omitted Terms and Contract Method, 67 Corn. L. Rev. 785, 785 (1982) (describing Restatement as "blueprint for judicial reasoning in the adjudication of contract disputes").

[31]*See* Kornhauser & Sager, "Unpacking the Court," (forthcoming Yale L. J. 1986).

[32]*See* Priest, "Selective Characteristics of Litigation," 9 J. Legal Stud. 399 (1980) (discussing effect of "substantive indeterminancy" on litigation decisions and development of law); Priest & Klein, "The Selection of Disputes for Litigation," 13 J. Legal Stud. 1 (1984). The other economic models of litigation are in substantial agreement on this point. *E.g.,* Cooter, Marks & Mnookin, "Bargaining in the Shadow of the Law: A Testable Model of Strategic Behavior," 11 J. Legal Stud. 225 (1982); Gould, "The Economics of Legal Conflicts," 2 J. Legal Stud. 279 (1973); Landes & Posner, "Adjudication as a Private Good," 8 J. Legal Stud. 235 (1979).

[33]The example makes a number of simplifying assumptions: uniform stake of the beneficiaries in the outcome of litigation (a potential gain of $100,000 for each); identical risk preferences, risk neutrality; no mechanism for pursuing the action collectively or forcing others to contribute; and fixed litigation costs.

[34]A sophisticated body of scholarship debates the extent to which a "selective litigation" effect makes the common law efficient, even without the help of judges. In brief, the claim is that the common law evolves toward efficiency because parties are more likely to litigate inefficient rules, which will eventually "mutate" under repeated judicial reexamination. For a useful summary of this controversial thesis and its criticism, *see* Elliott, "The Evolutionary Tradition in Jurisprudence," 85 Colum. L. Rev. 38, 62–71 (1985). This essay obviously seeks the help of judges to change an obsolete rule. The litigation effect claim here is more modest: A pattern of judicial decisions altering an obsolete, "inefficient" rule is more likely to emerge if judges are repeatedly pressed on the rule. For the reasons discussed in the text, an authoritative commentary makes that process of relitigation less likely.

[35]*E.g.,* First Ala. Bank of Montgomery v. Martin, 425 So. 2d 415, *cert. denied,* 461 U.S. 938 (1983); Chase v. Pevear, 419 N.E.2d 1358 (Mass. 1981); In re Morgan Guaranty Trust Co., 396 N.Y.S.2d 781 (Surr. 1977); In re Bank of N.Y., 364 N.Y.S.2d 164 (N.Y. 1974). *See* text accompanying notes 54–58 *infra.*

[36]As is evident from the citations in this essay, there are perhaps ten post-1965 cases that give serious consideration to the trustee's investment management.

[37]Beginning with the first edition (1939), the Treatise advised the trustee "to consider each individual investment not as an isolated transaction, but in relation to the whole estate. Thus . . . he should diversify the investments as to diminish the risk of serious losses." 2 Treatise (1st ed. 1939), § 227.12, at p. 1223. This familiar idea in the law of trusts is connected to portfolio theory only in a rudimentary way. It is not elaborated upon in subsequent editions of the Treatise. *See, e.g.,* 3 Treatise (3d ed. 1967), § 227, at p. 1809. In any event, this potential opening to portfolio theory does not appear in either of the Restatements.

[38]*See* note 3 *supra.*

[39]*See* note 8 *supra.*

[40]The cases to be discussed in the text are all drawn from the Treatise. Interestingly, the first Restatement cited no cases. Instead of the format of more recent restatements, in which reporters' notes followed the black letter and comments, the American Law Institute arranged for bar groups in different states to annotate the Restatement in light of respective state law. In some cases the annotators indicated clearly whether or not the Restatement was consistent with state law. *See, e.g.,* Massachusetts Annotations to the Restatement of Trusts (1936) (prepared by M.A. Shattuck). Of further interest is an unusual practice pertaining to tentative drafts of the first Restatement: for most sections the reporter circulated an appendix citing cases, research memoranda, and the like, generally in support of the black letter. For the predecessor section to § 227, there is no appendix entry. *See* Am. Law Inst., Restatement of Trusts, T.D. No. 4 (Feb. 1933).

[41]Treatise (1st ed. 1939), § 227.6, at p. 1207; 3 Treatise (2d ed. 1956), § 227.6, at p. 1607; 3 Treatise (3d ed. 1967), § 227.6, at p. 1816.

[42]31 N.H. 352 (1855).

[43]207 N.Y.S. 385 (4th Dep't 1925).

[44]44 A.2d 137 (Vt. 1945).

[45]169 N.Y.S. 853 (Surr. 1918).

[46]190 S.W. 333 (Mo. 1916).

[47]16 So. 126 (Ala. 1894).

[48]206 N.Y.S. 448 (2d Dep't 1924).

[49]Moreover, of the nineteenth and early twentieth century surcharge cases purporting to apply a prudent man rule not cited by the Treatise, virtually all are also consistent with a portfolio theory approach. A majority of the cases clearly involve a "speculative" investment comprising a disproportionately large portion of the portfolio. *E.g.,* Pray's Appeal, 14 Pa. (10 Casey) 100 (Sup. Ct. 1859) (50 percent of trust fund in start-up enterprise); English v. McIntyre, 51 N.Y.S. 697 (1898) (entire trust fund in heavily margined stock trading account); Michigan Home Missionary Soc'y v. Corning, 129 N.W. 686 (Mich. 1911) (entire trust fund in note of lumbering business); Durant v. Crowley, 189 N.Y.S. 385 (1st Dep't 1921) (50 percent of trust fund in start-up rubber recycling business, secured by mortgage on real estate without substantial value unless business was successful); Murphy-Bolanz Land & Loan Co. v. McKibben, 236 S.W. 78 (Comm. of App. Tex. 1922) (nearly 50 percent of trust fund in leveraged real estate purchase); In re Jenkins' Estate, 245 N.W. 508 (1932) (75 percent of trust fund in loan to single corporation, secured by mortgage on real estate of limited value). In a few other surcharge cases the facts as to the relative size of the impermissible investment are suggestive of consistency with portfolio theory, but too scanty for a definite conclusion. *E.g.,* Mattocks v. Moulton, 24 A. 1004 (Me. 1892) (investment in stocks and bonds of highly leveraged new business) (cited by Treatise); White v. Sherman, 48 N.E. 128 (1897) (investment in widely fluctuating railroad shares); Steele v. Leopold, 120 N.Y.S. 569 (1st Dep't 1909), *aff'd,* 54 N.E. 1099 (N.Y. 1911) (investment in heavily margined stock trading account). In only one case surcharging the trustee under the prudent man rule in the pre-Treatise era does it seem likely that the challenged investment constituted a relatively small portion of the portfolio. Morris v. Wallace, 3 Pa. (3 Barr.) 317 (1846) ($650 invested in stock of troubled bank, balance in mortgage).

[50]This is evidenced by the somewhat inconsistent position Scott takes on the risk/return trade-off. The Treatise claims that "The primary purpose of a trustee should be to preserve the trust estate, while receiving a reasonable amount of income, rather than taking risks for the pur-

pose of increasing the principal or income." 3 Treatise (3d ed. 1967), § 227.3, at p. 1811; *Accord* 2 Treatise (1st ed. 1939), § 227.3, at p. 1203; 3 Treatise (2d ed. 1956), § 227.3, at p. 1666. And in the Restatement, Scott criticizes as improper "a disposition which is speculative in character with a view to increasing his property instead of merely preserving it . . . because it is not a disposition which makes the preservation of the fund a primary consideration." Restatement (First) and (Second) of Trusts § 227, comment e. Yet in both the Treatise and the Restatement Scott countenances investments in other than government bonds, in light of a risk/return trade-off that is foreign to his system of capital preservation: "There are other securities which yield a higher return as to which the element of risk is sufficiently small so as to make them proper trust investments." 3 Treatise (3d ed. 1967), § 227.3, at p. 1812; *Accord* 2 Treatise (1st ed. 1939), § 227.3, at p. 1204; 3 Treatise (2d ed. 1956), § 227.3, at p. 1667. He has the intuition but lacks the necessary conceptual framework to quantify risk in a useful way.

[51] 25 N.E. 99 (Mass. 1890).

[52] *Id.* at 100 [emphasis added].

[53] *Dickinson* is not the only case reasoning in this fashion. In Appeal of Davis, 67 N.E. 604 (Mass. 1903), the court permitted an initial investment of approximately 20 percent of a $30,000 trust in stocks and bonds of a railroad company, but not a subsequent investment of an additional 20 percent. In Thayer v. Dewey, 69 N.E. 1074 (Mass. 1904), the court permitted investment of a "small part" of a $200,000 fund to be invested in Illinois real estate.

[54] 419 N.E.2d 1358 (Mass. 1981).

[55] 425 So. 2d 415 (Ala.), *cert. denied,* 461 U.S. 938 (1983).

[56] 470 A.2d 585 (Pa. Super. Ct. 1983).

[57] *Id.* at 593.

[58] 393 P.2d 96 (Hawaii 1964).

[59] 486 N.Y.S.2d 956 (2d Dep't 1985).

[60] Scott's flat declarations regarding speculation have had a similarly negative effect on the appropriate use of leverage in designing the optimum portfolio. Restatement (First) and (Second) of Trusts § 227, comment f identifies purchase of stock on margin as a clear speculation. *Accord* 3 Treatise (3d ed. 1967), § 227.6, at p. 1816; 2 Treatise (1st ed. 1939), § 227.6, at p. 1206–07; 3 Treatise (2d ed. 1956), § 227.6, at p. 1670–71. The case cited, In re Hirsch's Estate, 101 N.Y.S. 893 (1st Dep't 1906), *aff'd,* 81 N.E. 1165 (N.Y. 1907), would also be objectionable on portfolio theory grounds: The trust fund was levered to an extraordinarily high degree, such that payment of $52,000 of a fund of $80,000 was necessary to meet a margin call. The degree of leverage made the portfolio far too risky for a trust fund. The Treatise subsequently cites Merrill Lynch, Pierce, Fenner & Smith, Inc. v. Bocock, 247 F. Supp. 373 (S.D. Tex. 1965), which reasons that a "short sale is a margin account," that a margin account is less safe than a second mortgage (also on the Treatise's presumptively speculative list), and therefore that short selling or use of margin "are speculative to the extent that they can be termed 'rank gambles.'" Id. at 379, 380. The case gives no clear indication of the size of the trust, but it seems likely that the extent of the short selling left the fund highly levered. *See also* Chaner Estate, 26 D. & C.2d 450 (Pa. 1961) (citing Restatement section and comment). All the cases (and Scott) ignore the trustee's failure to monitor the investment position and cut losses at a particular point. Assuming that a trustee can invest an appropriate portion of portfolio assets in a particular stock on the basis of securities research that suggests the stock will hold a steady value or perhaps increase, then it follows that the trustee should be able to capitalize on research showing the opposite by selling the stock short. The problem arises where, as in *Hirsch* and *Bocock,* the trustee's failure to monitor exposes the portfolio to excessive risk of loss.

By condemning all uses of margin and short sales, Scott forecloses use of techniques that can be employed in a manner totally consistent with a low level of portfolio risk. *See* Elton & Gruber, *The Lessons of Modern Portfolio Theory,* Appendix A, *supra.* Moreover, in condemning categorically these particular instances of leverage, the Treatise calls into question new techniques, such as writing covered call or put options or using financial futures, which enhance the trustee's capacity to manage a portfolio at the lowest possible cost. See note 8 and text accompanying notes 23–24 *supra.*

[61] 396 N.Y.S.2d 781 (Surr. Ct. 1977).

[62]445 F. Supp. 670 (S.D.N.Y. 1978).

[63]In *Morgan Guaranty* the court refused to surcharge a bank for transactions in four particular securities (including Penn Central) in its administration of a common trust fund. It seems likely that the securities in question represented only a small percentage of the fund, which is likely to have been highly diversified, but the court focused instead on trust department structure and procedures.

In *Stark,* the court refused to surcharge a bank for retention of three particular securities in its administration of four private trusts. Although it is impossible from the opinion to determine the percentage of the fund represented by the three stocks, it seems unlikely that the trusts were highly diversified. The three stocks had been included in the trusts on the grantor's initiative and the trust instrument empowered the trustee to retain the stocks without regard to a claim of alleged overrepresentation in the fund. The court focused on the research procedures of the bank and the decision-making process of the bank trust officer in reviewing the fund's holdings.

[64]*See* note 78 *infra.*

[65]The initial theoretical work on portfolio theory was done by 1965. Among the seminal contributions were Markowitz, "Portfolio Selection," 7 J. Fin. 77 (1952); H. Markowitz, *Portfolio Selection: Efficient Diversification of Assets* (1959); Sharpe, "Capital Asset Prices: A Theory of Market Equilibrium Under Condition of Risk," 19 J. Fin. 425 (1964); Linter, "The Valuation of Risky Assets and the Selection of Risky Investments in Stock Portfolios and Capital Budgets," 47 Rev. Econ. & Stats. 13 (1964). By 1969 work on portfolio theory was carried on throughout the academic finance community. *See* M. Jensen, ed., *Studies in the Theory of Capital Markets* vii, 3–46 (1972) (summarizing 1969 conference and current state of capital market theory). Investment managers began to apply the theory in the late 1960s; by the 1970s it had become commonplace. *See, e.g.,* Treynor, "How to Rate Management of Investment Funds," 1965 Harv. Bus. Rev. 63 (1965); Treynor, Priest, Fisher, & Higgins, "Using Portfolio Composition to Estimate Risk," 24 Fin. Analysts J. 93 (1968); Block, "Elements of Portfolio Construction," 25 Fin. Analysts J. 123 (1969); Welles, "The Beta Revolution: Learning to Live With Risk," Institutional Investor 21 (Sept. 1971); Lorie, "Four Cornerstones of a New Investment Policy," Institutional Investor 48 (Nov. 1971). The theory was quickly funneled into the work of legal academics. *E.g..* Note, "The Regulation of Risky Investments," 83 Harv. L. Rev. 603 (1970); Cohen, "The Suitability Rule and Economic Theory," 80 Yale L.J. 1607 (1971).

[66]*See, e.g.,* Am. Stock Exch., *Options for Institutions: The Prudent Man Rule* (1978), which argues for the prudence of covered call writing under traditional trust principles: "If the stock goes up in price, the only sacrifice . . . is an opportunity for even greater profits. Since trust assets are not held for speculation and the highest profit, this possibility may be irrelevant. If the stock declines in value, writing covered calls . . . reduces the loss which would have been incurred on the underlying stock had the calls not been written. Therefore such an investment technique acts to conserve principal. If the price of the stock remains constant, the premium income adds to the yield on the investment, thus increasing the productivity of the property."

[67]For example, courts have recently employed one key claim of the modern finance paradigm, the efficient market hypothesis, in finding the reliance element in a securities fraud action satisfied by reliance on the market price—which on an EMH view impounds all relevant information—even if the plaintiff had not read the misleading prospectus. *See* Black, "Fraud on the Market: A Criticism of Dispensing With Reliance Requirements in Certain Open Market Transactions," 62 N.C.L. Rev. 435 (1984); Fischel, "Use of Modern Finance Theory in Securities Fraud Cases Involving Actively Traded Securities," 38 Bus. Law. 1 (1982).

By contrast, in the trusts area, only one judicial opinion bears the clear influence of portfolio theory, Hamilton v. Nielsen, 678 F.2d 709 (7th Cir. 1982), in which Judge Posner (author, inter alia, of *Economic Analysis of Law* (3d ed. 1985)) suggested that plaintiffs had missed a potential basis for surcharge by failing to employ portfolio theory.

[68]For example, Restatement (First) of Contracts § 164 stated that an assignee's acceptance of a contract ordinarily carries the assignee's promise to perform the assignor's duties under the contract. No distinction was drawn between contracts for the sale of goods or services and those for the sale of land. Nevertheless, courts drew such a distinction and rejected the rule in land

contracts. *E.g.,* Langel v. Betz, 164 N.E. 890 (N.Y. 1928). This is recognized in Restatement (Second) of Contracts § 328 (which retreats to a "no opinion" on the land contracts distinction) and the accompanying Reporter's Note. *See* 3 Williston, *Contracts* § 418A (3d ed. 1960); 4 Corbin, *Contracts* § 906 (1951 and Supps. 1971 & 1980).

To take another example, Restatement (First) of Contracts § 142 stated that a promisor's duty to a donee beneficiary could not be altered by any contrary agreement with the promisee, unless such a power was reserved in the initial agreement. Thus, for example, a party taking out a life insurance policy could not change the beneficiary unless the policy reserved such a right. Courts reject such irrevocability, as is recognized by Restatement (Second) of Contracts § 311 (which accepts the judicial view) and the accompanying Reporter's Note. *See* 2 Williston, *Contracts* §§ 396–97 (3d ed. 1959); 4 Corbin, *Contracts* §§ 813–15 (1951).

[69] A third factor—the limited incentives for beneficiaries and trustees to challenge the constrained rule by litigation or otherwise—may also be involved. *See* Gordon, The Puzzling Persistence of the Constrained Prudent Man Rule (Working paper, July 1986).

[70] Marsh, "Are Directors Trustees? Conflicts of Interest and Corporate Morality," 22 Bus. Law. 35, 39 (1966).

[71] *Id.*

[72] *Id.* at 40.

[73] *Id* at 41. Rhoads, "Personal Liability of Directors of Corporate Mismanagement," 65 U. Pa. L. Rev. 128 (1916).

[74] For example, assume an automobile manufacturer needs to purchase tires. If the owner (or director) of a tire manufacturer sits on the automobile manufacturer's board, the two companies can very easily discover one another's needs, capacities, reputation, and creditworthiness. Assuming some assurance that goods will be delivered at the market price and quality, a contract between these two firms would result in a savings in transaction costs and thus would be more "efficient." (The allocation of these savings between the two firms is another problem.)

[75] The claim that common-law courts (consciously or intuitively) adopt more efficient rules is controversial. *See, e.g.,* Note, "The Inefficient Common Law," 92 Yale L.J. 862, 862 ns. 1, 2 (1983) (citing literature making efficiency claims but proposing model of inefficiency). Some might claim that judges are motivated to favor certain groups or interests. *See generally* M. Horwitz, *The Transformation of American Law* 1780–1860 (1977). In the case of the director contracts rule change, one could propose judicial disposition to favor directors at the expense of shareholders. Given the original rule, however, this explanation seems a less plausible account of the *change* than the cost-savings explanation.

[76] This is not entirely the case, for example, in the case of certain uses of options and financial futures. Even without a full portfolio theory approach, a court might understand the gains from covered call writing or use of a financial futures contract to hedge a long-term Treasury bond. Options and futures exchanges argue strenuously that particular uses of these vehicles are consistent with the traditional understanding of prudence of the constrained rule. *See* note 66 *supra.*

[77] For example, the model employed by Scott analyzes "risk" in terms of the variance (or risk) of a particular security in isolation.

[78] *In re Morgan Guaranty* and *Stark v. U.S. Trust Co.,* notes 61 and 62 *supra,* which validated transactions in particular equity securities on the ground of the formal decision-making process of professional trustees, illustrate a typical judicial response to uncertainty about a substantive theory—reliance on process. But without a substantive theory as a guide, the court's reliance on process may encourage costly formal procedures and paper trails that do not contribute to beneficiary welfare. Moreover, the court's process standard may create difficulties for the fiduciary who believes that stock markets are highly efficient and undertakes to buy and hold a diversified portfolio that is a reasonable proxy for the market portfolio. He will not engage in extensive "fundamental research" about each portfolio security or constant review of portfolio holdings. A process standard uninformed by theory could conceivably find his reasonable approach imprudent.

The process approach of *Morgan Guaranty* and *Stark* may provide comfort for the trustee willing to live within the confines of the constrained rule and to follow a documented process of securities selection and retention. This approach provides little comfort, however, for the trustee who wishes to use new financial products and techniques, for which a demonstration of prudence depends upon an understanding of the theory behind an unconstrained rule.

[79]See text accompanying notes 65–67 *supra.* As discussed above, counsel may be influenced in their case presentation by the prior tailoring of conduct to fit into the conception of prudence set forth in the Restatement and the Treatise. *See* text accompanying notes 34–45 *supra.* If the trustee's decision-making process is not geared to a portfolio theory approach, it may be harder to present such a case, even in the alternative.

[80]*See* note 67 *supra;* Gordon & Kornhauser, "Efficient Markets, Costly Information, and Securities Research," 60, N.Y.U. L. Rev. 761, 810–23 (1985) (discussing, in addition, use by SEC in integrated disclosure scheme and shelf registration); D. Harrington, *Modern Portfolio Theory and the Capital Asset Pricing Model* 129 (1983) (public utility rate regulation).

[81]*See* text accompanying notes 54–67 *supra.*

[82]*But see* Hamilton v. Nielsen, 678 F.2d 709 (7th Cir. 1982) (Posner, J.).

One factor that might be linked to judicial reception of (or resistance to) complicated new theory into the law is what is taught in law school. *See generally* A. Watson, *The Evolution of Law* 118–19 (1985). (Legal development is determined by the culture of lawyers and lawmakers. "Social, economic, and political factors impinge on legal development only through their consciousness.") An examination of trusts casebooks published over a thirty-year period was made to see how they present the prudent man rule, especially through comment, leading questions, and case selection.

The dominant casebooks in the 1950s and 1960s emphasize the trustee's duty not only to earn a reasonable return, but to insure the safety of principal. The casebooks promote the prudent man rule over the legal list approach, to the extent of encouraging investments in seasoned securities, not speculation. *See* Scott, 4th ed. 1951, 5th ed. 1966 (with Scott); Bogert, 2d ed. 1951, 3d ed. 1958; Scoles, 1st ed. 1965. The 1970s casebooks signal a shift. The selected cases seem to place more emphasis on the procedures followed by the trustee, rather than the type of security or outcome. In particular, the appropriateness of trustee reliance on qualified investment advisers receives emphasis. *See* Scoles, 2d ed. 1973; Ritchie, Alford, & Effland, 4th ed. 1971, 5th ed. 1977. The 1980s casebooks generally quote significantly from recent literature on portfolio theory and the efficient market hypothesis. *See* Ritchie et al. 6th ed. 1982; McGovern, 1st ed. 1983; Wellman, 4th ed. 1983; Dukeminier & Johanson, 3d ed. 1984.

Of course, it is impossible to say what material is actually covered in classes, what gloss a professor may add, and how students respond. Nevertheless, a guess might be hazarded that the portfolio theory paradigm will become increasingly accepted as lawyers gain skill at its argument and judges (aided perhaps by law clerk discussion) become more familiar with alien theory. But currently sitting judges are likely to have been exposed to the prudent man rule in law school through Scott's conception.

[83]These are explored more fully at text accompanying notes 91–93 *infra.* These problems probably account for the continuing strictness of rules pertaining to trustee self-dealing.

[84]A similar argument on behalf of judicially manageable standards undoubtedly was a powerful inducement for courts to adopt a legal list approach. *See* King v. Talbot, 40 N.Y. 76 (1869).

[85]Some have argued that the restrictions on trust investment flexibility have derived principally from judicial perception of the incompetence of trustees. *See* H. Bines, *The Law of Investment Management* ¶¶ 1.02[2][a], 1.02[2][c] (1978). Indeed, many of the cases cited in the Treatise inveighing against speculative investments and new and untried enterprises seem clear examples of trustee incompetence or even self-dealing. *See* text accompanying notes 41–49 *supra.* On the other hand, most trust investment management activity today is carried out by professional trustees, such as banks or trust companies or investment advisers registered with the SEC. The potential incompetence is probably in a narrower compass.

[86]It may be helpful to cite another example drawn from the law of trusts that illustrates judicial receptivity to efficiency claims where assessment of potential gains and costs requires only incremental advance. In several instances courts have permitted trustees to invest in common stocks despite restrictions limiting investment to fixed income instruments, on the ground that inflation was rapidly eroding the real value of the trust estate. In re Trusteeship Under Agree-

ment With Mayo, 105 N.W.2d 900 (Minn. 1960); Carlick v. Keiler, 375 S.W.2d 397 (Ky. Ct. App. 1964); Davison v. Duke Univ., 194 S.E.2d 761 (N.C. 1973). *Contra* Stanton v. Wells Fargo Bank & Union Trust Co., 310 P. 2d 1010 (Cal. Ct. App. 1957); Toledo Trust Co. v. Toledo Hosp., 187 N.E.2d 36 (1962); Troost Ave. Cemetery Co. v. First Nat'l Bank, 409 S.W.2d 632 (Mo. 1966). The gains from such deviation from the trust instrument are easy to understand: The real value of a trust corpus consisting of long-term fixed income investments deteriorates in inflationary times; the addition of common stocks will help hold values constant. As to the costs, since the deviation grants the trustee the latitude of the constrained prudent man rule, not beyond it, the court faces no new discretion problems. The gains are readily graspable; the additional discretion minimal. This judicial flexibility, even in the face of express trust language, suggests once again the ordinary judicial response to comprehensible claims of "efficiency" and the extent to which the complexity of the portfolio theory model has made acceptance of an unconstrained rule more difficult.

[87]Restatement (Second) of Trusts § 227(a) and comments u, v; 3 Treatise (3d ed. 1967), § 227.14, at pp. 1848–54. *See* H. Bines, *The Law of Investment Management,* ¶ 5.02[2] n.16 (1978) (citing to exemplars of clauses expanding investment powers). However, courts are likely to construe strictly any purported authority to invest beyond the scope of the constrained rule. *See* Restatement (Second) of Trusts § 227, comments u, v, w; 3 Treatise (3d ed. 1967) § 227.14, at p. 1852. Thus expanded investment powers clauses in earlier-drafted instruments may not provide sufficient comfort for a trustee contemplating investment in instruments or vehicles that did not exist at the time the instrument was drafted. There may also be a lag time between the invention or availability of a new instrument and its inclusion in expanded powers clauses.

[88]*See, e.g.,* Comm. on Trusts, Estates & Surr. Cts., Ass'n of Bar, City of N.Y., Report No. 27 on S. 9572, A. 7114-A (1985) (prudent person standard drafted for professional trustees moves rule closer to business judgment rule).

[89]*See, e.g.,* American Law Institute, *Principles of Corporate Governance* § 4.01(d) (T. D. No. 3 1984).

[90]Restatement (Second) of Trusts § 227, comment e; 3 Treatise (3d ed. 1967), § 227.3, at pp. 1811–12.

[91]*See* Joy v. North, 692 F.2d 880, 885–86 (2d Cir. 1982), *cert. denied sub nom.,* Citytrust v. Joy, 460 U.S. 1051 (1983).

[92]The limits on shareholder monitoring of management performance in selling the company may account for the heightened judicial scrutiny of directors in Smith v. Van Gorkom, 488 A.2d 858 (Del. 1985).

[93]*See, e.g.,* Joy v. North, 692 F.2d 880 (2d Cir. 1982), *cert. denied sub nom.,* Citytrust v. Joy, 460 U.S. 1051 (1983) (construction loans were no-win proposition); Selheimer v. Manganese Corp. of Am., 224 A.2d 634 (Pa. 1966) (expenditures on economically unfeasible plant).

[94]Restatement (Second) of Trusts § 213; 3 Treatise (3d ed. 1967), § 213.1, at pp. 1712–17.

[95]*See* Fleming, "Prudent Investments: The Varying Standards of Prudence," 12 Real Prop. Prob. & Trust J. 243, 248–49 (1977) G. Bogert & G. Bogert, *Trusts & Trustees* § 671, at pp. 7–8 (2d ed. rev. 1980).

[96]364 N.Y.S.2d 164 (1974).

[97]*Id.* at 168.

[98]*Spitzer* contains some ambiguity on the extent to which its review of particular securities is portfolio based. *Id.* at 168. Nevertheless, criticisms of *Spitzer* as an unfair anti-netting rule (*see* Fleming, note 95 *supra*; Bogert, note 95 *supra*) are on the whole not well taken.

[99]Restatement (Second) of Trusts § 228; 3 Treatise (3d ed. 1967), § 228, at p. 1856.

[100]*E.g.,* In re Newhoff, 435 N.Y.S.2d 632 (Surr. Ct. 1980), *aff'd,* 486 N.Y.S.2d 956 (2d Dep't 1985) (noting New York does not require diversification but arguing it should). The New York position stems from Matter of Adriance, 260 N.Y.S. 173 (Surr. Ct. 1932), which noted conflicting views among investment experts on the wisdom of diversification and decided it could make no definite decision either way. "This divergence of sentiment in favor of either school of thought is an *ultra* hazardous undertaking." *Id.* at 181. *See* Note, "Trust Fund Investment in New York: The Prudent Man Rule and Diversification of Investments," 47 N.Y.U. L. Rev. 527 (1972).

[101]Strand, "New York's Partial Prudent Man Rule," 25 N.Y.U. L. Rev. 583, 591 (1950).

[102]For example, perhaps the settlor, a famed stockpicker, held a large block of stock in a particular firm and prefers, although does not require, the trust to retain the stock. Alternatively, one of the purposes of the trust might be for a family group to retain control over a firm, which would necessitate retaining a large block.

[103]486 N.Y.S.2d 956 (2d Dep't 1985).

[104]*See* Elton & Gruber, *The Lessons of Portfolio Theory,* Appendix A, *supra.*

[105]2 Treatise (1st ed. 1939), § 236, at pp. 1293–1325; 3 Treatise (2d ed. 1956), § 236, at pp. 1804–48; 3 Treatise (3d ed. 1967), § 236, at pp. 1967–2022. Also part of the standard rule is that all interest payments on fixed income instruments count as income (including increments in value because of original issue discount) and that repayment of the face amount (and gain or loss on a sale before maturity) counts as principal. 3 Treatise (3d ed. 1967), § 233.1, at pp. 1898–1902.

Most states have adopted either the Uniform Principal and Income Act of 1931 or the Revised Uniform Principal and Income Act of 1962. *See* Hirsch, "Inflation and the Law of Trusts," 18 Real Prop. Prob. & Tr. J. 601, 614 (1983).

[106]There is a split in the jurisdictions. Under the "Massachusetts rule," all cash dividends are treated as income, even if extraordinary. The "Pennsylvania rule" (repudiated by statute in Pennsylvania) bases an allocation on the extent to which the dividend came from earnings that accrued to the corporation during the period of the trust or prior thereto. *See* 3 Treatise (3d ed. 1967), § § 236.3, 236.4, at pp. 1975–89.

[107]The "Massachusetts rule" treats all stock dividends as principal. The "Pennsylvania rule" allocates as above. *See* 3 Treatise (3d ed. 1967), § § 236.3, 236.7, at pp. 1975–81, 1996–99. The Revised Uniform Principal and Income Act, § 5, opts in favor of the Massachusetts rule: "Corporate distributions of shares of the distributing corporation, including . . . a stock split or stock dividend, are principal. . . . [A]11 [other] corporate distributions are income, including cash dividends [and rights offerings]." *Compare* Restatement (Second) of Trusts § 236. *See* Annot., "Modern Status of Rule Governing Allocation of Stock Dividends or Splits Between Principal and Income," 81 A.L.R.3d 876 (1977). A few states have opted for the so-called "six percent rule," which arbitrarily declares that any stock dividend of less than (or "up to," in some versions) six percent counts as income. *E.g.,* N.Y. Estate, Powers & Trusts Law § 11-2.1(e) (2) (McKinney 1967). *See* Note, "Trust Allocation Doctrine and Corporate Stock: The Law Must Respond to Economics," 50 Tex. L. Rev. 747, 766–67 (1972).

[108]*See* Elton & Gruber, *The Lessons of Portfolio Theory,* Appendix A, *supra;* W. Cary & C. Bright, *The Law and the Lore of Endowment Funds* 28–32 (1969). A "total return" approach draws no distinction between realized and unrealized gains and losses. Unless otherwise indicated, references to gains in this section include realized and unrealized gains.

[109]For simplicity the text adopts a model requiring the trustee to distribute currently all income. Some trusts give the trustee power to accumulate income for subsequent payout. The principal and income allocation rules nevertheless require such a trustee to *treat* as income all dividends; i.e., dividends are subject to whatever rules the trust sets up for income.

[110]*See* 3 Treatise (3d ed. 1967), §§ 232, 239.2, 240, at pp. 1894–97, 2037–41, 2053–57.

[111]The standard allocation of principal and income fails even without regard to the claims of portfolio theory. The interest paid on a fixed income investment will include some element of compensation for expected inflation, to preserve the real value of the principal upon maturity. On the standard allocation rules, all such interest belongs to the life beneficiary, irrespective of the depreciation of principal. *See* note 102 *supra.* An investment of unreproachable prudence, short term Treasury notes, can work out to the remaindermen's severe disadvantage in inflationary times. A total return approach would address this problem.

A corollary that follows from the total return approach is the excision of statements in the Treatise and the Restatement about "prudence" as the "preservation" of capital and "speculation" as the effort to increase it. Restatement (Second) of Trusts § 227, comment e; 3 Treatise (3d ed. 1967), § 227.6, at p. 1816. The goal of the prudent fiduciary is to maximize returns while incurring no more than the appropriate level of risk for the particular fund under management. In many instances this entails investment choices made with the hope of capital gains.

[112]*See, e.g.,* W. Cary & C. Bright, *The Developing Law of Endowment Funds: The "Law and*

the Lore" Revisited 7–12 (1974); Yale Univ. Financial Statements and Supplemental Schedules 7 (for year ending 1982) (determination of amount spent from endowment, including "University Equation Method"). The Uniform Management of Institutional Funds Act, § 2, adopts a total return approach in permitting the trustees of a nonprofit institution to count appreciation, realized and unrealized, in the value of the fund, as moneys available for appropriation.

[113]Ease of administration is frequently a powerful argument. It may be possible to understand judicial hostility to common stock ownership by trusts as a defensive response to the problems they knew would arise in the fair allocation of capital gains between income and remainder interests. Indeed, the logic of the "Pennsylvania rule" on the allocation of cash dividends argues for the allocation of gains as well, on the view that the gains are the result of income earned and retained during the income beneficiary's entitlement. *See* 3 Treatise (3d ed. 1967), § 236.3, at p. 1983.

[114]A recent article argues strenuously, but not entirely convincingly, that the present Uniform Act permits sufficient trustee discretion in the allocation of income to at least protect the principal against erosion from inflation. Hirsch, "Inflation and the Law of Trusts," 18 Real Prop. Prob. & Tr. J. 601, 647–49 (1983).

[115]*See* Note, "Effectuating the Settlor's Intent: A Formula for Providing More Income for the Life Beneficiary," 33 U. Chi. L. Rev. 783, 783–84 (1966).

[116]*See* J. Dukeminier & S. Johanson, *Wills, Trusts and Estates* 905–06 (3d ed. 1984).

[117]126 N.W.2d 614 (Wis. 1964).

[118]*See, e.g.,* Carpenter, "The 'Fixed-Income,' 'Annuity' and 'Modernized' Types of Trust," 5 L. & Contemp. Prob. 368, 371 (1938).

[119]Corporate trustees have vigorously opposed the adoption of a discretionary rule as a general substitute for the uniform act. See the panel discussion reprinted in Uniform Revised Principal and Income Act, 101 Tr. & Estates 894, 896 (1962).

[120]A version of this proposal was made in Carpenter, "The 'Fixed Income,' 'Annuity,' and 'Modernized' Types of Trust," 5 L. & Contemp. Probs. 368 (1938).

[121]In addition to the inflation assumptions discussed in the text, any return assumptions also obviously depend on the specific portfolio, particularly the level of risk. Questions about appropriate returns assumptions for a trusteed portfolio are raised in connection with the financial study proposed *infra*.

[122]For example, assume that the settlor establishes a testamentary trust. Believing that the sustainable long term nominal yield is 6 percent, but being uncertain as to the size of the trust corpus at the time of his death, the settlor sets a payout percentage of 6 percent of the trust corpus rather than a fixed dollar amount. Under the fixed nominal payout approach, the payout would be fixed at the dollar amount equal to 6 percent of the trust corpus *at the trust's effective date.* This contrasts to the approach described below of a fixed portfolio percentage payout, in which the dollar amount of the payout would vary.

[123]Perhaps it bears emphasis that the fixed income approach contemplates possible invasion of the corpus if necessary to make the prescribed payout. The extent of the payout could vary, even holding inflation assumptions constant, depending on the settlor's concern about potential erosion of the corpus either because of the ultimate effect on income beneficiaries (the funds might run out) or on remaindermen (not as much wealth will be passed to them).

Observe that the interests of income beneficiaries will always be to receive the largest possible payout as soon as possible. To the extent they are concerned about future income (and inflation), they could presumably take appropriate steps. In establishing a trust, as opposed to a direct gift or bequest, the settlor expresses an intention somewhat at odds with the income beneficiary.

[124]There would be the usual problems in determining the appropriate measure of general inflation: consumer vs. producer prices, quarterly vs. yearly adjustments, regional vs. national prices. In addition there is the problem that the inflation rate may vary across different expenditures faced by life beneficiaries at different stages of their lives: Housing costs may not increase significantly for the widow in the house that is paid for, but medical costs may be increasing significantly faster than general inflation rate. A general inflation assumption deals imperfectly with the changing market basket of goods and services a life beneficiary will require across his or her life.

Calls for real fixed payout approaches have been made by, *e.g.,* Barclay, "Lot of the Income Beneficiary—Part 3," 107 Tr. & Estates 389 (1968); Note, "Common Stocks in Trust," 113 U. Pa. L. Rev. 228 (1964).

[125]Such an assumption is made more plausible by portfolio management that could shift among investment vehicles in light of changing conditions and the effectiveness of particular inflation hedges—from stocks to bonds to real estate to precious metals.

[126]The analogy is not exact. The insurance company, unlike the remaindermen, also guarantees the making of the payout, even beyond exhaustion of the "corpus" (its fee).

[127]A version of this proposal was made in David, "Principal and Income—Obsolete Concepts," 43 Pa. B.A.Q. 247, 251 (1972); Clark, Power to Invest Without Yield, 100 Tr. & Estates 495 (1961); Carpenter, "The 'Fixed Income,' 'Annuity,' and 'Modernized' Types of Trust," 5 L. & Contemp. Prob. 368 (1938).

A twist on this proposal is offered by a student note that suggests that the current allocation rules continue to apply, subject to a minimum and a maximum portfolio percentage payout. Note, "Range of Returns: A New Approach to the Allocation of Trust Gains and Losses," 21 Stan. L. Rev. 420 (1969). The problems are that continued reliance in any manner on the current allocation rules is likely to interfere with acceptance of modern portfolio management, and that the various percentages proposed have no necessary relation to sustainable real yields.

[128]The capital gains and losses referred to in the text include unrealized as well as a realized gains and losses. This would obviously require a change in the customary trust law practice of focusing on realized gains and losses. *See* 3 Treatise (3d ed. 1967) §§ 236.11, 236.12, at pp. 2008–11.

[129]A similar proposal is found in Note, "Trust Allocation Doctrine and Corporate Stock: The Law Must Respond to Economics," 50 Tex. L. Rev. 747 (1972). Another student note makes a related proposal: to set an annual payout based on the sum of the current average annual dividend yield of all stocks and the long term average annual real capital gain for such stocks. Note, "Effectuating the Settlor's Intent: A Formula for Providing More Income for the Life Beneficiary," 33 U. Chi. 783, 793 (1966). This payout in effect assumes that the benchmark trusteed portfolio consists of the market index of equity securities; debt is not considered. It is not obvious that a portfolio of this level of risk is the appropriate benchmark. Moreover, to require annual payout of this amount could rapidly erode corpus in a period of declining market conditions.

[130]"Simple trusts," which are required under the terms of their governing instruments to distribute all income currently, are entitled to a deduction of that amount in computing taxable income. 26 U.S.C. § 651. "Complex trusts," whose governing instruments may have additional provisions, are entitled to a deduction for required distributions up to the "distributable net income of the trust." 26 U.S.C. § 661.

[131]26 U.S.C. § § 652 (simple trusts); 662 (complex trusts).

[132]"[For relevant parts] the term 'income' . . . means the amount of income of the . . . trust for the taxable year determined under the terms of the governing instrument and applicable local law." 26 U.S.C. § 643(b).

[133]Treas. Regs. § 1.651(a)–2(a). *See also* Treas. Regs. § 1.661(a)–2(b).

[134]In this connection, the regulations provide that, for the determination of whether income is required to be distributed currently, "if the trust instrument provides that the trustee in determining the distributable income shall first retain a reserve for depreciation or otherwise make due allowance for keeping the trust corpus intact by retaining a reasonable amount of the current income for that purpose, the retention of current income for that purpose will not disqualify the trust from being a 'simple' trust." Treas. Reg. § 1.651(a)–2(a). The payout under an adjusted real yield approach involves even less trustee discretion than these regulations permit.

[135]For estates of decedents dying before January 1, 1982 (or for spousal gifts made before that date), the bequest (or gift) had to confer on the spouse the equivalent of absolute ownership, or at the very least, all income from the property plus a general power of appointment. A 'terminable interest," such as a life estate, did not qualify for the deduction. 26 U.S.C. §§ 2056(b)(1) (bequests); 2523(b) (gifts); Cum. Bull. 1960–2, p. 77. For estates of decedents dying after this date (and for spousal gifts made after this date), provisions added by the Economic Recovery Tax Act of 1981 permit bequests (or gifts) of "qualified terminable interests" in property, such as a life

estate, to qualify for the marital deduction. 26 U.S.C. §§ 2056(b)(7) (bequests); 2523(f) (gifts). Under both regimes qualification for the marital deduction (for bequests and gifts) requires that the spouse recipient receive "all income" from the property for life. This raises the question of whether the payout under the adjusted fixed yield approach satisfies the statutory standard.

[136]Treas. Reg. § 20.2056(b)–5(f)(1). The trust must assure the surviving spouse " . . . substantially that degree of beneficial enjoyment of the trust property during her life which the principles of the law of trusts accord to a person who is unqualifiedly designated as the life beneficiary of a trust. Such degree of enjoyment is given only if it was the decedent's intention, as manifested by the terms of the trust instrument and the surrounding circumstances, that the trust should produce for the surviving spouse during her life such an income . . . as is consistent with the value of the trust corpus and with its preservation. . . . "

These regulations apply to standard marital deduction trusts, not to the Qualified Terminable Interest Property (QTIP) trusts permitted as of 1981. See note 135 supra. However, proposed QTIP regulations indicate that the earlier regulations will generally apply in determining "if the surviving spouse is entitled for life to all the income from the property." Prop. Treas. Reg. § 20.2056(b)–7(c)(1).

[137]Treas. Reg. § 20.2056(b)–5(f)(4) (standard marital deduction trust). Note also the need to argue that the adjusted yield approach does not entail "accumulation" that would deny the surviving spouse "all income." Treas. Reg. § 20.2056(b)–5(f)(7). As to all these problems, Jackson v. United States, 376 U.S. 503 (1964), indicating that the marital deduction is not to be broadly construed, sounds a cautionary note.

[138]A similar problem may arise under state laws that reduce a surviving spouse's "elective share" against a decedent's will by property previously transferred to the surviving spouse as a life estate. As in the marital deduction case, a statutory change could address the problem but is arguably unnecessary on the grounds that a settlor-crafted allocation formula on the adjusted fixed yield approach is not in derogation of the spouse's life estate. Both the standard marital deduction and the elective share questions are discussed in greater detail in Hirsch, "Inflation and the Law of Trusts," 18 Real Prop., Prob. & Tr. J. 601, 643–46 (1983).

[139]It could also be the case that the life beneficiaries received a payout greater than current "income" (i.e., interest and cash dividends) or total retained "income," depending on economic conditions and the composition of the trust portfolio.

[140]See Restatement (Second) of Property § 2.2(1) (comments and reporter's notes exhaustively treating).

[141]See id., § 2.2 (3) (comments and reporter's notes exhaustively treating); 2 Treatise (3d ed. 1967), § 182, at pp. 1466–68. Buried in this question is the further question about retroactive effect of any such change in the allocation formula. See text accompanying notes 143–45 infra.

[142]Restatement (Second) of Property § 2.2 (4), comments j, k; reporter's notes 8, 9, 12, 13. See also 2 G. Bogert, Trusts and Trustees, § 217 (2d ed. 1965) (creation of reserve for later payout is not an accumulation). Indeed, it would be entirely consistent with an investor's expectation in purchasing a high-yielding fixed income instrument during inflationary times that part of the interest is compensation for erosion in the real value of the principal. In a sense the adjusted real yield approach merely broadens that insight into a mode of "judicious trust management."

[143]3 Treatise (3d ed. 1967), § 227.13, at p. 1843.

[144]In re Estate of Stillman, 366 N.Y.S. 2d 934, 938 (Surr. 1975). The court continues: "Where the instrument is silent or contains only permissive language with respect to investments, the statutory authorization in existence at the time of any particular investment will control."

[145]For example, the settlor may have adopted a provision implementing a total return approach, but used a nominal fixed payout scheme. Or the settlor may not intend the usual division of current benefits of trust assets to life beneficiaries, corpus to remaindermen.

APPENDIX C

Results of the Study Questionnaire

It has been one purpose of this study to identify gaps between legal notions of investment prudence and those now prevailing in the marketplace for investments and in financial theory. In the summer of 1985, in an effort to learn what investment opportunities fiduciaries subject to the prudent man rule consider themselves constrained from using, as well as other views of fiduciaries about portfolio management and how those views differed among groups of fiduciaries subject to different versions of the prudent man rule, a survey of fiduciaries was conducted. Letters, shown in Exhibits A and B, and the questionnaire (Questionnaire), shown in Exhibit C, were mailed to the fifty largest of each of the following categories of fiduciaries: bank trust departments (subject to the traditional prudent man rule in their administration of personal trust assets); college and university endowments (subject to state law of charitable corporations and to the Uniform Management of Institutional Funds Act of 1972 (UMIFA) in those states that have adopted it); private foundations (subject to the regulations under Section 4944 of the Internal Revenue Code as well as state law of charitable corporations); and corporate pension fund sponsors (subject to the Employee Retirement Income Security Act of 1974 (ERISA)). Asset size was determined in each case from generally used 1985 sources. The Questionnaire contains questions directed to perceptions of constraint by the law, use of internal and external delegation of investment management, the extent of efforts to outperform the market and specific methods used to that end, the use of outside consultants to assist in selection of investment managers and evaluation of investment performance, use of various investment theories in portfolio design, and finally the degree to which specific investment products and techniques were considered to be precluded or questionable by the applicable rules of prudence. Ninety-five institutions, or about one-half of those polled, returned the Questionnaire over the course of the summer.

Analysis of Numerical Summary of Results

Schedule 1 contains a numerical survey of the results. The following conclusions emerge from that data.

In response to the Questionnaire's first question, which read "How often, in your opinion, does the form of prudent man rule that applies to you operate to preclude investment opportunities that you would otherwise seek to pursue in what you believe to be the proper discharge of your duties?", to which the possible answers were "often," "sometimes," and "never," no respondents answered "often," about one-third responded "sometimes," and 61 percent answered "never." When the answers are analyzed by category of respondent, it appears, not surprisingly, that bank trust departments reported the most discomfort with applicable legal standards and pension funds the least, with educational and foundation endowments in the middle.

However, in response to specific questions about what their portfolios actually contained, most respondents reported that they did not use a number of unconventional and legally problematic investments such as options, futures, or index funds. Surprisingly, foundations turned out to be the most conservative, even more than bank trust departments. They reported the smallest use by far of options, futures, repurchase agreements, index funds, venture capital, real estate, or foreign equities.

When asked with reference to specific investment products and techniques whether they would consider the product or technique legally precluded, questionable, permissible, or had no opinion, the majority of respondents felt that the following unconventional investments and techniques were either precluded or questionable: commodity futures, commodity futures pools, Old Masters and other collectibles, short selling, margin purchases, other forms of leverage, naked put writing, naked call writing, and put or call purchases other than to hedge. Although most respondents said that naked put writing was either precluded or questionable, only 12 percent thought covered call writing would be precluded or questionable.

The survey results also indicate that some of the basic propositions of modern portfolio theory, including the efficient market hypothesis, are not widely accepted. For example, in response to a question about the practice of particular investment theories, 79 percent of the respondents indicated that they practiced value-oriented fundamental analysis, while less than one-half indicated use of technical analysis, market timing, or modern portfolio theory. Most respondents believed that some managers can consistently outperform the market (87 percent) and that it is possible to select those managers in advance (86 percent); and most respondents stated that it is their objective to outperform the standard market indices (84 percent). Moreover, about one-third had retained consultants either to assist in selecting investment managers or in monitoring or evaluating the performance of investment managers. It thus appears that the great majority of these fiduciaries believe that, despite the claims of efficient market theorists, it is possible to beat the market and worthwhile to try.

Further, the opinions of most fiduciaries surveyed are at odds with some basic propositions of modern portfolio theory, including, in particular, the capital asset pricing model. For example, while 84 percent said that they established or tried to establish an overall risk level for their portfolio, only 48 percent said they attempted to differentiate between the diversifiable and nondiversifiable elements of risk. Also, as noted above, two practices advocated by the capital asset pricing model, short selling and leveraged purchases of securities, are considered legally precluded or questionable by most respondents.

Analysis of Written Responses

Perception of Constraint (Questions 1 and 15)

These questions asked for written elaborations as to the types of investments that were perceived to be precluded by the law and as to distinctions drawn between different versions of the prudent man rule in regard to flexibility. Not surprisingly, bank trust departments supplied the most detailed list of investments that they felt precluded from using and on the whole reported the greatest degree of constraint. The types of investments most frequently reported as precluded were non-income securities in general, nondividend paying stocks in particular, and investments that might be viewed as speculative if examined in isolation. Other banks mentioned, as investment opportunities that they believed might be precluded, venture capital, options, futures, "low quality" investments, small companies or companies with weak financials, or investments not widely used by others. One bank reported that the high cost of defending against challenges to prudence itself operates as a constraint; as a result, that bank reports that it makes a special effort to obtain more liberal provisions in governing trust instruments.

The most striking aspect of the bank trust department responses, however, is that those banks that offered separate answers in their capacity as pension fund managers consistently indicated that they considered themselves decidedly less contrained when operating under the ERISA rule than under the traditional prudent man rule. Educational endowments and foundations reported significantly fewer categories of precluded investment opportunities, and pension fund sponsors reported virtually none. Foundations reported more such categories than did endowments or pension fund sponsors, possibly reflecting the influence of the "special scrutiny" list of investments contained in the Section 4944 regulations. For example, foundations reported that options and futures, short selling, and borrowing transactions were among precluded investment opportunities. One foundation reported that its legal counsel had advised that Section 4944 precluded venture capital investments. A number of foundations indicated that many categories of unconventional investments were precluded by restrictions on the boards of directors or that many of the kinds of investments inquired about in the Questionnaire simply had not been considered.

Some educational endowments also reported that they considered themselves constrained not by law but by internal policy. A number of universities and colleges had restrictions on investments in the securities of companies disfavored on social responsibility grounds. One educational endowment reported that it considered venture capital investments suspect, and another remarked that the exhaustive legal review that had to be accorded unconventional investments resulted on some occasions in missed opportunities due to the disappearance of the investment opportunity by the time the legal review was completed.

Interestingly, as noted above, the pension fund sponsors reported virtually no investments as precluded, one such sponsor reported that it considered itself precluded from only those investment opportunities that "are so unique they have not been done by anyone else. The ERISA concept of prudence tends to cause one to think twice about doing anything untried or unproven."

Delegation Issues (Questions 2 and 3)

As would be predicted by the nature of the legal standards, bank trust departments in their management of personal trust funds reported themselves the most constrained in the use of external delegation. Some, however, said that they do use some outside managers in specialized areas such as real estate and international investments. In some cases, it was not possible to be certain whether those responses were meant to describe personal trust activities or pension money management.

Foundations and educational endowments, on the other hand, very frequently used multiple external investment managers, especially for foreign investments, real estate, and venture capital. A number of educational endowments said that they delegated to outside managers responsibility for the bulk of the endowment, often with written guidelines creating restrictions on permitted types of investments as well as on the degree of concentration in any particular investment. Pension fund sponsors offered similar answers as to delegation, although internal management appeared to be more frequent in the case of pension funds than in that of educational and foundation endowments.

Performance in Relation to the Market (Questions 5, 6, 9 and 10)

As noted in the analysis of numerical results, the overwhelming majority of respondents believed that it is possible to outperform the market and worthwhile to try. This belief is share more or less evenly across categories of fiduciaries. Each category of respondent remarked with some consistency, in response to the question as to whether it was possible for some managers to consistently outperform the indices, in the manner of one respondent who said "the long-term records of some managers speak for themselves." Respondents repeatedly cited the records of the Templeton Funds, the Magellan Fund, Value Line, and the Windsor Fund as evidence that consistent superior performance is possible. In their own portfolio management, fiduciaries consistently said that they used the Standard & Poor's (S&P) 500, the Dow Jones, NASDAQ, and the Shearson Lehman Government/Corporate Bond index as the indices whose performance they seek at least to equal with their own portfolios. Most respondents, however, stressed that consistent superior performance was extremely rare and that selection of such superior performers was extremely difficult; one respondent likened that search to looking for a needle in a haystack. The consensus view appears to be that the keys to identifying those who will provide superior performance are a good long-term track record, stable management, and a disciplined and logical investment approach. Contrarian and value-oriented investment philosophies were also thought by a significant number of respondents to hold the best promise for superior performance. Past performance appears to be very widely and heavily relied upon as an indicator of future performance, although a number of respondents believe that it is an unreliable predictor at best. A period of at least five years appears to be the consensus view as the minimum period in which consistent superior performance can be expected.

Use of Consultants (Questions 7 and 8)

As noted above, about one-third of the respondents had retained consultants either to assist in selecting investment managers or in monitoring or evaluating their performance. These consultants appeared to be valued by all categories of respondents principally for the pool of information they possess concerning other portfolios and for the independence they bring to the evaluation process. For example, one respondent said that consultants provided a "universe of comparable portfolios, and statistical analysis of performance that it would be difficult to produce in-house." In this way, consultants were thought to be helpful in keeping the fiduciaries abreast of the marketplace by comparing their portfolio with others and, in that way, serving as an extension of the in-house research ability. One fiduciary remarked that consultants were helpful in navigating the investment manager selection decision in light of the thousands of potential managers. Not surprisingly, banks, which used outside managers least often, reported a correspondingly smaller use of selection consultants.

It seems that consultants are looked to for assistance in handling politically sensitive situations within the internal hierarchy of a fund. One foundation respondent said that consultants are able to say things to a fund's investment committee that an insider could not. Another said of selection advisers: "They can be very helpful to trustees of funds who are inexperienced or subject to political pressures." Finally, the aid of consultants in monitoring the performance of investment managers is frequently cited as a reason for their retention.

Portfolio Design and Investment Philosophies (Questions 11 to 13)

Use of the tools of modern portfolio theory to measure and regulate portfolio risk appears to be quite common. A substantial number of respondents, principally fiduciaries other than bank trust departments managing personal trust assets, reported using some form of beta measure, such as those supplied by BARRA, both to regulate the risk of the portfolio and to provide risk-adjusted performance measures for their managers. However, many (although fewer) respondents expressly disclaim use of modern portfolio theory in their management of risk. A typical answer to this effect was that of one fiduciary who reported that "objective risk measures" were used instead. Bank trust departments that answered both in their capacities as manager of personal trust assets and of pension fund monies frequently reported that in the case of personal trusts, the need for current income played an important role in establishing the portfolio's overall risk level and that in the case of pension funds, risk levels were established by consultation with each pension fund sponsor and appropriate tailoring of the portfolio as a consequence.

Exhibit A

June 6, 1985

Attention: Name
            Title

Dear

      I am writing to acquaint you with a project
that will be of interest to anyone responsible for making
investments in a fiduciary capacity and to ask you to
take a few moments to complete a questionnaire in connection with that project.

      Bevis Longstreth, until recently a Commissioner
of the Securities and Exchange Commission and now a senior partner at the New York law firm of Debevoise &
Plimpton, is directing a study of the conflicts between
the legal standards governing investments by fiduciaries
and the rapidly developing new products and strategies in
the financial marketplace. Mr. Longstreth will conduct
the study, whose working title is "Modern Investment
Management and the Prudent Man Rule," in collaboration
with the Salomon Brothers Center for the Study of Financial Institutions, of which I am the Director. The study
is funded by grants from the Alfred P. Sloan Foundation,
the Carnegie Corporation of New York, The Ford Foundation, the William and Flora Hewlett Foundation, and the
Rockefeller Foundation.

      It has been suggested that the legal standards
governing fiduciaries subject to some version of the
"prudent man" standard--such as trustees and investment
managers for charitable foundations, university endowments, not-for-profit corporations, personal trusts,
and pension funds--have come to lag unrealistically and
even dangerously behind recent developments in financial
analysis and in the marketplace for investments. The
purpose of this study is to investigate the pervasiveness
and validity of that perception and to advance a modern
interpretation of the governing legal standards, thereby
providing a basis for trustees and investment managers to
pursue investment techniques and strategies unfettered by
outmoded legal doctrine.

      The attached questionnaire is being sent to you
and a limited number of other institutional investors
who, we believe, could importantly contribute to and
benefit from the study. We are seeking to collect data,
for use in the study, from the most economically significant fiduciaries subject to some form of the prudence
standard. (Variations of this standard include, in addition to the common-law "prudent man rule" governing the
trustees of personal trusts, the Uniform Management of
Institutional Funds Act, ERISA, and the provisions of

Section 4944 of the Internal Revenue Code governing foundations.) We intend to tabulate and publish this data as
part of the book that results from the study. Of course,
we will preserve the anonymity of the respondents in all
respects. In addition, you will receive without charge,
if you participate in the survey, a summary of its results well in advance of publication (now scheduled for
the summer of 1986).

        A wide response to this survey will be of ines-
timable value to the study. Please take the time to
complete the enclosed questionnaire and return it in the
enclosed envelope to Thomas Kelly by July 1, 1985. If
you have any questions about the survey or about any
aspect of the study, please call Mr. Longstreth at (212)
909-6651 or Mr. Kelly at (212) 909-6907.

        Thank you for your cooperation.

                        Sincerely,

                        Arnold W. Sametz
                        Director

Exhibit B

                                        July 12, 1985

Attention: Name
             Title

Dear

        As you may recall, I wrote to you some weeks
ago to describe a study of modern investment management
and the prudent man rule, with particular emphasis on the
conflicts between the legal standards governing investments by fiduciaries and the rapidly developing new products and strategies in the financial marketplace. I also
asked that you participate in a survey whose results will
eventually be reported in the published study but which
will be provided in a special report to respondents well
in advance of publication.

        The high response rate to date (almost one-
third) assures the value of the report both to the study
and the respondents. Of course, we are seeking a substantially higher rate and to that end have extended the

response date to August 1, 1985. Because we have not yet received a response from your institution, I am writing to ask that you return a completed questionnaire by that date. (An additional copy is enclosed for your convenience.) I hope that you will able to participate in the survey.

In case my original letter went astray, some of the additional information included there is repeated below. The study is being directed by Bevis Longstreth (until recently a Commissioner of the Securities and Exchange Commission and now a senior partner in the New York law firm of Debevoise & Plimpton) in collaboration with the Salomon Brothers Center for the Study of Financial Institutions, of which I am the Director. The study is funded by grants from the Alfred P. Sloan Foundation, the Carnegie Corporation of New York, The Ford Foundation, the William and Flora Hewlett Foundation and the Rockefeller Foundation.

The study's purpose is to investigate the pervasiveness and validity of the claim that the legal standards governing fiduciaries subject to some version of the "prudent man" standard--such as trustees and investment managers for charitable foundations, university endowments, not-for-profit corporations, personal trusts and pension funds--have come to lag unrealistically and even dangerously behind recent developments in financial analysis and in the marketplace for investments. In accordance with its findings, the study will advance a modern interpretation of the governing legal standards.

The attached questionnaire was sent to you and a limited number of other institutional investors who, we believe, could importantly contribute to and benefit from the study. We are seeking to collect data, for use in the study, from the most economically significant fiduciaries subject to some form of the prudence standard. (Variations of this standard include, in addition to the common-law "prudent man rule" governing the trustees of personal trusts, the Uniform Management of Institutional Funds Act, ERISA, and the provisions of section 4944 of the Internal Revenue Code governing foundations.) We intend to tabulate and publish this data as part of the book that results from the study. Of course, we will preserve the anonymity of the respondents in all respects. As I mentioned, you will receive without charge, if you participate in the survey, a summary of its results well in advance of publication (now scheduled for the summer of 1986).

Because of the selective nature of the survey group, we would value your response highly. Please take the time to complete the enclosed questionnaire and return it in the enclosed envelope to Thomas Kelly by August 1, 1985. If you have any questions about the survey or about any aspect of the study, please call Mr.

Longstreth at (212) 909-6651 or Mr. Kelly at (212) 909-6907.

Thank you for your cooperation.

Sincerely,

Arnold W. Sametz
Director

Enclosures

Exhibit C   Questionnaire for Study on Modern Investment Management and the Prudent Man Rule

1. How often, in your opinion, does the form of prudent man rule that applies to you operate to preclude investment opportunities that you would otherwise seek to pursue in what you believe to be the proper discharge of your duties?

    Often _____   Sometimes _____   Never _____

    Please list the investment opportunities, if any, that you believe may be precluded.

2. Does the form of prudent man rule that applies to you obstruct arrangements for the delegation of investment authority that you would otherwise seek to use?

    Yes _____   No _____

    If you answered "Yes" please elaborate.

3. Do you delegate investment authority to any outside managers?

    Yes _____   No _____

    Please describe the systems of delegation, both internal and external, that you use.

4. Please indicate whether your portfolio contains any of the following and the approximate percentage where indicated:

		Yes	No	
(a)	options	____	____	
(b)	futures	____	____	
(c)	repos	____	____	
(d)	reverse repos	____	____	

		Yes	No	Approximate Percentage
(e)	index funds	____	____	____
(f)	venture capital	____	____	____
(g)	real estate	____	____	____
(h)	foreign equities	____	____	____
(i)	other equities	____	____	____
(j)	debt securities	____	____	____

5. Do you believe that certain investment managers can, after transaction costs are taken into account, consistently out-perform the standard stock market indices?

    Yes _____   No _____

    Please elaborate.

6. Do you believe it is possible to select those managers?

    Yes _____   No _____

    Please elaborate.

7. Have you retained a consultant to assist you in selecting investment managers?

    Yes _____   No _____

8. Have you retained a consultant to assist you in monitoring
    or evaluating the performance of investment managers acting
    on your behalf?

    Yes _____   No _____

    Please elaborate as to whether and in what ways you believe
    such consultants are useful.

9. Is it the objective of your fund to outperform the standard
    market indices?

    Yes _____   No _____

    If you answered "Yes" please explain how you go about se-
    lecting managers to meet that objective.

10. Is there a standard market index whose performance you seek
    at least to equal?

    Yes _____   No _____

    If you answered "Yes," which index?

11. Do you try to establish an acceptable level of risk for your
    overall portfolio?

    Yes _____   No _____

    Please elaborate.

12. Do you attempt to differentiate between the diversifiable and nondiversifiable elements of risk?

                    Yes _____   No _____

     Please elaborate.

13. Do you attempt to practice investment techniques based upon any of the following theories?

                                                    Yes   No

     (a) Value-oriented fundamental analysis   ___   ___

     (b) Technical analysis   ___   ___

     (c) Market timing   ___   ___

     (d) Modern Portfolio Theory:

          (i)   holding a diversified passive
                portfolio, leveraged or unlev-
                eraged   ___   ___

          (ii) holding a diversified passive
                portfolio in combination with
                stock-picking of securities
                regarded as undervalued because
                their expected returns are higher
                than that predicted by their betas   ___   ___

     If appropriate, please elaborate on any of your answers.

14. With respect to each of the following investment instruments and investment techniques, do you believe that the form of prudent man rule that applies to you would preclude, render questionable, or permit its use (assuming the instrument or technique was one that you would otherwise seek to pursue in what you believe to be the proper discharge of your duties)?

                              Precluded Questionable Permissible No Opinion

     Investment Instruments

     (a) options on stocks   ____   ____   ____   ____

		Precluded	Questionable	Permissible	No Opinion
(b)	options on stock indices	____	____	____	____
(c)	options on index futures	____	____	____	____
(d)	debt options	____	____	____	____
(e)	options on debt futures	____	____	____	____
(f)	foreign currency options	____	____	____	____
(g)	options on foreign currency futures	____	____	____	____
(h)	commodity futures	____	____	____	____
(i)	commodity futures pools	____	____	____	____
(j)	financial futures generally	____	____	____	____
(k)	futures on stock indices	____	____	____	____
(l)	debt futures	____	____	____	____
(m)	foreign currency futures	____	____	____	____
(n)	foreign currency forward contracts	____	____	____	____
(o)	repos	____	____	____	____
(p)	reverse repos	____	____	____	____
(q)	index funds	____	____	____	____
(r)	new and untried enterprises	____	____	____	____
(s)	venture capital pools	____	____	____	____
(t)	real estate	____	____	____	____
(u)	real estate pools (such as real estate investment trusts)	____	____	____	____
(v)	foreign equities	____	____	____	____
(w)	foreign equity pools	____	____	____	____

		Precluded	Questionable	Permissible	No Opinion
(x)	gold	___	___	___	___
(y)	Old Master paintings and other collectibles	___	___	___	___

Investment Techniques

(a)	short selling	___	___	___	___
(b)	margin purchases of securities	___	___	___	___
(c)	other forms of leverage	___	___	___	___
(d)	options for hedging purposes generally	___	___	___	___
(e)	options for market timing purposes generally	___	___	___	___
(f)	options for arbitrage purposes generally	___	___	___	___
(g)	covered call writing	___	___	___	___
(h)	protective put purchases	___	___	___	___
(i)	naked put writing	___	___	___	___
(j)	naked call writing	___	___	___	___
(k)	put or call purchases other than to hedge	___	___	___	___
(l)	straddles	___	___	___	___
(m)	spreads	___	___	___	___
(n)	futures for hedging purposes generally	___	___	___	___
(o)	futures for market timing purposes generally	___	___	___	___
(p)	futures for arbitrage purposes generally	___	___	___	___
(q)	futures on stock indices for purposes of market timing	___	___	___	___

	Precluded	Questionable	Permissible	No Opinion
(r) futures on stock indices for purposes of arbitrage	____	____	____	____
(s) risk arbitrage (e.g., tender offer plays)	____	____	____	____

If appropriate, please elaborate on any of your answers.

15. If you are subject to more than one variation of the prudent man rule, do you draw distinctions between the types of investments permissible under each?

Yes _____   No _____

    Please explain which variation(s) of the rule you are subject to and, if you answered "Yes" above, explain what distinctions you draw.

Institution: _____

By: _____

Title: _____

Date: _____

Schedule 1   Responses to Questionnaire for Study on Modern Investment Management and the Prudent Man Rule

Abbreviations	No. of Respondents	Response Rate (%)
Bt - Banks (personal trust assets)	27	54%

Bp - Banks (pension fund assets)	8	*
E - Educational Endowments	24	49
F - Foundations	17	34
P - Pension Funds	27	54
Total	105**	53

1. How often, in your opinion, does the form of prudent man rule that applies to you operate to preclude investment opportunities that you would otherwise seek to pursue in what you believe to be the proper discharge of your duties?

	Often	Sometimes	Never	No Response***
Bt	0%	63%	33%	4%
Bp	0	50	38	12
E	0	17	75	8
F	0	24	64	12
P	0	19	81	0
Total	0	32	61	7

*   Although the survey did not specifically solicit responses from banks as pension fund managers, eight of the fifty bank trust departments surveyed volunteered separate responses in their capacity as pension fund managers.

**   Two respondents did not identify themselves or the category of fiduciary to which they belonged. Therefore their responses are reflected only in the totals.

***   This column indicates the percentage of those who responded to the questionnaire but did not respond to this question.

2. Does the form of prudent man rule that applies to you obstruct arrangements for the delegation of investment authority that you would otherwise seek to use?

	Yes	No	No Response
Bt	15%	81%	4%
Bp	25	63	12

E	0	92	8
F	0	100	0
P	0	100	0
Total	6	90	4

3. Do you delegate investment authority to any outside managers?

	Yes	No	No Response
Bt	41%	56%	3%
Bp	38	50	12
E	88	8	4
F	82	18	0
P	96	4	0
Total	72	24	4

4. Please indicate whether your portfolio contains any of the following:

(a) Options

	Yes	No	No Response
Bt	48%	44%	8%
Bp	63	12	25
E	46	46	8
F	12	88	0
P	48	52	0
Total	42	51	7

(b) Futures

	Yes	No	No Response
Bt	30%	63%	7%
Bp	50	25	25
E	25	62	13
F	12	88	0

P	59	37	4
Total	35	56	9

(c) Repos

	Yes	No	No Response
Bt	67%	26%	7%
Bp	50	12	38
E	59	33	8
F	29	71	0
P	81	19	0
Total	60	32	8

(d) Reverse Repos

	Yes	No	No Response
Bt	26%	63%	11%
Bp	38	38	24
E	42	50	8
F	6	94	0
P	41	56	3
Total	30	61	9

(e) Index Funds

	Yes	No	No Response
Bt	33%	63%	4%
Bp	50	25	25
E	21	66	13
F	18	82	0
P	70	30	0
Total	38	55	7

(f) Venture Capital

	Yes	No	No Response
Bt	33%	59%	8%

Bp	38	50	12
E	79	17	4
F	35	65	0
P	70	30	0
Total	54	41	5

(g)   Real Estate

	Yes	No	No Response
Bt	74%	19%	7%
Bp	50	38	12
E	79	17	4
F	35	59	6
P	93	7	0
Total	70	24	6

(h)   Foreign Equities

	Yes	No	No Response
Bt	74%	19%	7%
Bp	88	0	12
E	54	42	4
F	35	59	6
P	81	19	0
Total	65	30	5

(i)   Other Equities

	Yes	No	No Response
Bt	85%	4%	11%
Bp	88	0	12
E	96	0	4
F	76	18	6
P	93	7	0
Total	87	7	6

(j) Debt Securities

	Yes	No	No Response
Bt	89%	4%	7%
Bp	88	0	12
E	96	0	4
F	88	12	0
P	100	0	0
Total	92	3	5

5. Do you believe that certain investment managers can, after transaction costs are taken into account, consistently outperform the standard stock market indices?

	Yes	No	No Response
Bt	89%	7%	4%
Bp	50	38	12
E	96	0	4
F	88	6	6
P	93	7	0
Total	87	9	4

6. Do you believe it is possible to select those managers?

	Yes	No	No Response
Bt	81%	15%	4%
Bp	63	25	12
E	92	0	8
F	88	0	12
P	96	4	0
Total	86	8	6

7. Have you retained a consultant to assist you in selecting investment managers?

	Yes	No	No Response
Bt	8%	81%	11%
Bp	0	88	12
E	50	46	4
F	29	71	0
P	44	56	0
Total	30	64	6

8. Have you retained a consultant to assist you in monitoring or evaluating the performance of investment managers acting on your behalf?

	Yes	No	No Response
Bt	19%	74%	7%
Bp	13	74	13
E	42	54	4
F	35	65	0
P	59	41	0
Total	37	58	5

9. Is it the objective of your fund to outperform the standard market indices?

	Yes	No	No Response
Bt	89%	0%	11%
Bp	75	0	25
E	88	4	8
F	82	18	0
P	85	15	0
Total	84	9	7

10. Is there a standard market index whose performance you seek at least to equal?

	Yes	No	No Response
Bt	92%	4%	4%
Bp	75	0	25

	Yes	No	No Response
E	84	8	8
F	76	24	0
P	81	19	0
Total	82	12	6

11. Do you try to establish an acceptable level of risk for your overall portfolio?

	Yes	No	No Response
Bt	92%	4%	4%
Bp	74	13	13
E	88	4	8
F	65	35	0
P	89	11	0
Total	84	11	5

12. Do you attempt to differentiate between the diversifiable and nondiversifiable elements of risk?

	Yes	No	No Response
Bt	59%	30%	11%
Bp	63	25	12
E	37	46	17
F	29	65	6
P	56	44	0
Total	48	43	9

13. Do you attempt to practice investment techniques based upon any of the following theories?

   (a) Value-Oriented Fundamental Analysis

	Yes	No	No Response
Bt	89%	7%	4%
Bp	50	25	25

	Yes	No	No Response
E	83	4	13
F	59	35	6
P	93	7	0
Total	79	13	8

(b)   Technical Analysis

	Yes	No	No Response
Bt	48%	48%	4%
Bp	25	50	25
E	37	46	17
F	24	64	12
P	30	63	7
Total	34	54	12

(c)   Market Timing

	Yes	No	No Response
Bt	37%	59%	4%
Bp	38	38	24
E	42	29	29
F	29	59	12
P	52	44	4
Total	40	47	13

(d)   Modern Portfolio Theory:

   (i)   holding a diversified passive portfolio,
          leveraged or unleveraged

	Yes	No	No Response
Bt	22%	59%	19%
Bp	50	25	25
E	17	58	25
F	12	76	12

	Yes	No	No Response
P	49	44	7
Total	28	55	17

(ii) holding a diversified passive portfolio in combination with stock-picking of securities regarded as undervalued because their expected returns are higher than that predicted by their betas

	Yes	No	No Response
Bt	37%	52%	11%
Bp	50	25	25
E	17	58	25
F	18	76	6
P	26	67	7
Total	27	59	14

14. With respect to each of the following investment instruments and investment techniques, do you believe that the form of prudent man rule that applies to you would preclude, render questionable, or permit its use (assuming the instrument or technique was one that you would otherwise seek to pursue in what you believe to be the proper discharge of your duties)?

Investment Instruments

(a) Options on Stocks

	Precluded	Questionable	Permissible	No Opinion	No Response
Bt	15%	15%	67%	0%	3%
Bp	0	0	88	0	12
E	0	4	83	0	13
F	12	41	35	0	12
P	4	11	85	0	0
Total	7	14	71	0	8

(b) Options on Stock Indices

	Precluded	Questionable	Permissible	No Opinion	No Response
Bt	15%	26%	52%	4%	3%
Bp	0	0	88	0	12
E	0	29	63	0	8

	Precluded	Questionable	Permissible	No Opinion	No Response
F	18	40	24	6	12
P	4	15	74	7	0
Total	7	24	58	4	7

(c) Options on Index Futures

	Precluded	Questionable	Permissible	No Opinion	No Response
Bt	19%	26%	33%	19%	3%
Bp	0	0	88	0	12
E	4	25	54	4	13
F	18	34	24	12	12
P	4	15	70	11	0
Total	10	22	50	10	8

(d) Debt Options

	Precluded	Questionable	Permissible	No Opinion	No Response
Bt	19%	22%	52%	4%	3%
Bp	0	0	88	0	12
E	4	4	75	4	13
F	12	40	18	18	12
P	4	15	70	11	0
Total	9	17	59	8	7

(e) Options on Debt Futures

	Precluded	Questionable	Permissible	No Opinion	No Response
Bt	22%	22%	33%	19%	4%
Bp	0	0	88	0	12
E	4	21	54	8	13
F	18	40	18	12	12
P	4	15	66	15	0
Total	10	21	49	12	8

(f) Foreign Currency Options

	Precluded	Questionable	Permissible	No Opinion	No Response
Bt	37%	26%	22%	11%	4%
Bp	0	0	75	13	12
E	8	17	41	21	13
F	18	46	12	12	12
P	7	11	56	22	4
Total	16	21	38	16	9

(g) Options on Foreign Currency Futures

	Precluded	Questionable	Permissible	No Opinion	No Response
Bt	37%	26%	22%	11%	4%
Bp	0	12	63	13	12
E	8	21	37	21	13
F	18	52	6	12	12
P	7	15	56	22	0
Total	16	25	35	16	8

(h) Commodity Futures

	Precluded	Questionable	Permissible	No Opinion	No Response
Bt	44%	37%	7%	7%	5%
Bp	0	37	37	7	6
E	8	17	41	17	17
F	24	58	0	6	12
P	19	26	29	26	0
Total	22	32	23	14	9

(i) Commodity Futures Pools

	Precluded	Questionable	Permissible	No Opinion	No Response
Bt	41%	41%	3%	12%	3%
Bp	0	50	13	25	12
E	13	13	36	21	17
F	24	58	0	6	12
P	22	26	26	26	0
Total	23	33	18	17	9

(j) Financial Futures Generally

	Precluded	Questionable	Permissible	No Opinion	No Response
Bt	22%	30%	41%	4%	3%
Bp	0	0	75	13	12
E	8	13	58	8	13
F	18	46	12	12	12
P	4	4	84	4	4
Total	11	19	54	7	9

(k) Futures on Stock Indices

	Precluded	Questionable	Permissible	No Opinion	No Response
Bt	15%	33%	41%	7%	4%
Bp	0	0	88	0	12

	Precluded	Questionable	Permissible	No Opinion	No Response
E	8	13	62	4	13
F	18	29	29	12	12
P	4	11	81	4	0
Total	10	19	58	6	7

(1) Debt Futures

	Precluded	Questionable	Permissible	No Opinion	No Response
Bt	19%	30%	41%	7%	3%
Bp	0	0	88	0	12
E	8	13	62	4	13
F	18	34	24	12	12
P	4	11	81	4	0
Total	10	19	57	6	8

(m) Foreign Currency Futures

	Precluded	Questionable	Permissible	No Opinion	No Response
Bt	33%	33%	19%	11%	4%
Bp	0	13	63	12	12
E	13	13	44	17	13
F	18	46	6	18	12
P	11	7	63	19	0
Total	17	22	38	15	8

(n) Foreign Currency Forward Contracts

	Precluded	Questionable	Permissible	No Opinion	No Response
Bt	30%	33%	22%	11%	4%
Bp	0	13	63	12	12
E	13	8	53	13	13
F	18	46	6	18	12
P	7	7	67	19	0
Total	15	21	42	14	8

(o) Repos

	Precluded	Questionable	Permissible	No Opinion	No Response
Bt	0%	11%	82%	4%	3%
Bp	0	0	88	0	12
E	0	0	87	0	13
F	6	24	58	0	12

	Precluded	Questionable	Permissible	No Opinion	No Response
P	4	0	96	0	0
Total	2	7	83	1	7

(p)   Reverse Repos

	Precluded	Questionable	Permissible	No Opinion	No Response
Bt	3%	7%	67%	19%	3%
Bp	0	0	88	0	12
E	0	13	79	0	8
F	12	35	35	6	12
P	4	11	81	4	0
Total	4	13	70	7	6

(q)   Index Funds

	Precluded	Questionable	Permissible	No Opinion	No Response
Bt	0%	7%	89%	0%	4%
Bp	0	0	88	0	12
E	0	8	79	0	13
F	0	6	82	0	12
P	0	0	100	0	0
Total	0	5	88	0	7

(r)   New and Untried Enterprises

	Precluded	Questionable	Permissible	No Opinion	No Response
Bt	37%	37%	22%	0%	4%
Bp	0	25	63	0	12
E	0	29	50	8	13
F	18	40	18	12	12
P	4	22	55	19	0
Total	13	31	39	9	8

(s)   Venture Capital Pools

	Precluded	Questionable	Permissible	No Opinion	No Response
Bt	22%	37%	37%	0%	4%
Bp	0	0	88	0	12
E	0	4	83	0	13
F	12	18	64	0	6
P	0	4	92	4	0
Total	8	14	70	2	6

(t)   Real Estate

	Precluded	Questionable	Permissible	No Opinion	No Response
Bt	0%	4%	93%	0%	3%
Bp	0	0	88	0	12
E	0	0	87	0	13
F	0	0	94	0	6
P	0	0	100	0	0
Total	0	2	92	0	6

(u)   Real Estate Pools (such as real estate investment trusts)

	Precluded	Questionable	Permissible	No Opinion	No Response
Bt	0%	4%	93%	0%	3%
Bp	0	0	88	0	12
E	0	4	83	0	13
F	0	0	88	0	12
P	0	0	100	0	0
Total	0	3	90	0	7

(v)   Foreign Equities

	Precluded	Questionable	Permissible	No Opinion	No Response
Bt	4%	4%	89%	0%	3%
Bp	0	0	88	0	12
E	4	0	83	0	13
F	0	6	82	0	12
P	0	4	96	0	0
Total	2	3	88	0	7

(w)   Foreign Equity Pools

	Precluded	Questionable	Permissible	No Opinion	No Response
Bt	4%	11%	82%	0%	3%
Bp	0	0	88	0	12
E	4	4	75	4	13
F	0	0	82	6	12
P	0	4	96	0	0
Total	2	5	84	2	7

(x) Gold

	Precluded	Questionable	Permissible	No Opinion	No Response
Bt	19%	33%	41%	4%	3%
Bp	0	0	88	0	12
E	4	13	62	8	13
F	0	24	58	6	12
P	4	37	48	11	0
Total	7	25	54	7	7

(y) Old Master Paintings
and Other Collectibles

	Precluded	Questionable	Permissible	No Opinion	No Response
Bt	26%	41%	11%	19%	3%
Bp	0	25	37	25	13
E	4	25	37	17	17
F	6	35	29	12	18
P	7	59	11	19	4
Total	11	39	23	17	10

Investment Techniques

(a) Short Selling

	Precluded	Questionable	Permissible	No Opinion	No Response
Bt	70%	15%	4%	7%	4%
Bp	50	13	13	12	12
E	13	33	37	0	17
F	35	35	18	0	12
P	55	19	19	7	0
Total	45	24	18	5	8

(b) Margin Purchases of Securities

	Precluded	Questionable	Permissible	No Opinion	No Response
Bt	70%	19%	4%	4%	3%
Bp	25	37	25	0	13
E	25	33	17	8	17
F	41	35	12	0	12
P	67	19	7	7	0
Total	50	26	11	5	8

(c)   Other Forms of Leverage

	Precluded	Questionable	Permissible	No Opinion	No Response
Bt	37%	48%	4%	7%	4%
Bp	13	50	25	0	12
E	13	40	17	13	17
F	35	35	12	6	12
P	33	37	11	19	0
Total	28	41	12	11	8

(d)   Options for Hedging
      Purposes Generally

	Precluded	Questionable	Permissible	No Opinion	No Response
Bt	4%	37%	52%	4%	3%
Bp	0	0	88	0	12
E	4	13	62	8	13
F	12	29	29	12	18
P	0	11	89	0	0
Total	4	20	63	5	8

(e)   Options for Market
      Timing Purposes Generally

	Precluded	Questionable	Permissible	No Opinion	No Response
Bt	11%	37%	44%	4%	4%
Bp	0	13	75	0	12
E	4	21	62	0	13
F	6	52	18	12	12
P	0	26	74	0	0
Total	5	30	54	3	8

(f)   Options for Arbitrage
      Purposes Generally

	Precluded	Questionable	Permissible	No Opinion	No Response
Bt	22%	33%	33%	8%	4%
Bp	0	0	88	0	12
E	8	4	62	13	13
F	18	34	24	12	12
P	11	26	59	4	0
Total	13	22	50	8	7

(g) Covered Call Writing

	Precluded	Questionable	Permissible	No Opinion	No Response
Bt	4%	19%	74%	0%	3%
Bp	0	0	88	0	12
E	0	4	83	0	13
F	6	12	70	0	12
P	4	4	88	0	4
Total	3	9	80	0	8

(h) Protective Put Purchases

	Precluded	Questionable	Permissible	No Opinion	No Response
Bt	11%	22%	56%	7%	4%
Bp	0	0	88	0	12
E	0	4	83	0	13
F	6	18	40	18	18
P	4	7	85	4	0
Total	5	11	70	6	8

(i) Naked Put Writing

	Precluded	Questionable	Permissible	No Opinion	No Response
Bt	56%	33%	0%	7%	4%
Bp	25	25	37	0	13
E	17	36	17	13	17
F	29	47	0	12	12
P	33	41	11	15	0
Total	33	38	10	11	8

(j) Naked Call Writing

	Precluded	Questionable	Permissible	No Opinion	No Response
Bt	59%	30%	0%	7%	4%
Bp	25	25	37	0	13
E	17	36	17	13	17
F	29	47	0	12	12
P	37	41	7	15	0
Total	35	37	9	11	8

(k) Put or Call Purchases Other Than to Hedge

	Precluded	Questionable	Permissible	No Opinion	No Response
Bt	26%	56%	4%	11%	3%
Bp	13	12	63	0	12
E	4	17	58	4	17
F	18	46	6	12	18
P	19	44	22	15	0
Total	16	38	27	10	9

(l) Straddles

	Precluded	Questionable	Permissible	No Opinion	No Response
Bt	22%	44%	8%	22%	4%
Bp	0	13	63	12	12
E	0	17	49	21	13
F	12	34	18	24	12
P	15	22	30	33	0
Total	11	28	30	24	7

(m) Spreads

	Precluded	Questionable	Permissible	No Opinion	No Response
Bt	22%	44%	11%	19%	4%
Bp	0	13	63	12	12
E	0	17	49	21	13
F	12	40	12	24	12
P	15	19	30	36	0
Total	11	28	30	24	7

(n) Futures for Hedging Purposes Generally

	Precluded	Questionable	Permissible	No Opinion	No Response
Bt	11%	41%	33%	11%	4%
Bp	0	0	88	0	12
E	0	25	62	0	13
F	6	46	18	18	12
P	4	7	89	0	0
Total	5	26	56	6	7

(o)   Futures for Market Timing
Purposes Generally

	Precluded	Questionable	Permissible	No Opinion	No Response
Bt	19%	44%	26%	7%	4%
Bp	0	13	75	0	12
E	8	21	58	0	13
F	18	40	18	12	12
P	7	15	78	0	0
Total	11	28	50	4	7

(p)   Futures for Arbitrage
Purposes Generally

	Precluded	Questionable	Permissible	No Opinion	No Response
Bt	22%	48%	15%	11%	4%
Bp	0	13	75	0	12
E	4	21	49	13	13
F	12	40	18	18	12
P	15	22	59	4	0
Total	13	30	40	10	7

(q)   Futures on Stock Indices
for Purposes of Market Timing

	Precluded	Questionable	Permissible	No Opinion	No Response
Bt	15%	44%	26%	11%	4%
Bp	0	13	75	0	12
E	8	25	54	0	13
F	24	40	12	12	12
P	0	22	78	0	0
Total	10	30	48	5	7

(r)   Futures on Stock Indices
for Purposes of Arbitrage

	Precluded	Questionable	Permissible	No Opinion	No Response
Bt	22%	37%	22%	15%	4%
Bp	0	13	75	0	12
E	4	29	46	8	13
F	24	34	18	12	12
P	7	26	63	4	0
Total	12	30	42	9	7

(s) Risk Arbitrage (e.g.,
     Tender Offer Plays)

	Precluded	Questionable	Permissible	No Opinion	No Response
Bt	33%	33%	19%	11%	4%
Bp	13	0	63	12	12
E	4	13	53	17	13
F	18	34	24	6	18
P	11	22	48	19	0
Total	16	23	39	13	9

15. If you are subject to more than one variation of
    the prudent man rule, do you draw distinctions
    between the types of investments permissible under
    each?

	Yes	No	No Response
Bt	41%	37%	22%
Bp	63	25	12
E	13	45	42
F	6	70	24
P	4	52	44
Total	21	48	31

Index

Table of Cases

[References are to the page of text containing discussion of the case, followed, in parentheses, by the location of the footnote containing the case citation]